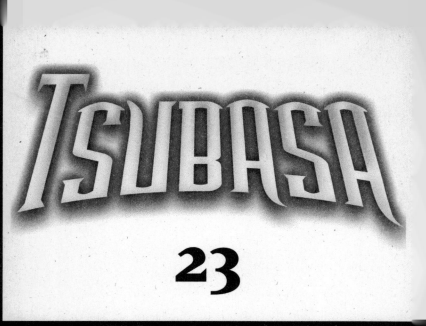

# TSUBASA

# 23

## CLAMP

TRANSLATED AND ADAPTED BY
**William Flanagan**

LETTERED BY
**Dana Hayward**

BALLANTINE BOOKS • NEW YORK

A Del Rey Manga/Kodansha Trade Paperback Original

*Tsubasa*, volume 23 copyright © 2008 CLAMP
English translation copyright © 2009 CLAMP

Published in the United States by Del Rey Books, an imprint of The Random House Publishing Group, a division of Random House, Inc., New York.

DEL REY is a registered trademark and the Del Rey colophon is a trademark of Random House, Inc.

Publication rights arranged through Kodansha Ltd.

First published in Japan in 2008 by Kodansha Ltd., Tokyo

ISBN 978-0-345-51230-7

Printed in the United States of America

www.delreymanga.com

9 8 7 6 5 4 3 2 1

Translator/Adapter—William Flanagan
Lettering—Dana Hayward

# Contents

*Tsubasa* crosses over with *xxxHOLiC*. Although it isn't necessary to read *xxxHOLiC* to understand the events in *Tsubasa*, you'll get to see the same events from different perspectives if you read both series!

# Honorifics Explained

Throughout the Del Rey Manga books, you will find Japanese honorifics left intact in the translations. For those not familiar with how the Japanese use honorifics and, more important, how they differ from American honorifics, we present this brief overview.

Politeness has always been a critical facet of Japanese culture. Ever since the feudal era, when Japan was a highly stratified society, use of honorifics—which can be defined as polite speech that indicates relationship or status—has played an essential role in the Japanese language. When you address someone in Japanese, an honorific usually takes the form of a suffix attached to one's name (example: "Asuna-san"), is used as a title at the end of one's name, or appears in place of the name itself (example: "Negi-sensei," or simply "Sensei!").

Honorifics can be expressions of respect or endearment. In the context of manga and anime, honorifics give insight into the nature of the relationship between characters. Many English translations leave out these important honorifics and therefore distort the feel of the original Japanese. Because Japanese honorifics contain nuances that English honorifics lack, it is our policy at Del Rey not to translate them. Here, instead, is a guide to some of the honorifics you may encounter in Del Rey Manga.

**-san:** This is the most common honorific and is equivalent to Mr., Miss, Ms., or Mrs. It is the all-purpose honorific and can be used in any situation where politeness is required.

**-sama:** This is one level higher than "-san" and is used to confer great respect.

**-dono:** This comes from the word "tono," which means "lord." It is an even higher level than "-sama" and confers utmost respect.

**-kun:** This suffix is used at the end of boys' names to express familiarity or endearment. It is also sometimes used by men among friends, or when addressing someone younger or of a lower station.

**-chan:** This is used to express endearment, mostly toward girls. It is also used for little boys, pets, and even among lovers. It gives a sense of childish cuteness.

**Bozu:** This is an informal way to refer to a boy, similar to the English terms "kid" and "squirt."

**Sempai/Senpai:** This title suggests that the addressee is one's senior in a group or organization. It is most often used in a school setting, where underclassmen refer to their upperclassmen as "sempai." It can also be used in the workplace, such as when a newer employee addresses an employee who has seniority in the company.

**Kohai:** This is the opposite of "sempai" and is used toward under-classmen in school or newcomers in the workplace. It connotes that the addressee is of a lower station.

**Sensei:** Literally meaning "one who has come before," this title is used for teachers, doctors, or masters of any profession or art.

**-[blank]:** This is usually forgotten in these lists, but it is perhaps the most significant difference between Japanese and English. The lack of honorific means that the speaker has permission to address the person in a very intimate way. Usually, only family, spouses, or very close friends have this kind of permission. Known as *yobisute*, it can be gratifying when someone who has earned the intimacy starts to call one by one's name without an honorific. But when that intimacy hasn't been earned, it can be very insulting.

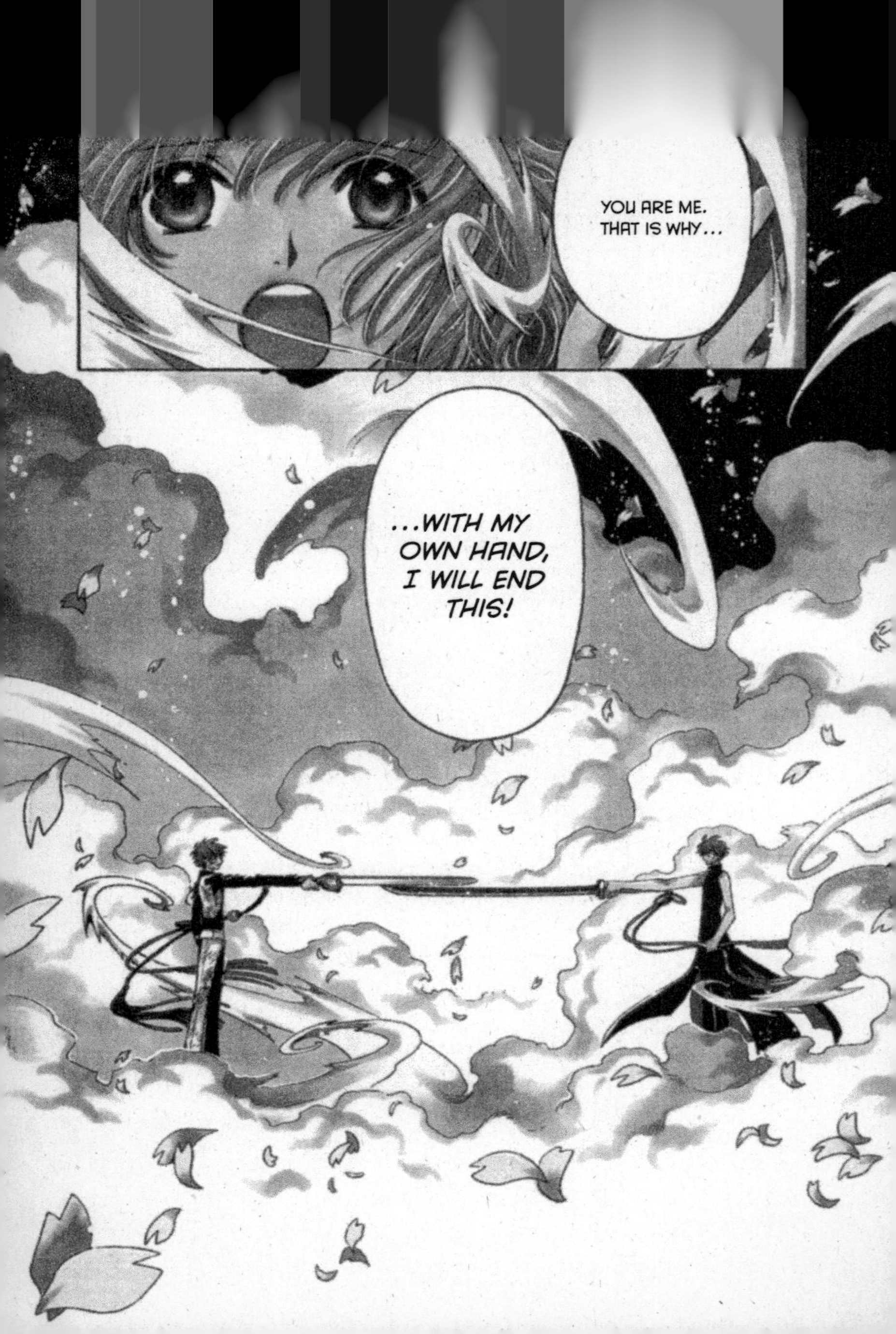
YOU ARE ME.
THAT IS WHY...
...WITH MY OWN HAND, I WILL END THIS!

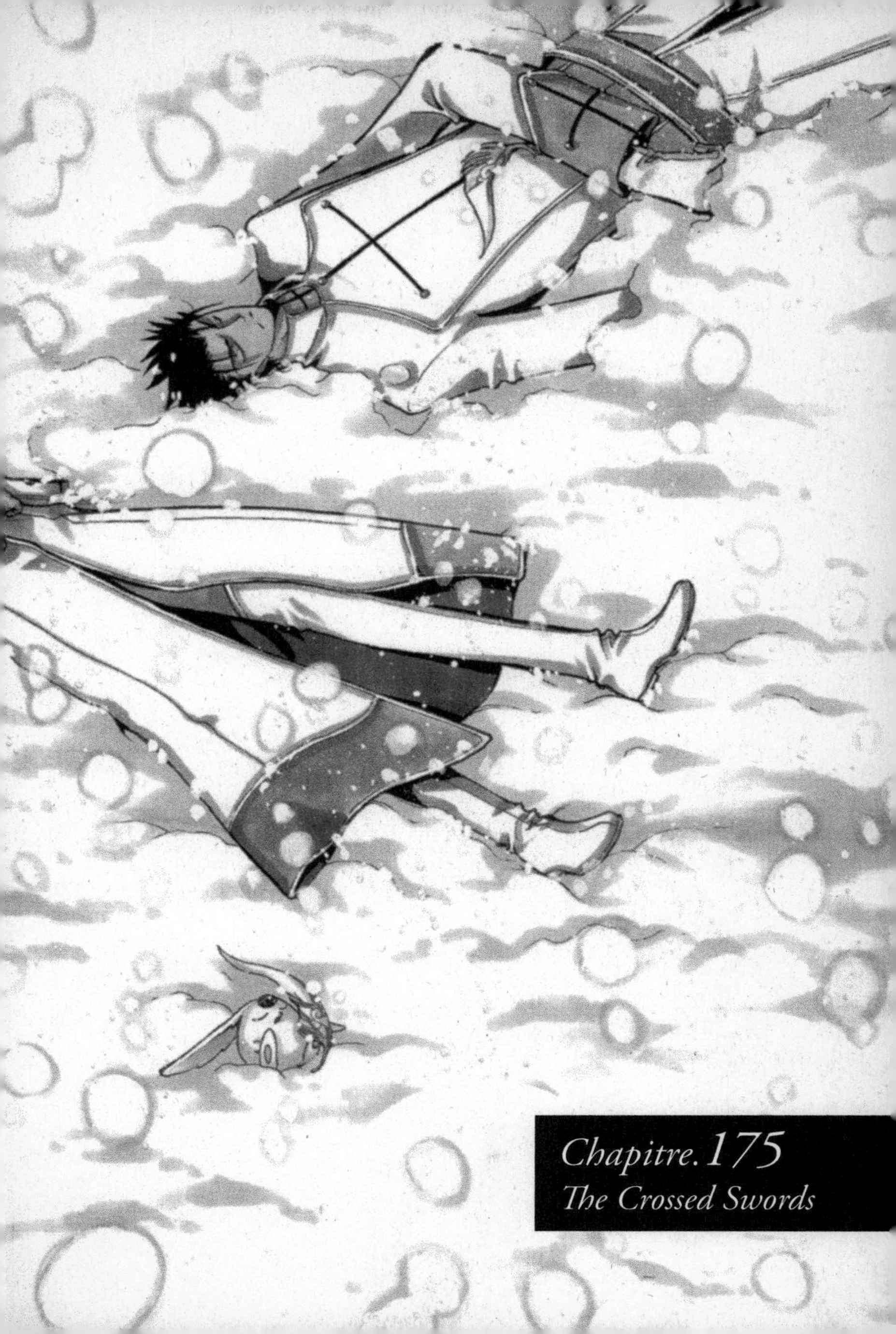
Chapitre. 175
The Crossed Swords

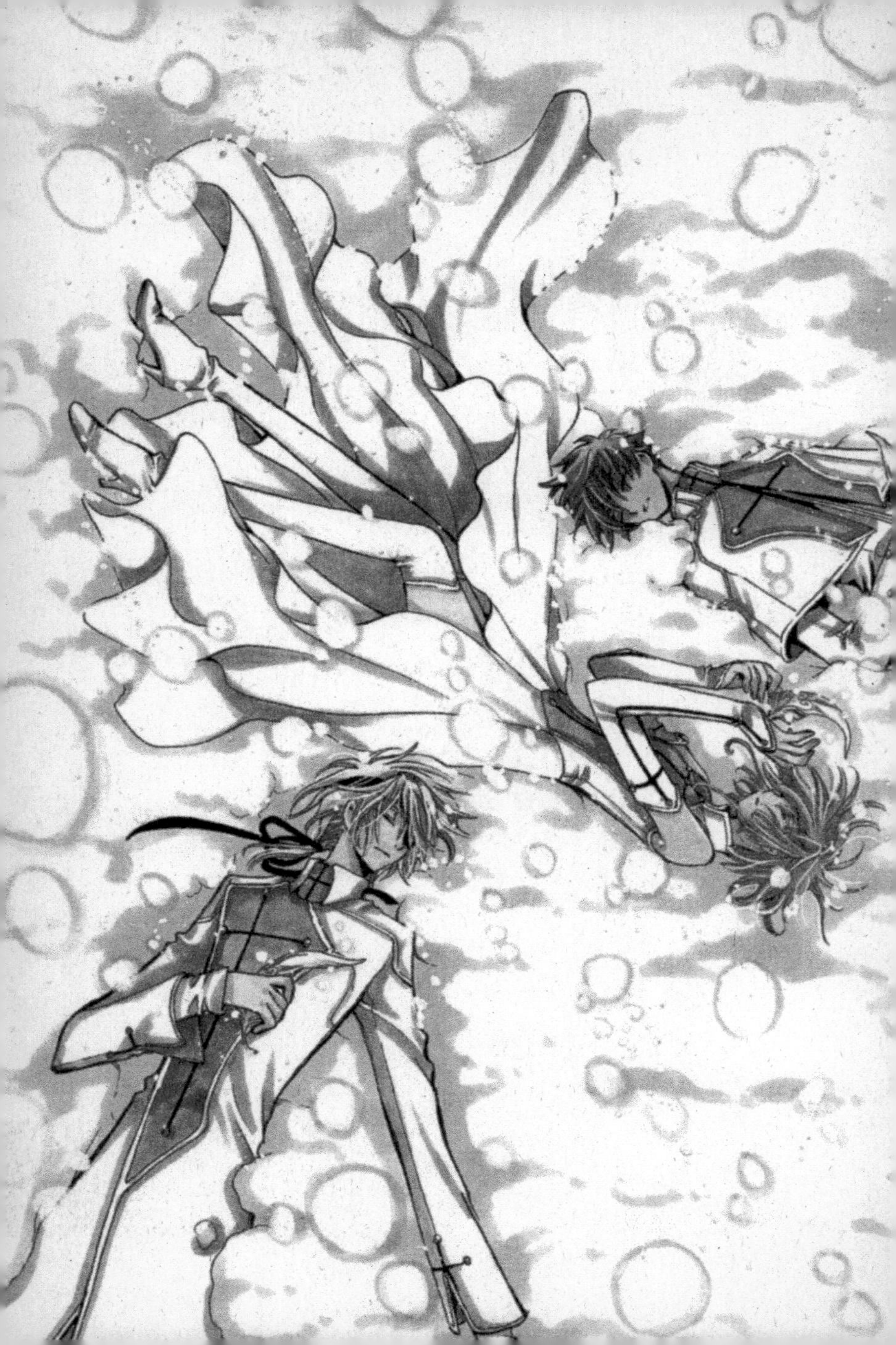

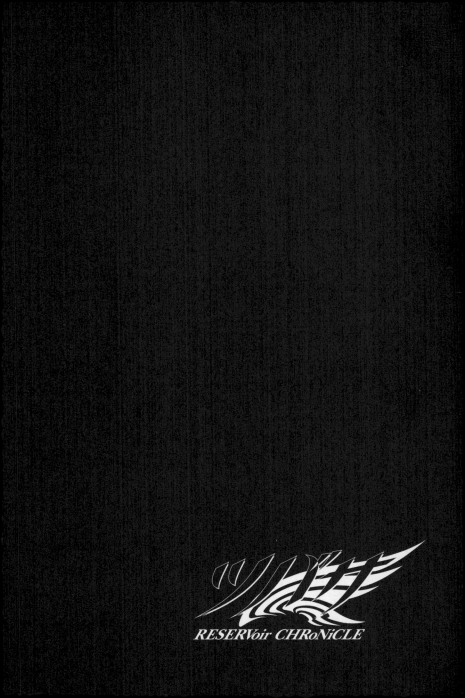

RESERVoir CHRoNiCLE

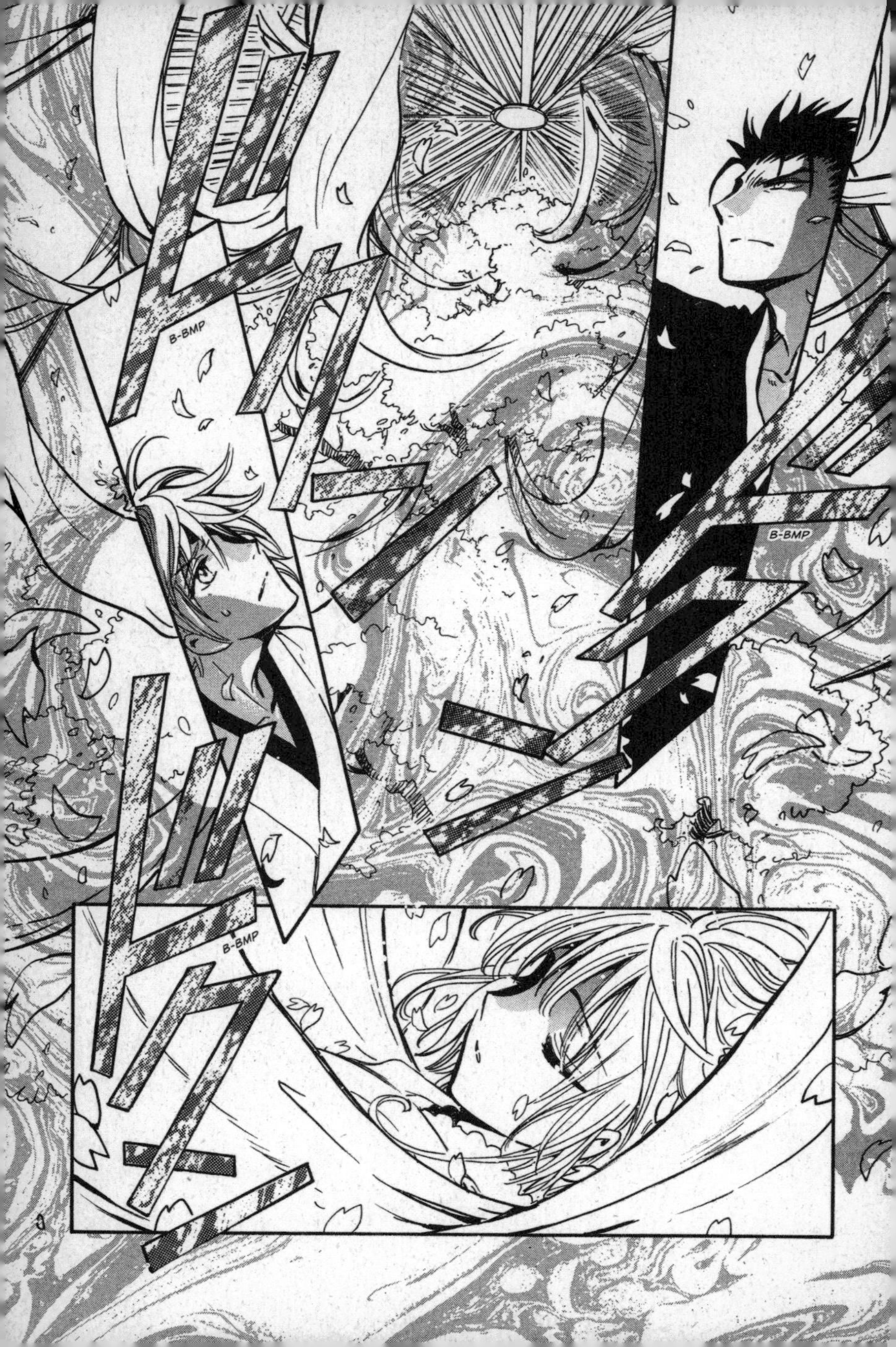
B-BMP
B-BMP
B-BMP

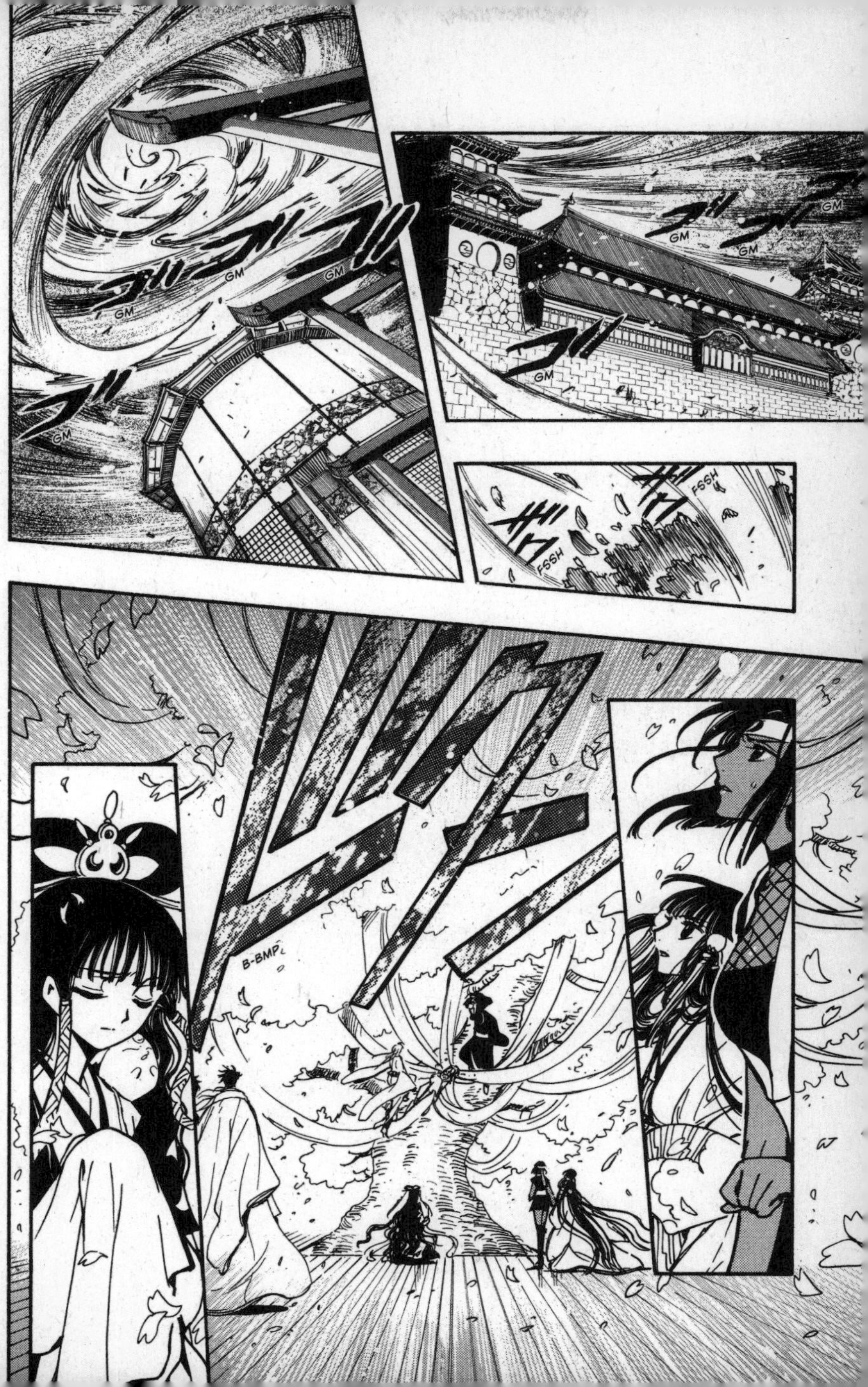
GM
GM
GM
GM
FSSH
FSSH
GM
GM
GM
GM
B-BMP

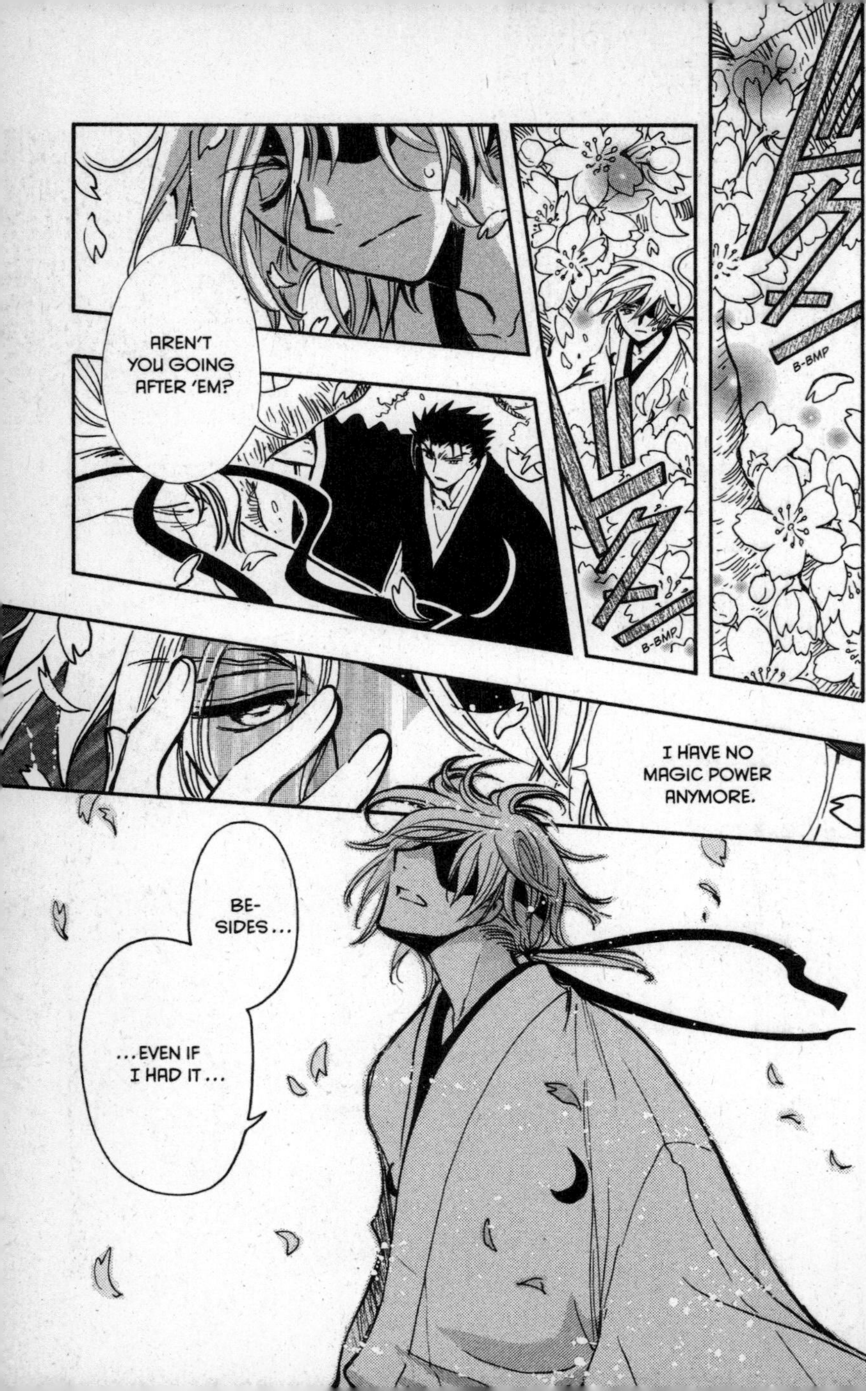
B-BMP
B-BMP
AREN'T YOU GOING AFTER 'EM?
I HAVE NO MAGIC POWER ANYMORE.
BE-SIDES...
...EVEN IF I HAD IT...

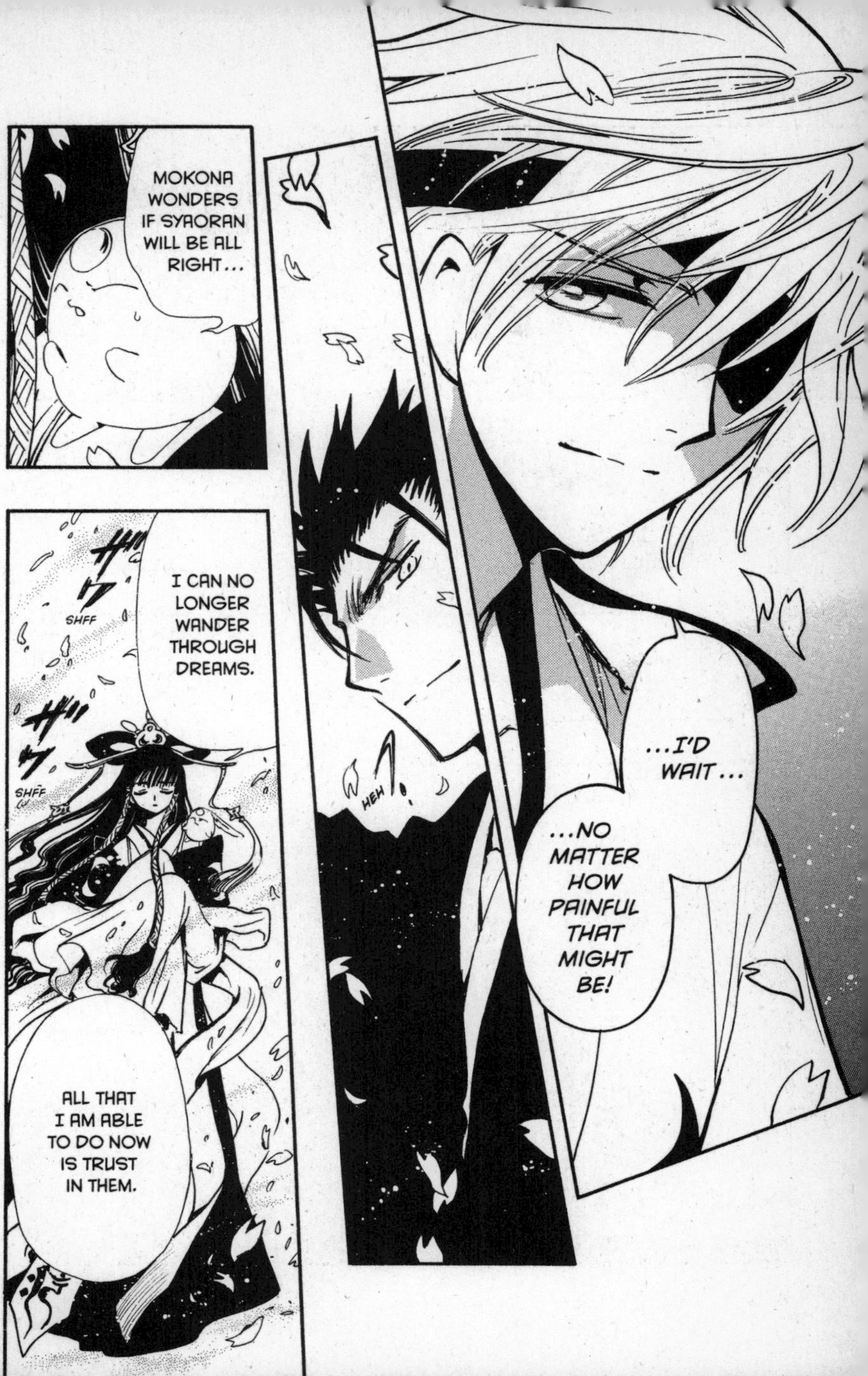
...I'D WAIT...
...NO MATTER HOW PAINFUL THAT MIGHT BE!
HEH
MOKONA WONDERS IF SYAORAN WILL BE ALL RIGHT...
SHFF
SHFF
I CAN NO LONGER WANDER THROUGH DREAMS.
ALL THAT I AM ABLE TO DO NOW IS TRUST IN THEM.

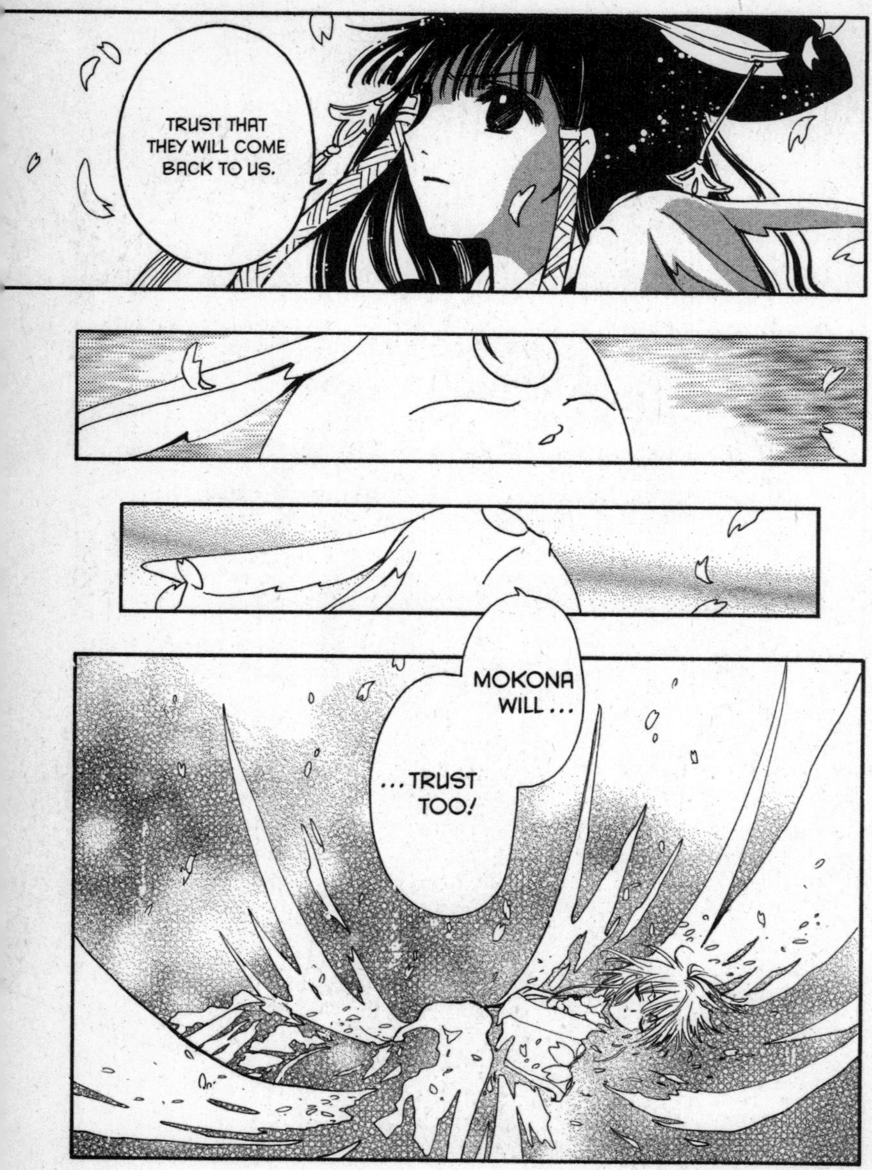
TRUST THAT THEY WILL COME BACK TO US.
MOKONA WILL . . .
. . . TRUST TOO!

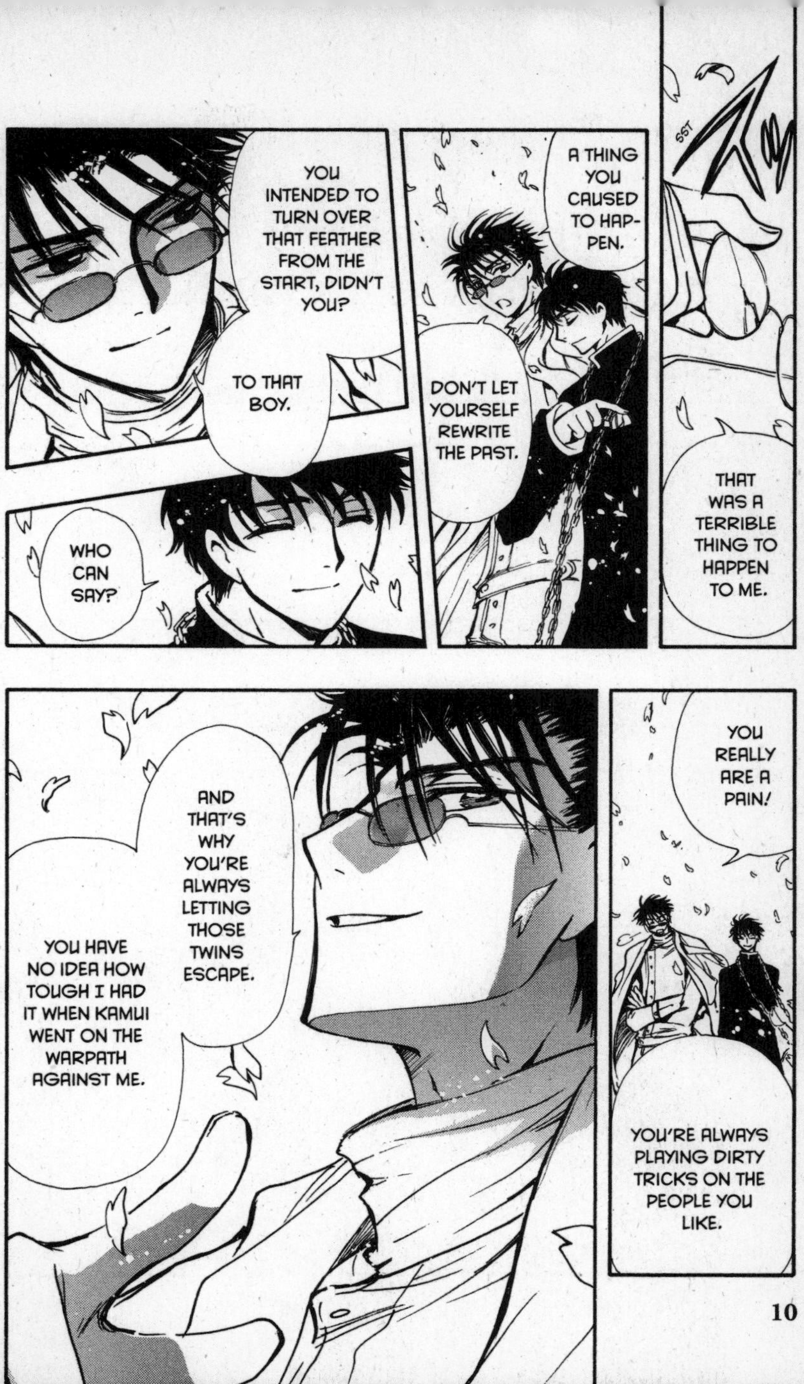
SST
THAT WAS A TERRIBLE THING TO HAPPEN TO ME.
A THING YOU CAUSED TO HAP- PEN.
DON'T LET YOURSELF REWRITE THE PAST.
YOU INTENDED TO TURN OVER THAT FEATHER FROM THE START, DIDN'T YOU?
TO THAT BOY.
WHO CAN SAY?
YOU REALLY ARE A PAIN!
YOU'RE ALWAYS PLAYING DIRTY TRICKS ON THE PEOPLE YOU LIKE.
AND THAT'S WHY YOU'RE ALWAYS LETTING THOSE TWINS ESCAPE.
YOU HAVE NO IDEA HOW TOUGH I HAD IT WHEN KAMUI WENT ON THE WARPATH AGAINST ME.

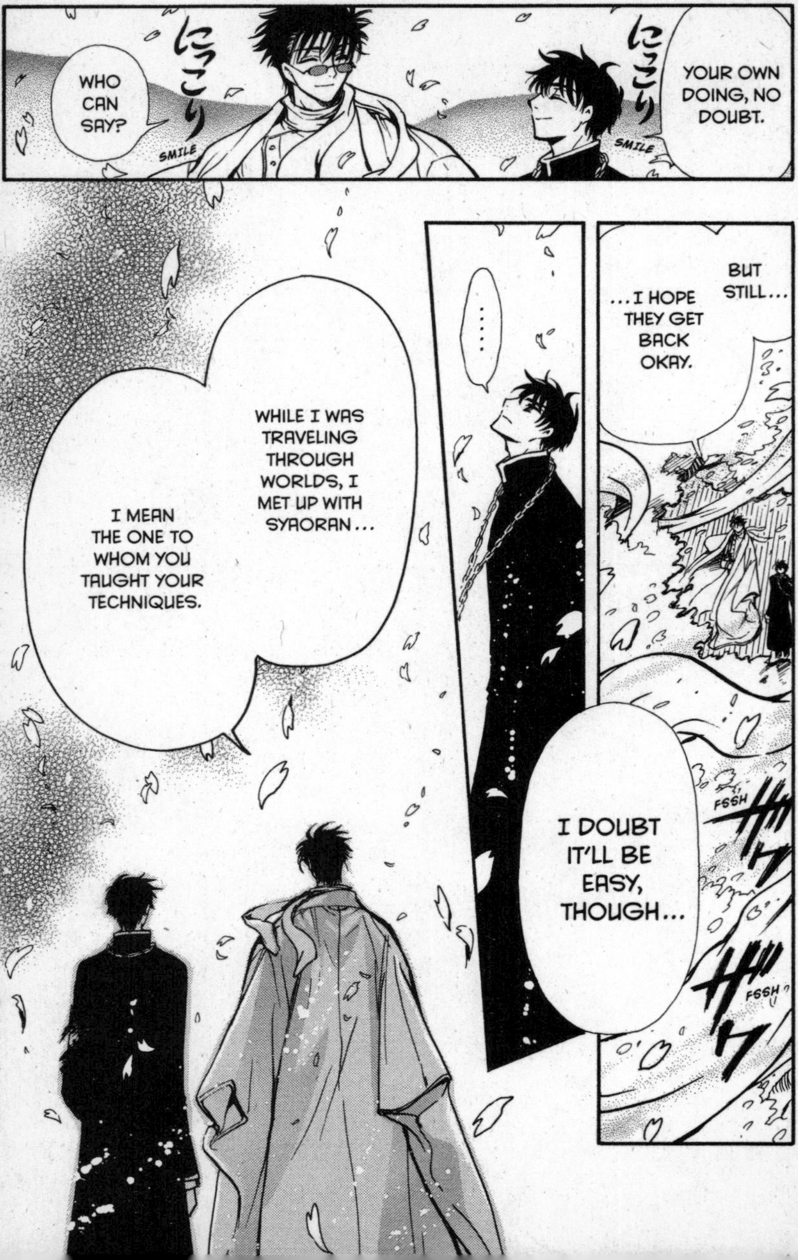
にっこり
YOUR OWN DOING, NO DOUBT.
SMILE
にっこり
WHO CAN SAY?
SMILE
BUT STILL...
...I HOPE THEY GET BACK OKAY.
I DOUBT IT'LL BE EASY, THOUGH...
FSSH
FSSH
......
WHILE I WAS TRAVELING THROUGH WORLDS, I MET UP WITH SYAORAN...
I MEAN THE ONE TO WHOM YOU TAUGHT YOUR TECHNIQUES.

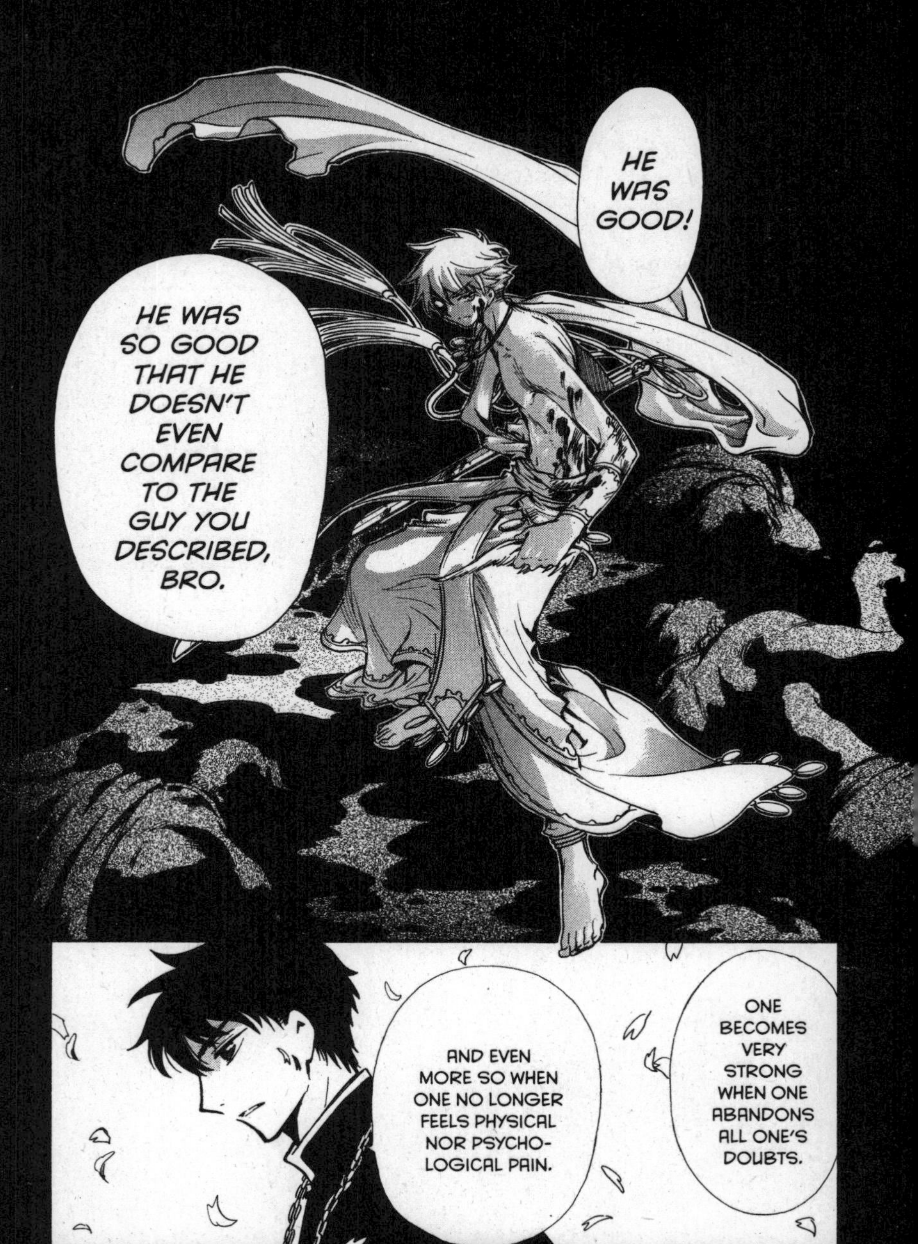
HE WAS GOOD!
HE WAS SO GOOD THAT HE DOESN'T EVEN COMPARE TO THE GUY YOU DESCRIBED, BRO.
ONE BECOMES VERY STRONG WHEN ONE ABANDONS ALL ONE'S DOUBTS.
AND EVEN MORE SO WHEN ONE NO LONGER FEELS PHYSICAL NOR PSYCHO-LOGICAL PAIN.

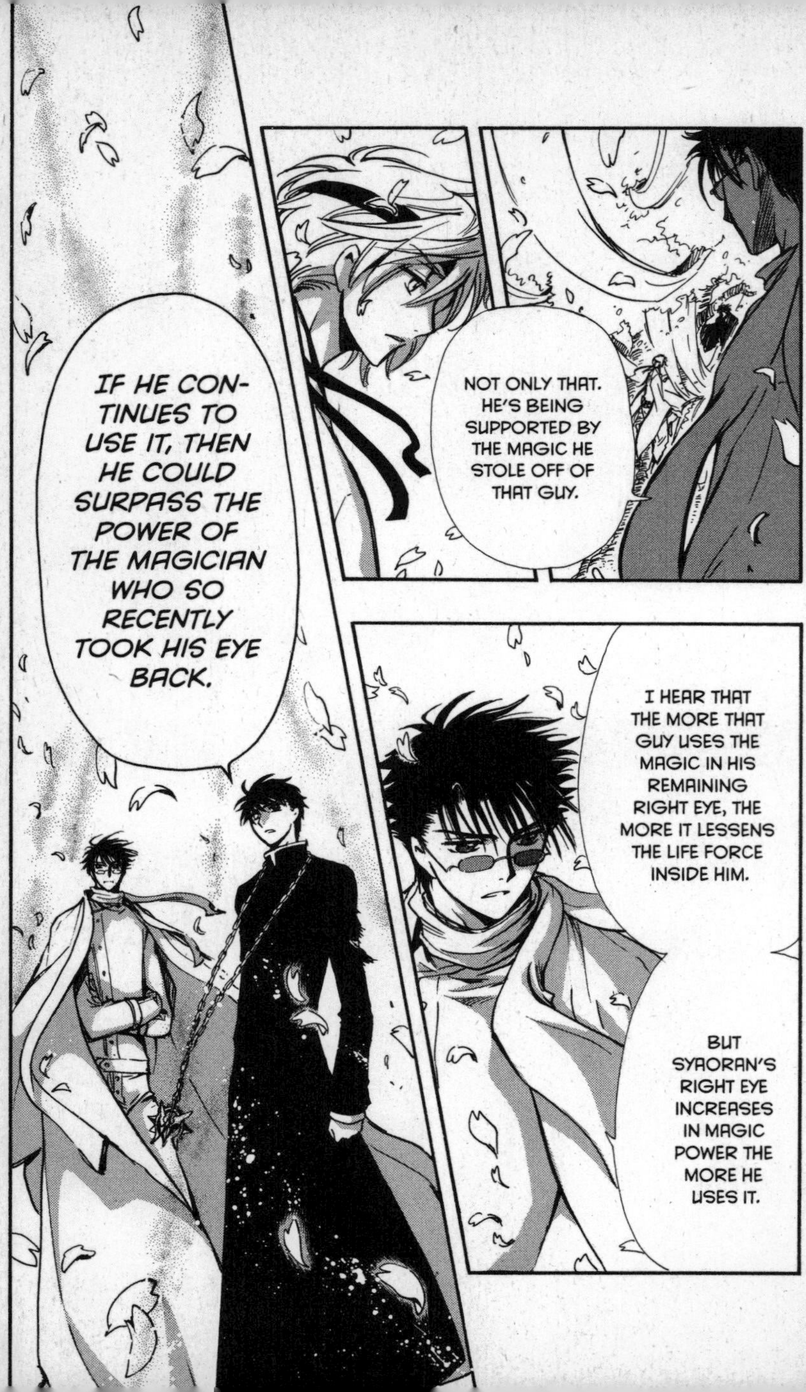
NOT ONLY THAT. HE'S BEING SUPPORTED BY THE MAGIC HE STOLE OFF OF THAT GUY.
I HEAR THAT THE MORE THAT GUY USES THE MAGIC IN HIS REMAINING RIGHT EYE, THE MORE IT LESSENS THE LIFE FORCE INSIDE HIM.
BUT SYAORAN'S RIGHT EYE INCREASES IN MAGIC POWER THE MORE HE USES IT.
IF HE CONTINUES TO USE IT, THEN HE COULD SURPASS THE POWER OF THE MAGICIAN WHO SO RECENTLY TOOK HIS EYE BACK.

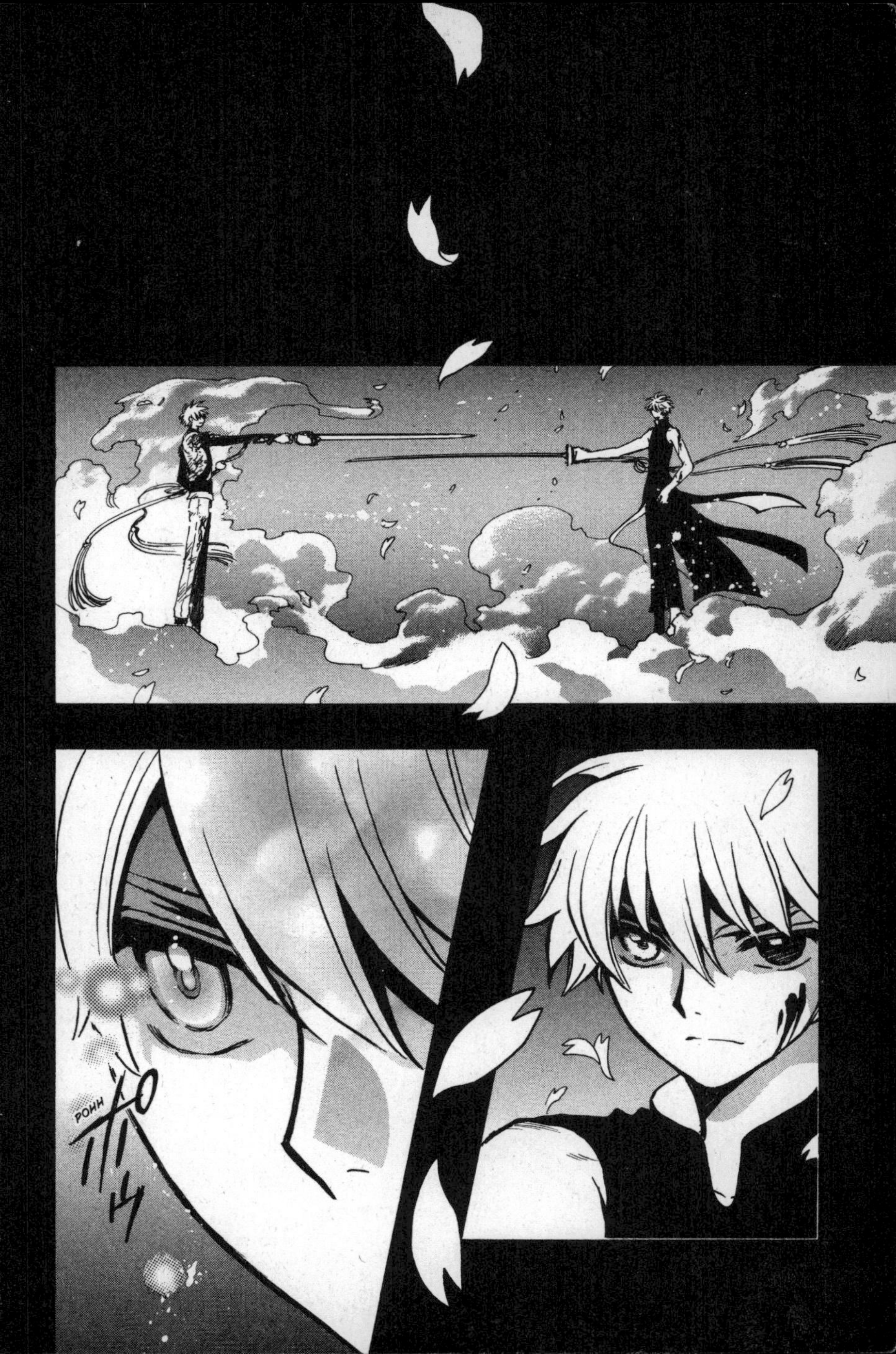
POHH

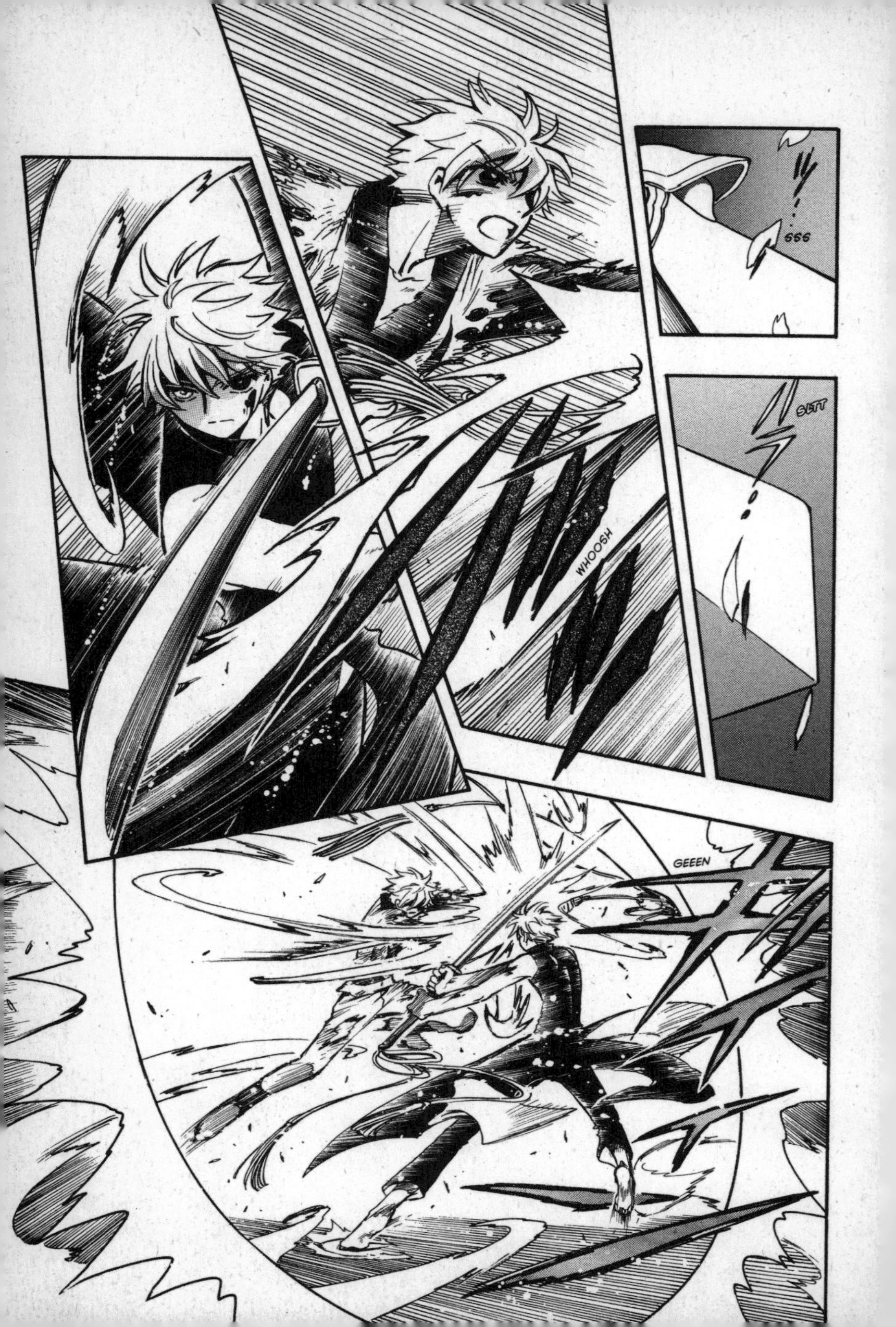
SSS
SLTT
WHOOSH
GEEEN

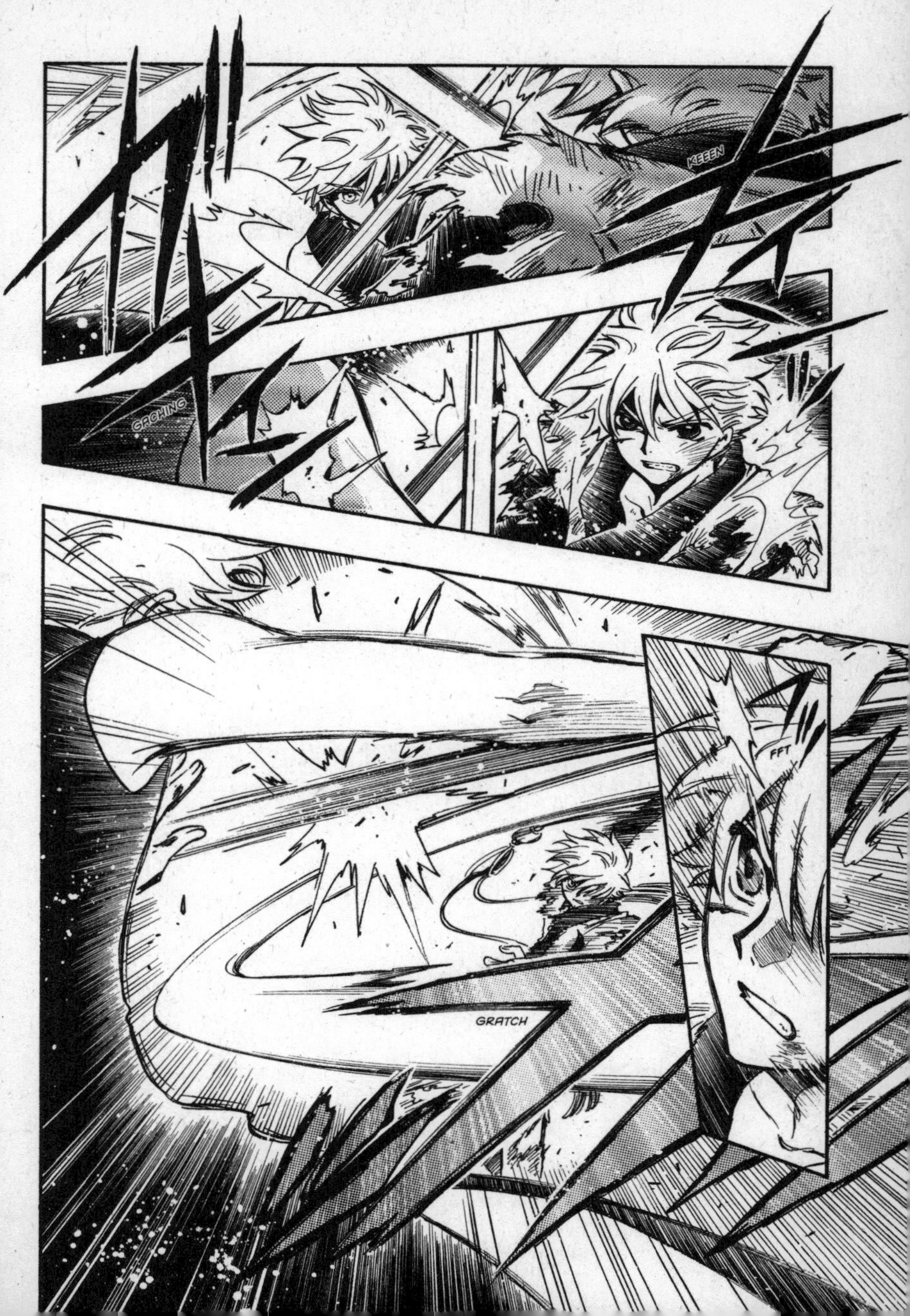
KEEEN
GACHING
FFT
GRATCH

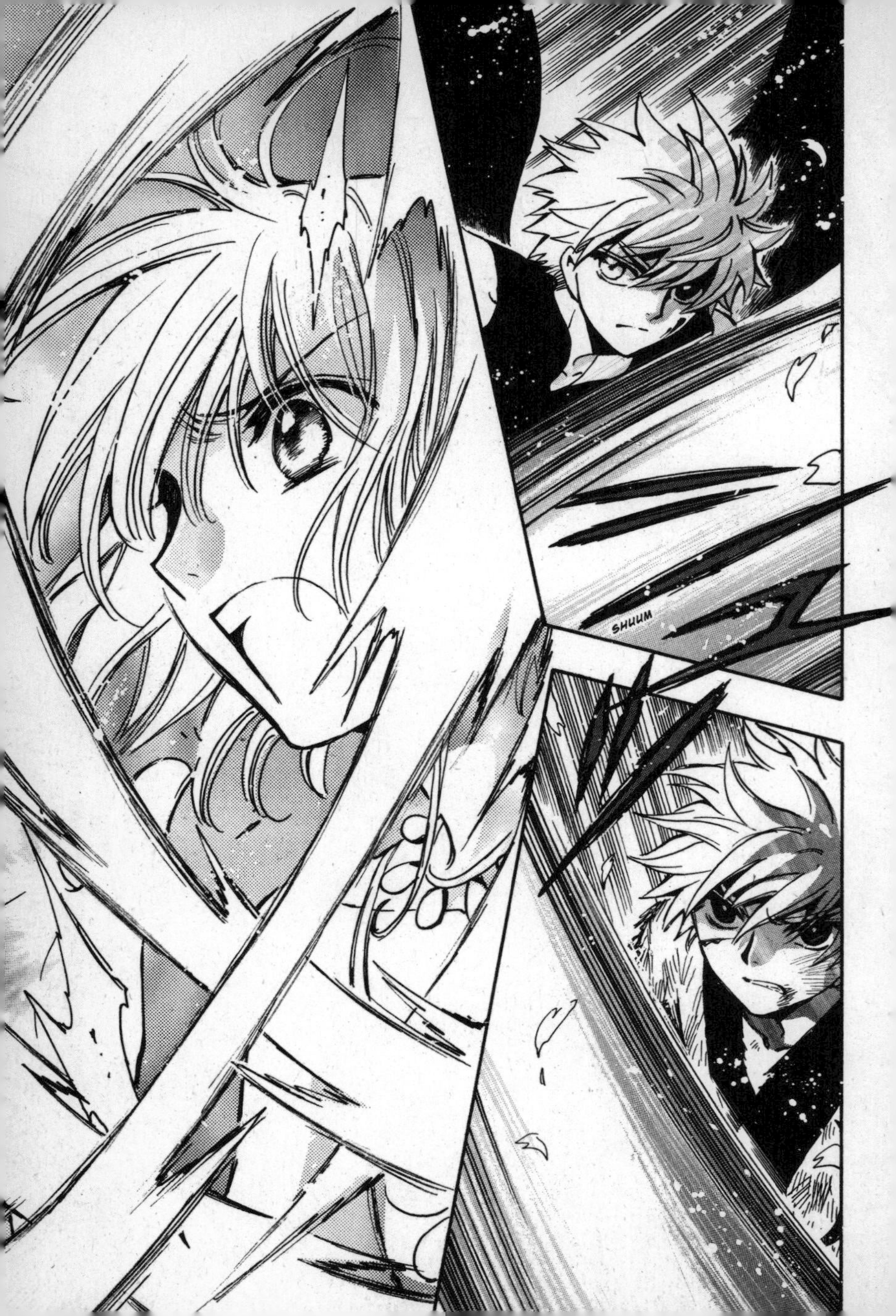
SHUUM

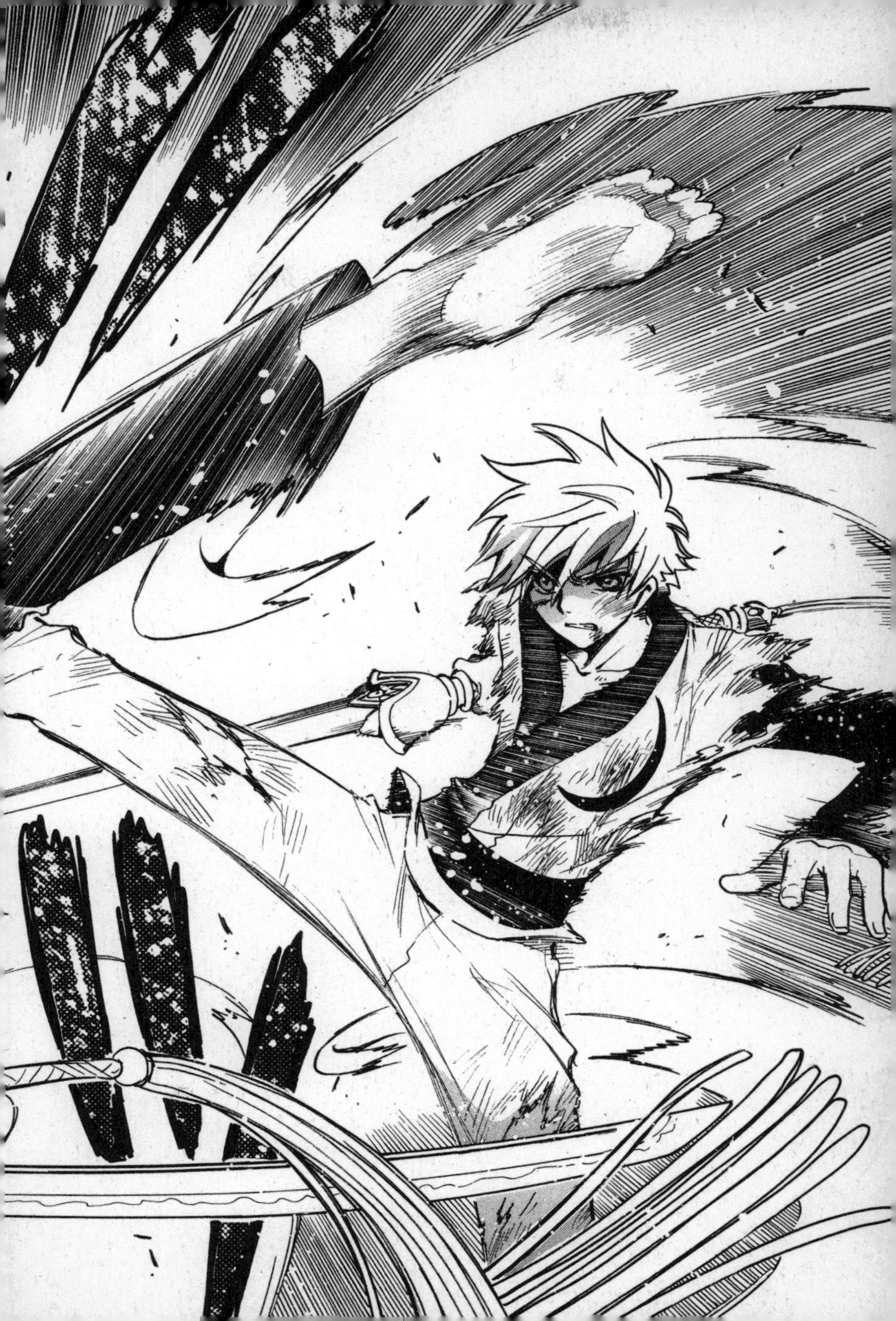

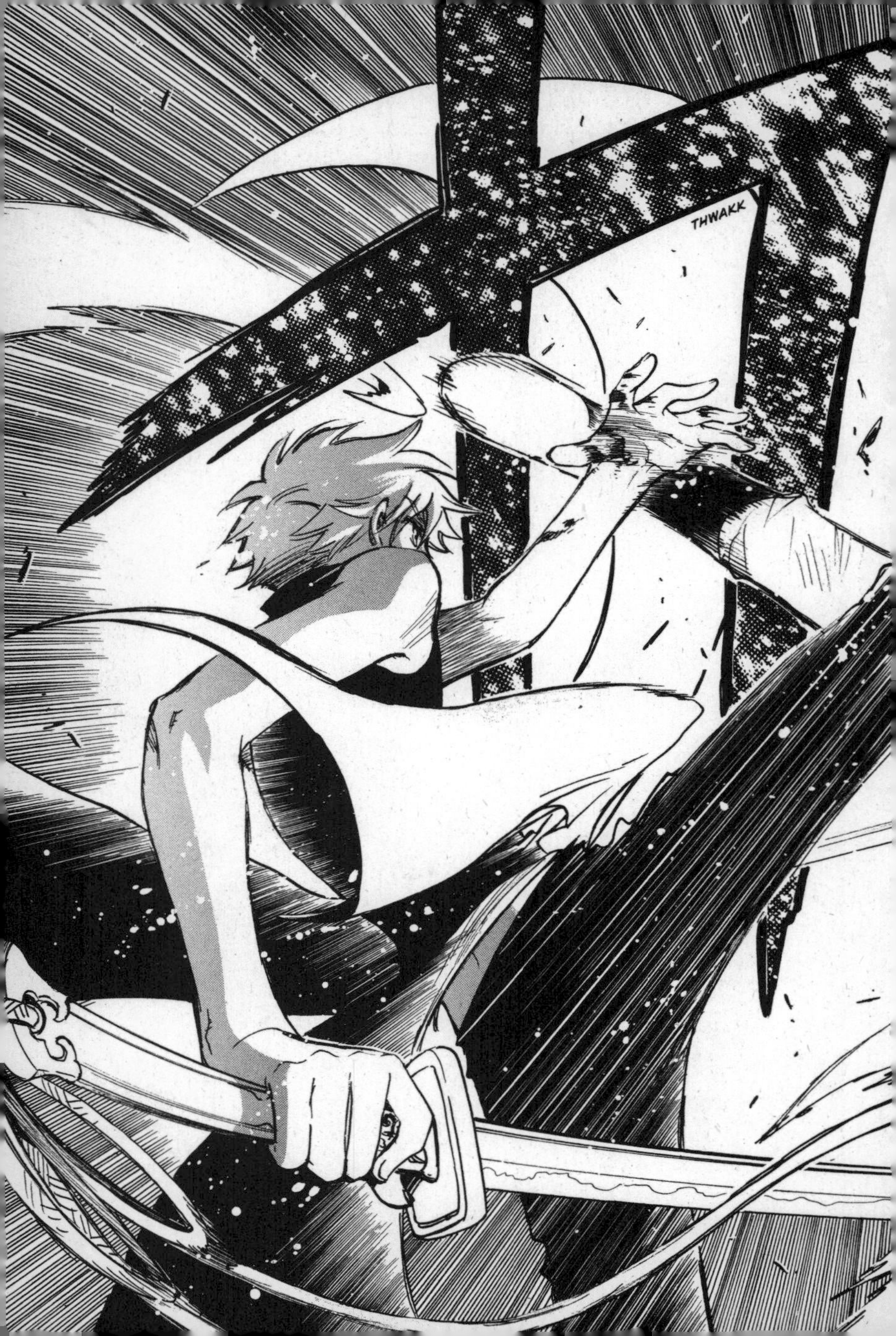
THWAKK

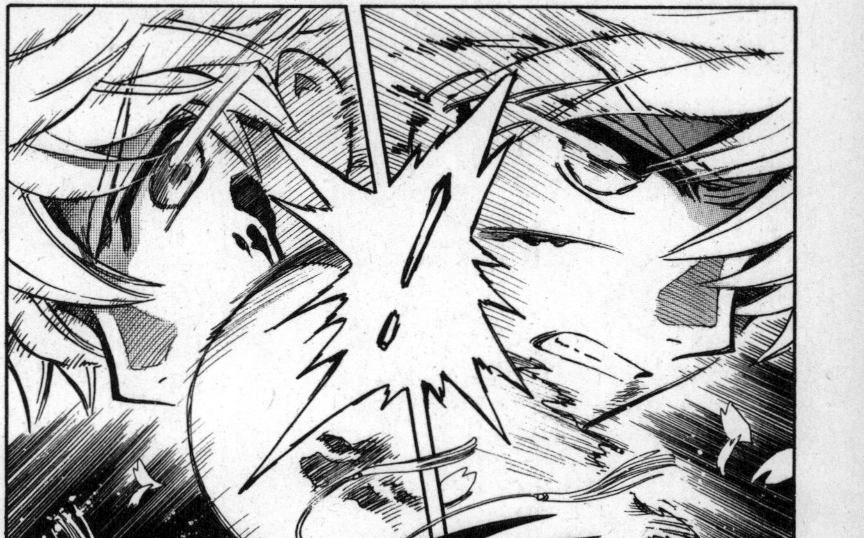
SHKK

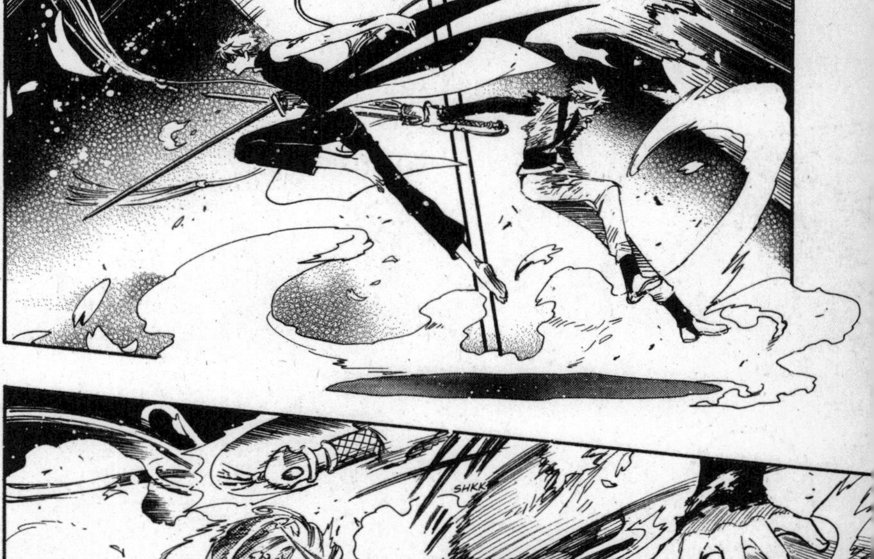
SHKK

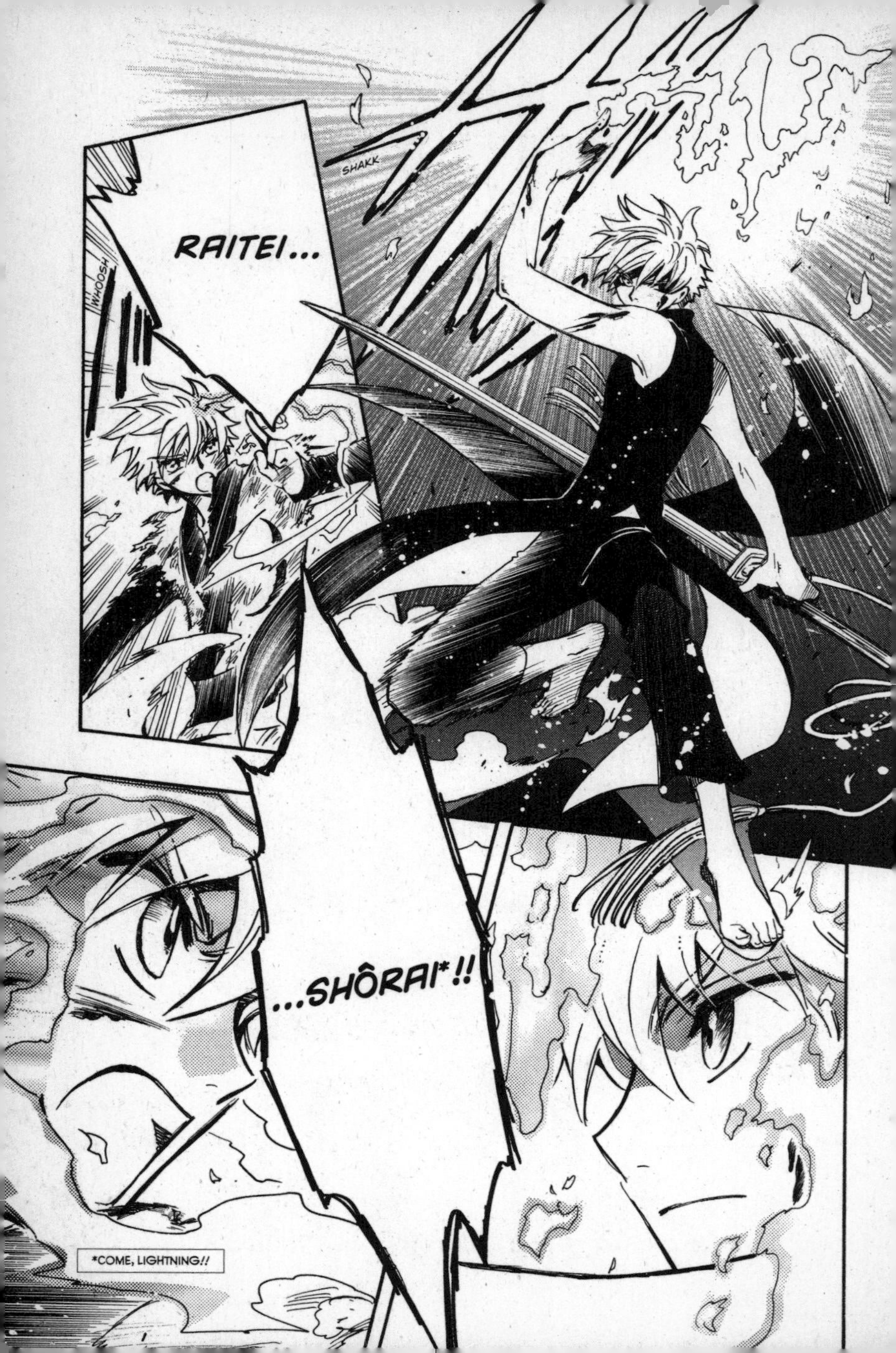
SHAKK
RAITEI...
WHOOSH
...SHÔRAI*!!
*COME, LIGHTNING!!

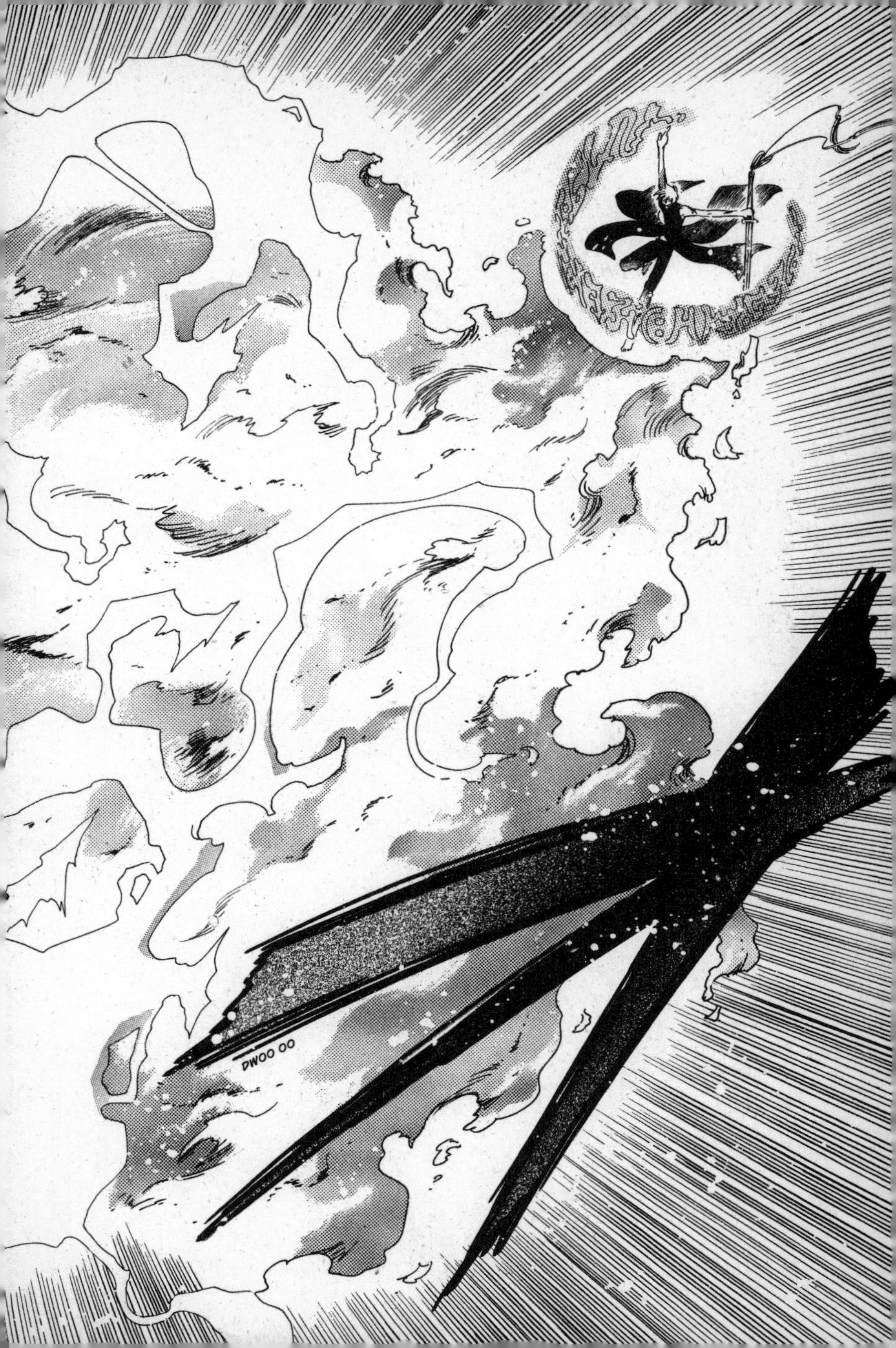
DWOO OO

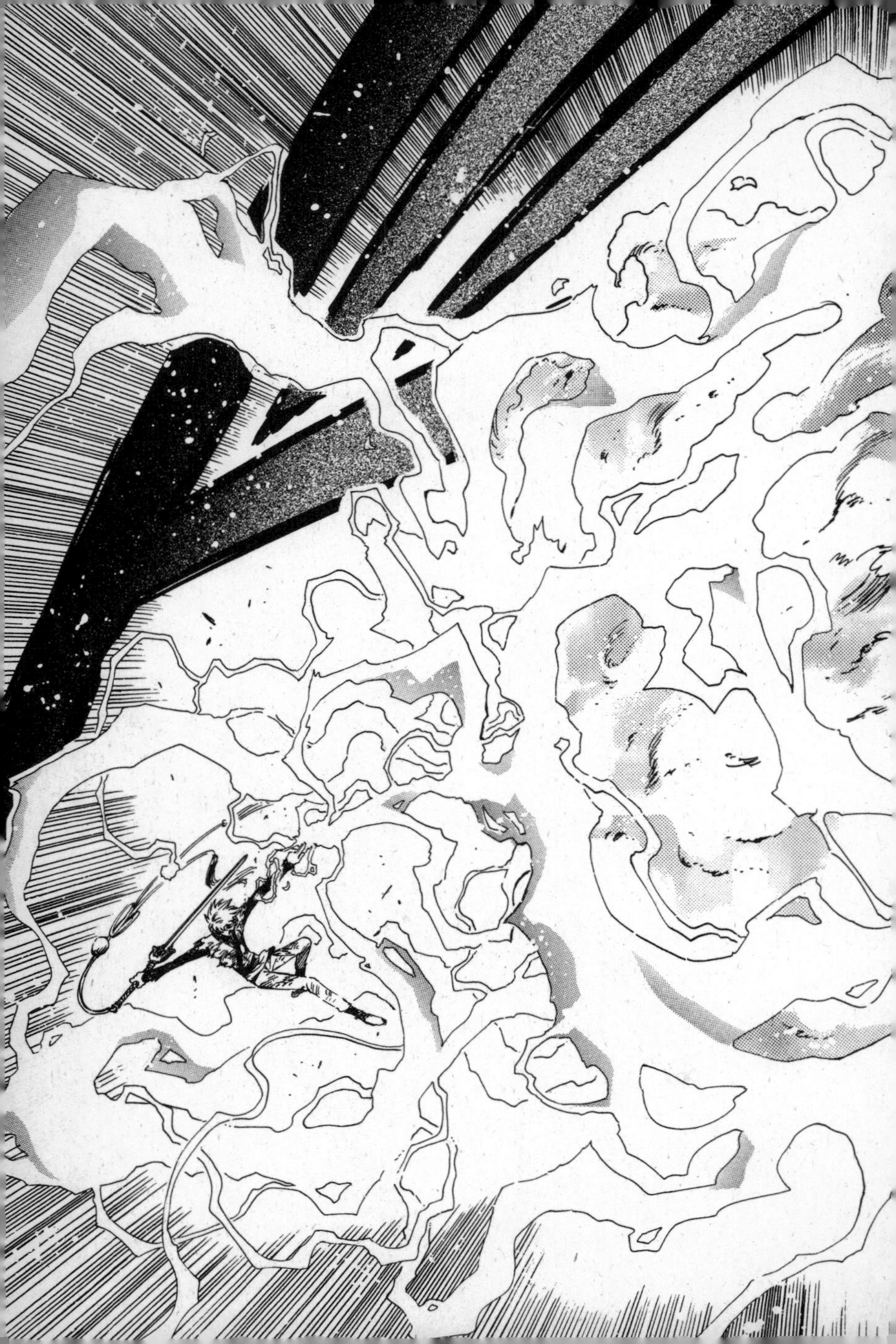

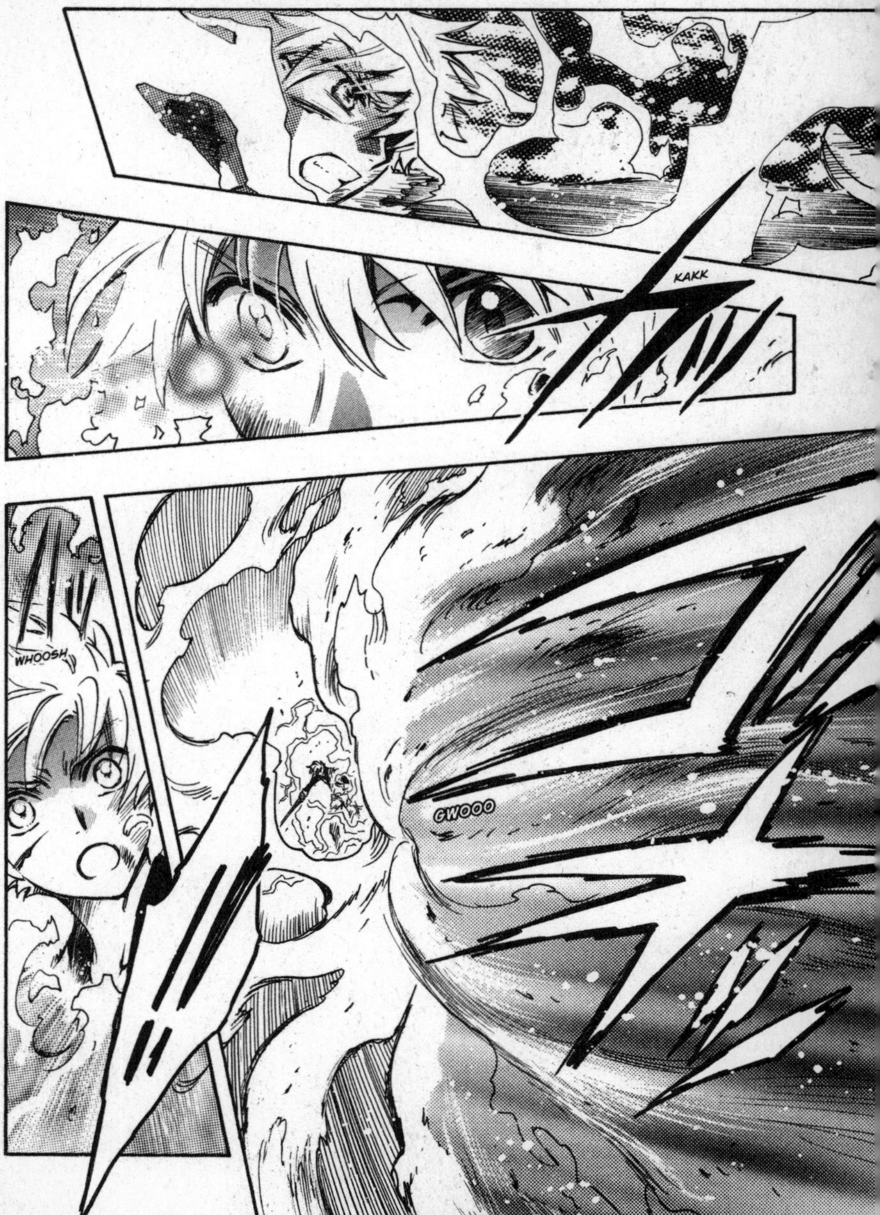
KAKK
GWOOO
WHOOSH

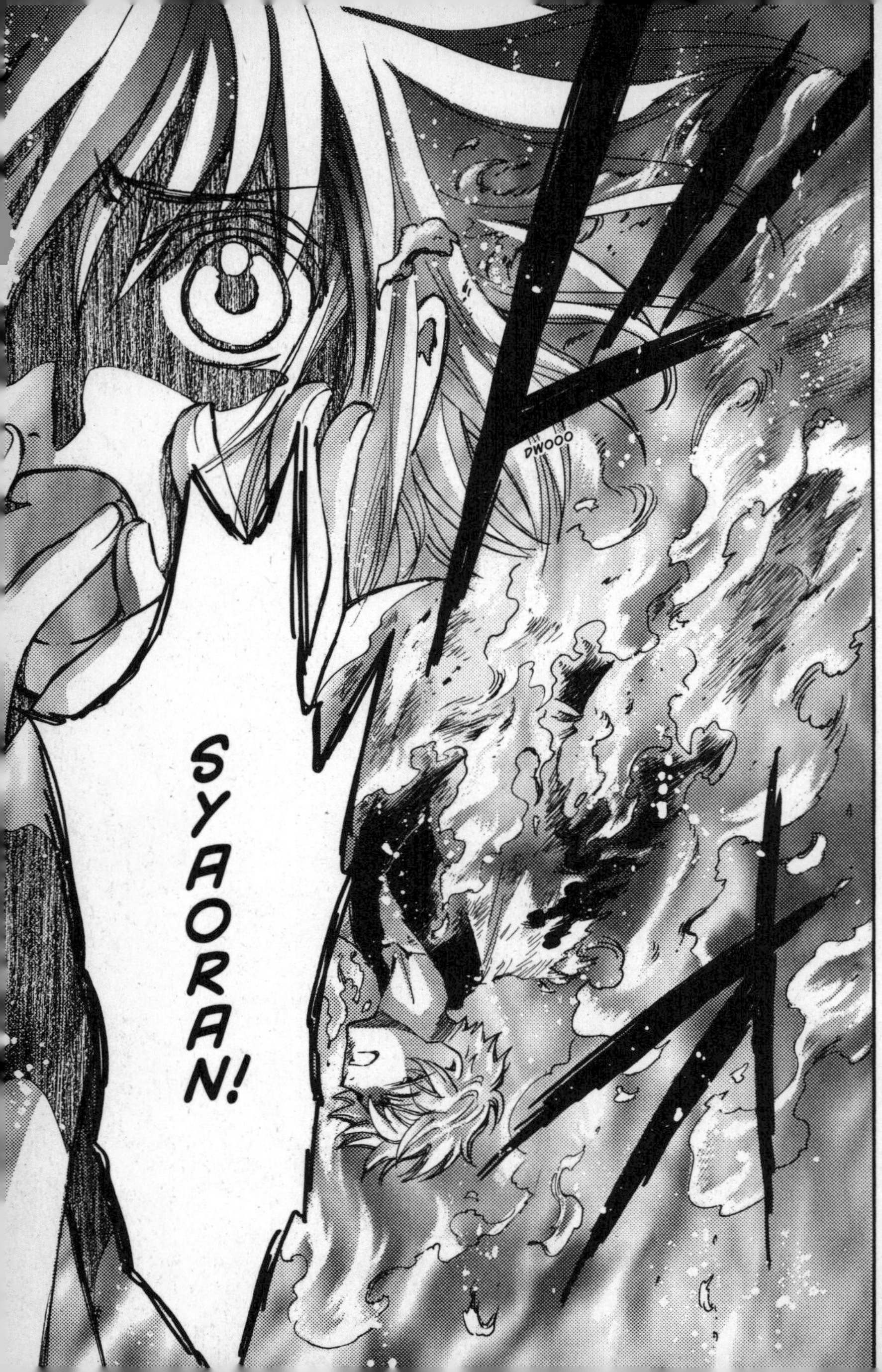
DWOOO
SYAORAN!

ツバサ

RESERVoir CHRoNiCLE

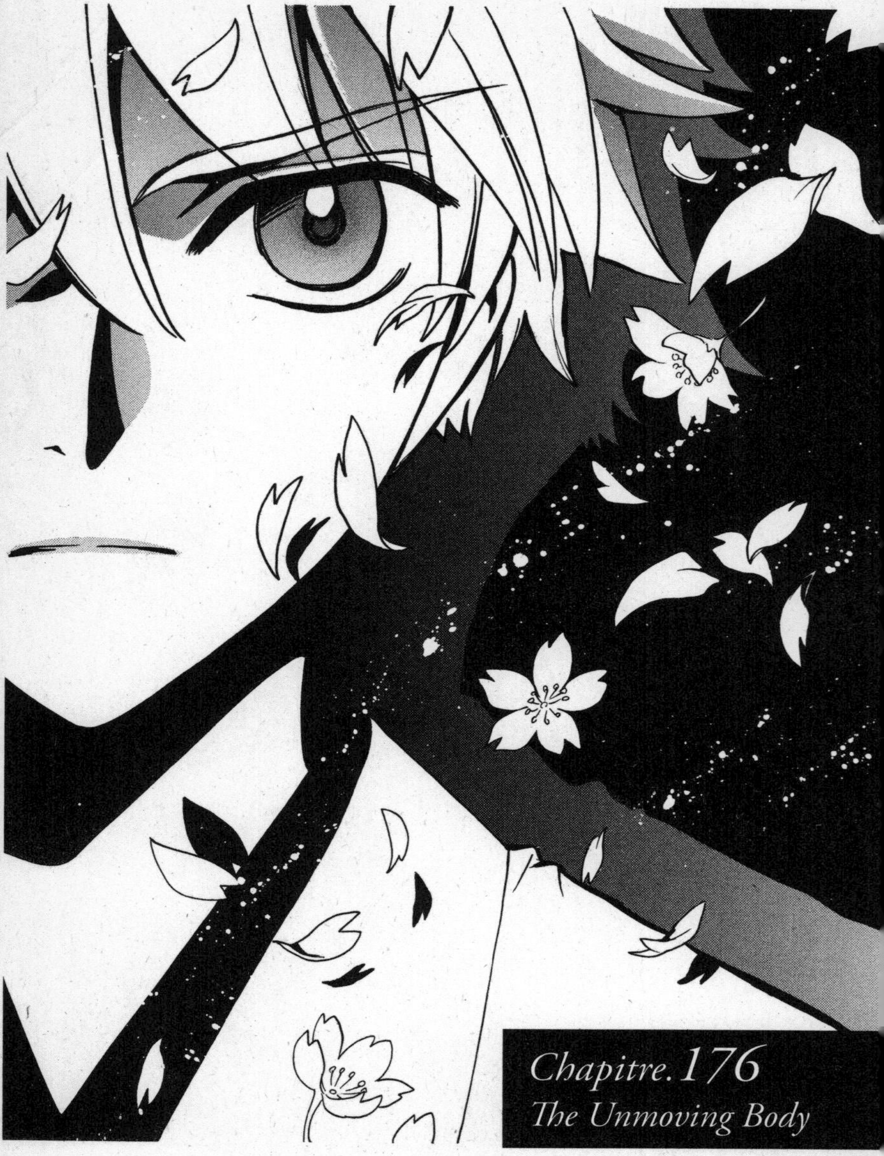
Chapitre. 176
The Unmoving Body

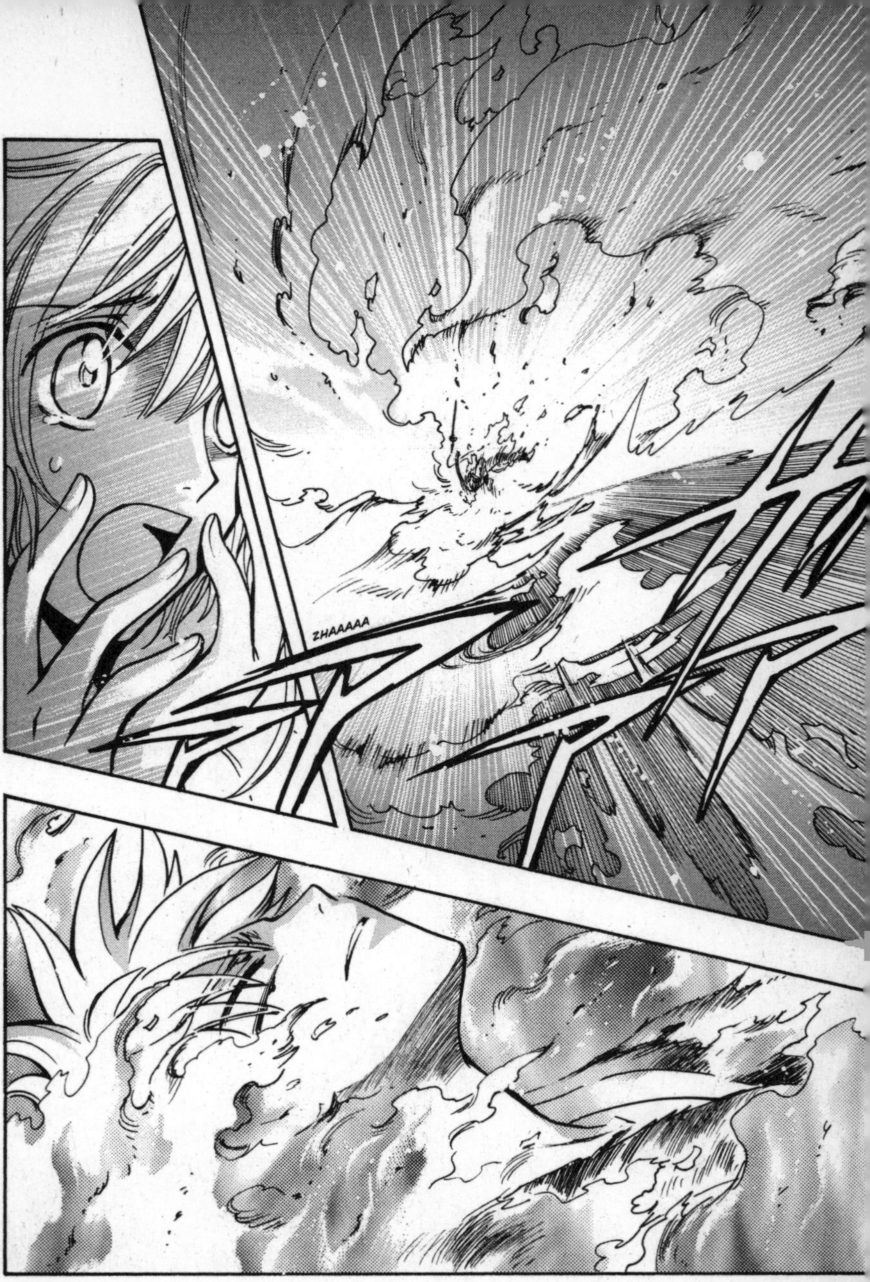
ZHAAAAA

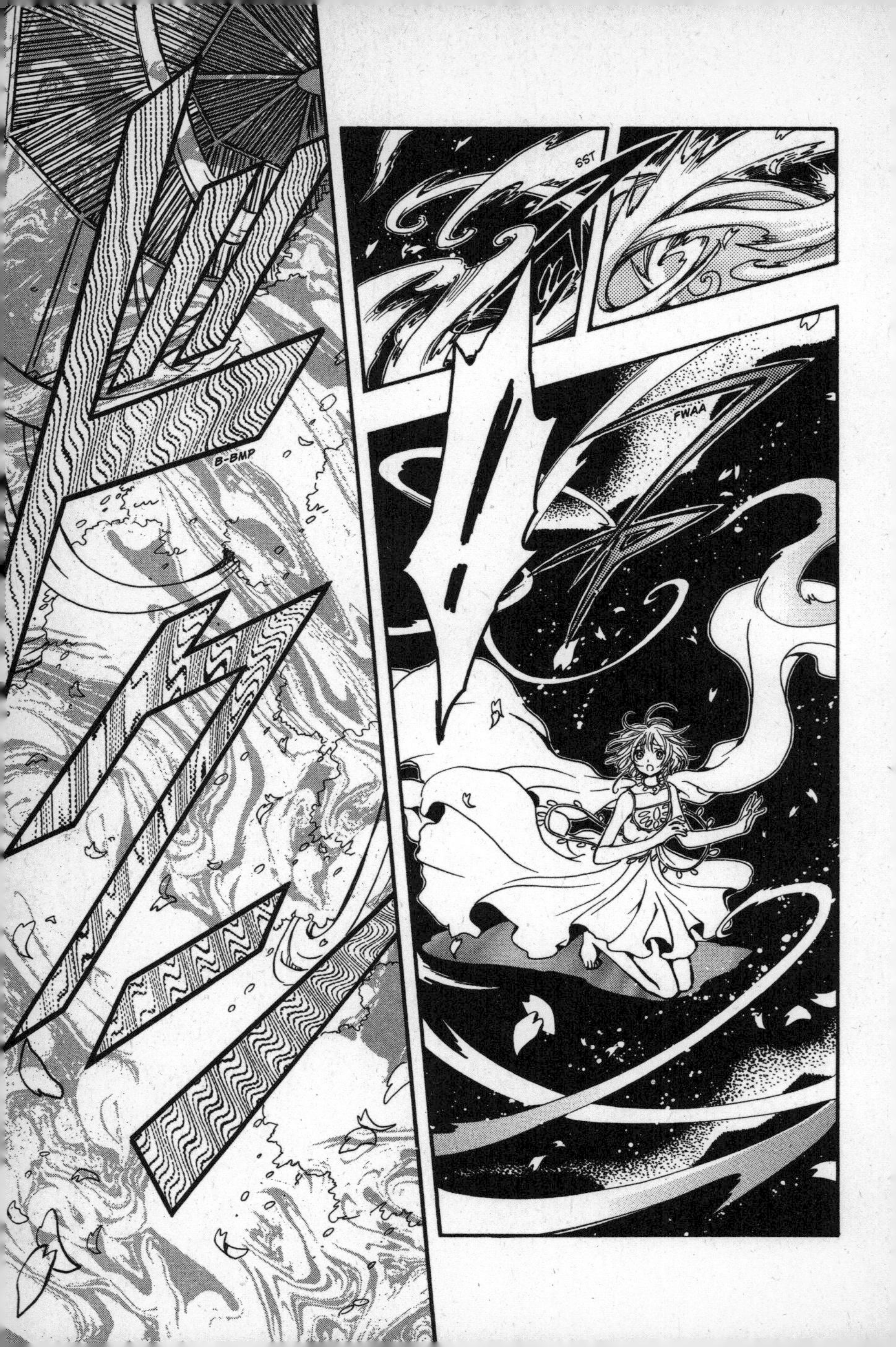
SST
FWAA
B-BMP

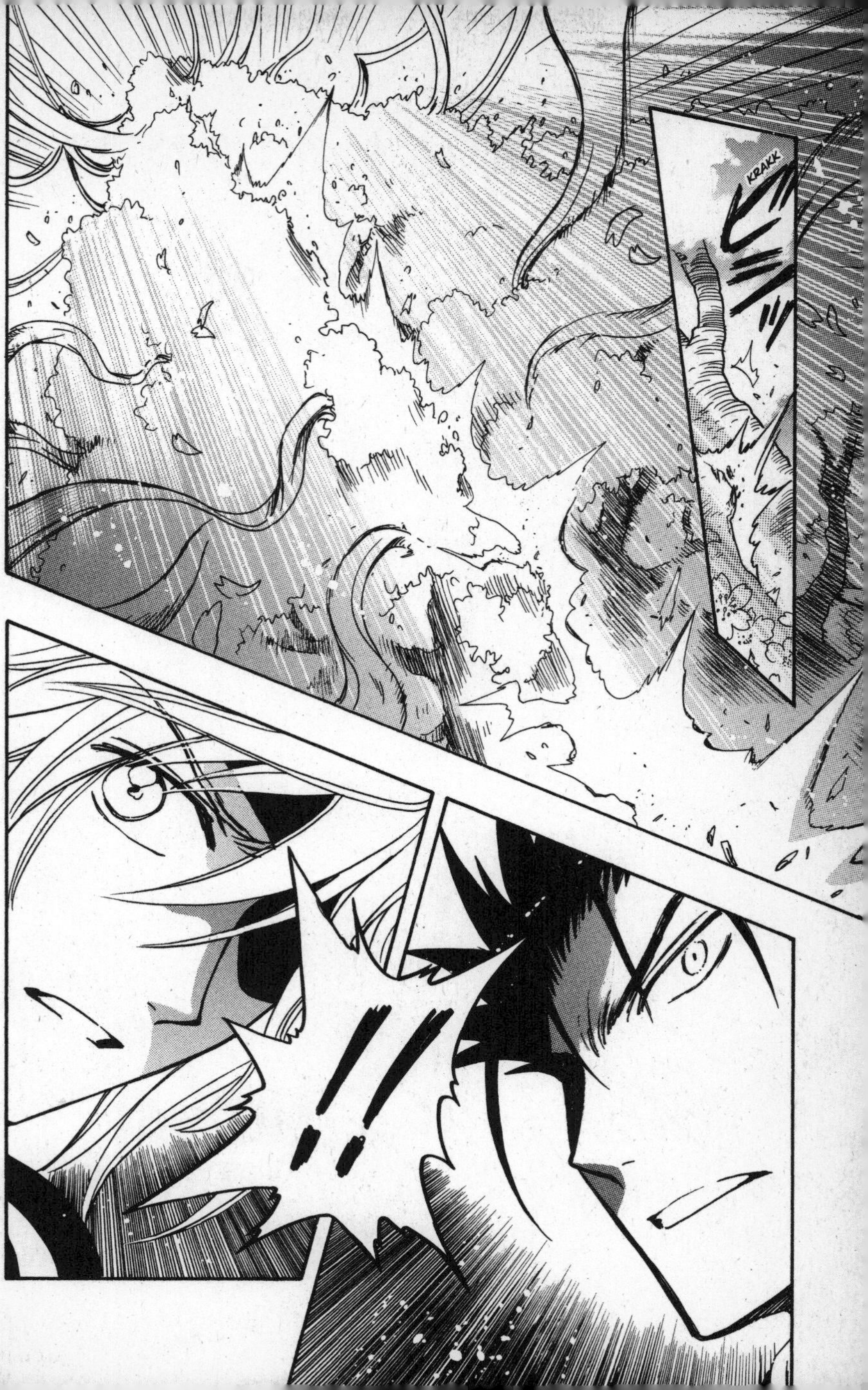
KRAKK

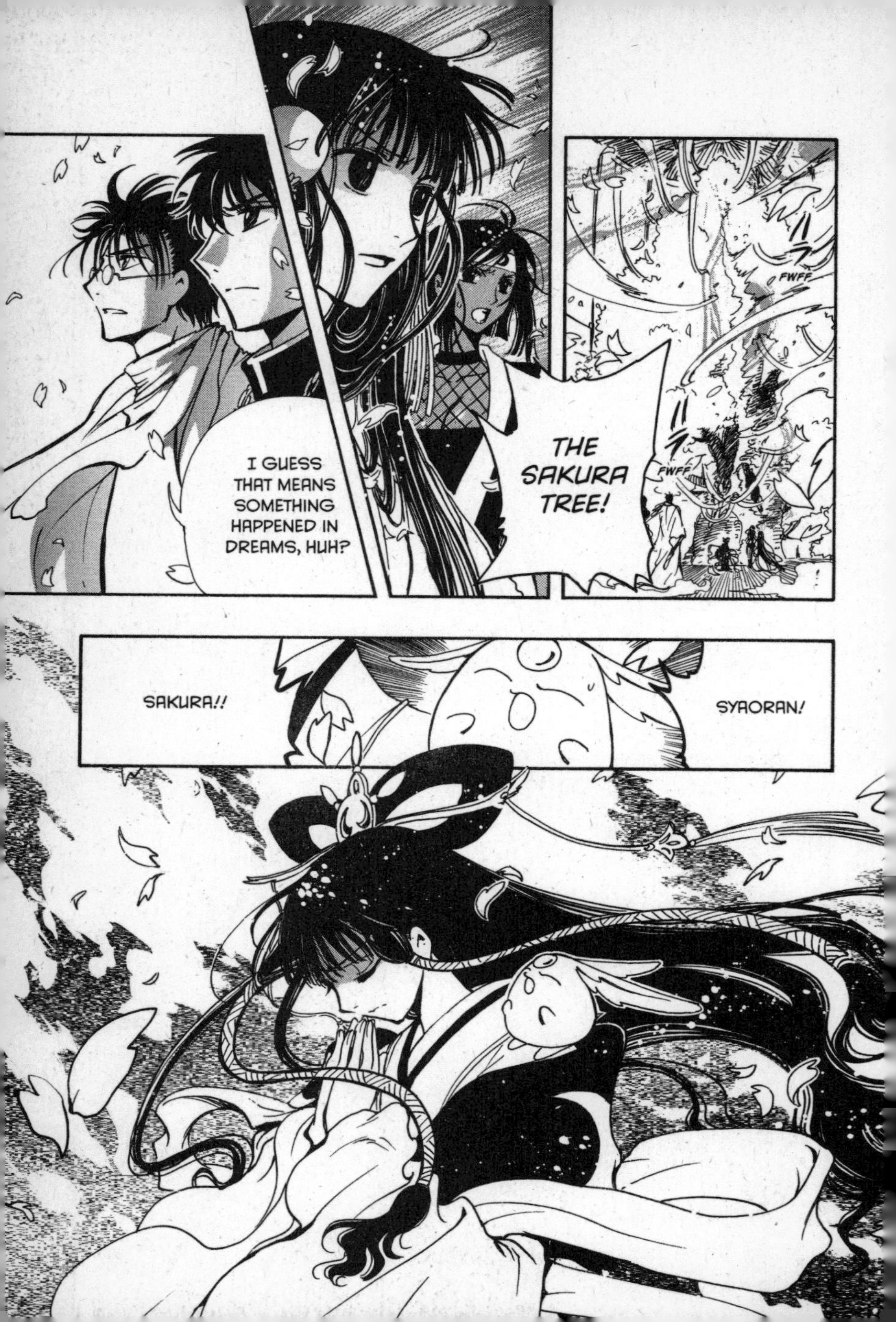
FWFF
FWFF
THE SAKURA TREE!
I GUESS THAT MEANS SOMETHING HAPPENED IN DREAMS, HUH?
SYAORAN!
SAKURA!!

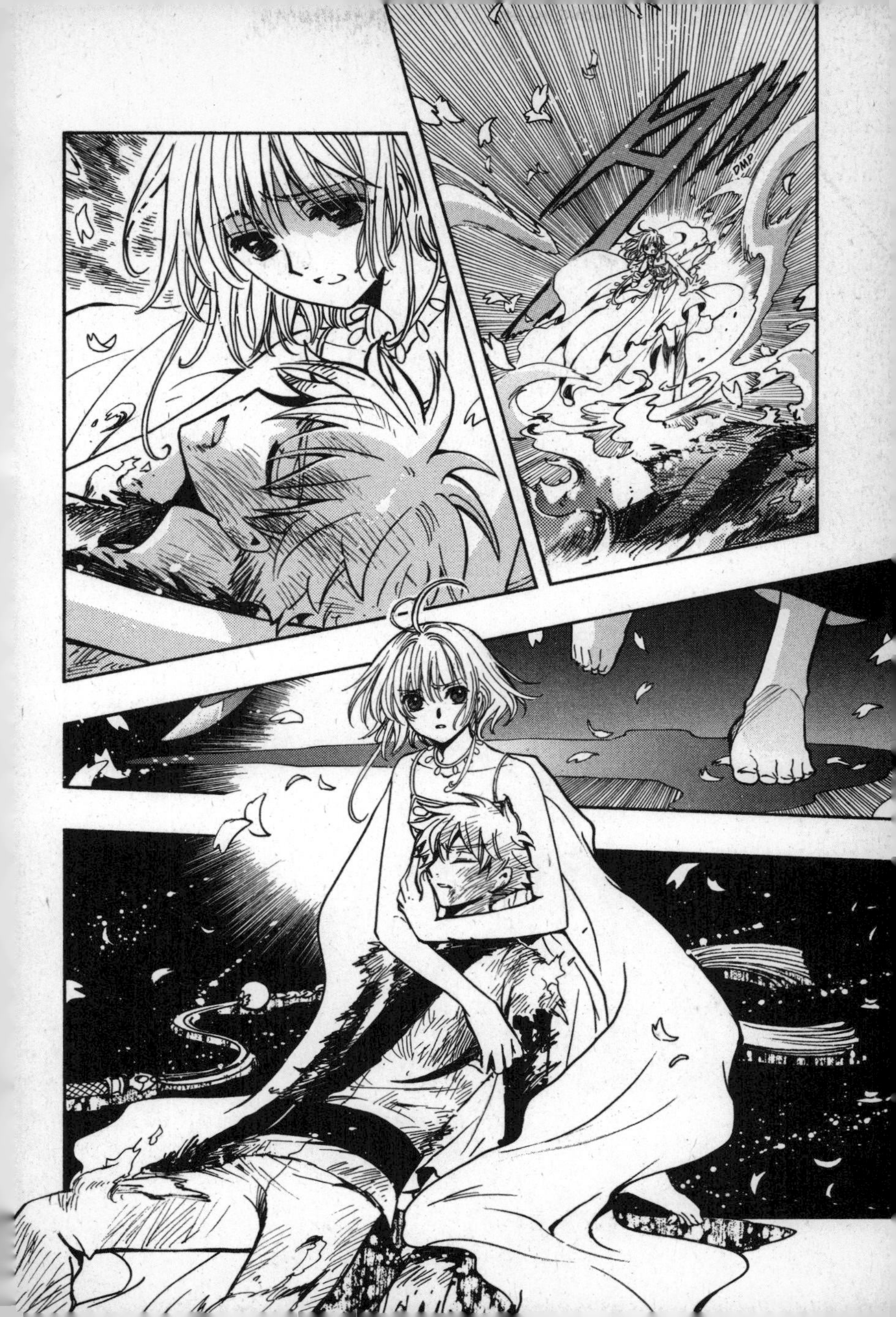
DMP

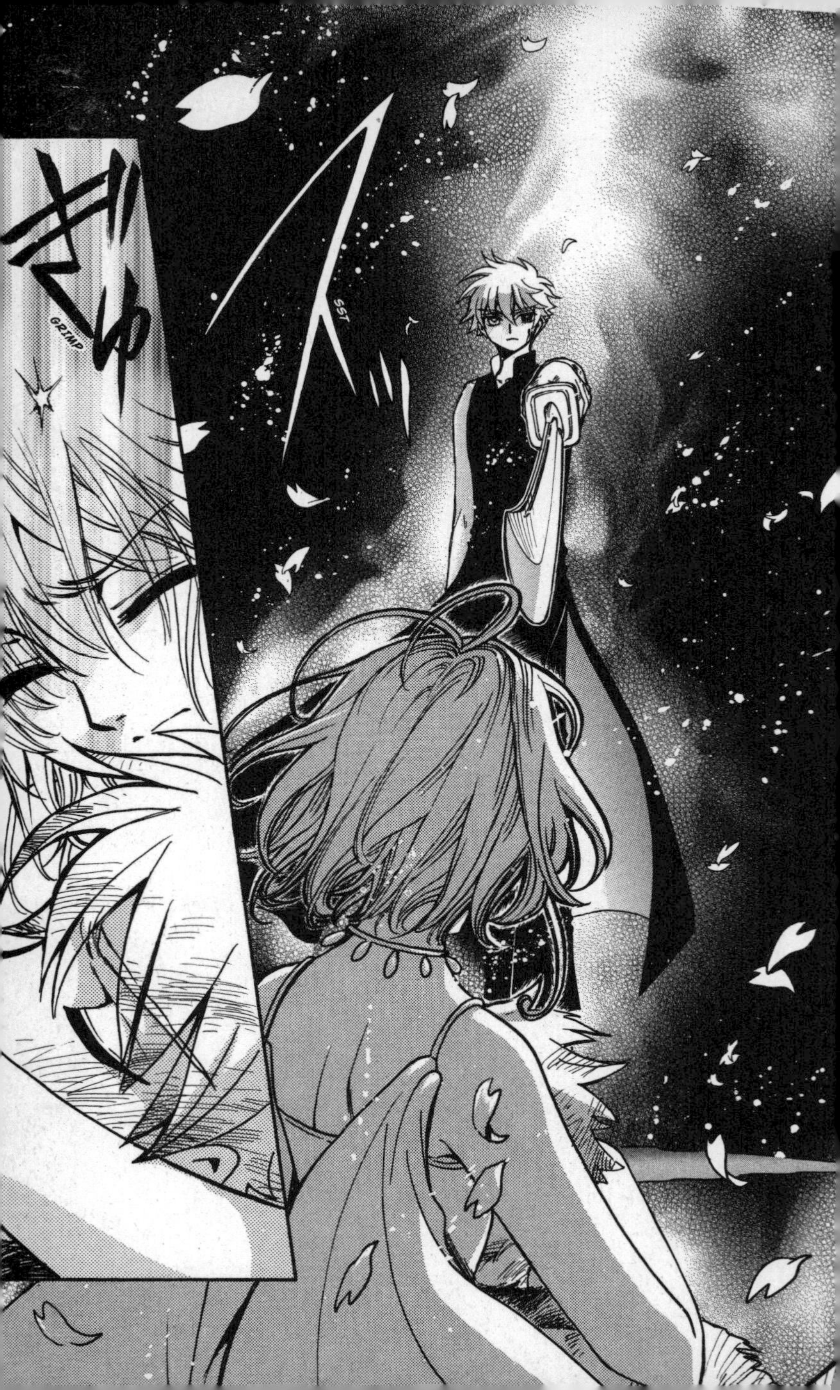
ス
SST
ぎゅ
GRIMP

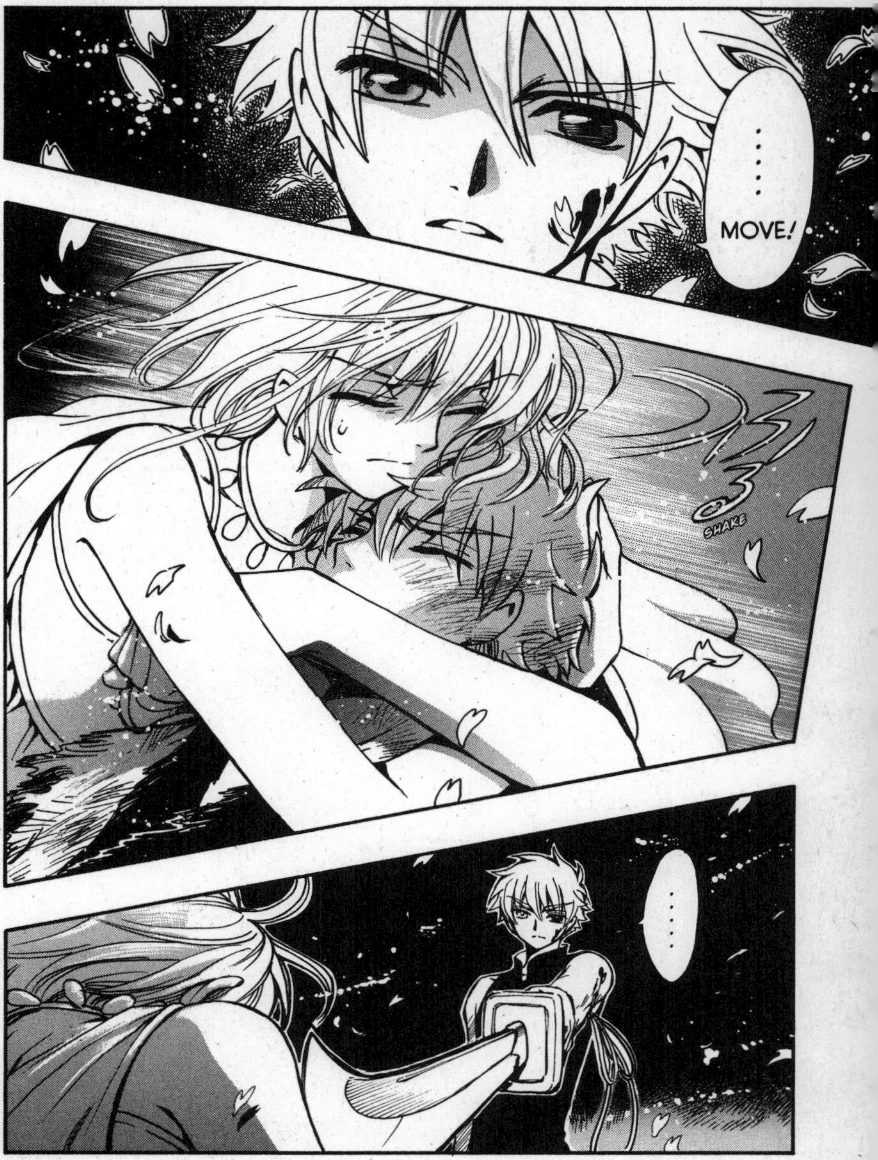
......
MOVE!
SHAKE
......

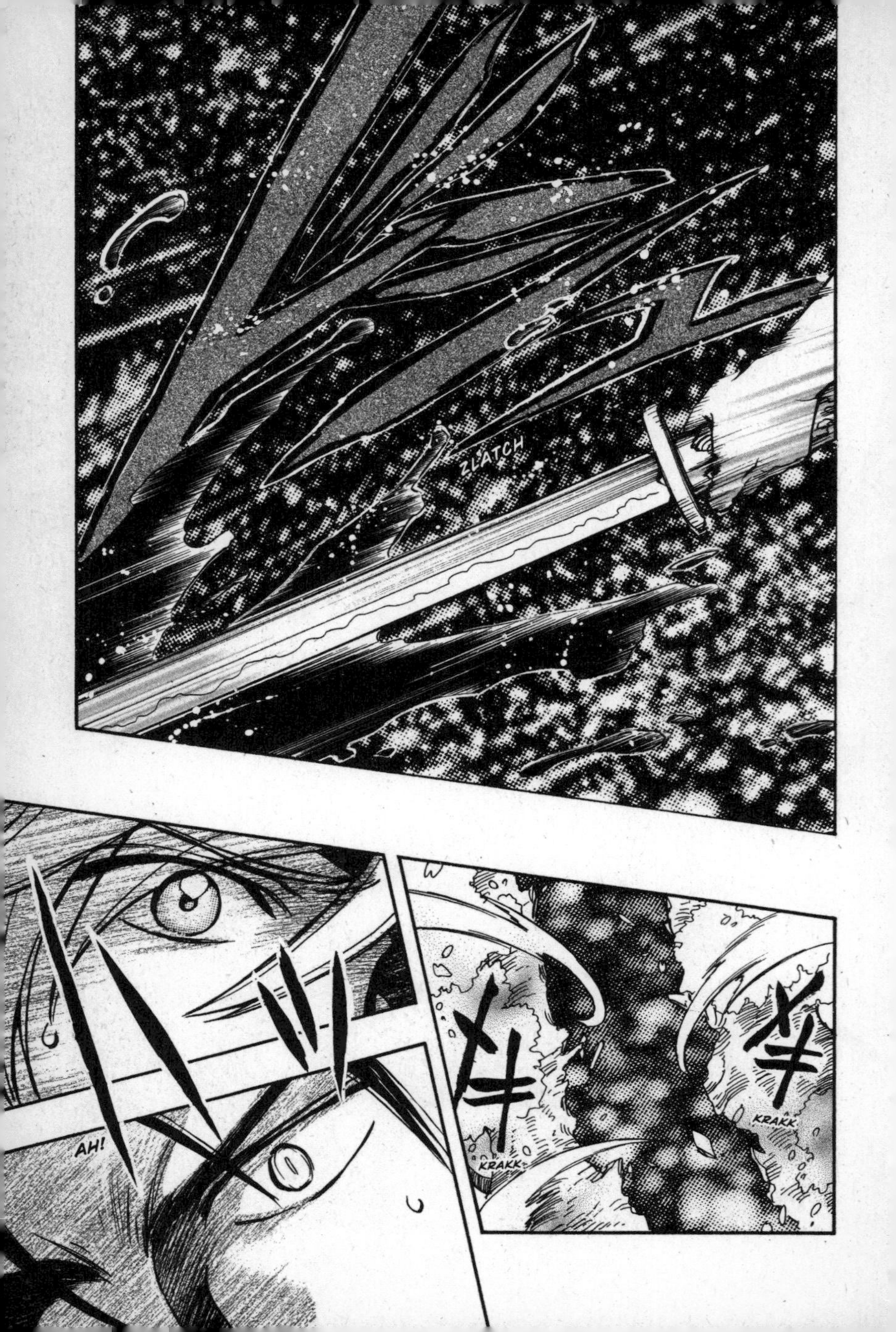
ZLATCH
KRAKK
KRAKK
AH!

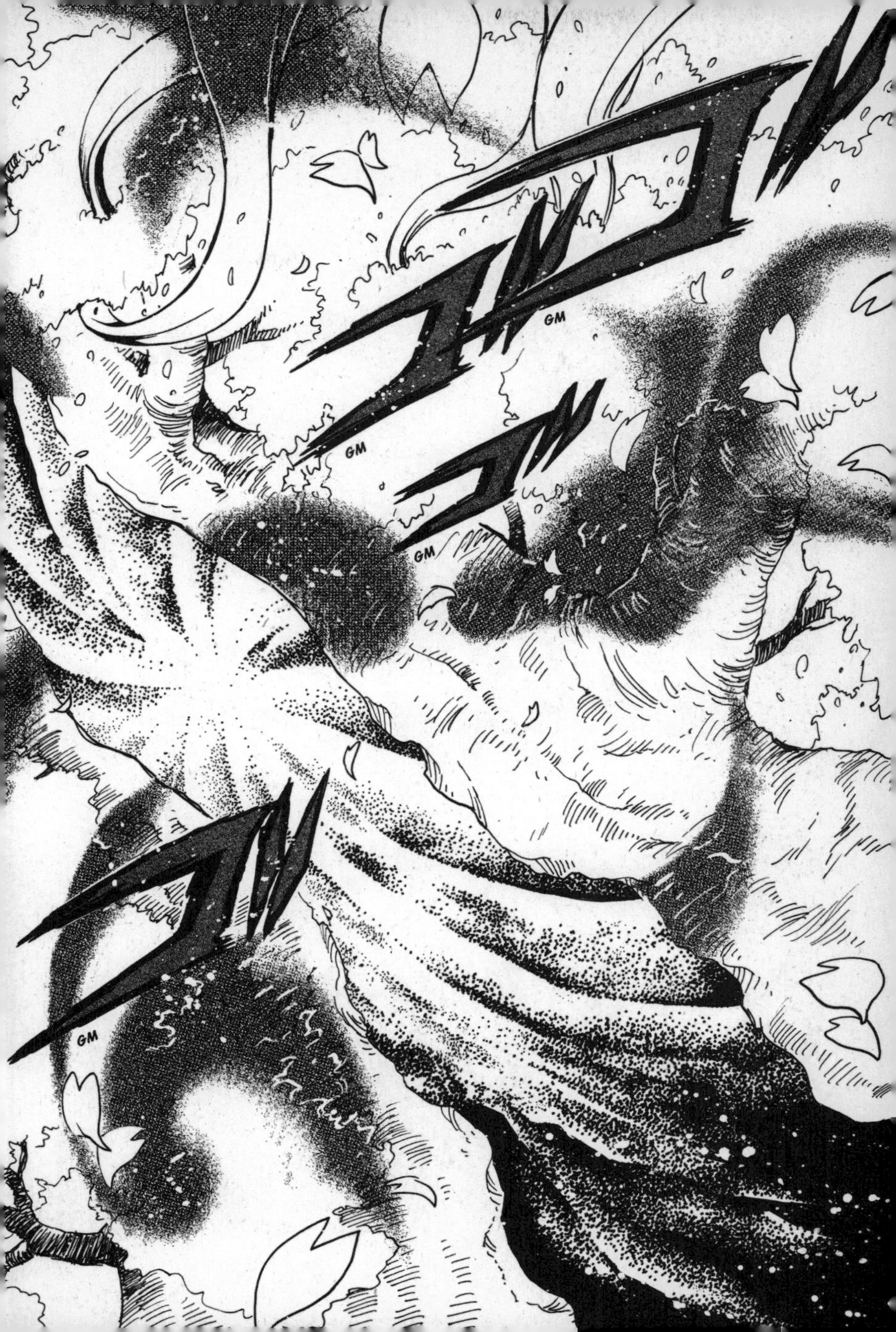
GM
GM
GM
GM

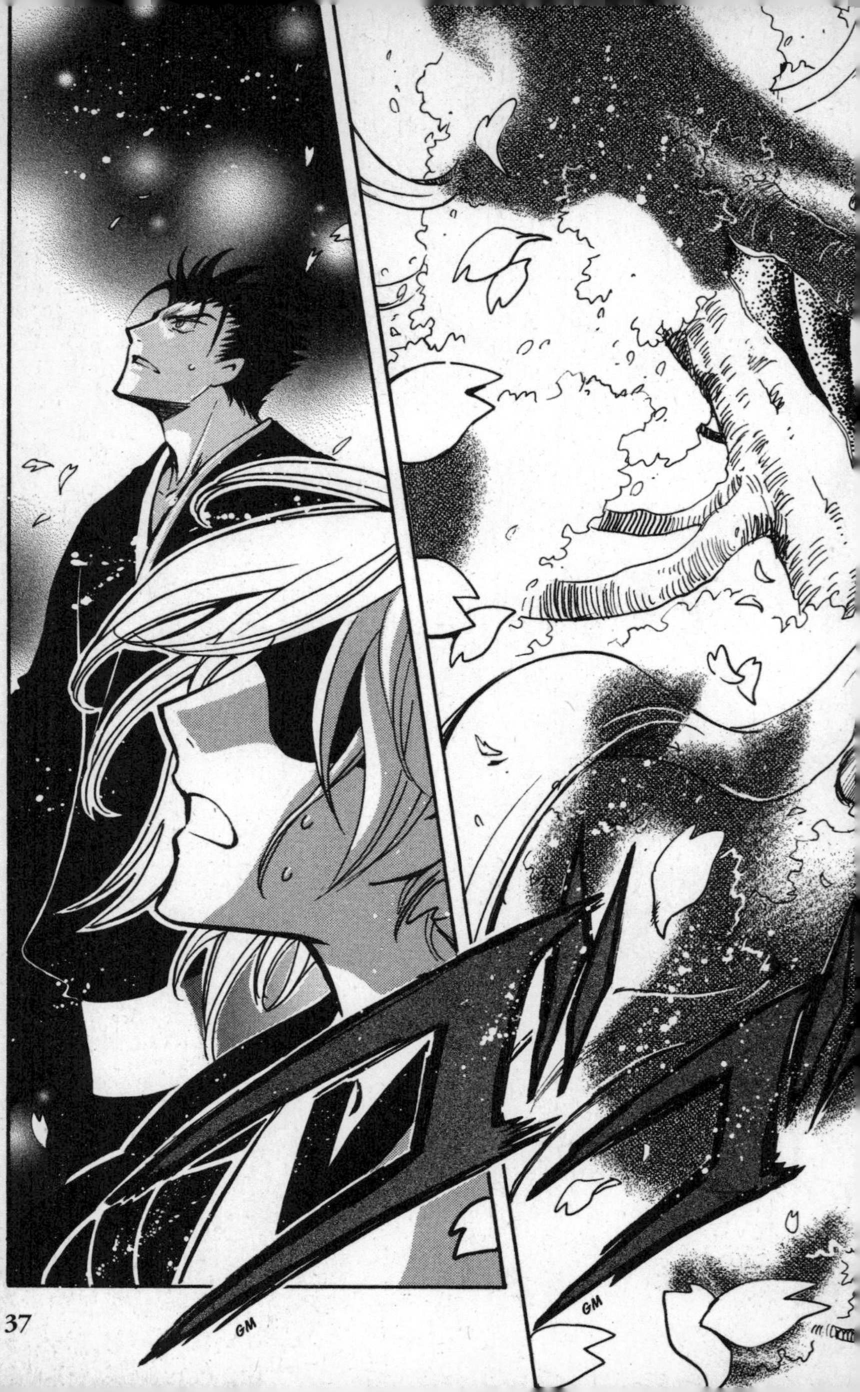

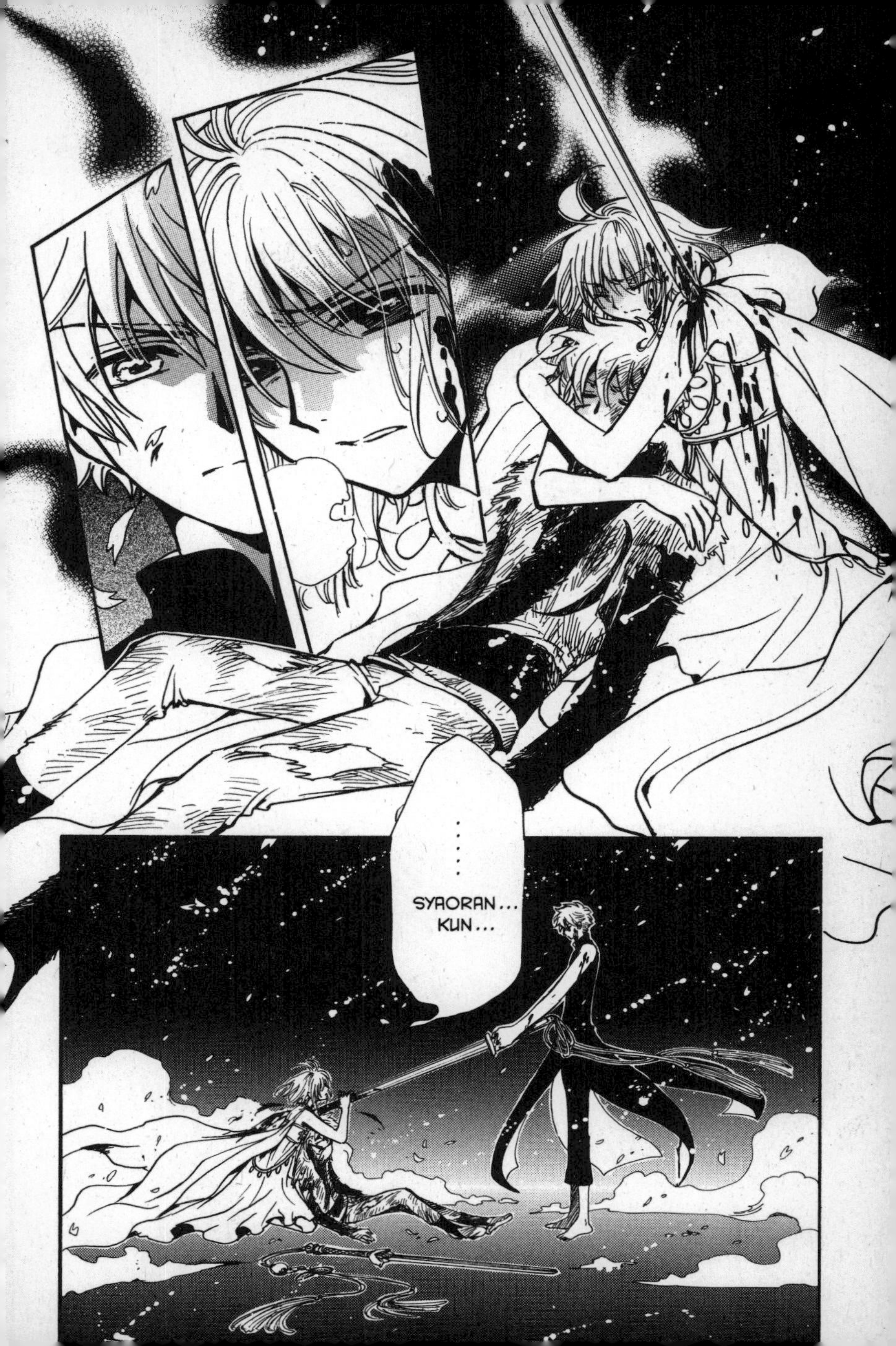
. . . . .
SYAORAN... KUN...

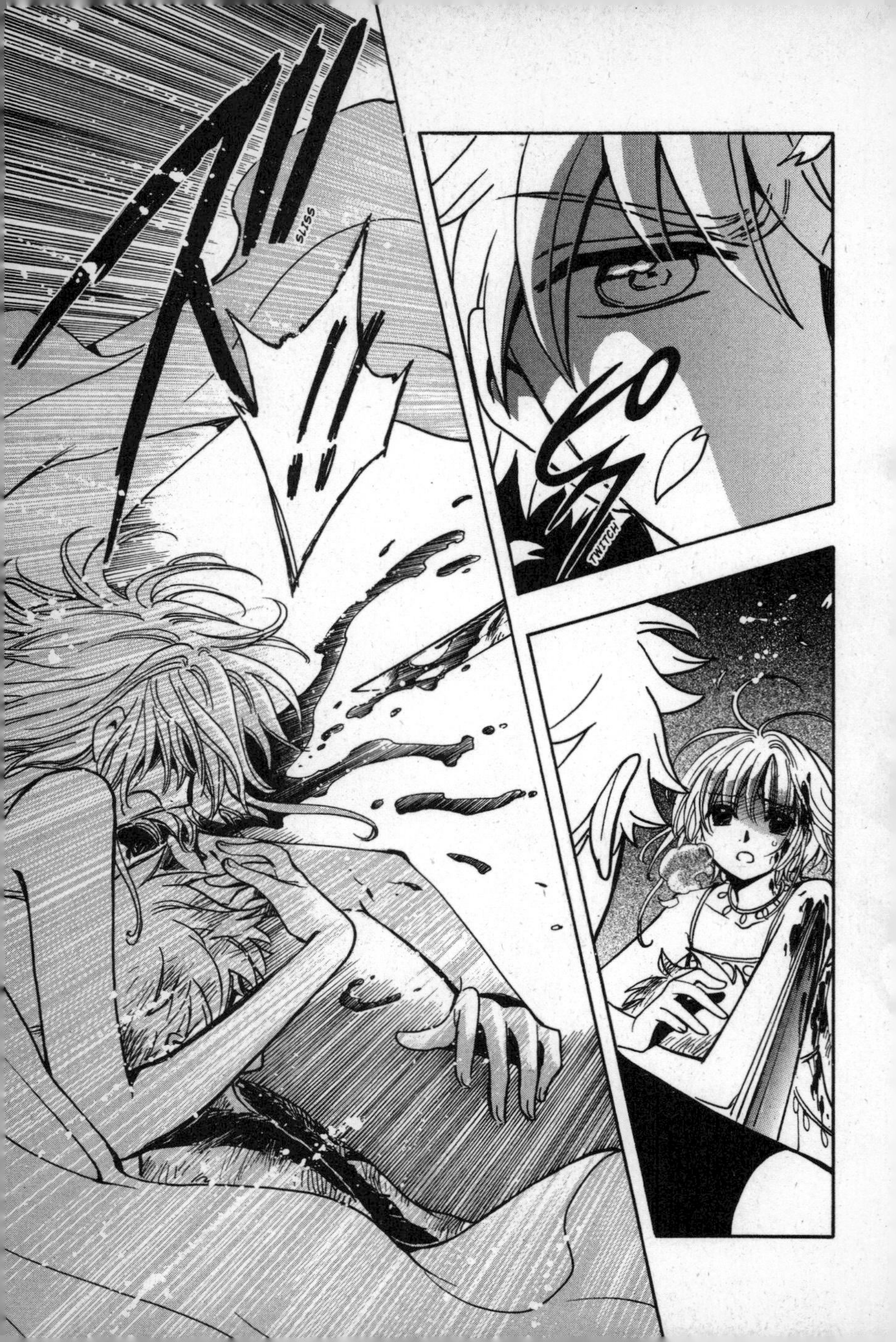
TWITCH
SLISS

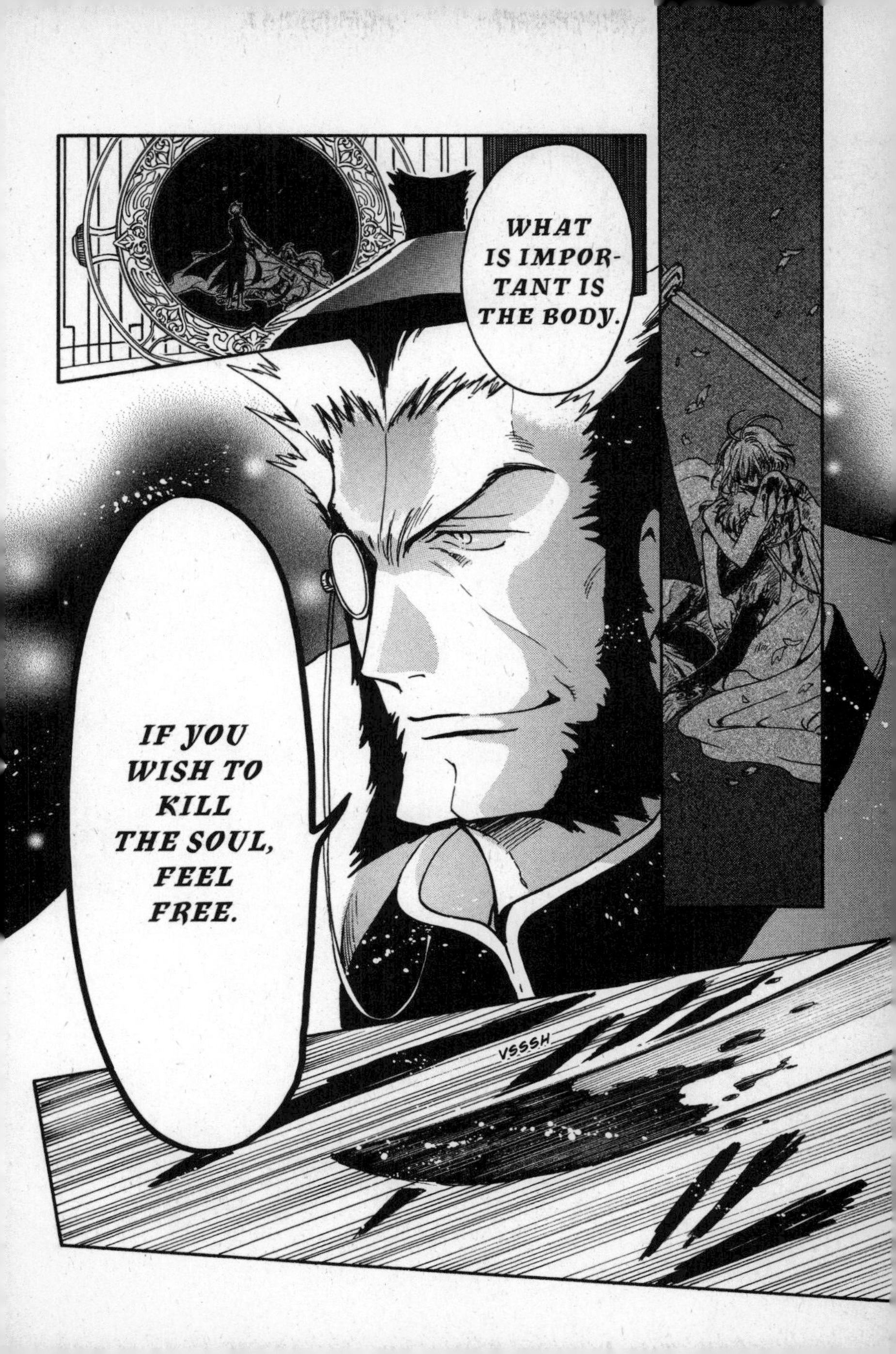
WHAT IS IMPORTANT IS THE BODY.
IF YOU WISH TO KILL THE SOUL, FEEL FREE.
VSSSH

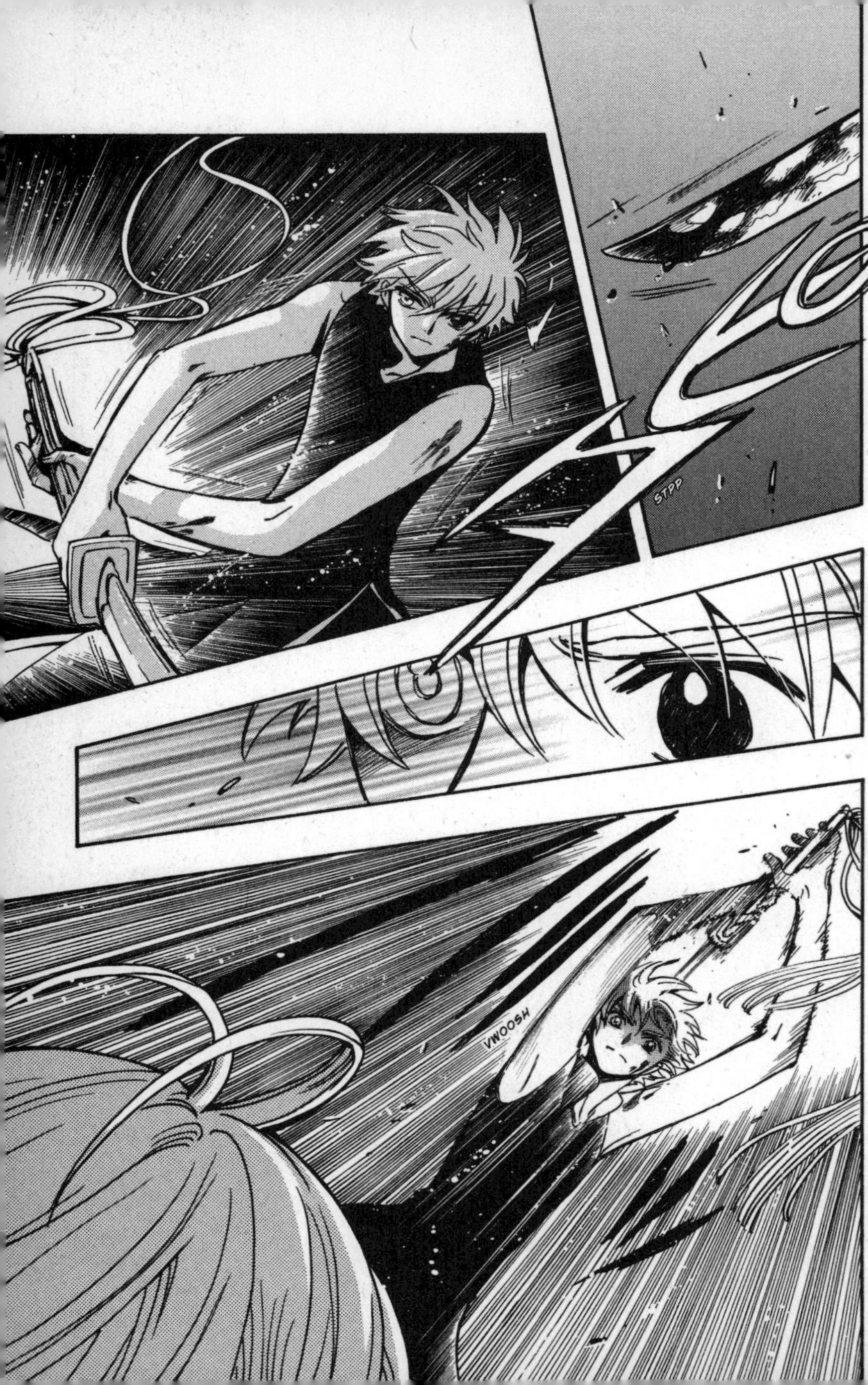
STPP
VWOOSH

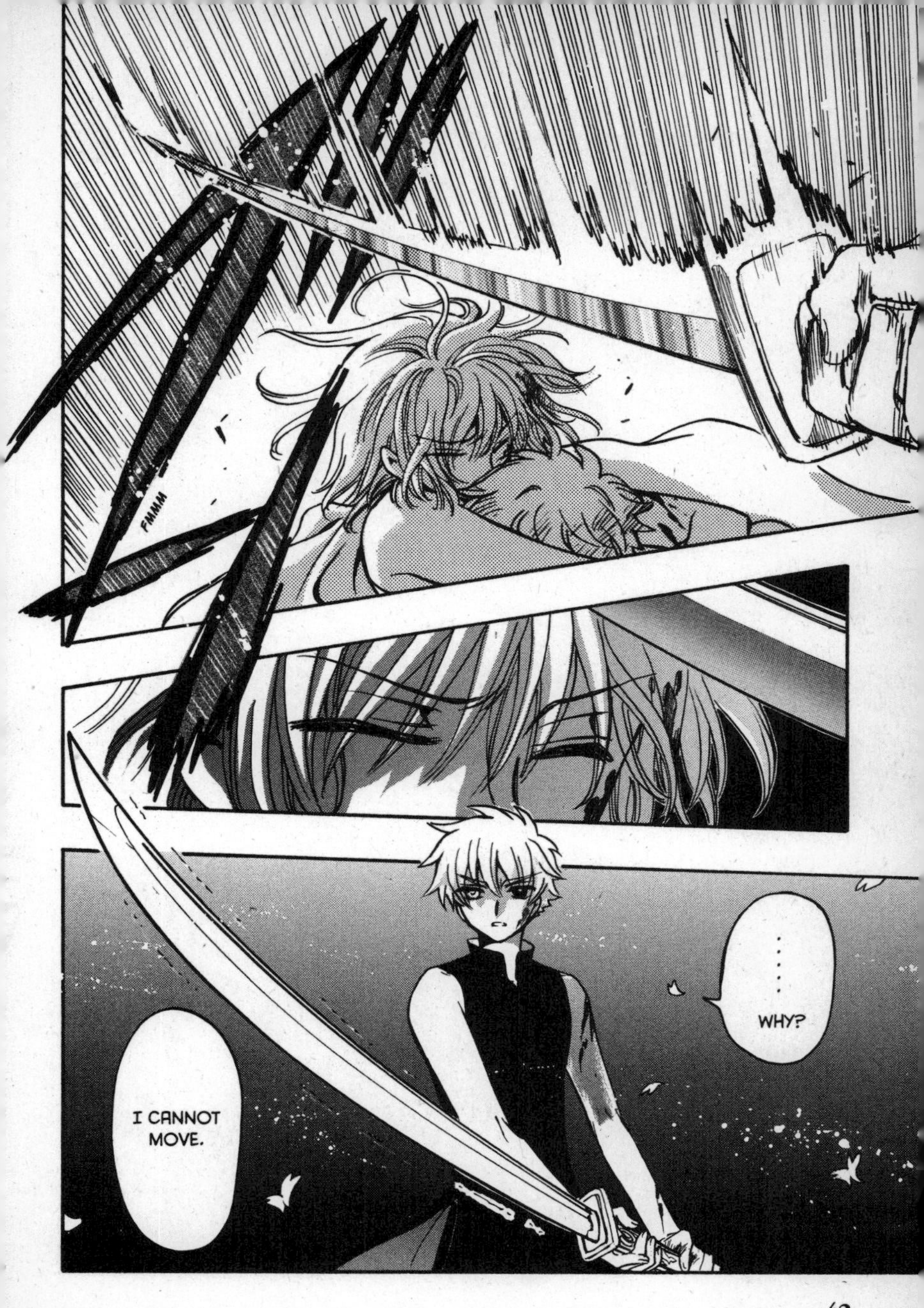
FMMM
...... WHY?
I CANNOT MOVE.

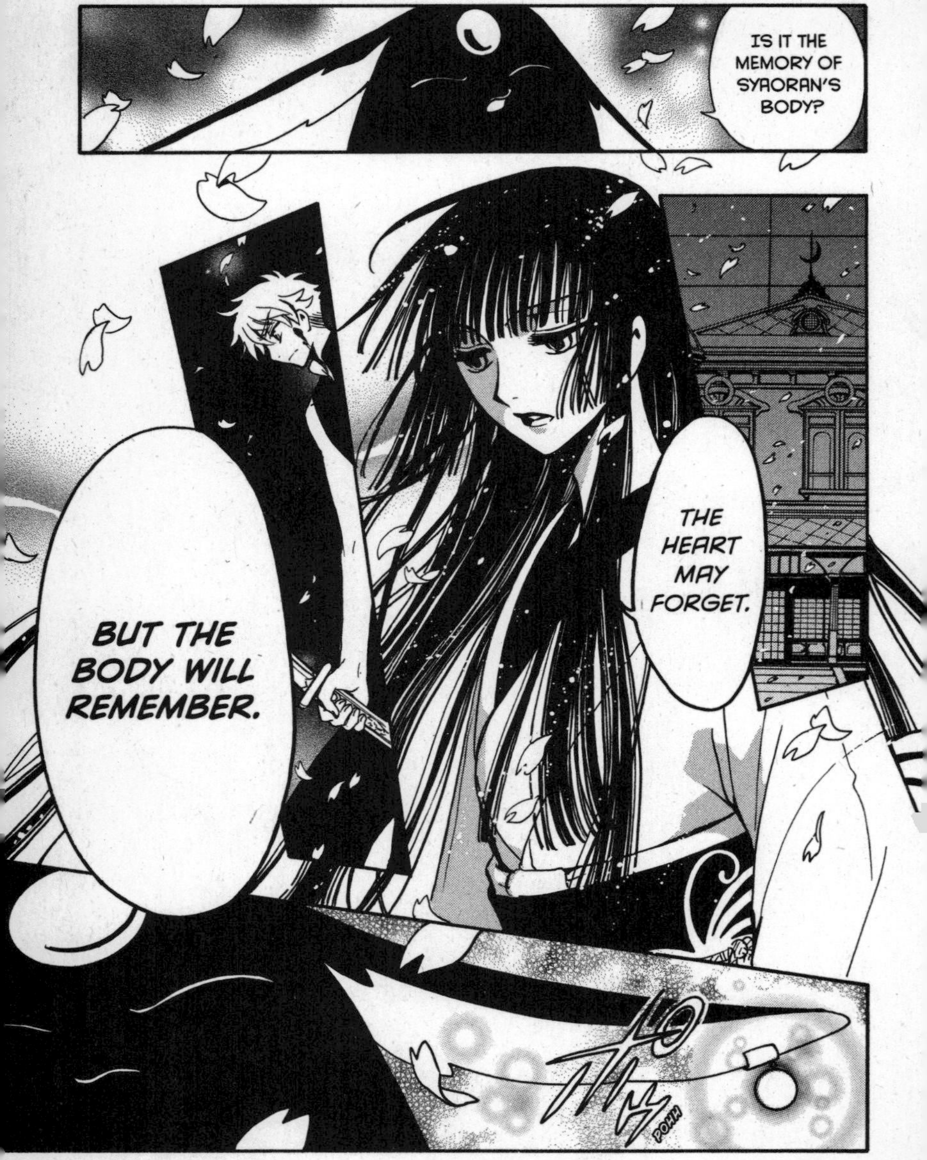
IS IT THE MEMORY OF SYAORAN'S BODY?
THE HEART MAY FORGET.
BUT THE BODY WILL REMEMBER.
POHH

ツバサ
RESERVoir CHRoNiCLE

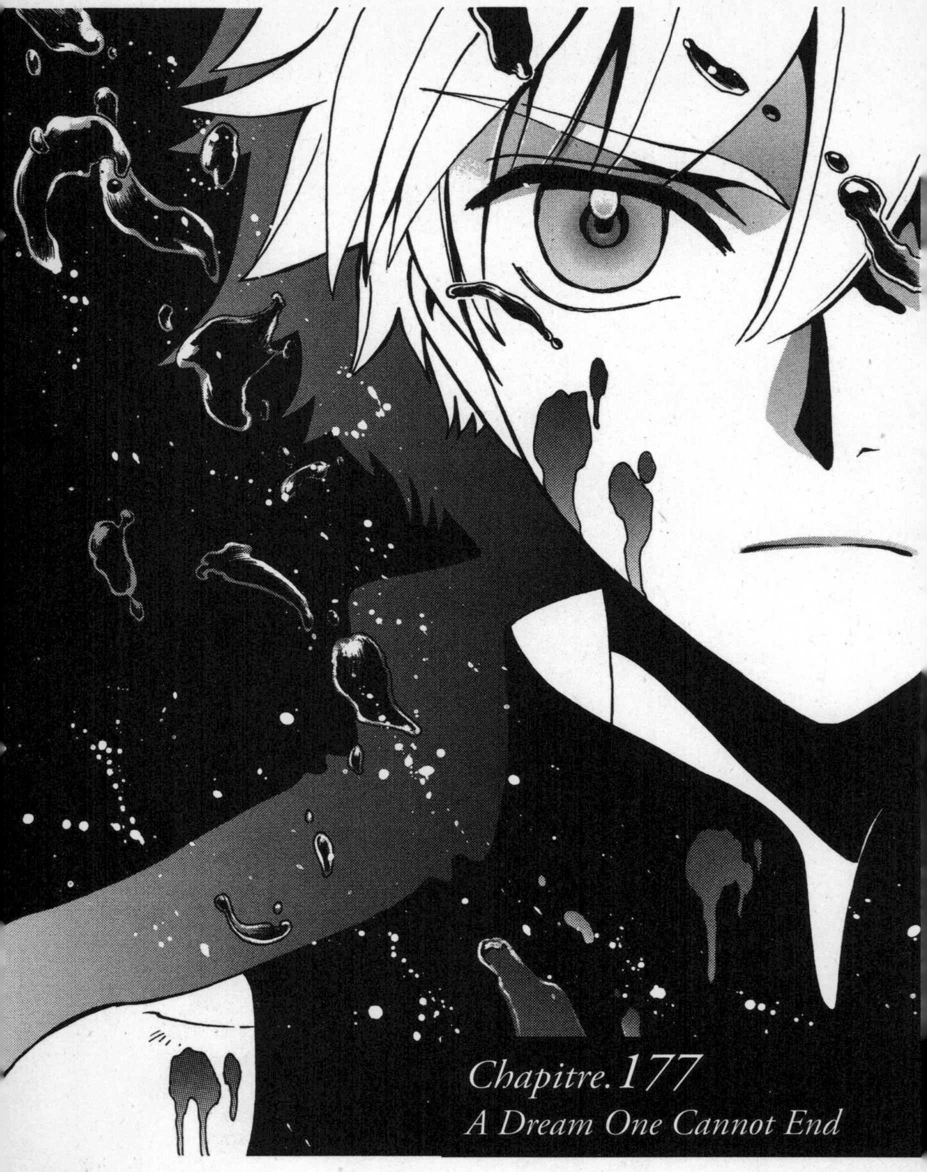
Chapitre. 177
A Dream One Cannot End

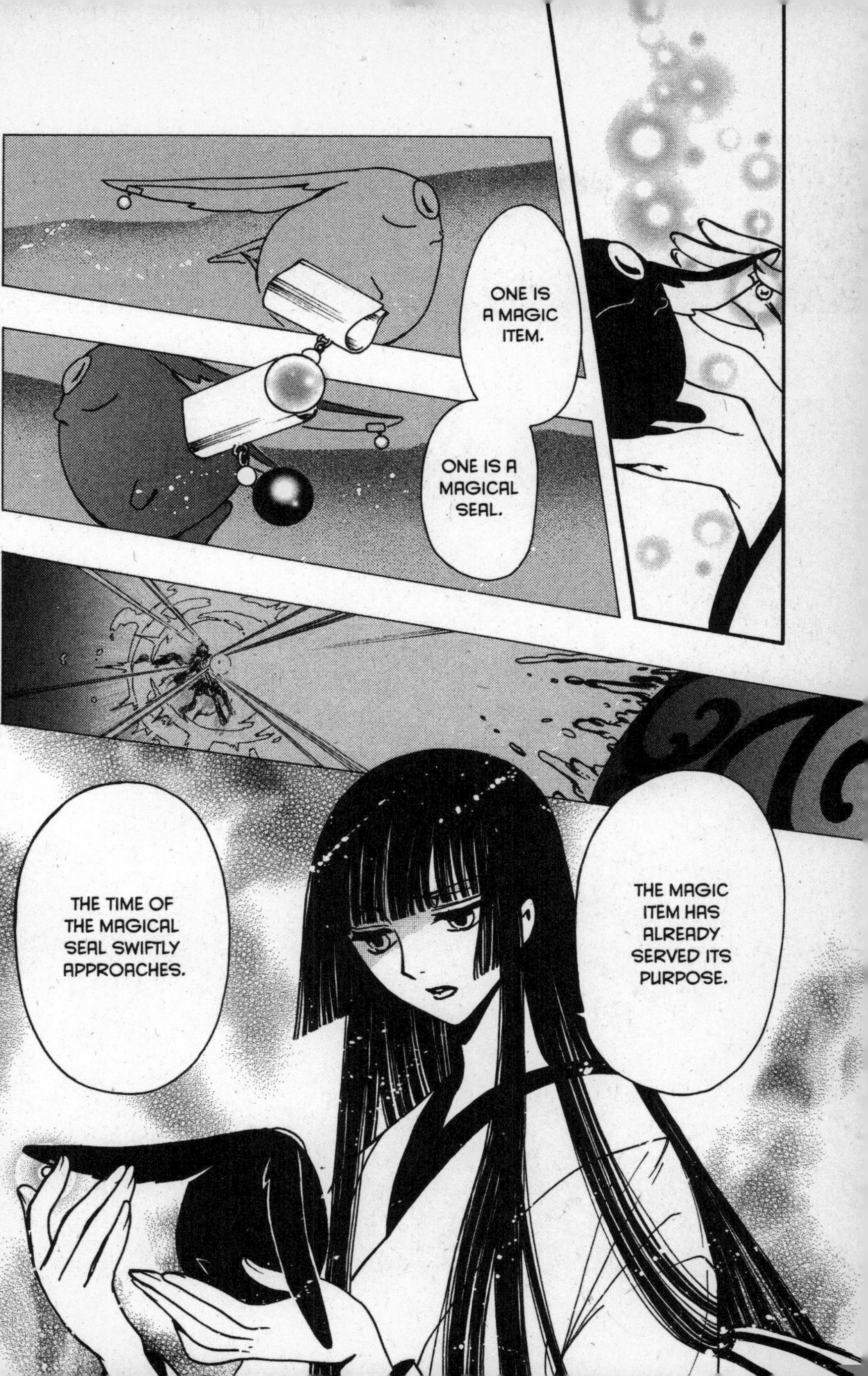
ONE IS A MAGIC ITEM.
ONE IS A MAGICAL SEAL.
THE MAGIC ITEM HAS ALREADY SERVED ITS PURPOSE.
THE TIME OF THE MAGICAL SEAL SWIFTLY APPROACHES.

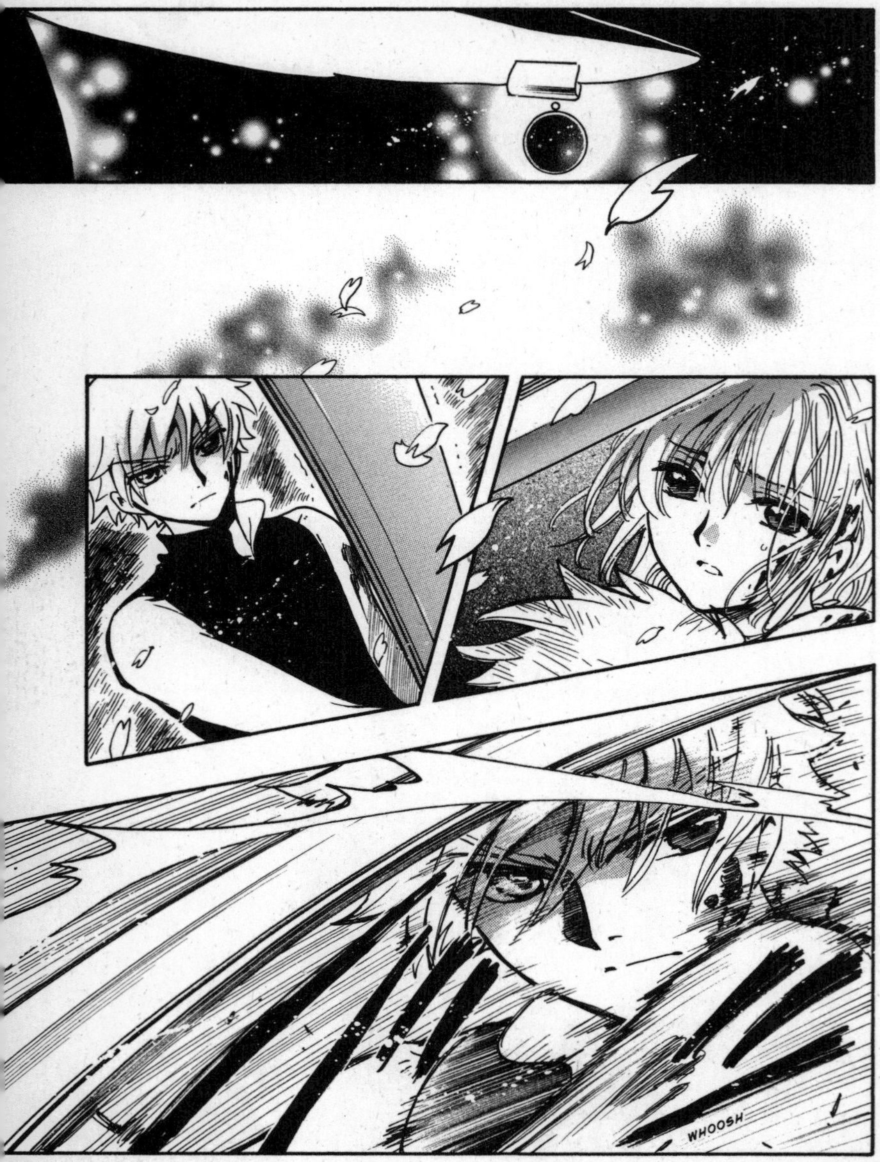
WHOOSH

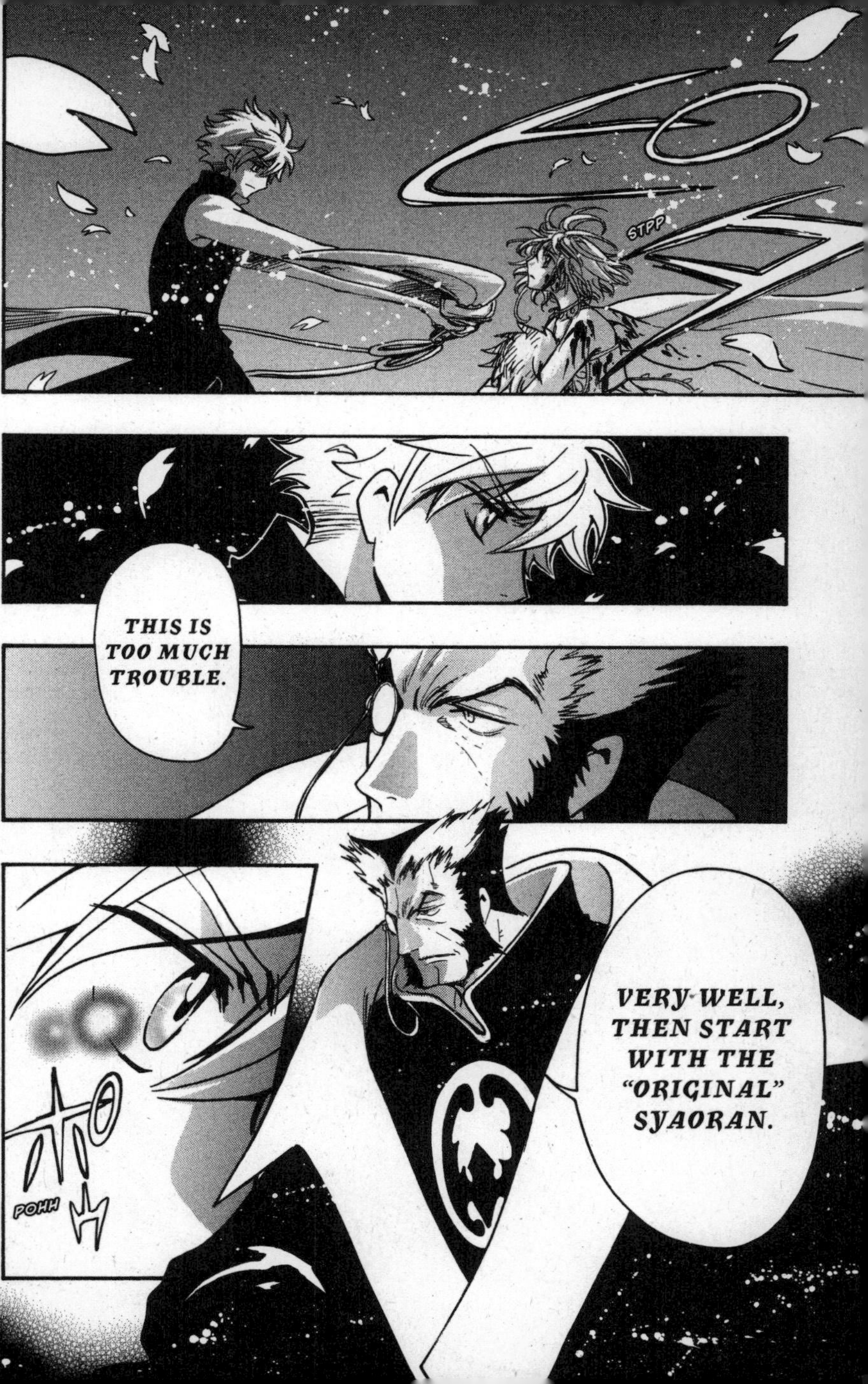
STPP
THIS IS TOO MUCH TROUBLE.
VERY WELL, THEN START WITH THE "ORIGINAL" SYAORAN.
POHH

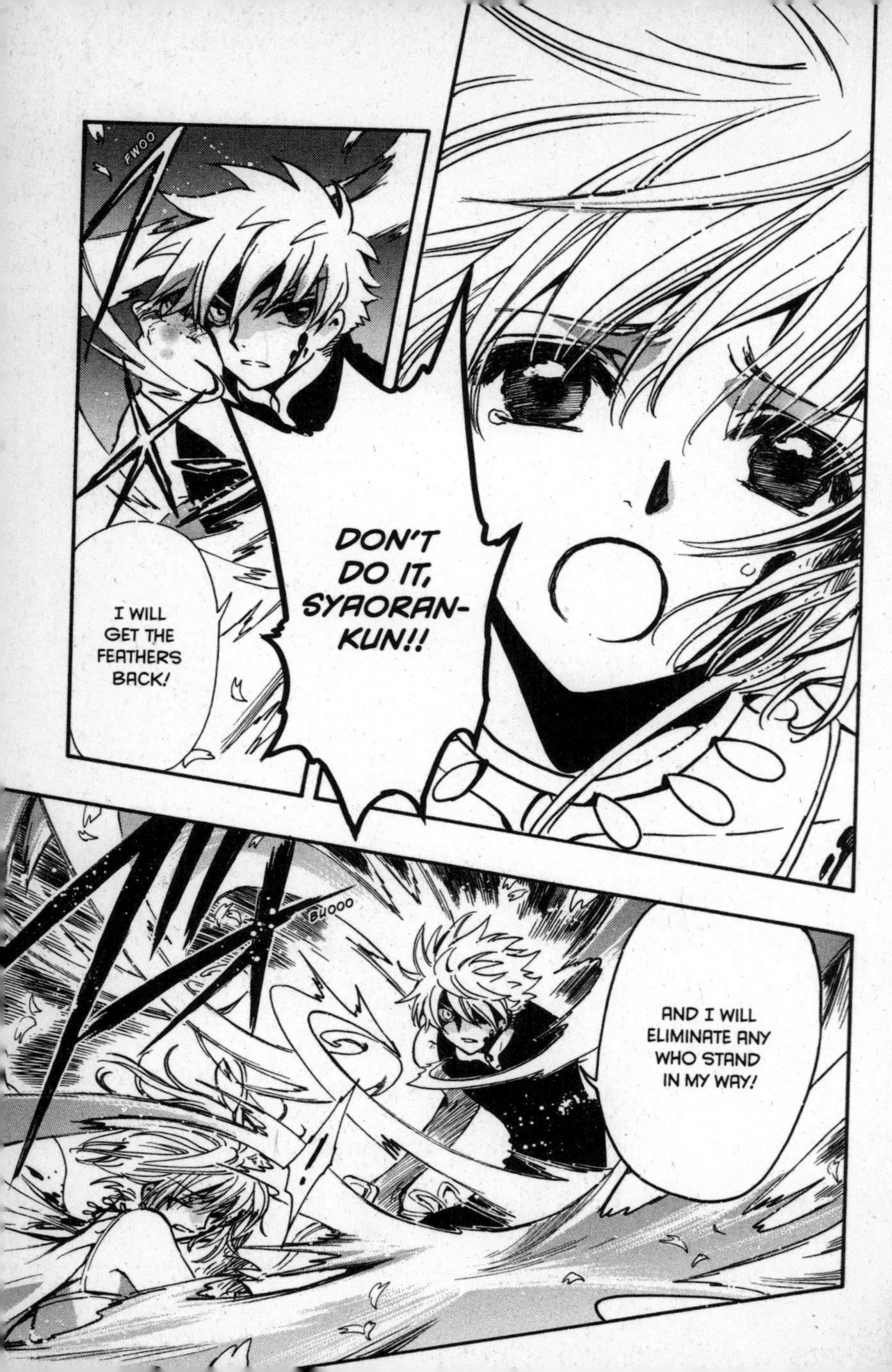
DON'T DO IT, SYAORAN-KUN!!
FWOO
I WILL GET THE FEATHERS BACK!
BUOOO
AND I WILL ELIMINATE ANY WHO STAND IN MY WAY!

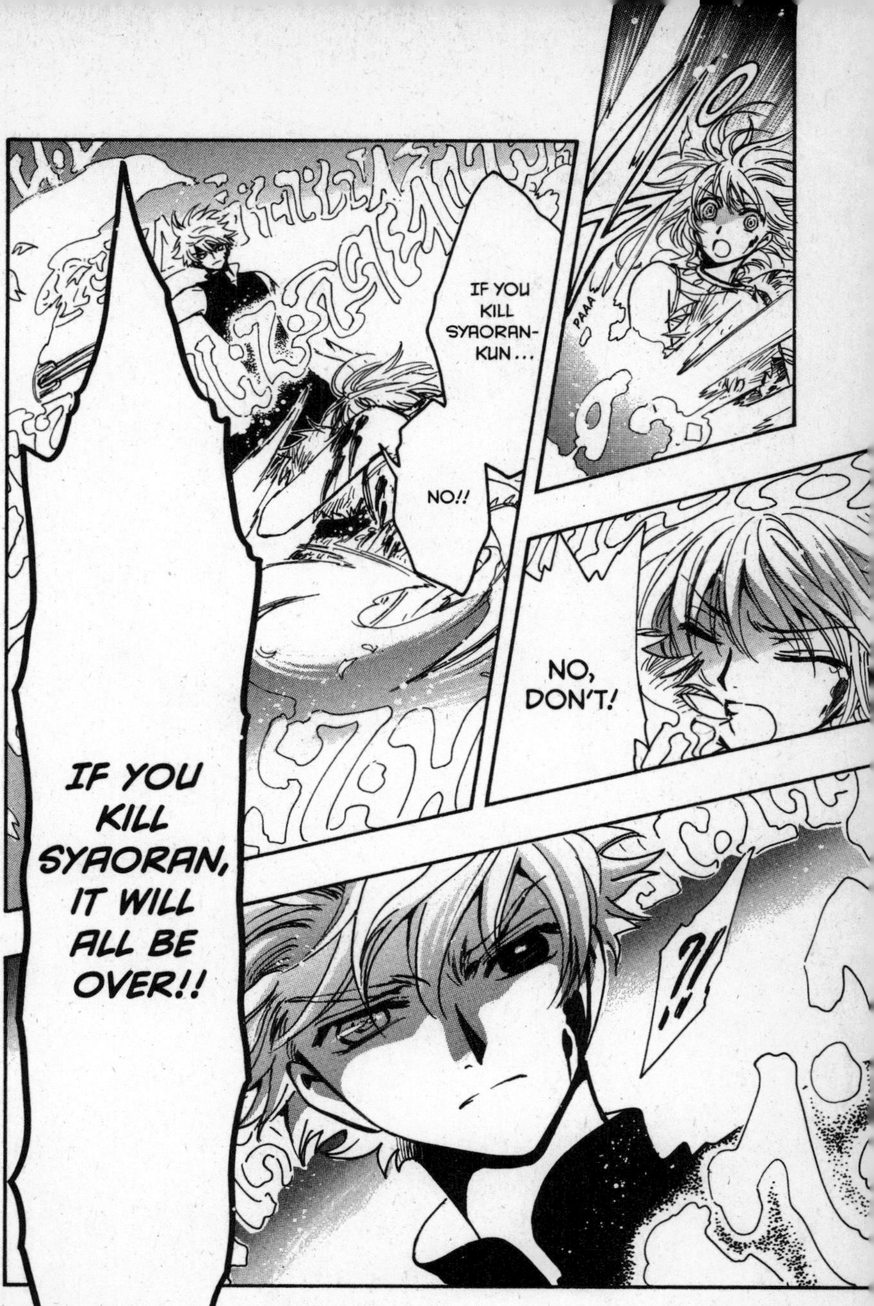
PAAA
IF YOU KILL SYAORAN-KUN...
NO!!
NO, DON'T!
IF YOU KILL SYAORAN, IT WILL ALL BE OVER!!
?!

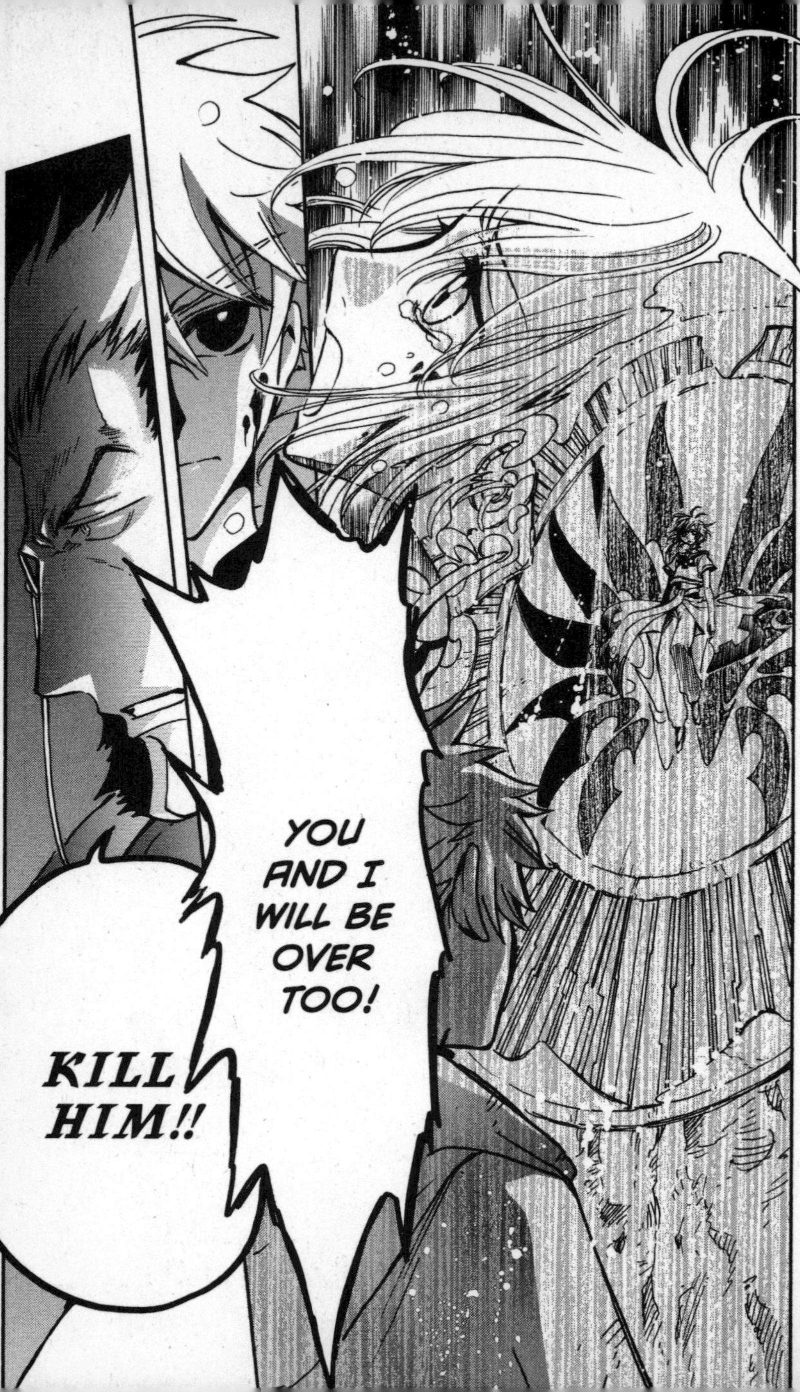
YOU AND I WILL BE OVER TOO!
KILL HIM!!

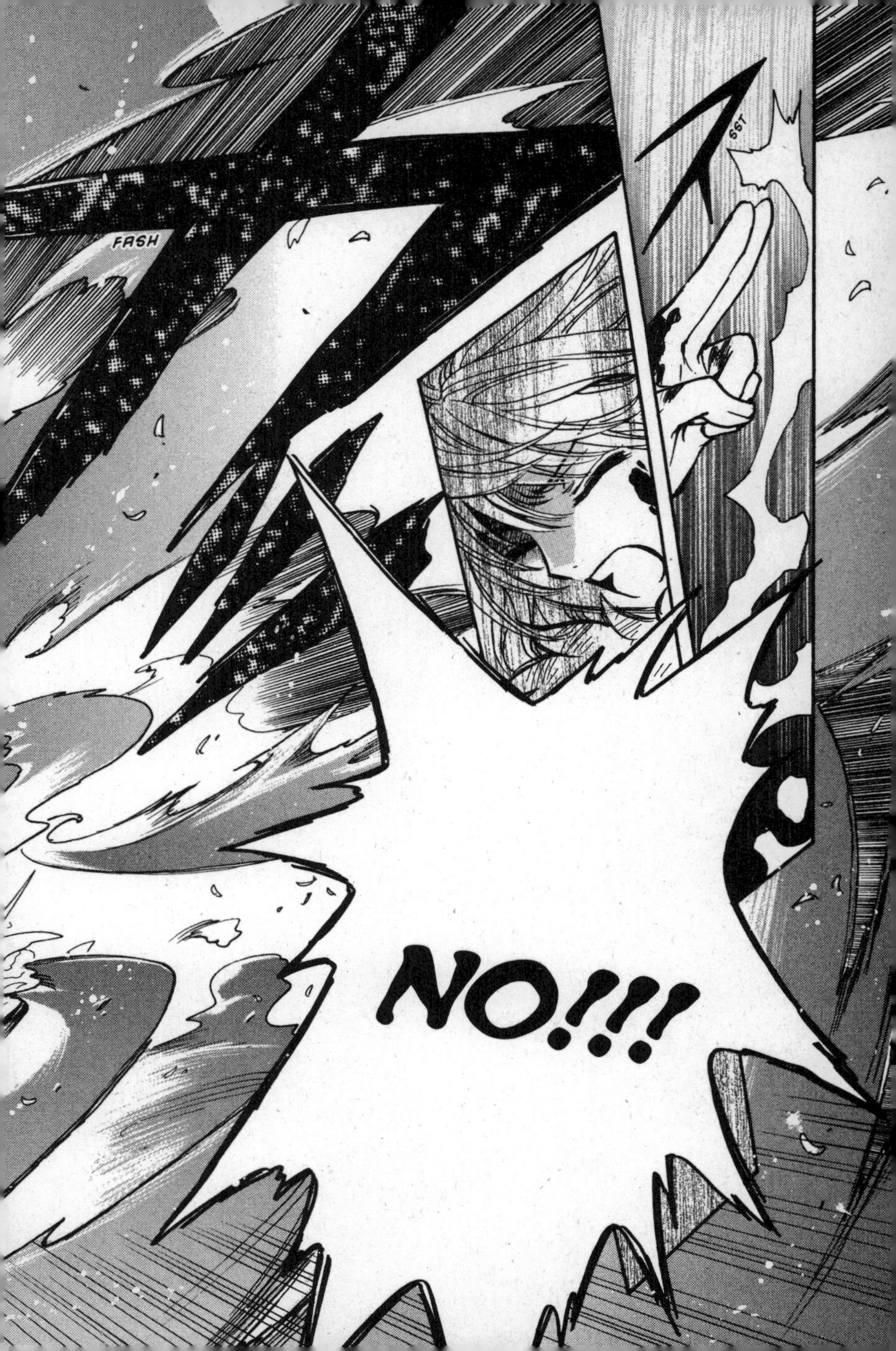
SST
FASH
NO!!!

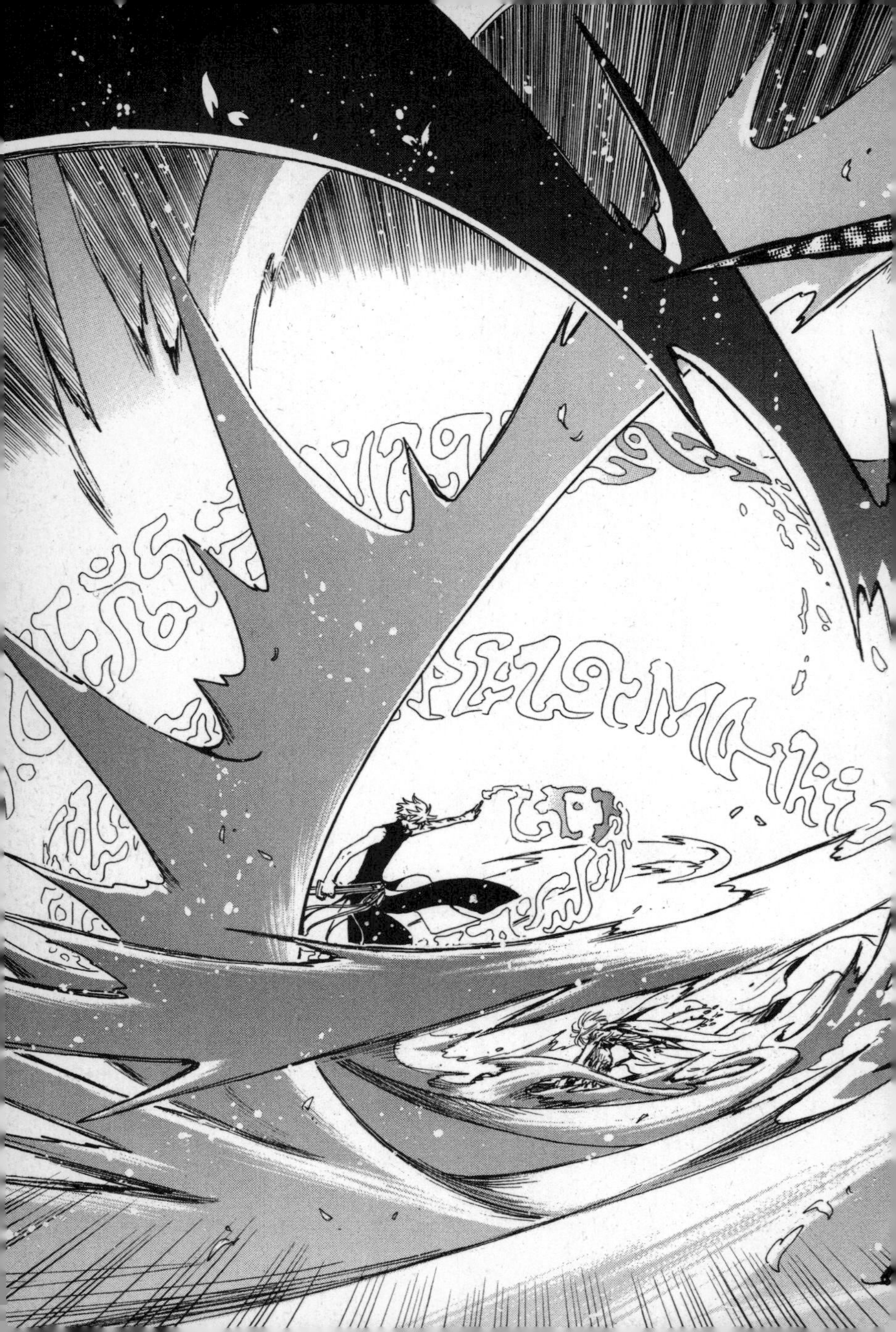

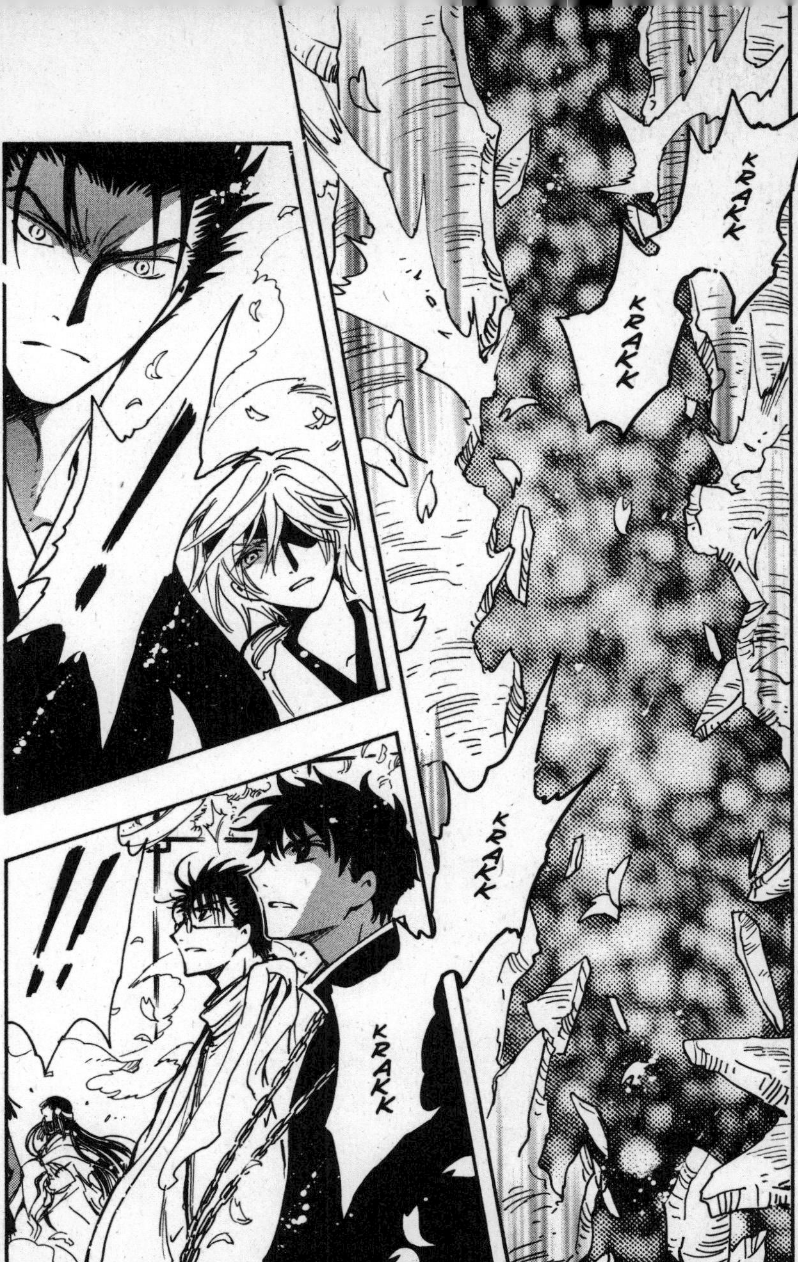

KRAKK
KRAKK
KRAKK
KRAKK
!!

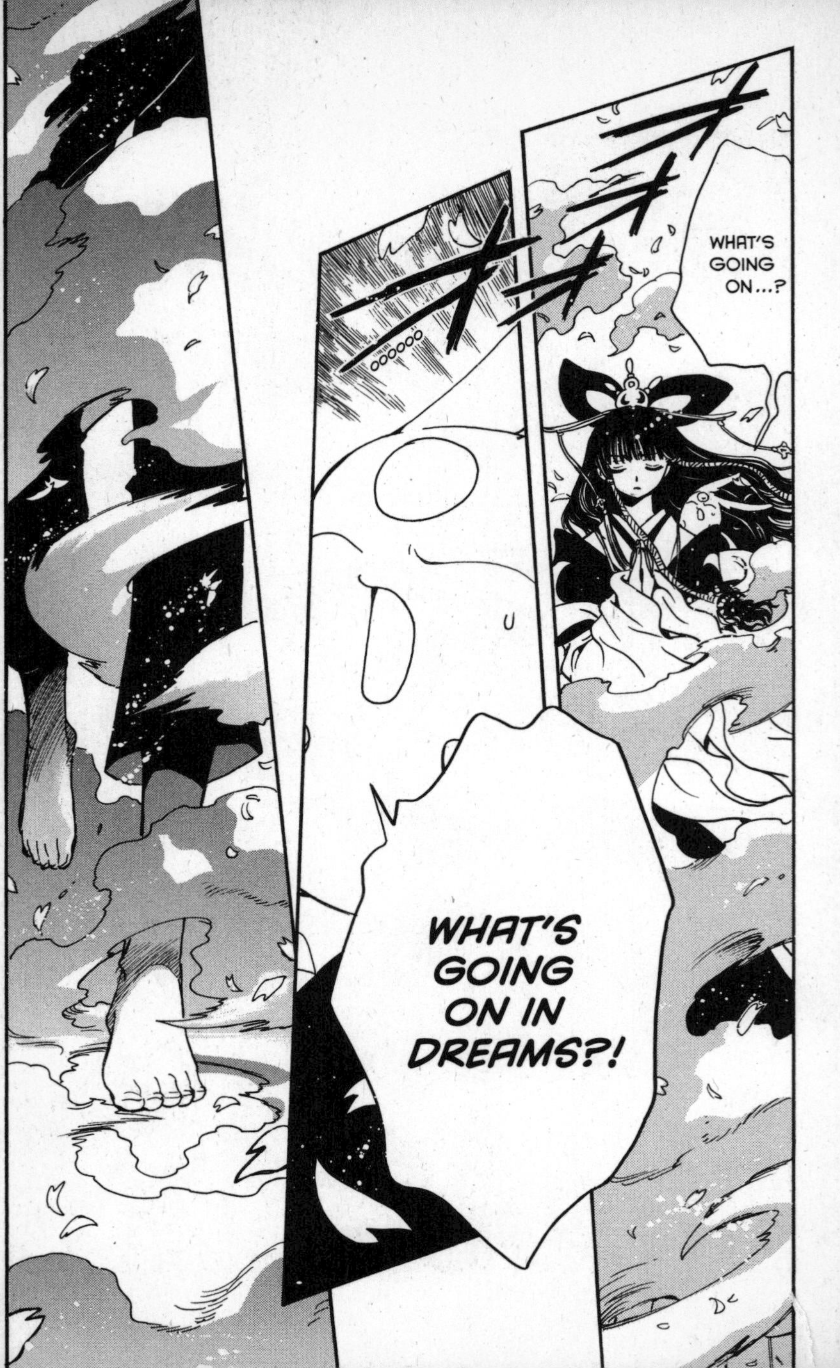
WHAT'S GOING ON...?
OOOOOO
WHAT'S GOING ON IN DREAMS?!

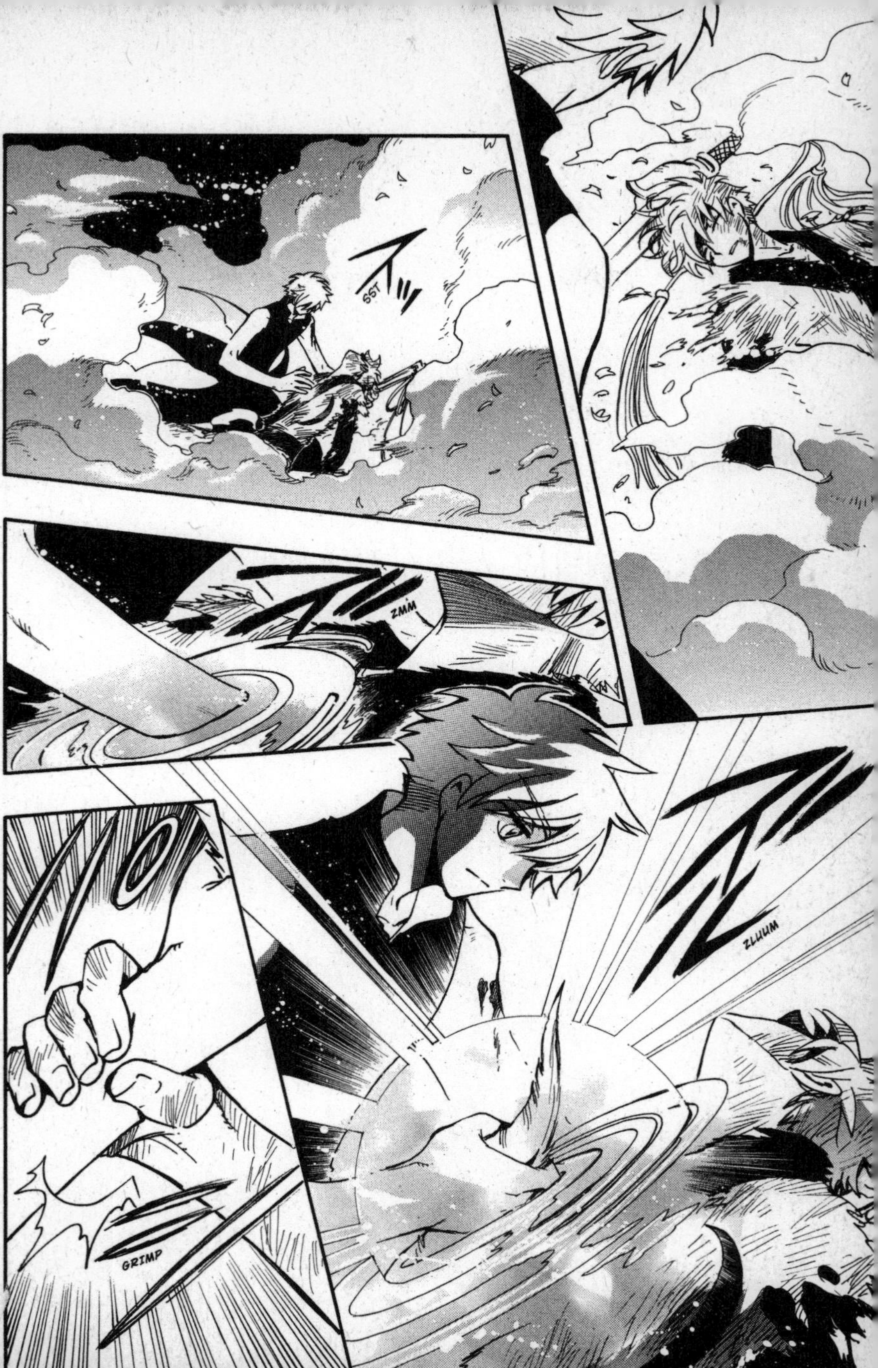
SST
ZMM
ZLUUM
GRIMP

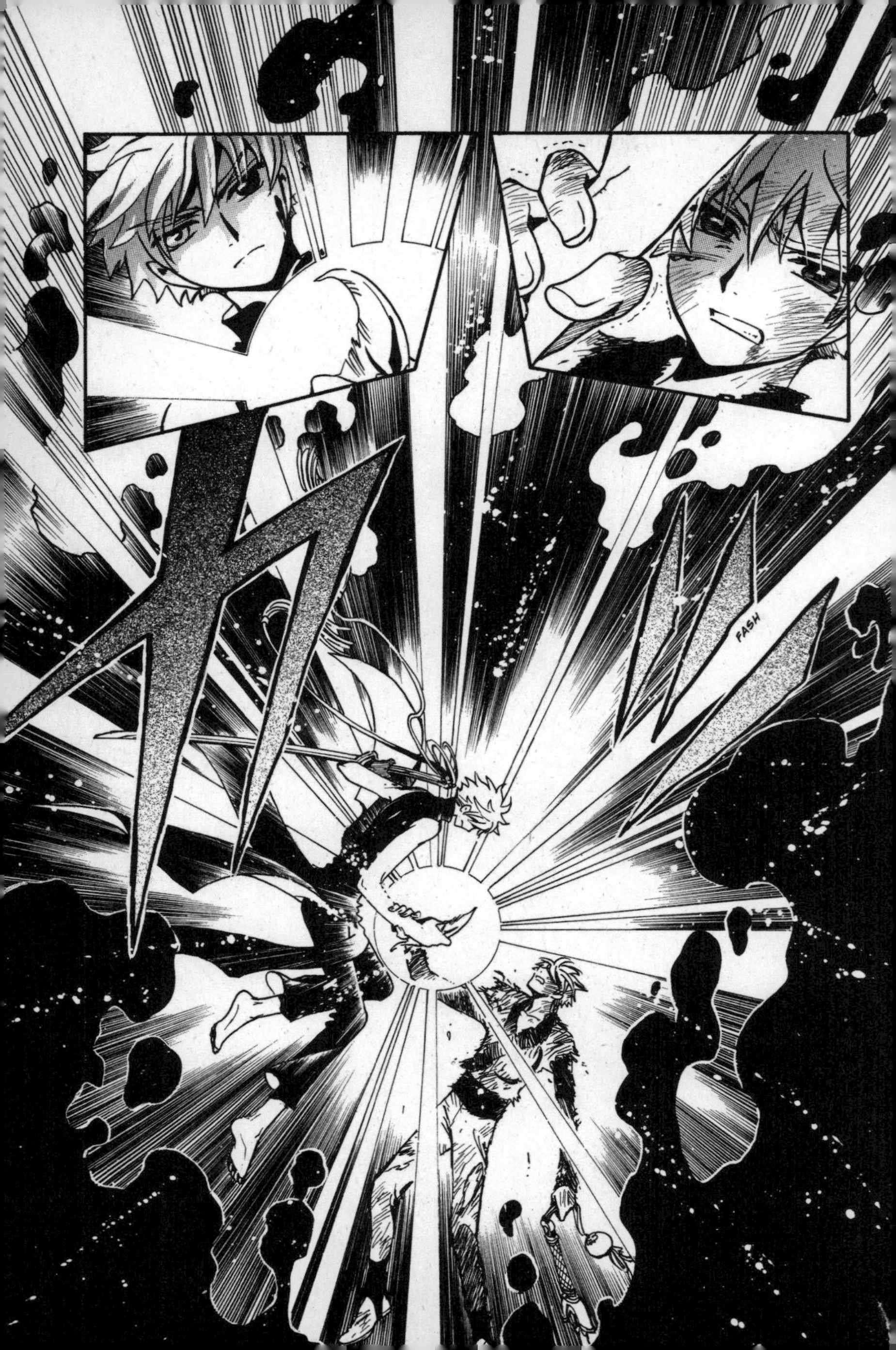
FASH

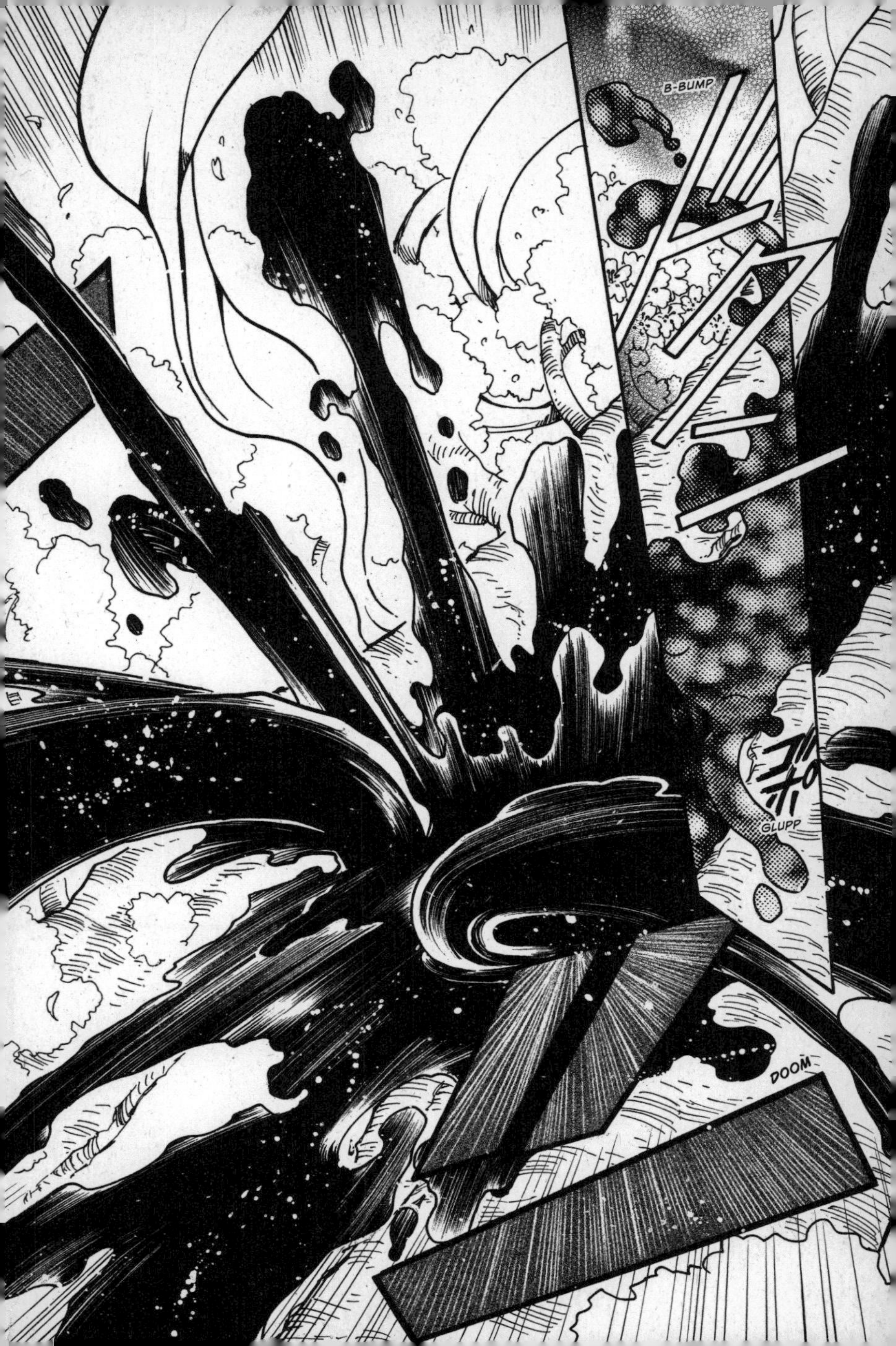
B-BUMP
GLUPP
DOOM

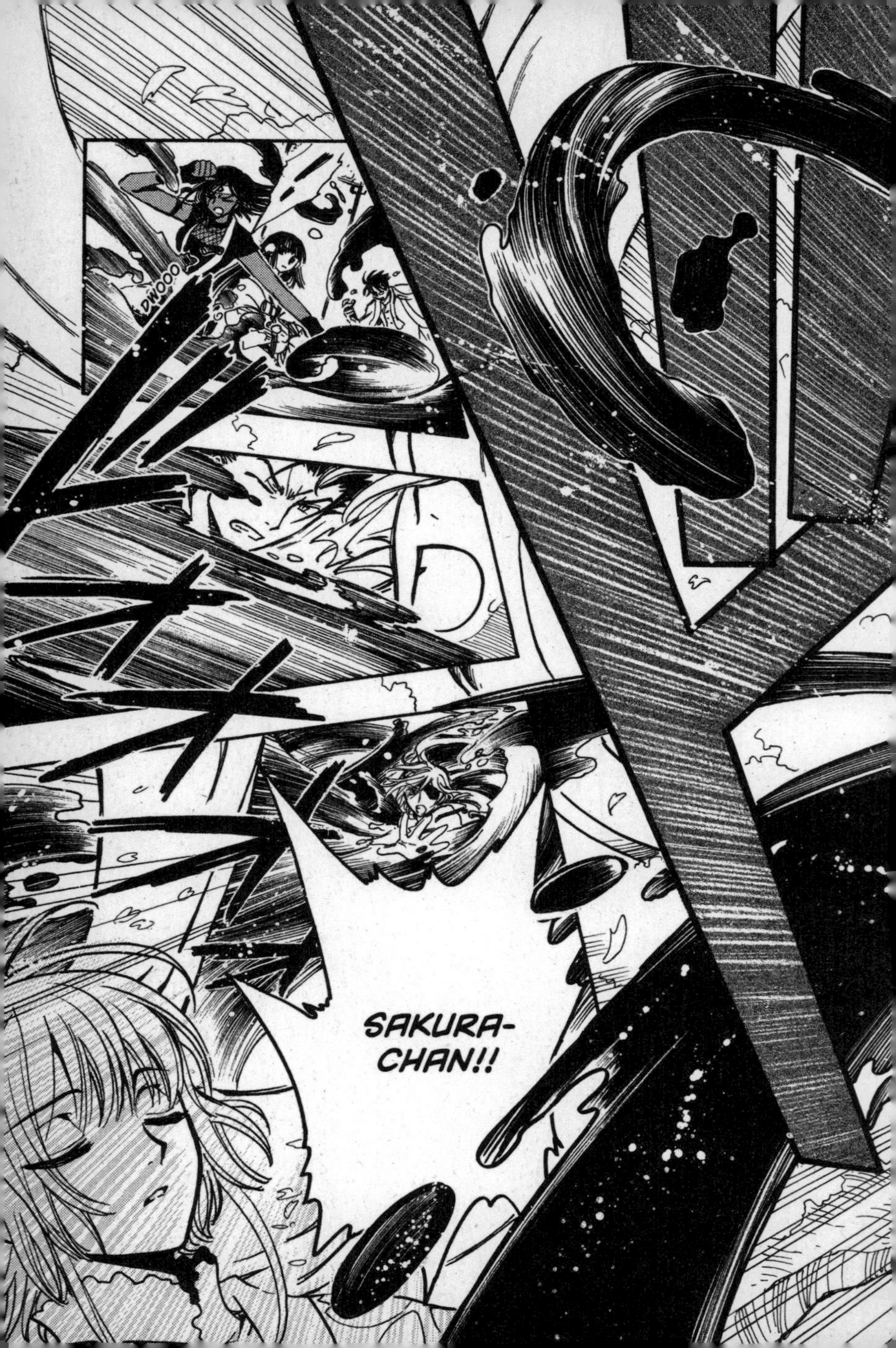
DWOOO
SAKURA-
CHAN!!

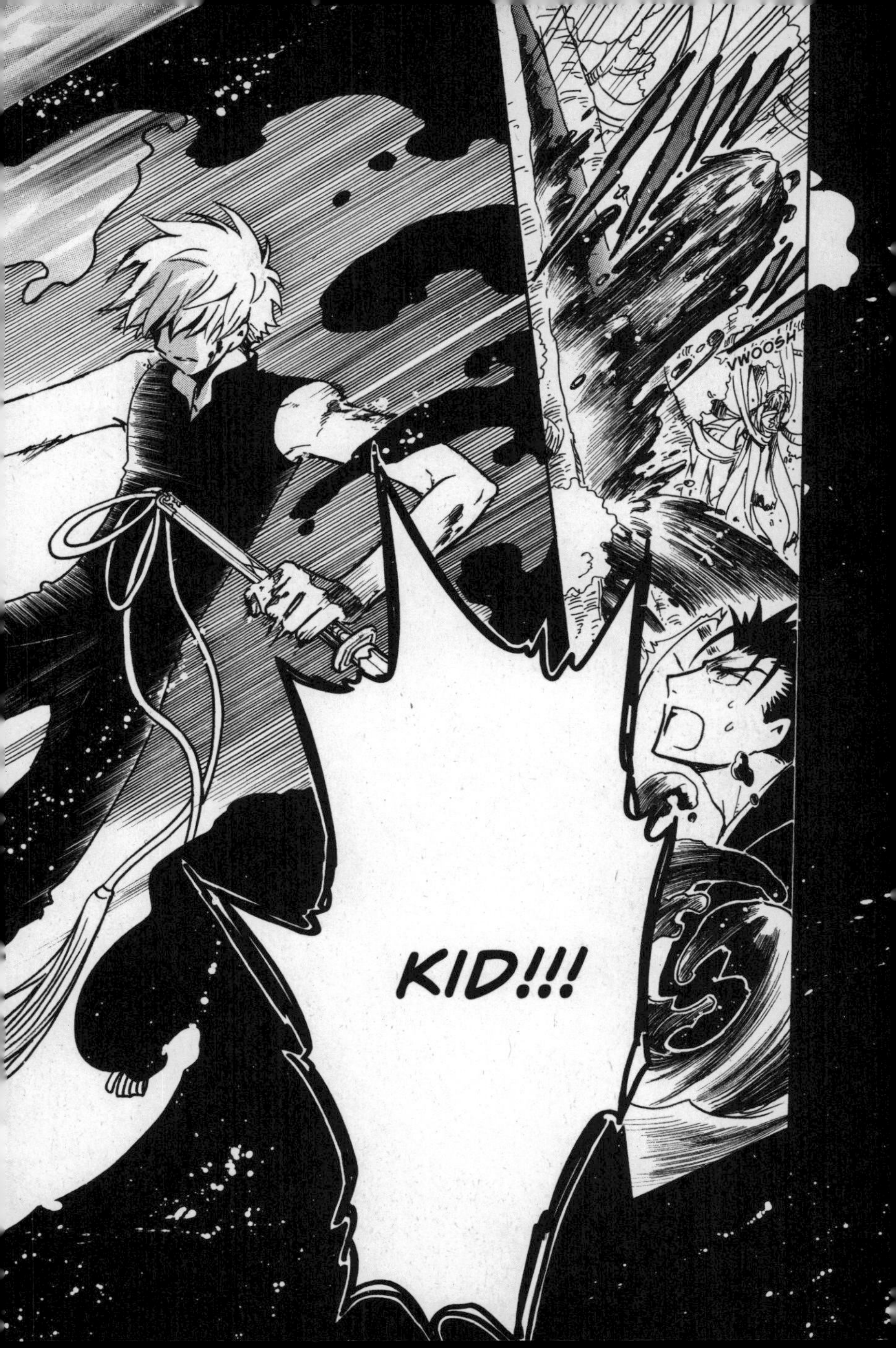
VWOOSH
KID!!!

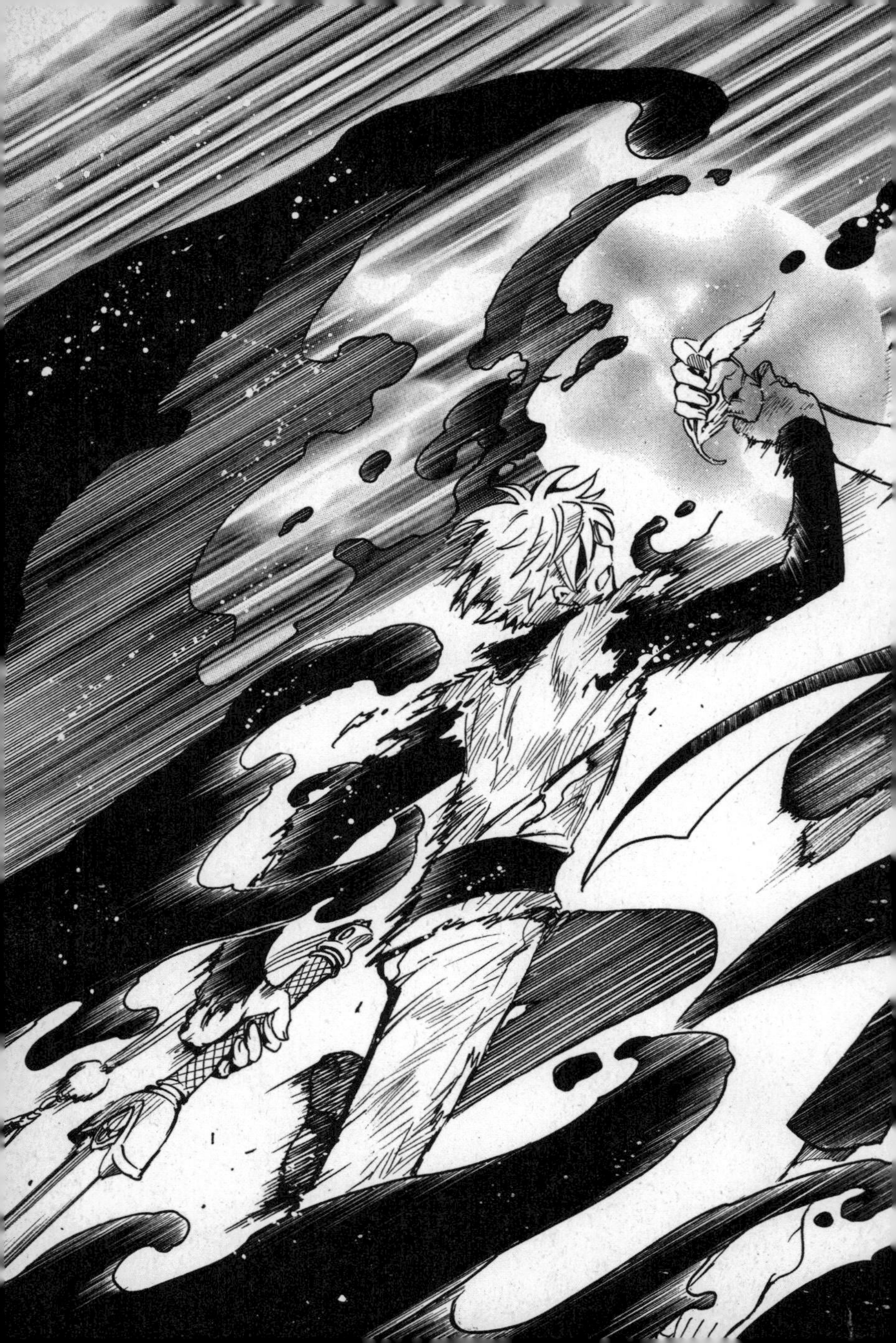

RESERVoir CHRoNiCLE

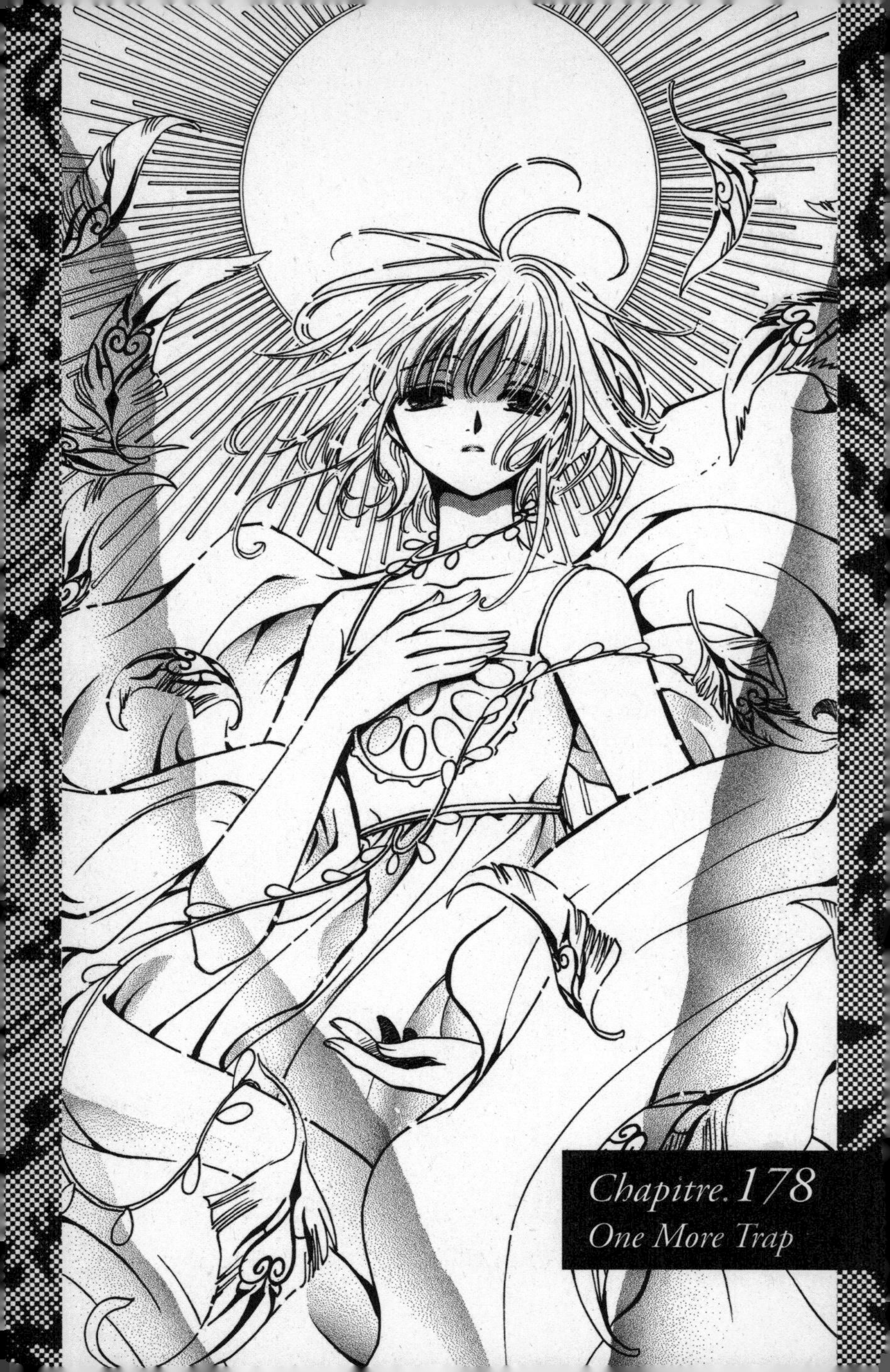
Chapitre.178
One More Trap

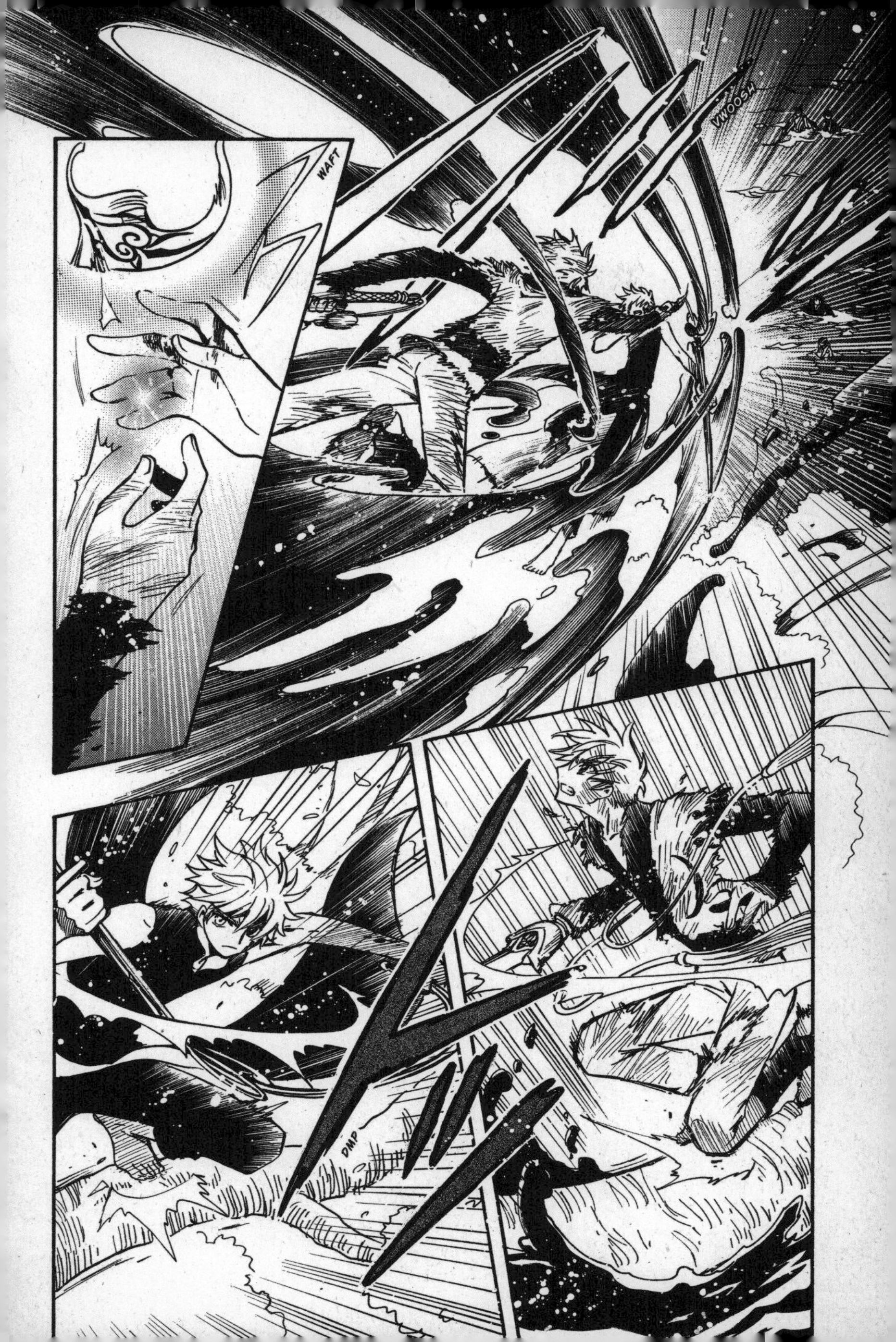
VWOOSH
WAFT
DMP

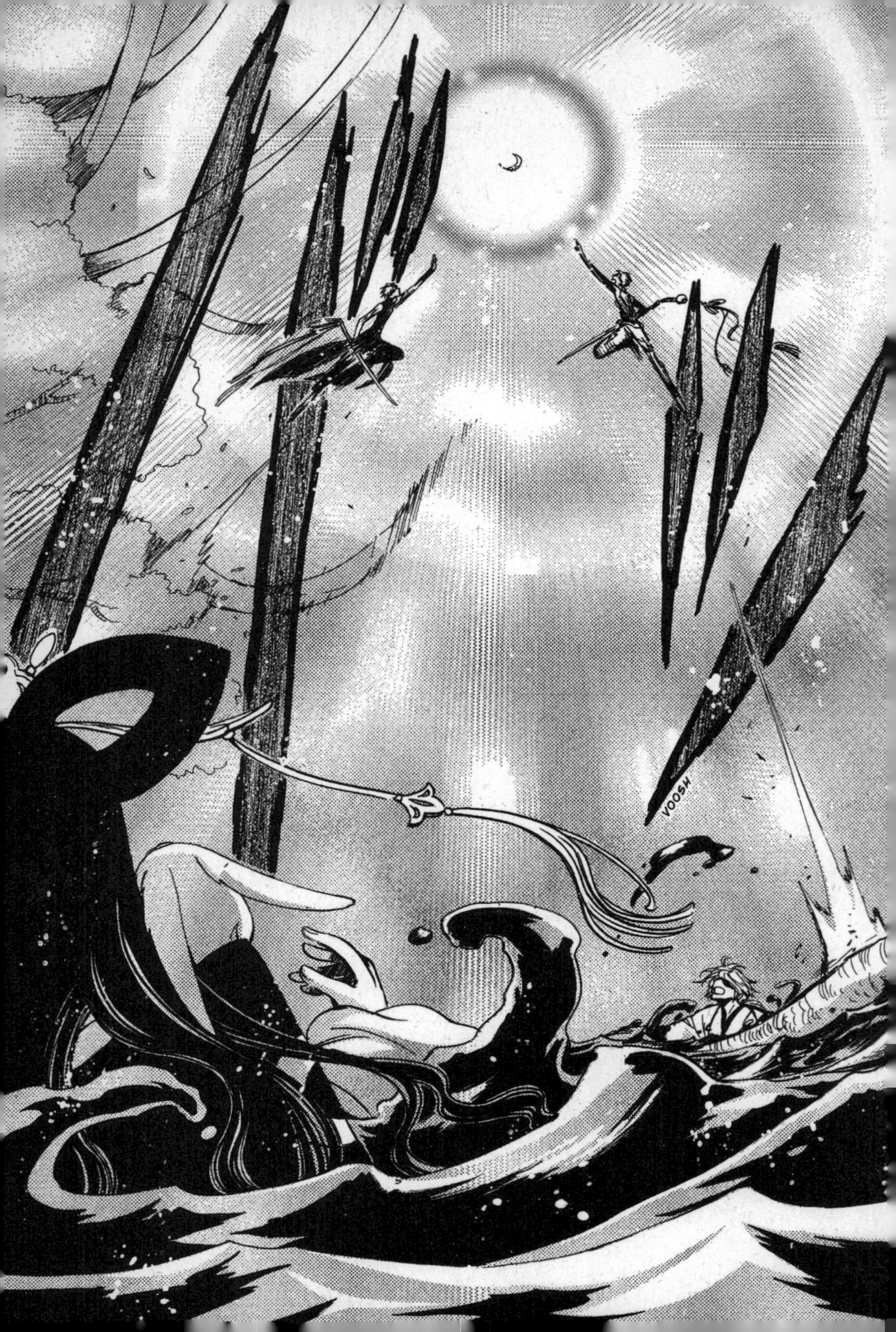
VOOSH

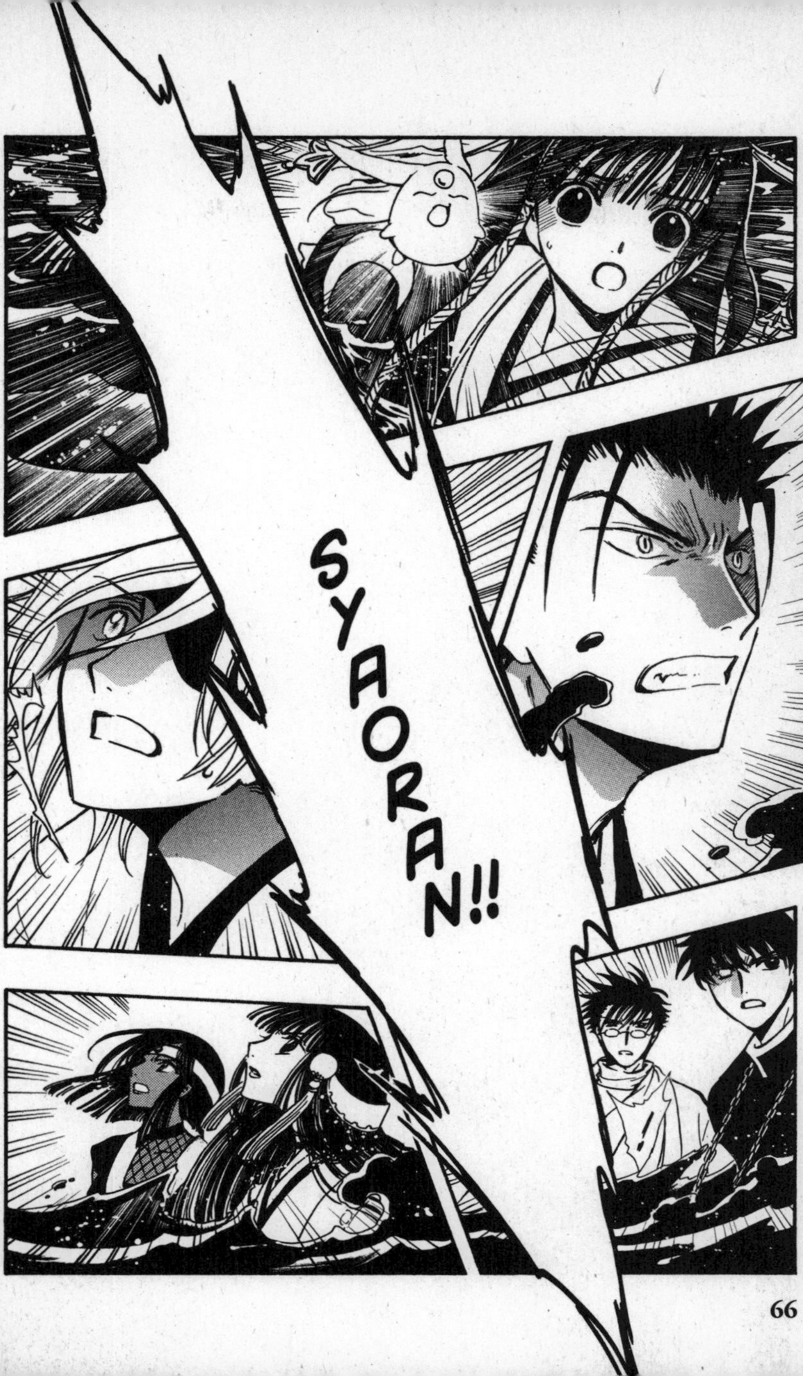
SYAORAN!!

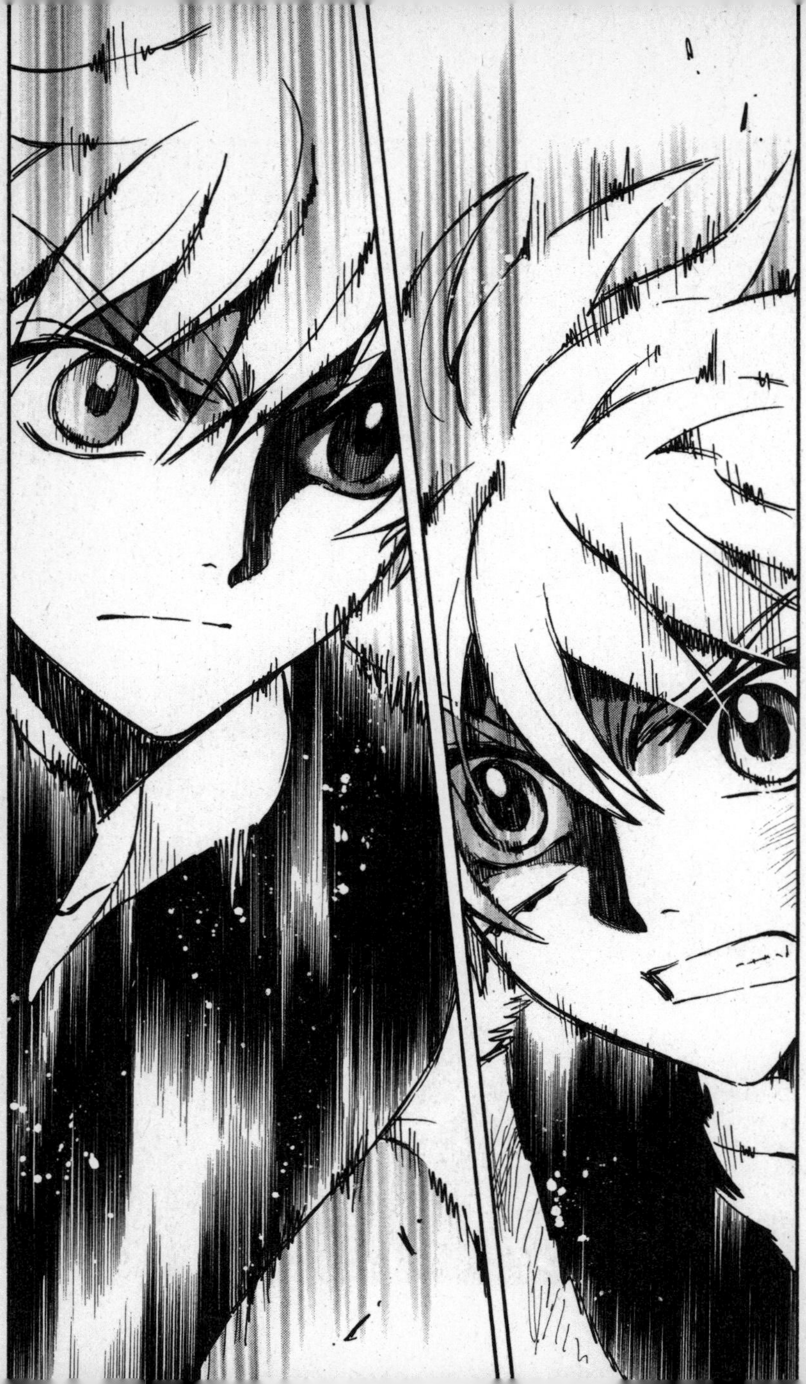

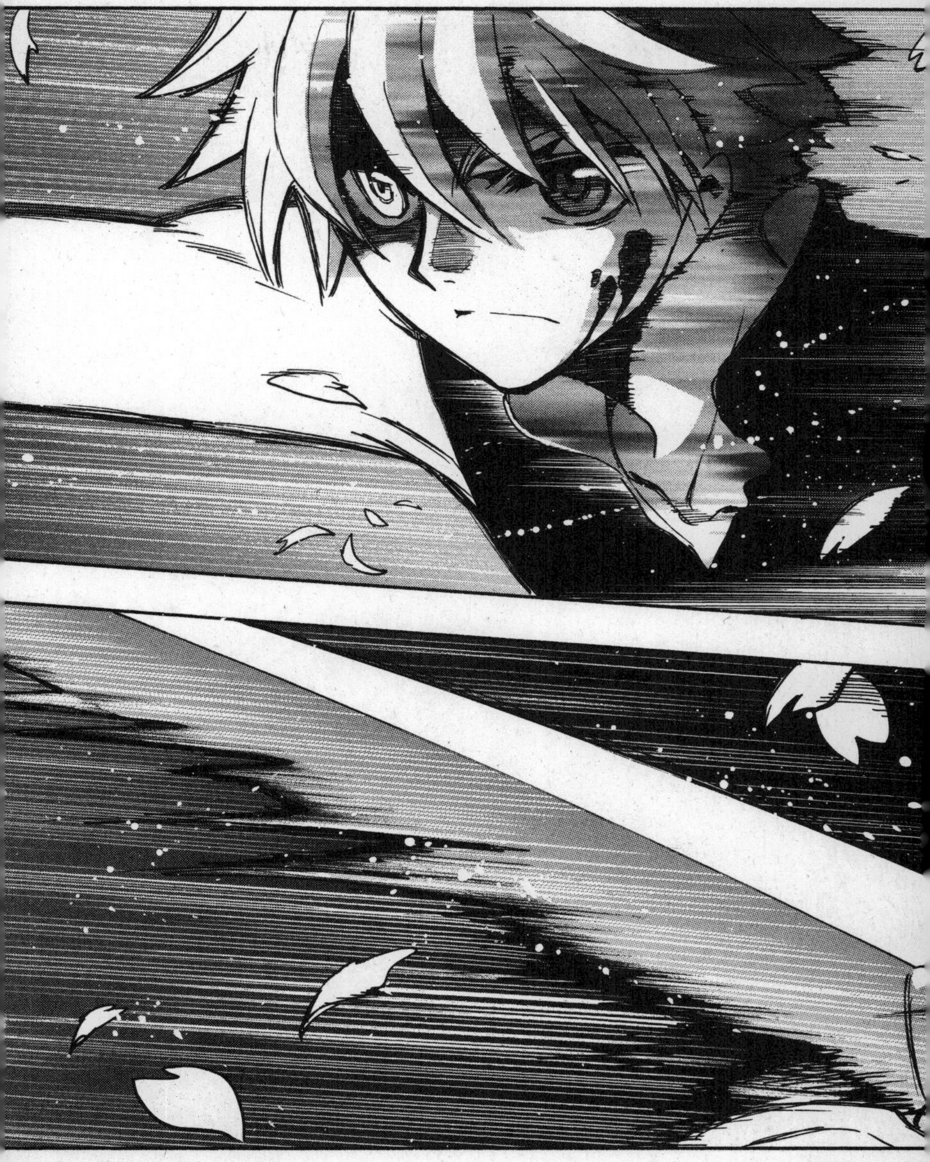

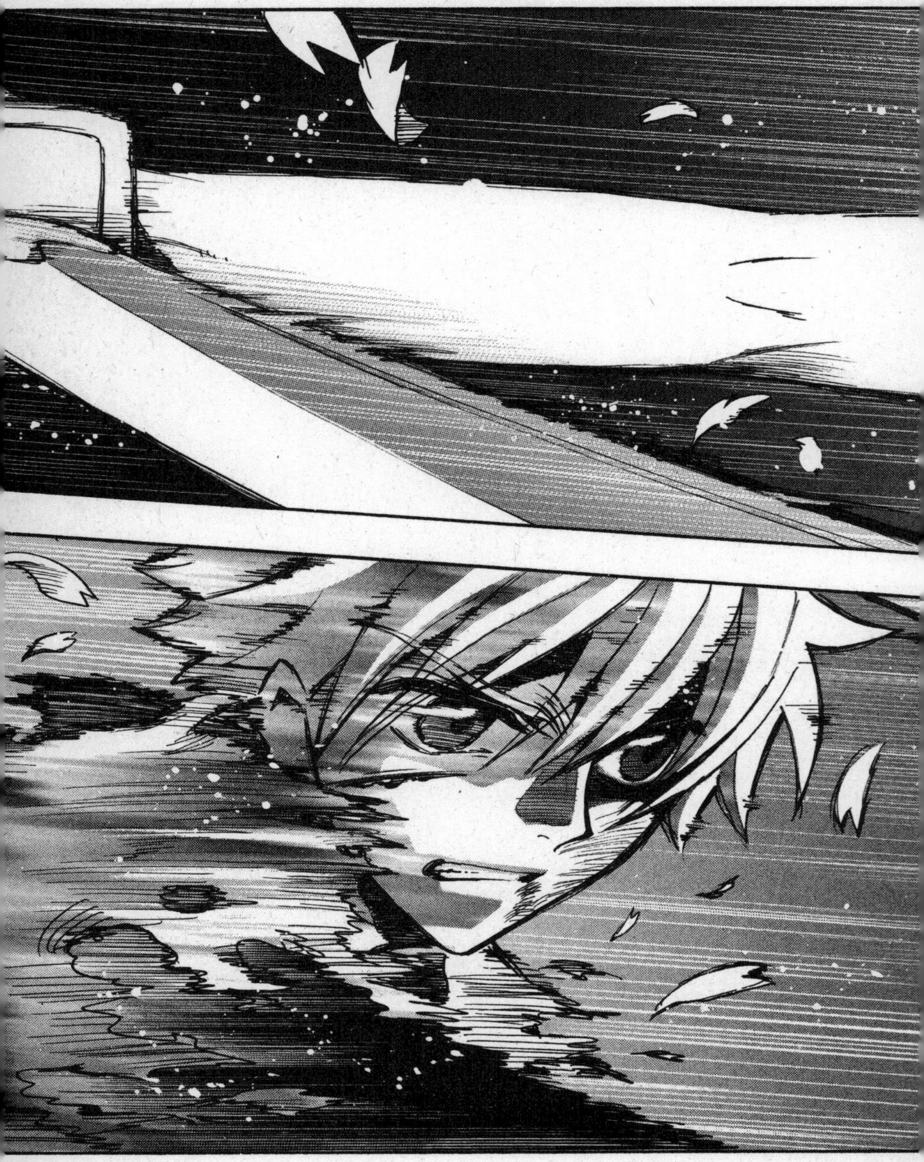

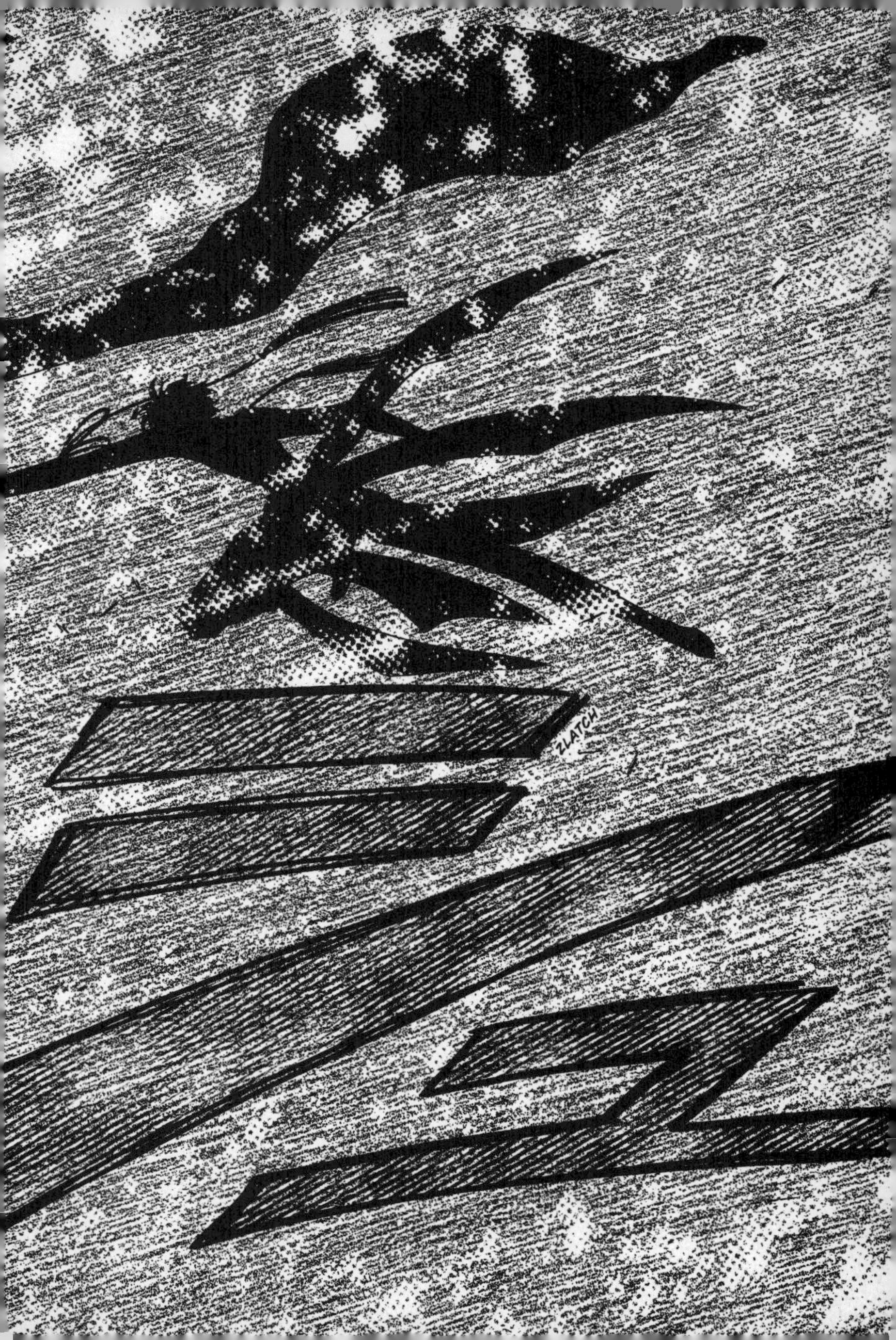
ZLATCH

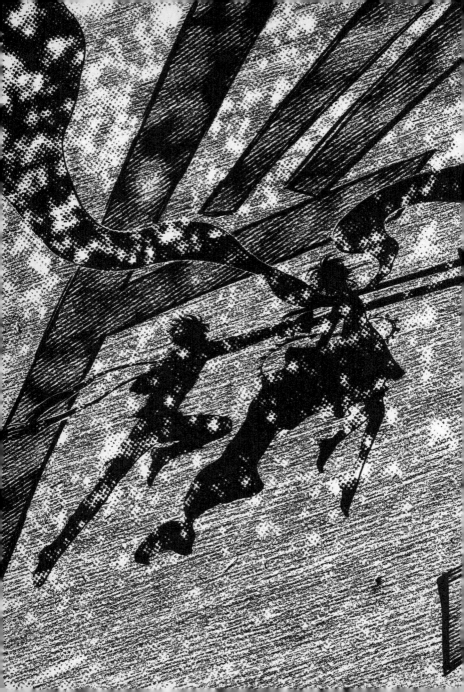

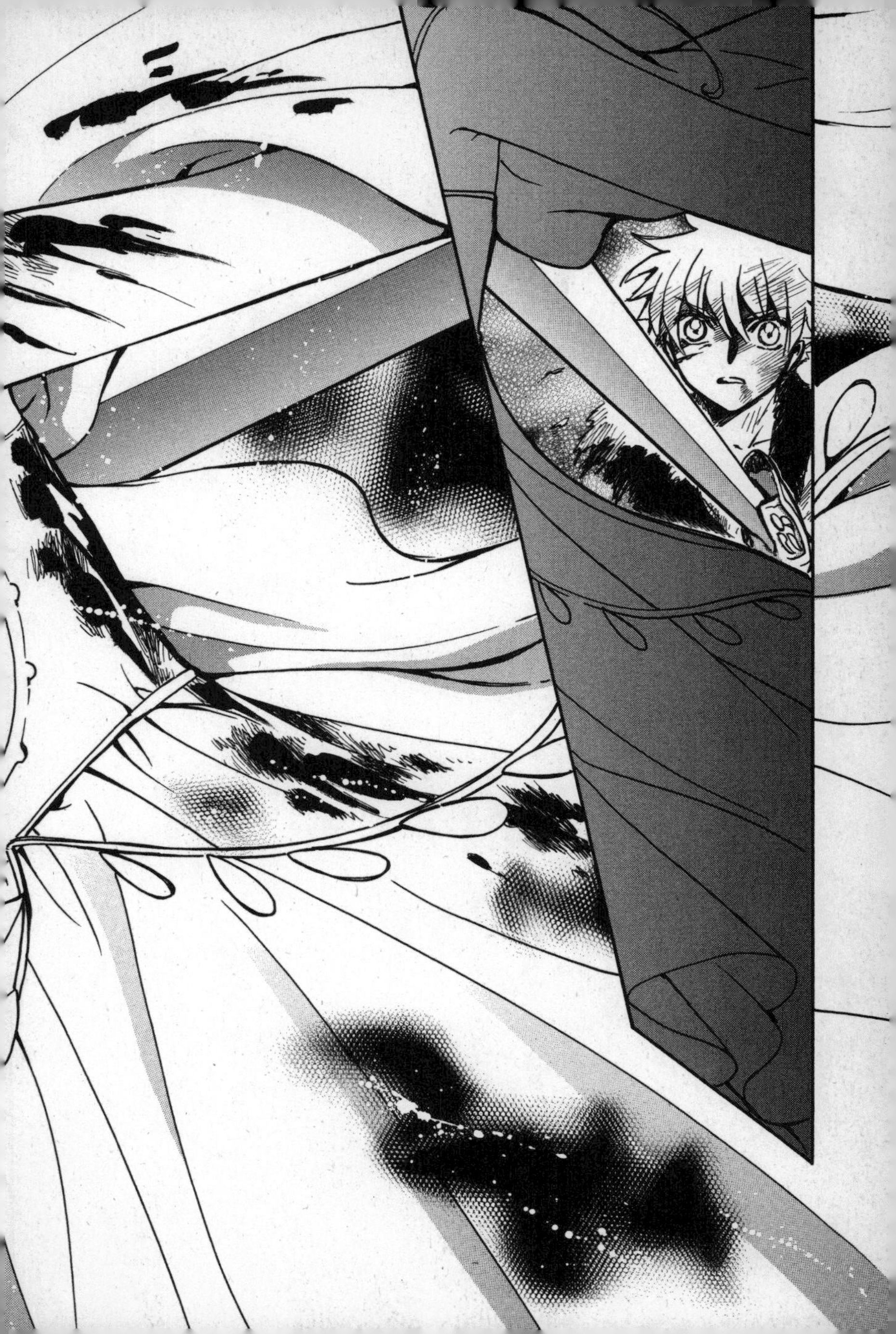

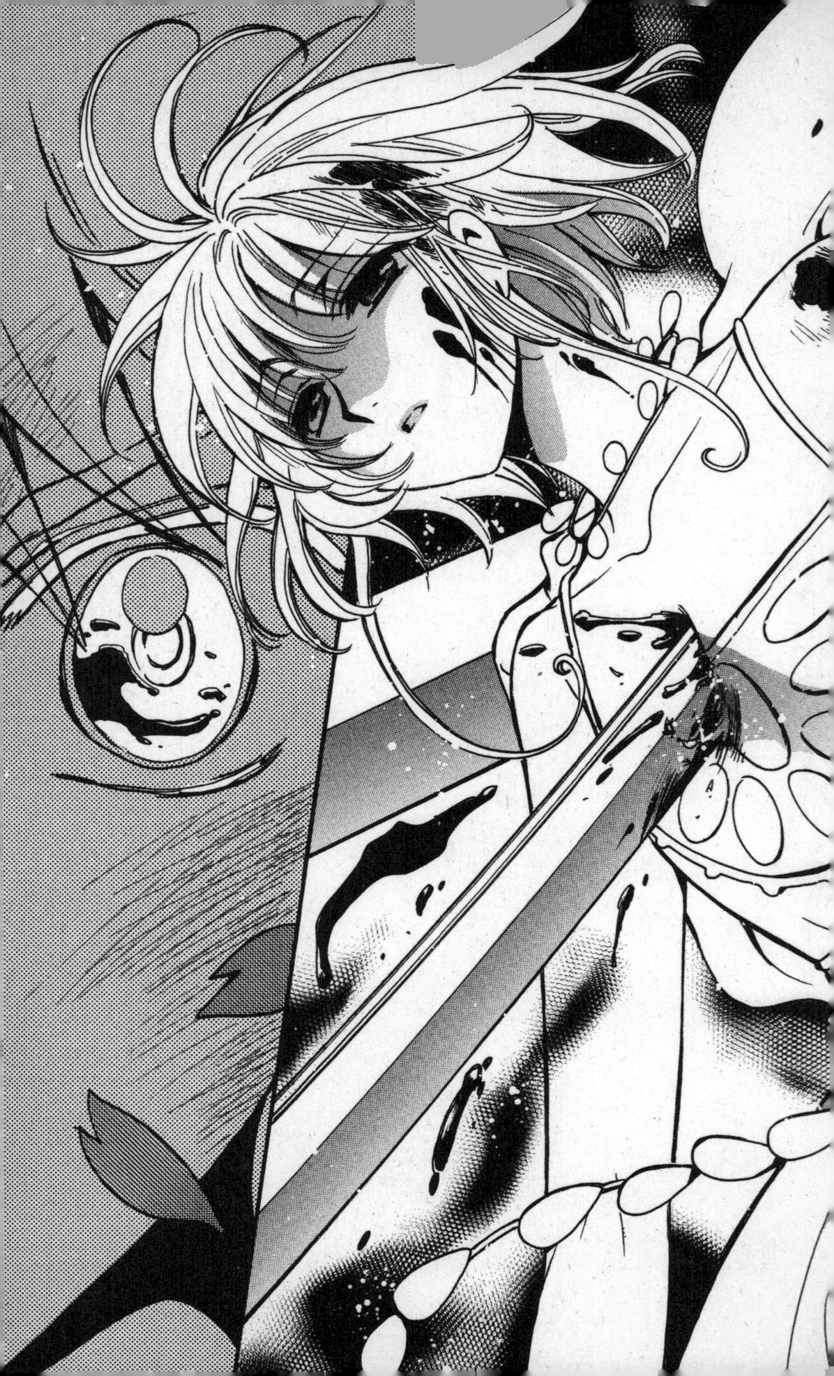

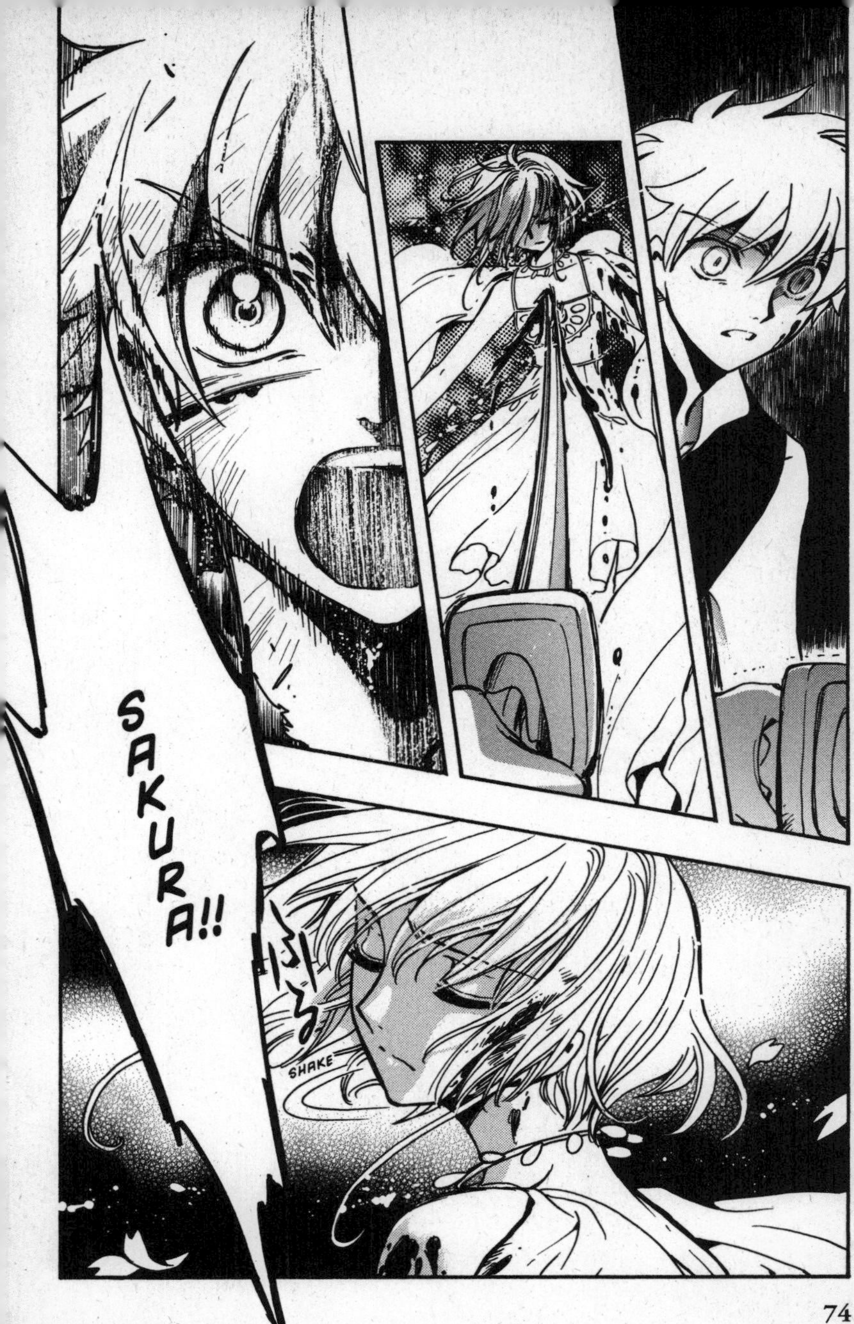
SAKURA!!
SHAKE

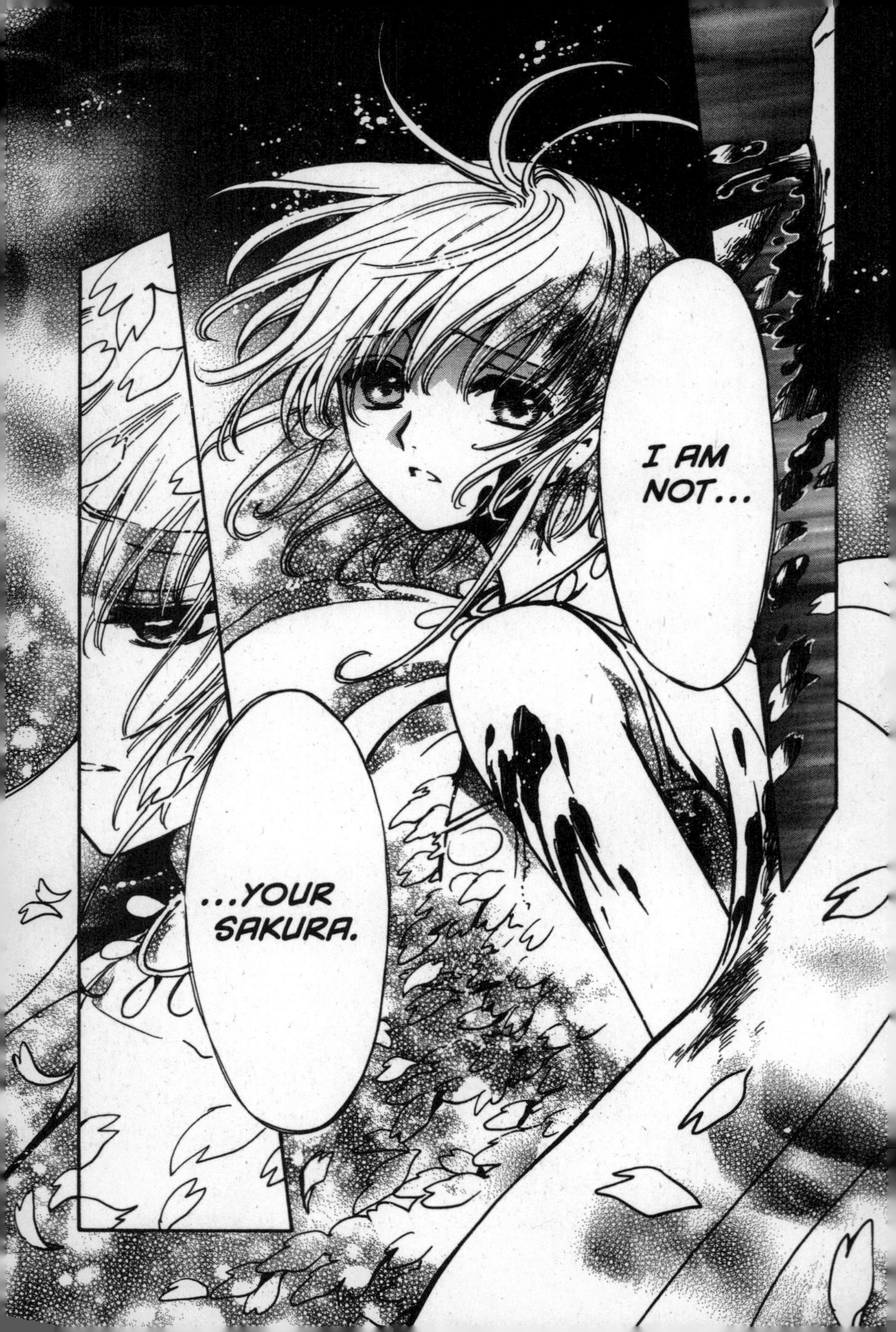
I AM NOT...
...YOUR SAKURA.

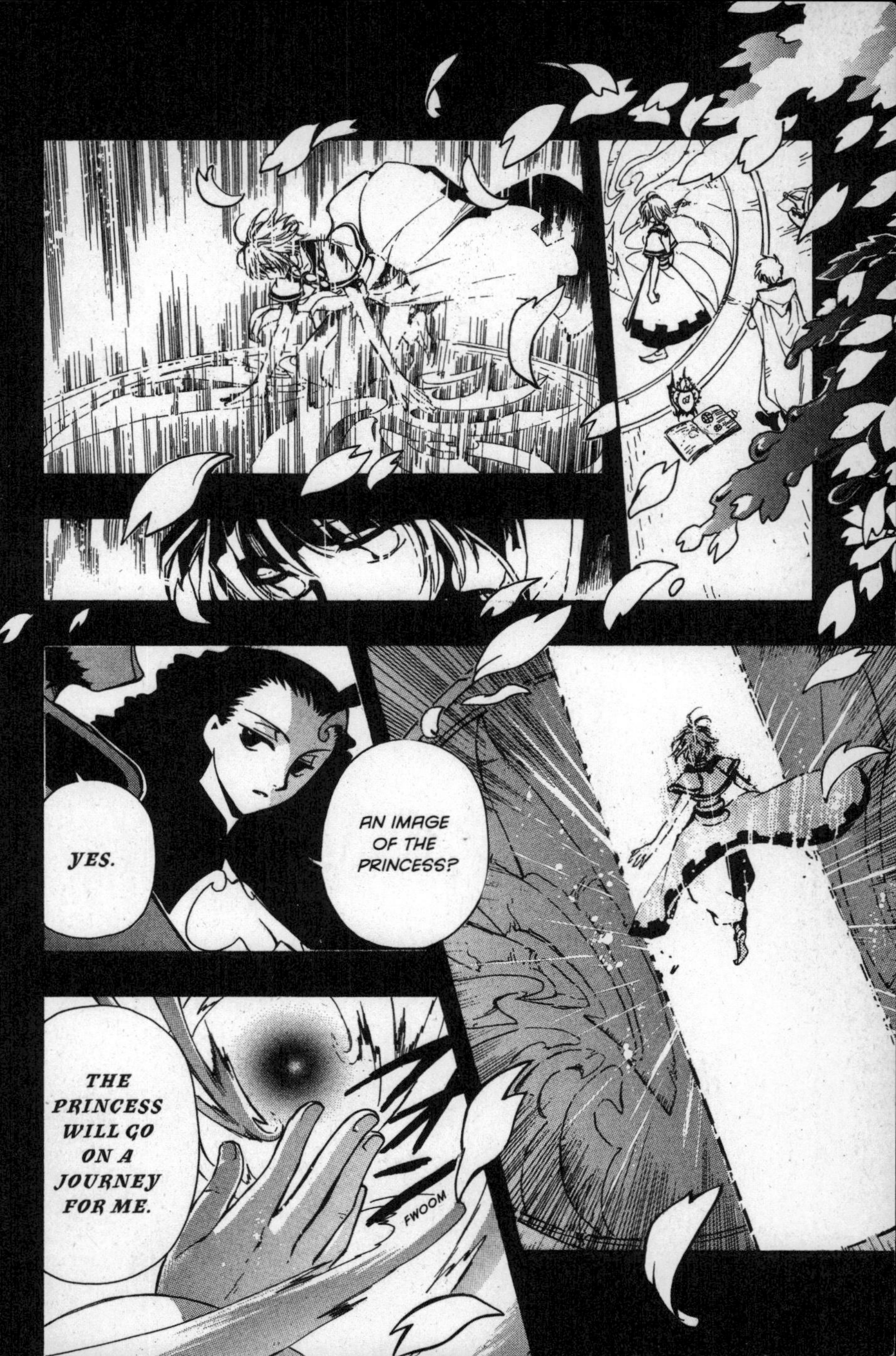
AN IMAGE OF THE PRINCESS?
YES.
THE PRINCESS WILL GO ON A JOURNEY FOR ME.
FWOOM

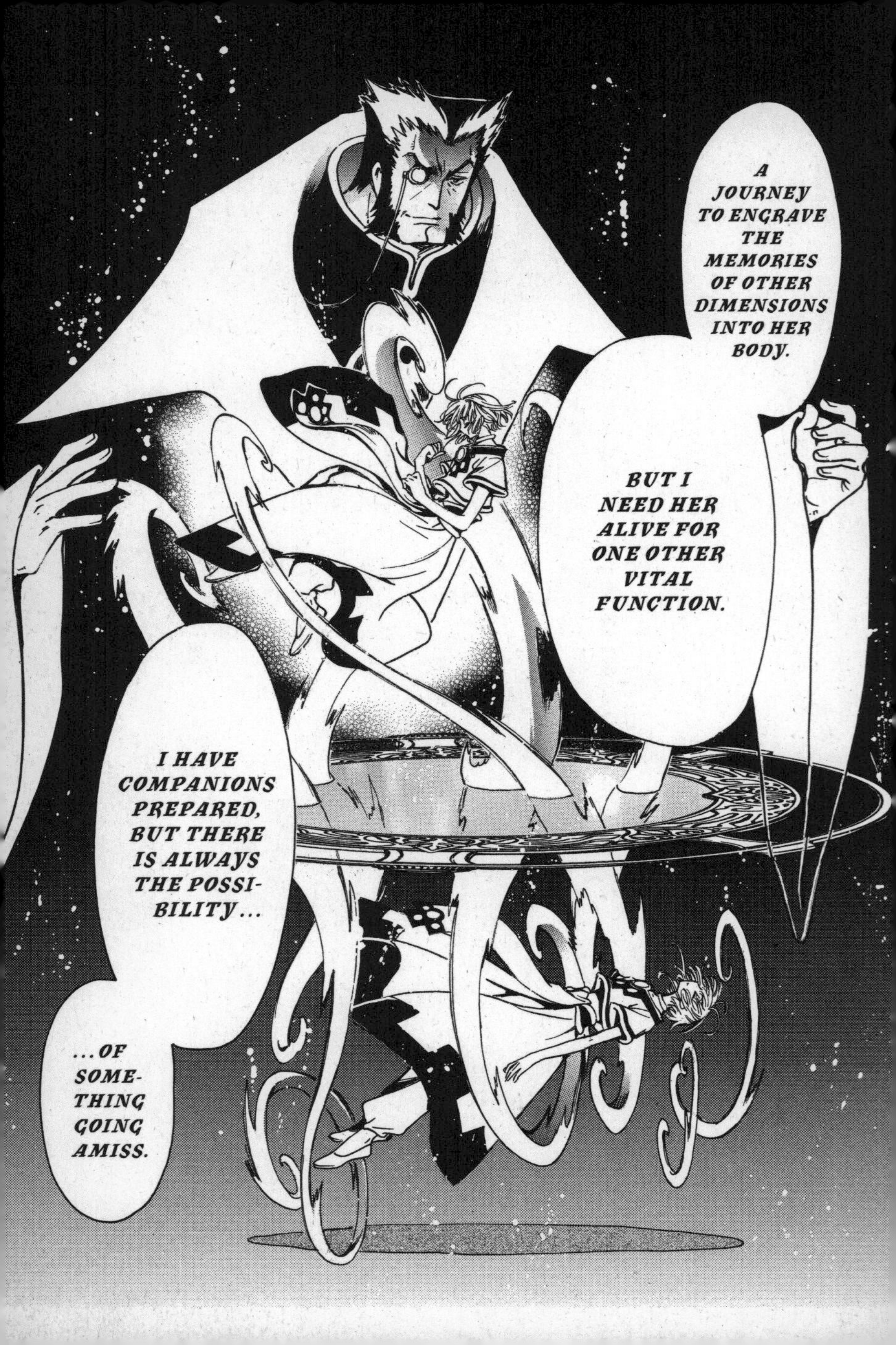
A JOURNEY TO ENGRAVE THE MEMORIES OF OTHER DIMENSIONS INTO HER BODY.
BUT I NEED HER ALIVE FOR ONE OTHER VITAL FUNCTION.
I HAVE COMPANIONS PREPARED, BUT THERE IS ALWAYS THE POSSI-BILITY...
...OF SOME-THING GOING AMISS.

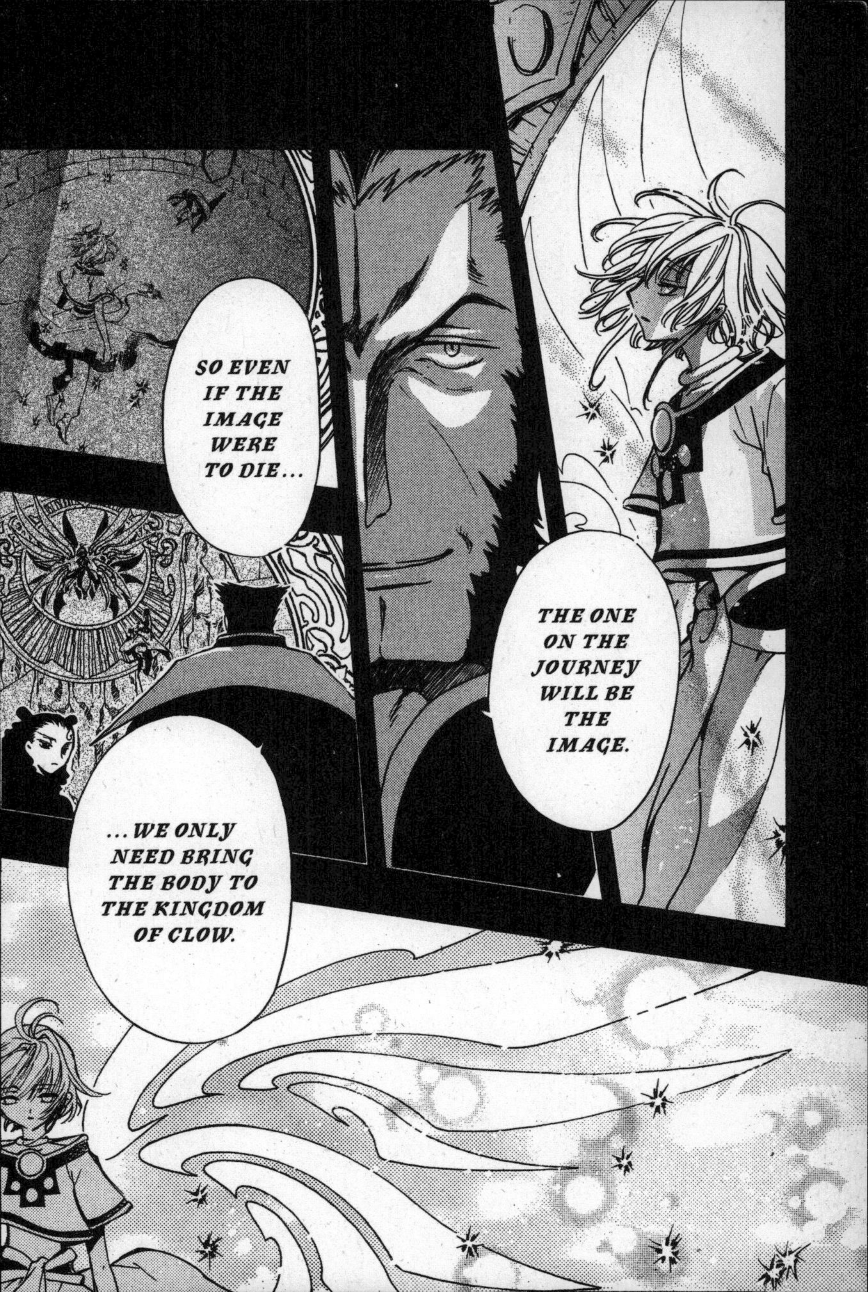
THE ONE ON THE JOURNEY WILL BE THE IMAGE.
SO EVEN IF THE IMAGE WERE TO DIE...
...WE ONLY NEED BRING THE BODY TO THE KINGDOM OF CLOW.

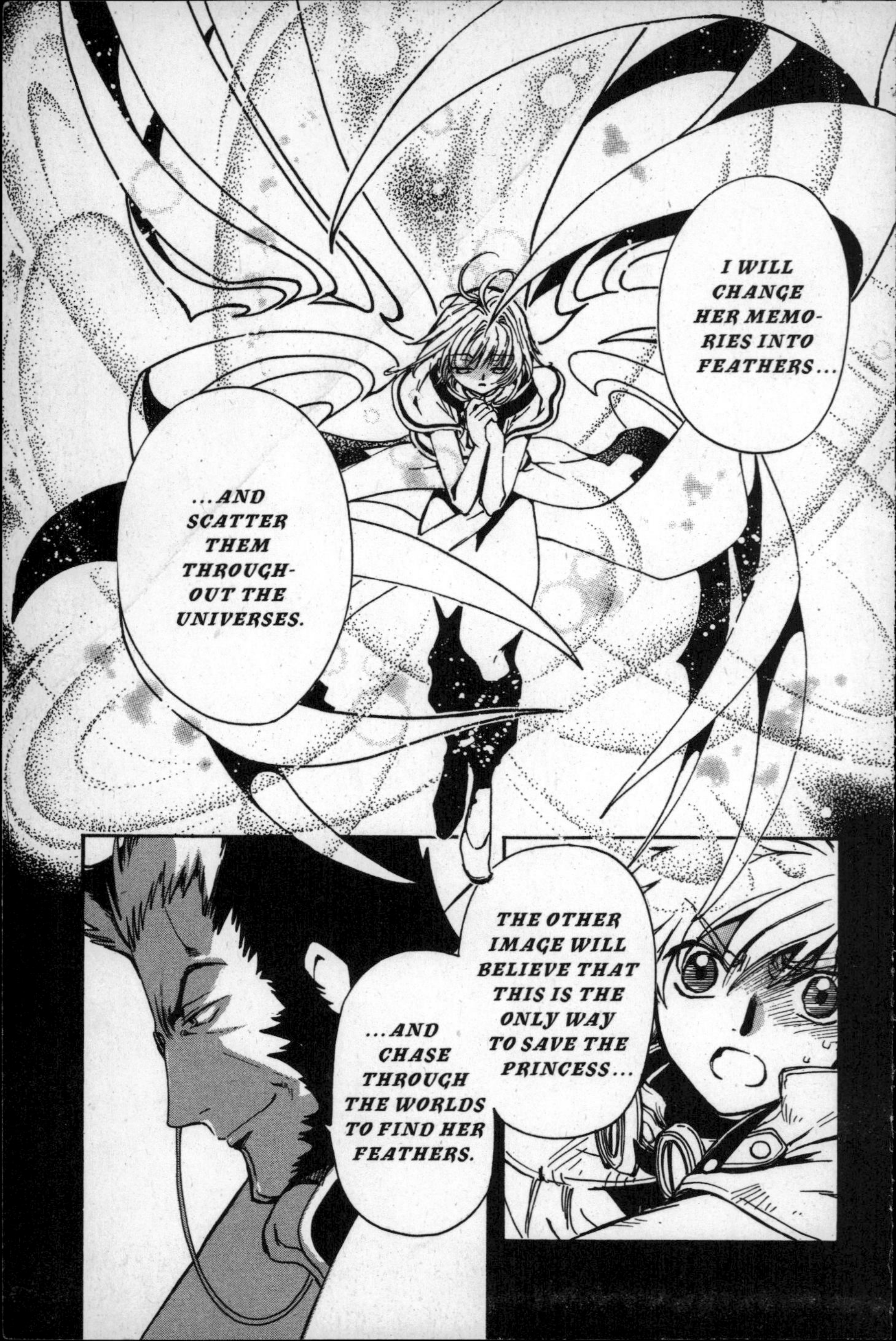
I WILL CHANGE HER MEMO-RIES INTO FEATHERS...
...AND SCATTER THEM THROUGH-OUT THE UNIVERSES.
THE OTHER IMAGE WILL BELIEVE THAT THIS IS THE ONLY WAY TO SAVE THE PRINCESS...
...AND CHASE THROUGH THE WORLDS TO FIND HER FEATHERS.

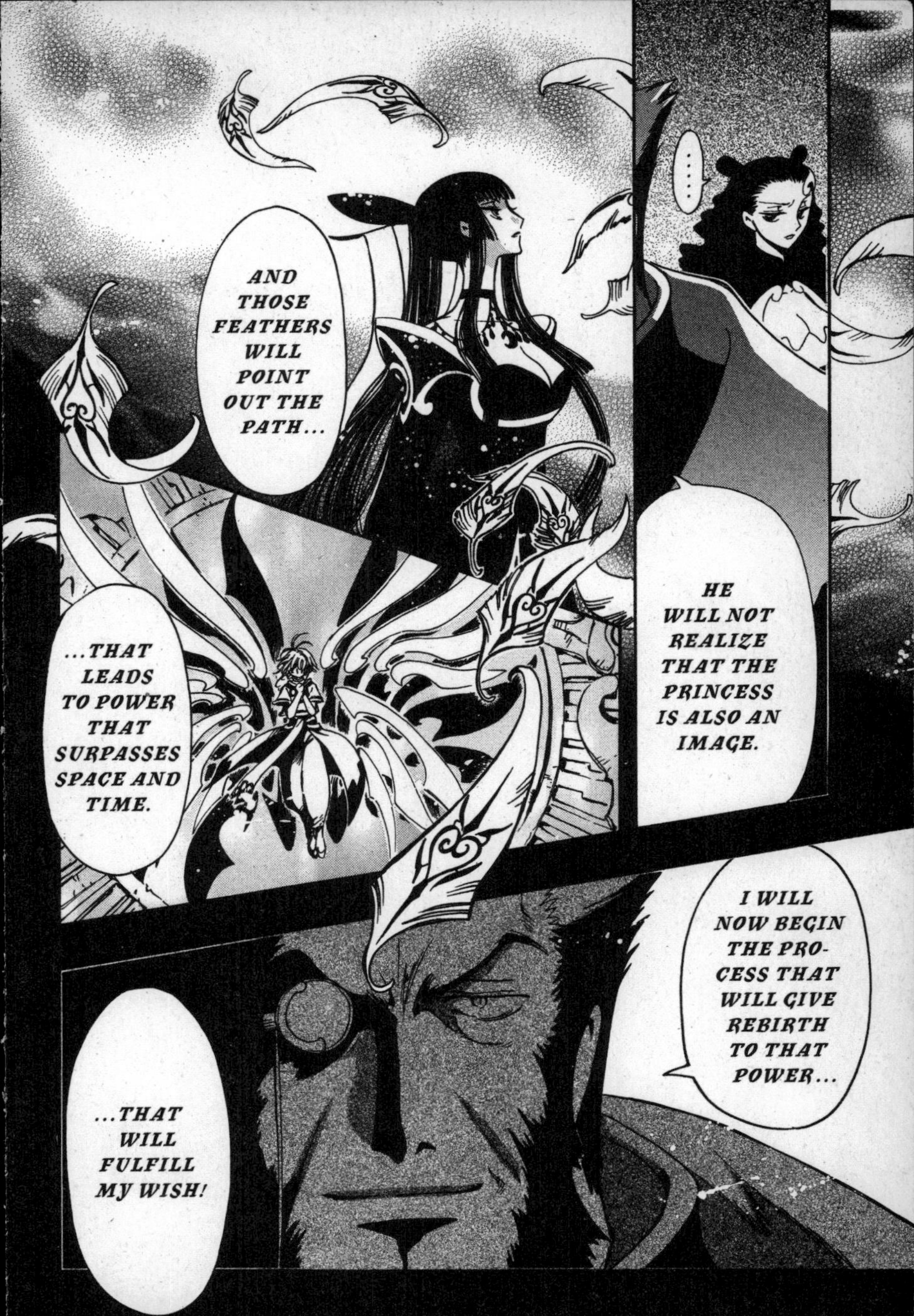
.....
HE WILL NOT REALIZE THAT THE PRINCESS IS ALSO AN IMAGE.
AND THOSE FEATHERS WILL POINT OUT THE PATH...
...THAT LEADS TO POWER THAT SURPASSES SPACE AND TIME.
I WILL NOW BEGIN THE PRO-CESS THAT WILL GIVE REBIRTH TO THAT POWER...
...THAT WILL FULFILL MY WISH!

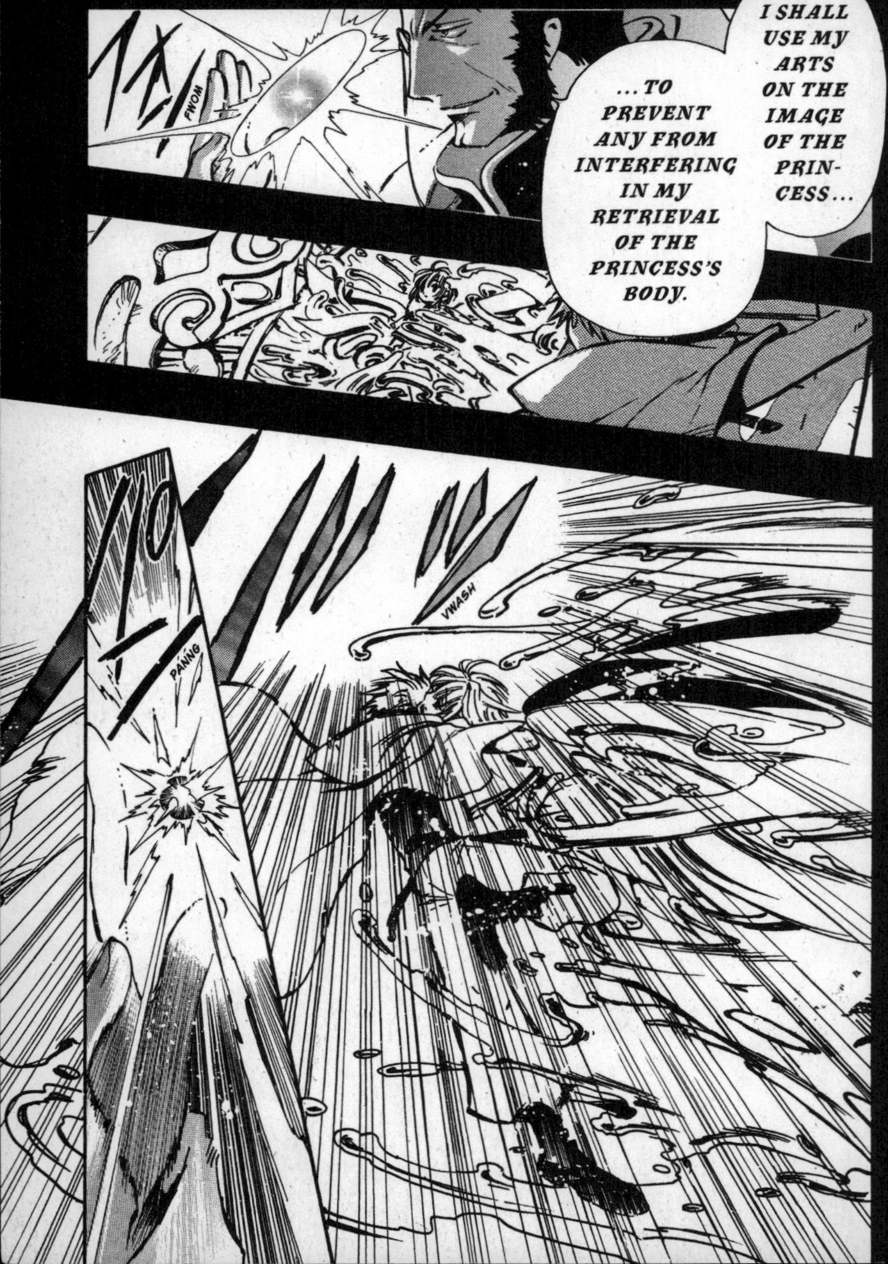
I SHALL USE MY ARTS ON THE IMAGE OF THE PRINCESS...
...TO PREVENT ANY FROM INTERFERING IN MY RETRIEVAL OF THE PRINCESS'S BODY.
FWOM
VWASH
PANNG

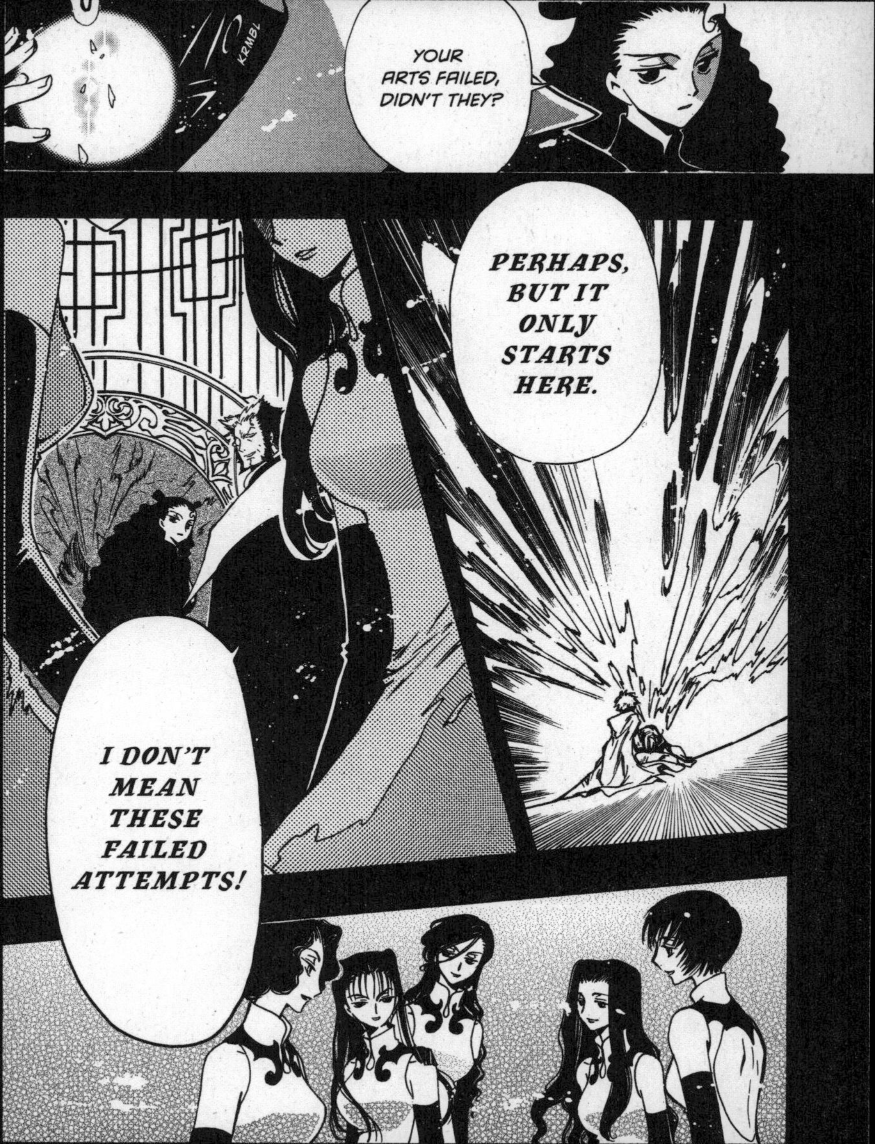
KRMBL
YOUR ARTS FAILED, DIDN'T THEY?
PERHAPS, BUT IT ONLY STARTS HERE.
I DON'T MEAN THESE FAILED ATTEMPTS!

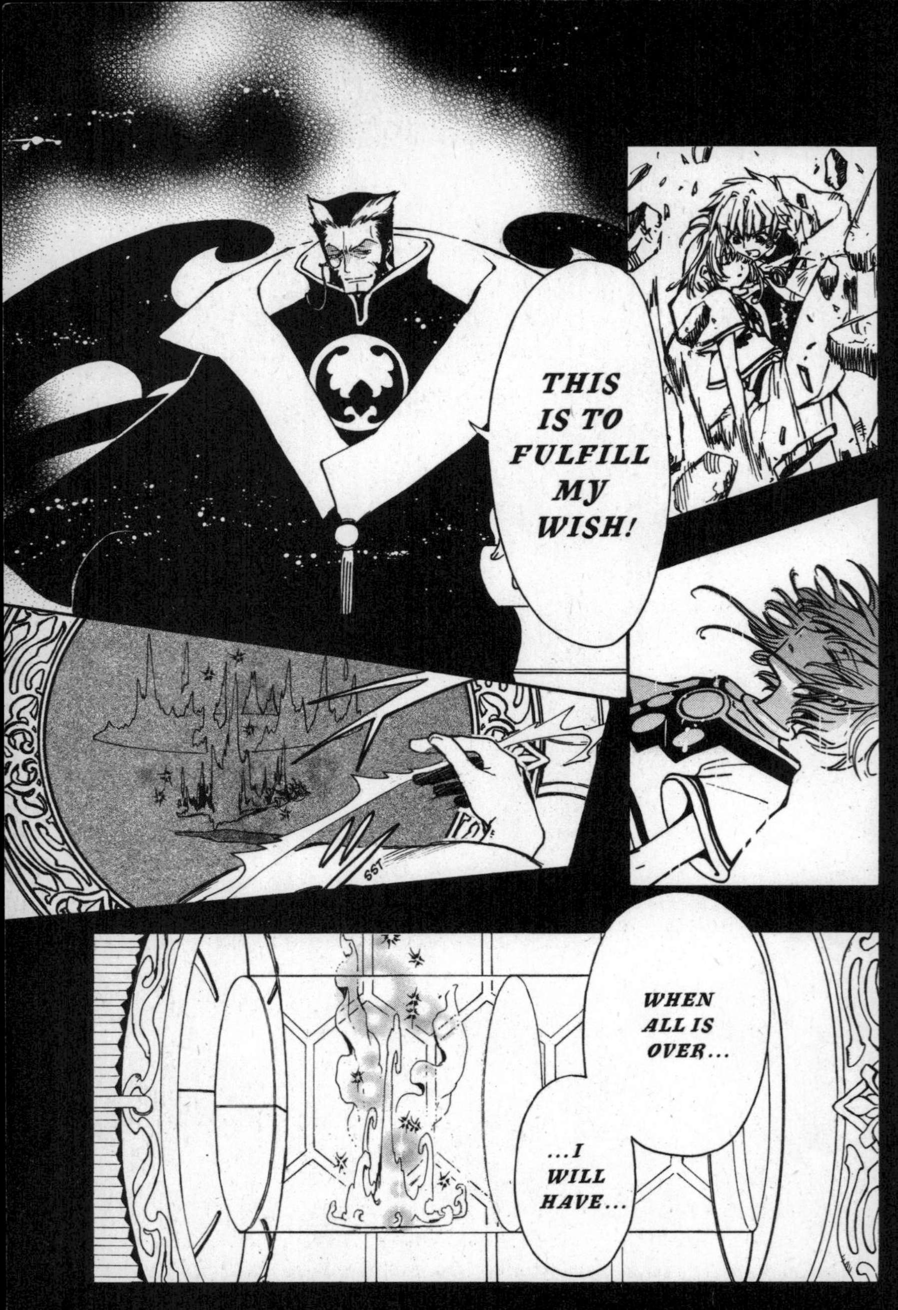
THIS IS TO FULFILL MY WISH!
SST
WHEN ALL IS OVER...
...I WILL HAVE...

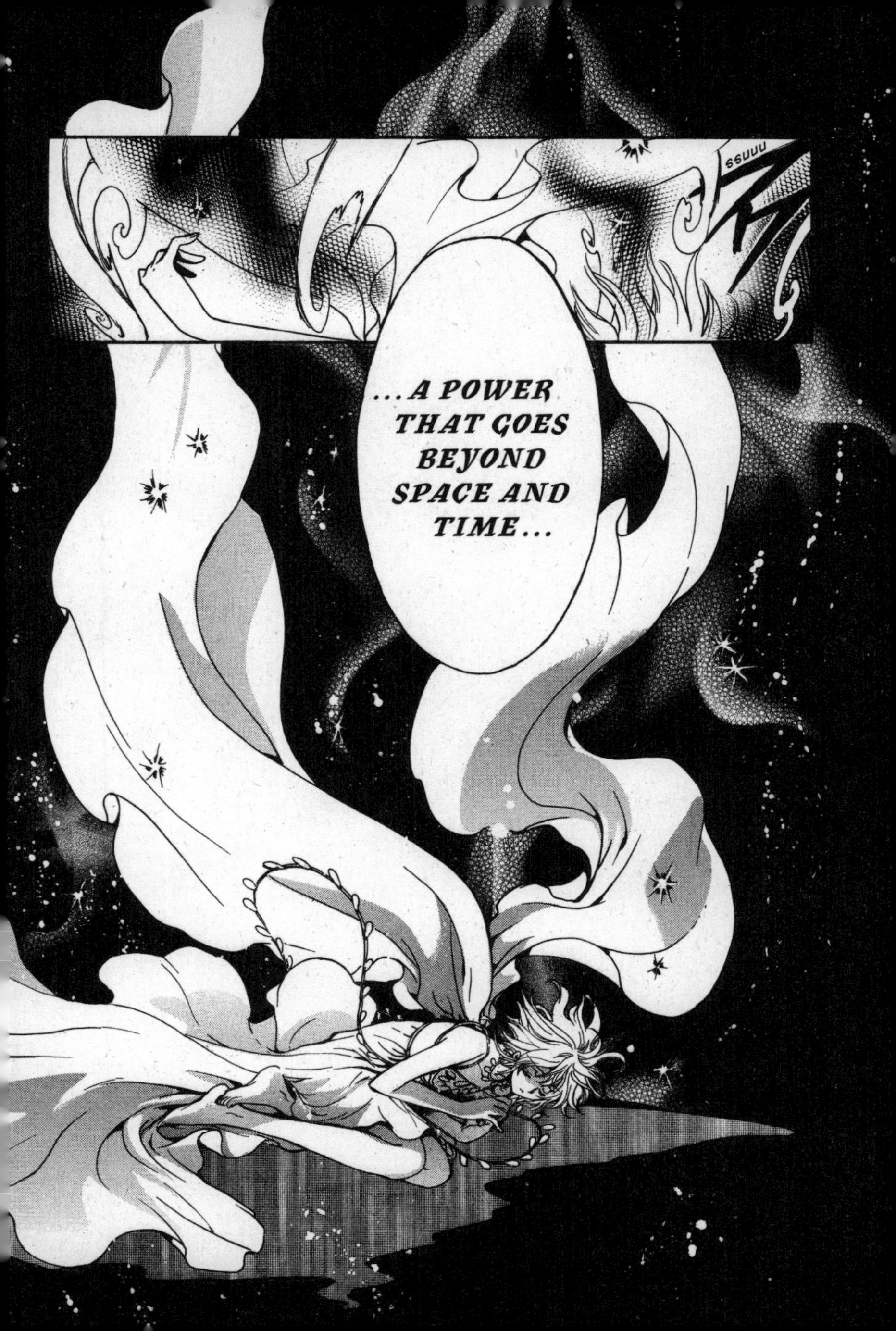
SSUUU
...A POWER THAT GOES BEYOND SPACE AND TIME...

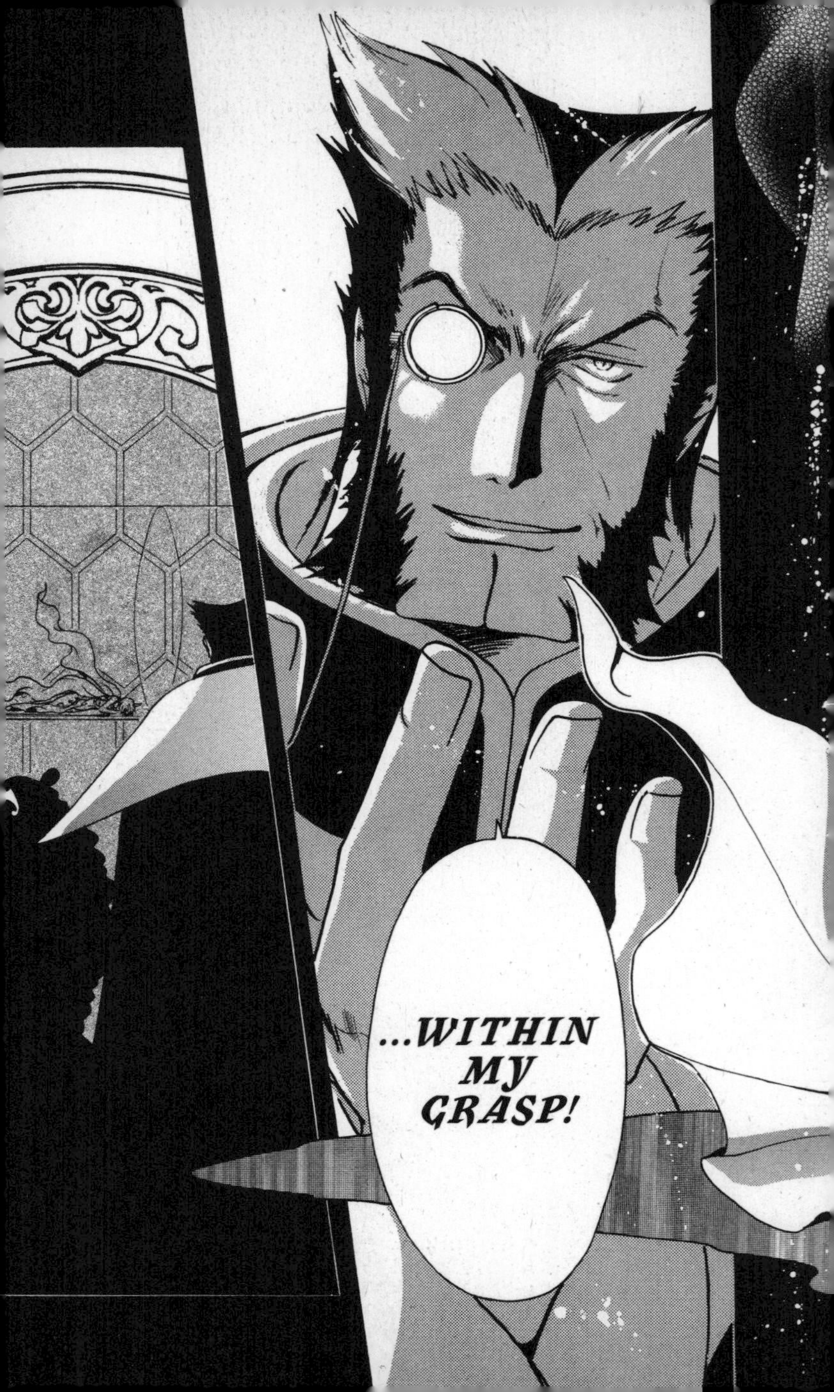
...WITHIN MY GRASP!

ツバサ

RESERVoir CHRoNiCLE

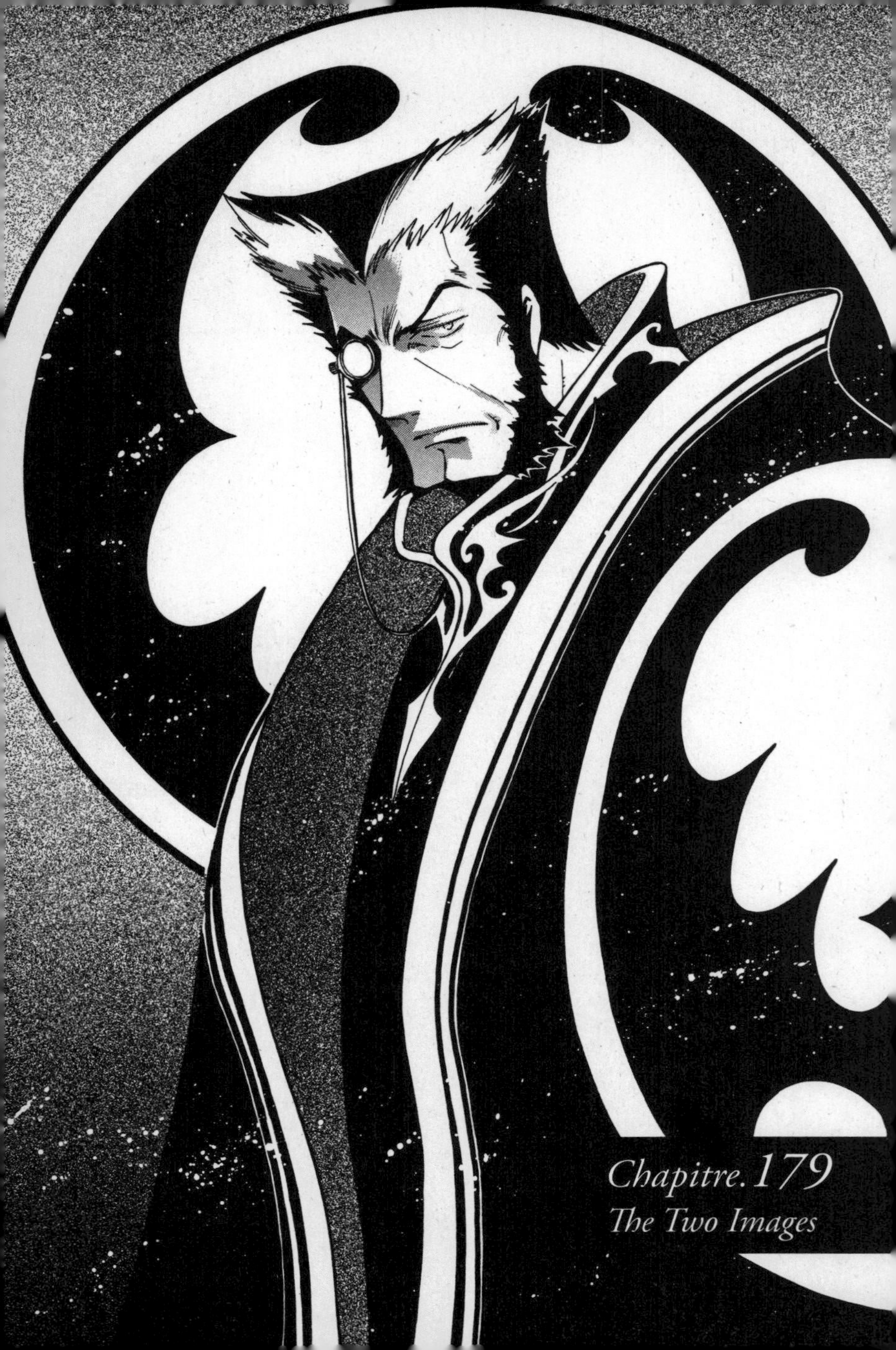

## Chapitre. 179
### The Two Images

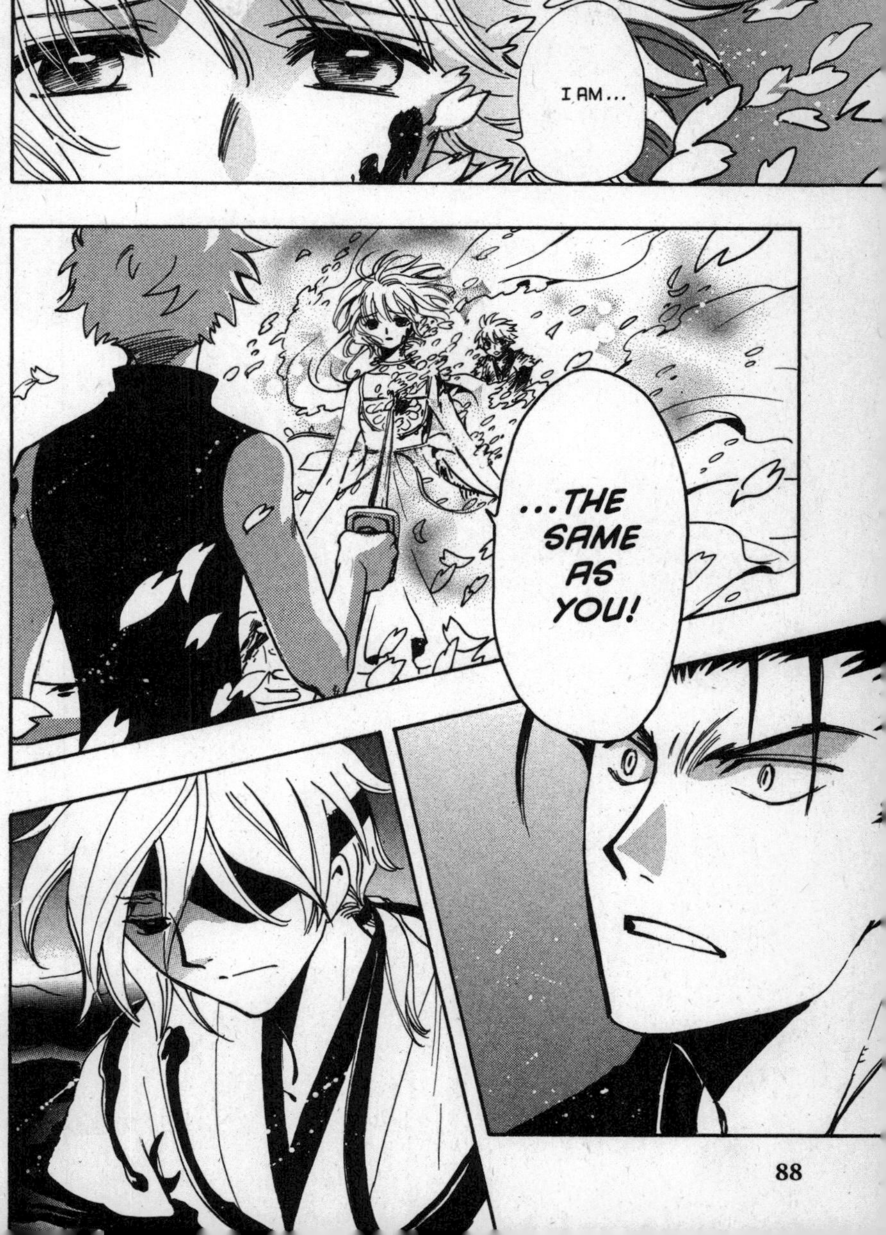
I AM...
...THE SAME AS YOU!

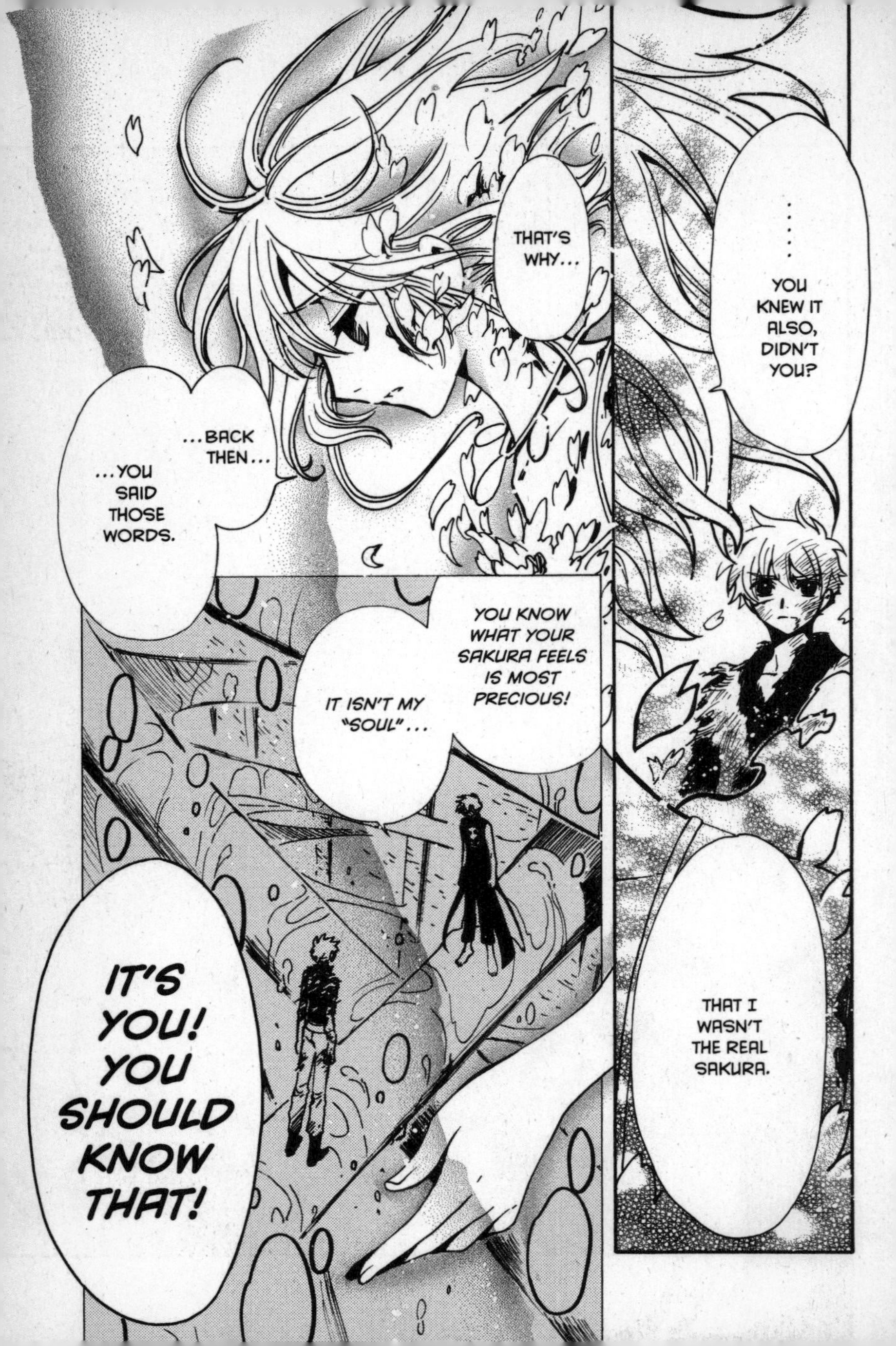

......
YOU KNEW IT ALSO, DIDN'T YOU?
THAT I WASN'T THE REAL SAKURA.
THAT'S WHY...
...BACK THEN... ...YOU SAID THOSE WORDS.
YOU KNOW WHAT YOUR SAKURA FEELS IS MOST PRECIOUS!
IT ISN'T MY "SOUL"...
IT'S YOU! YOU SHOULD KNOW THAT!

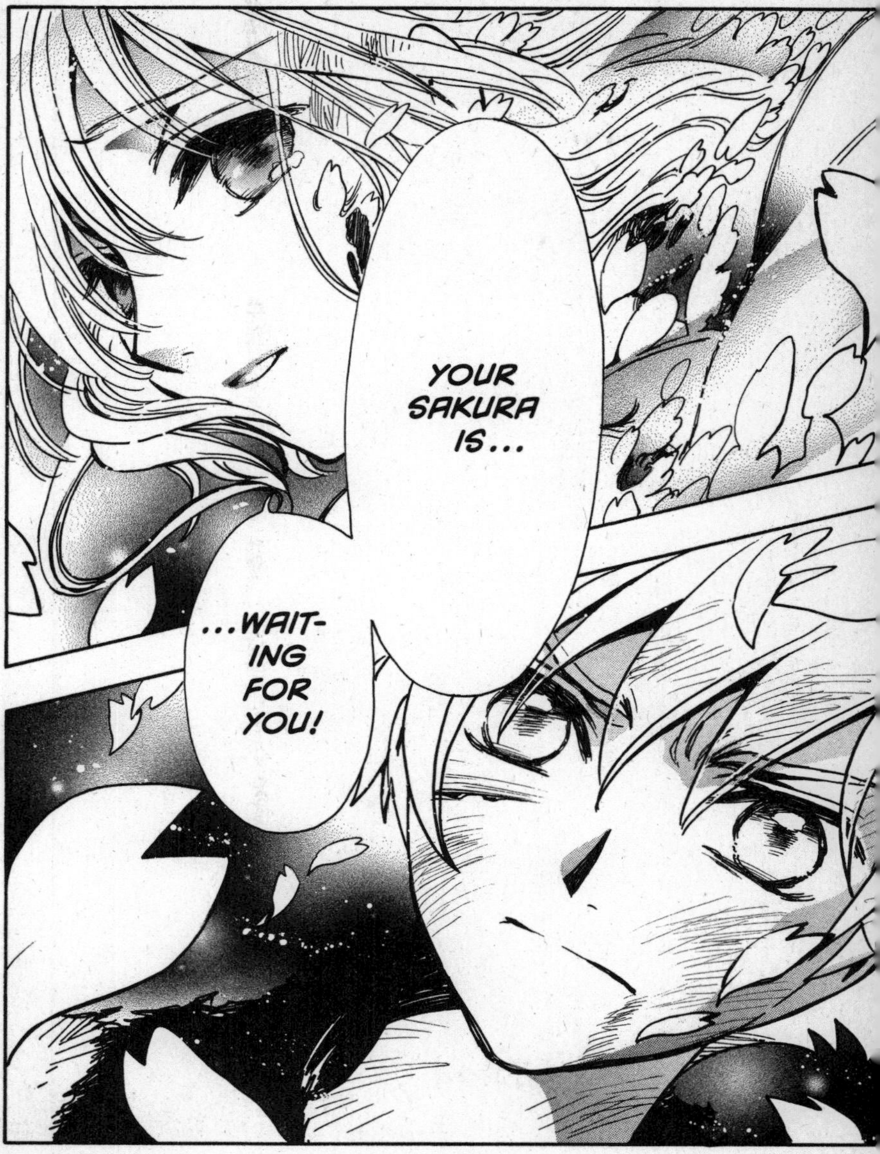
YOUR SAKURA IS...
...WAIT-ING FOR YOU!

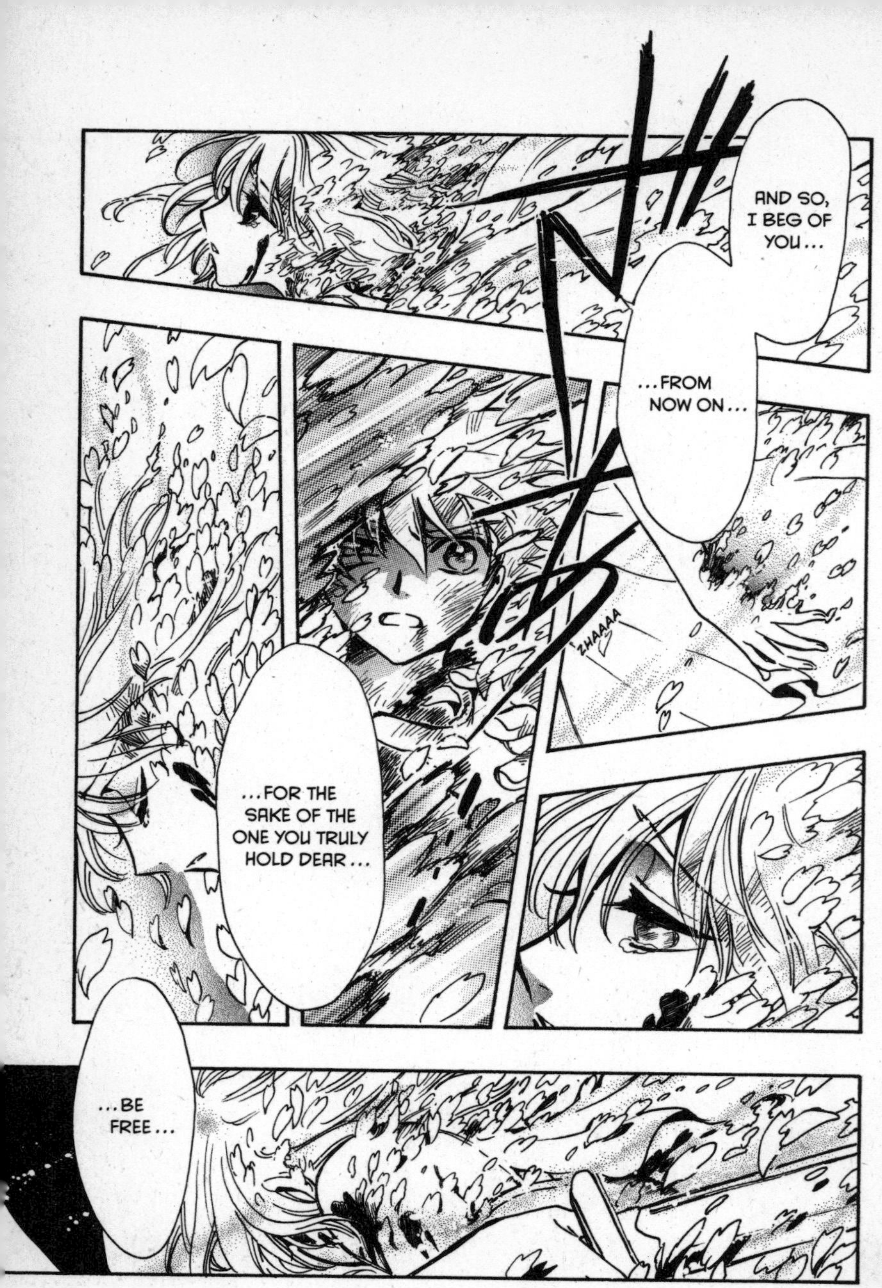
AND SO, I BEG OF YOU...
...FROM NOW ON...
ZHAAAA
...FOR THE SAKE OF THE ONE YOU TRULY HOLD DEAR...
...BE FREE...

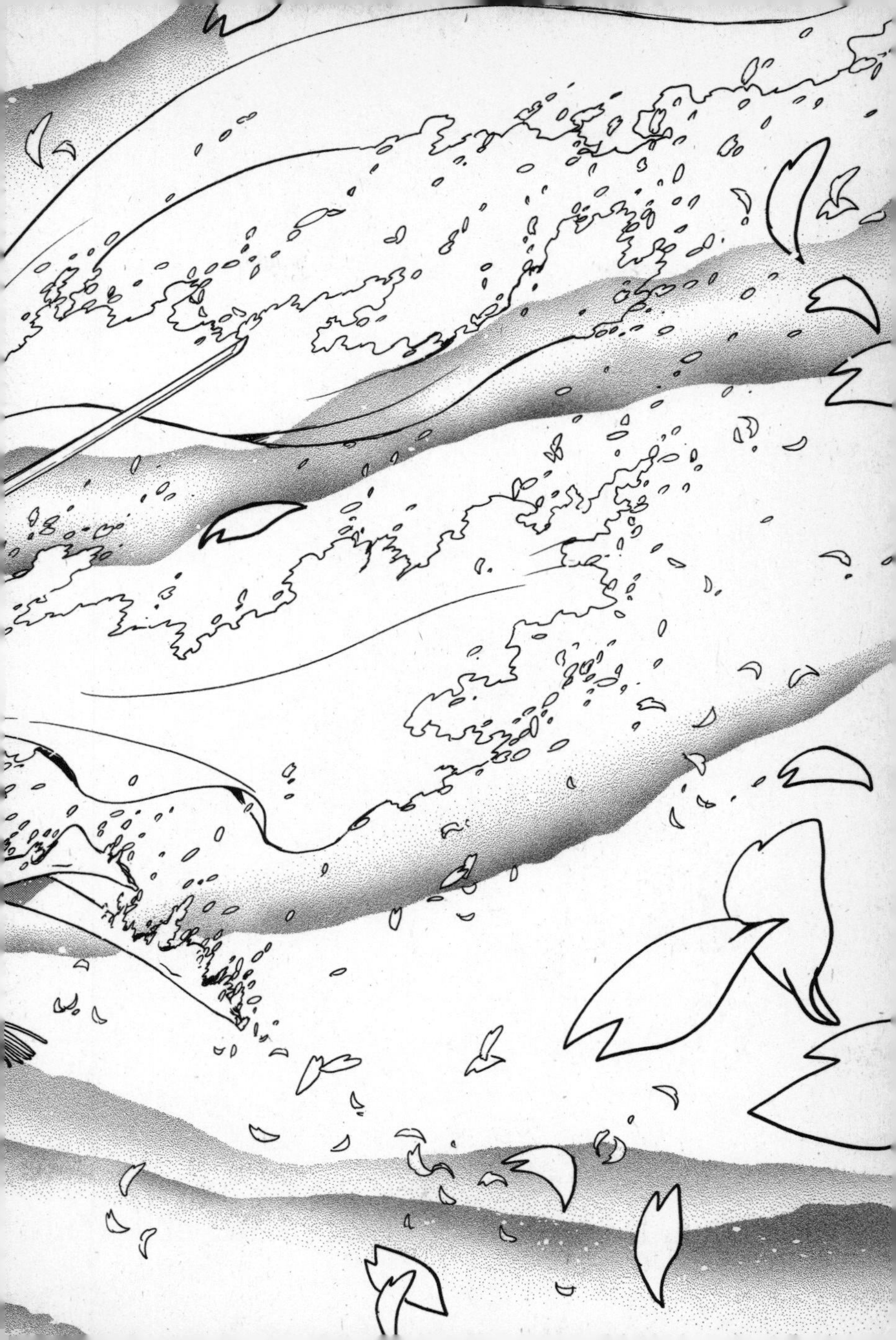

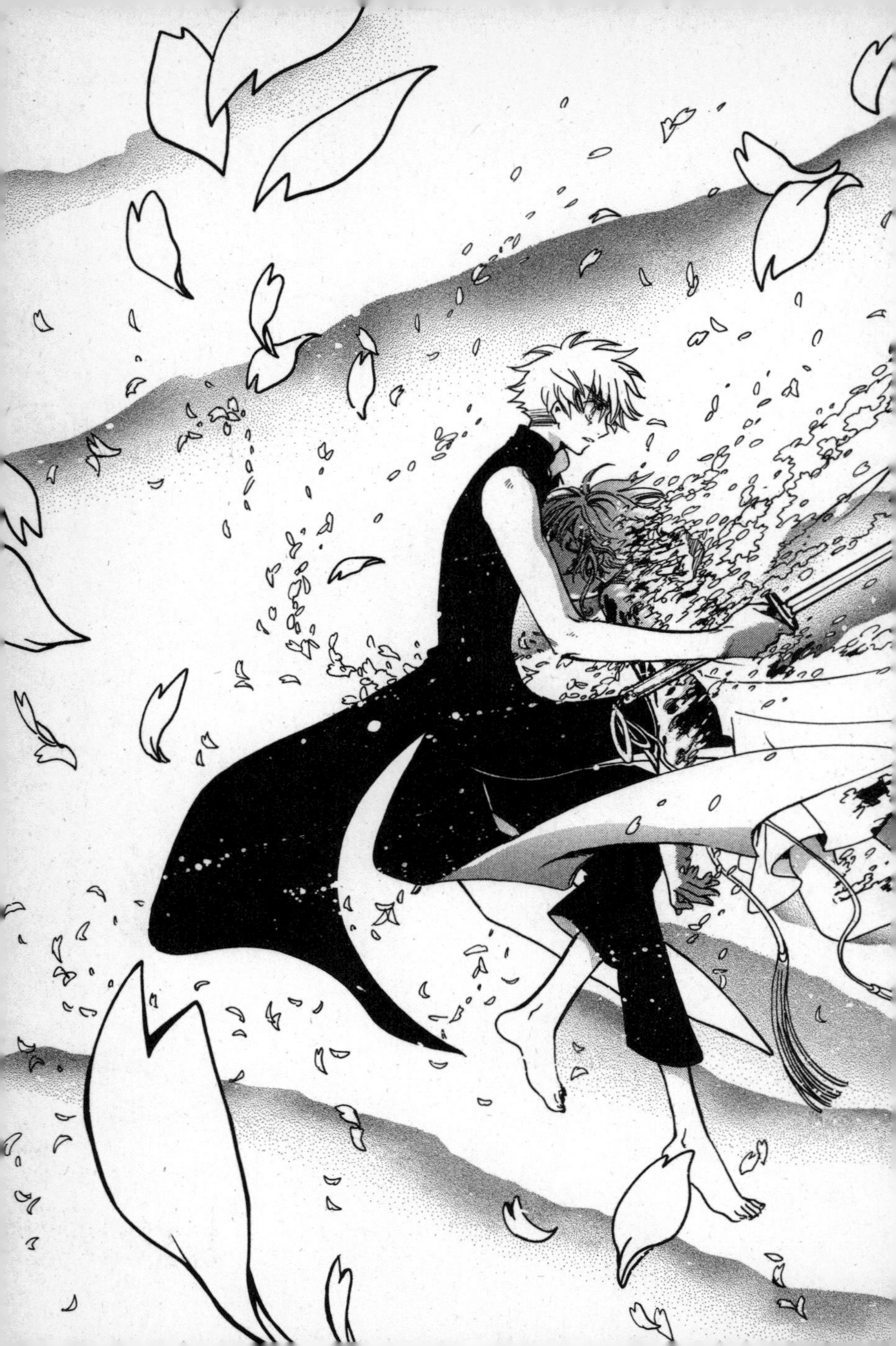

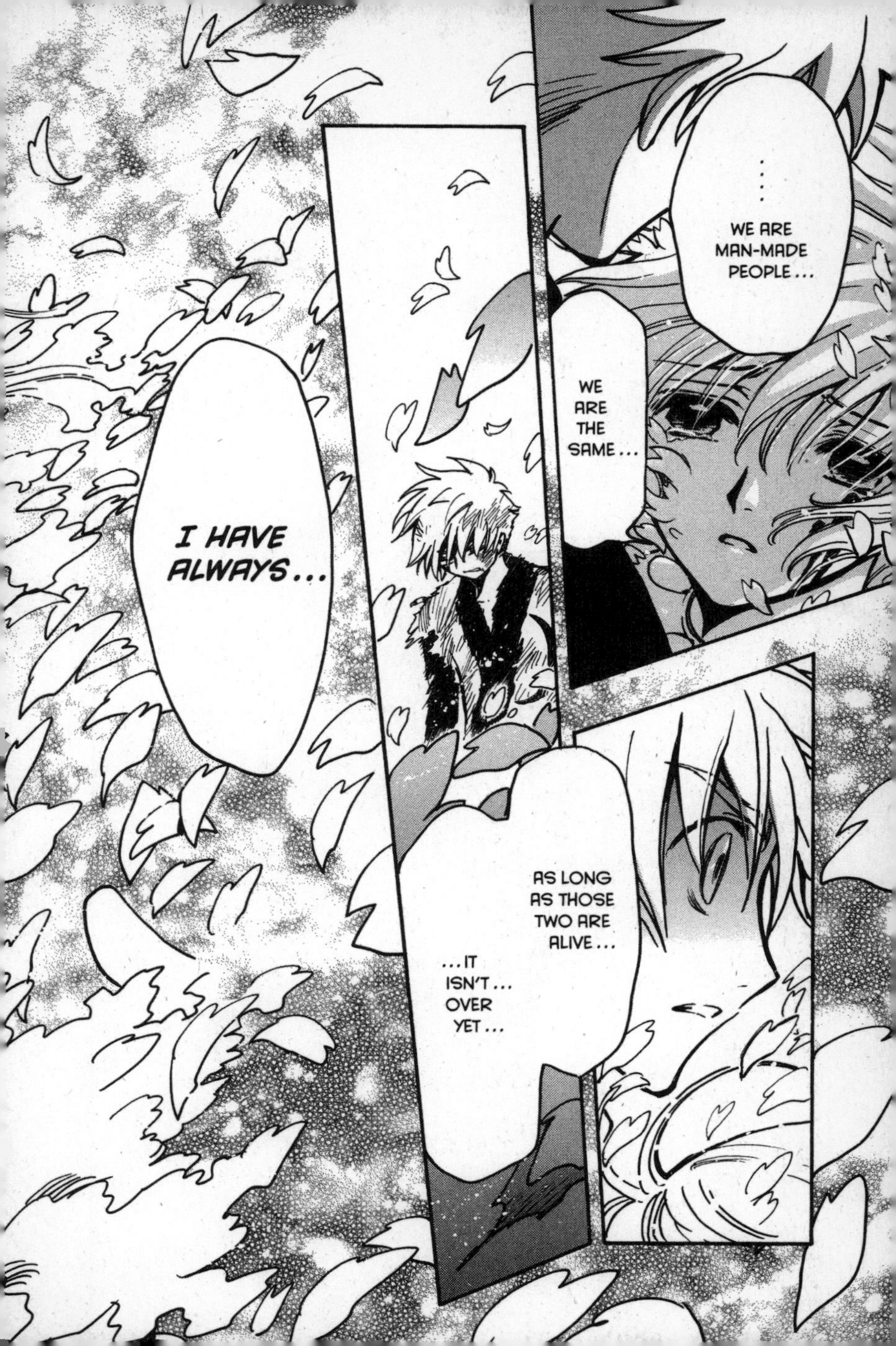
. . . .
WE ARE MAN-MADE PEOPLE...
WE ARE THE SAME...
AS LONG AS THOSE TWO ARE ALIVE...
...IT ISN'T... OVER YET...
I HAVE ALWAYS...

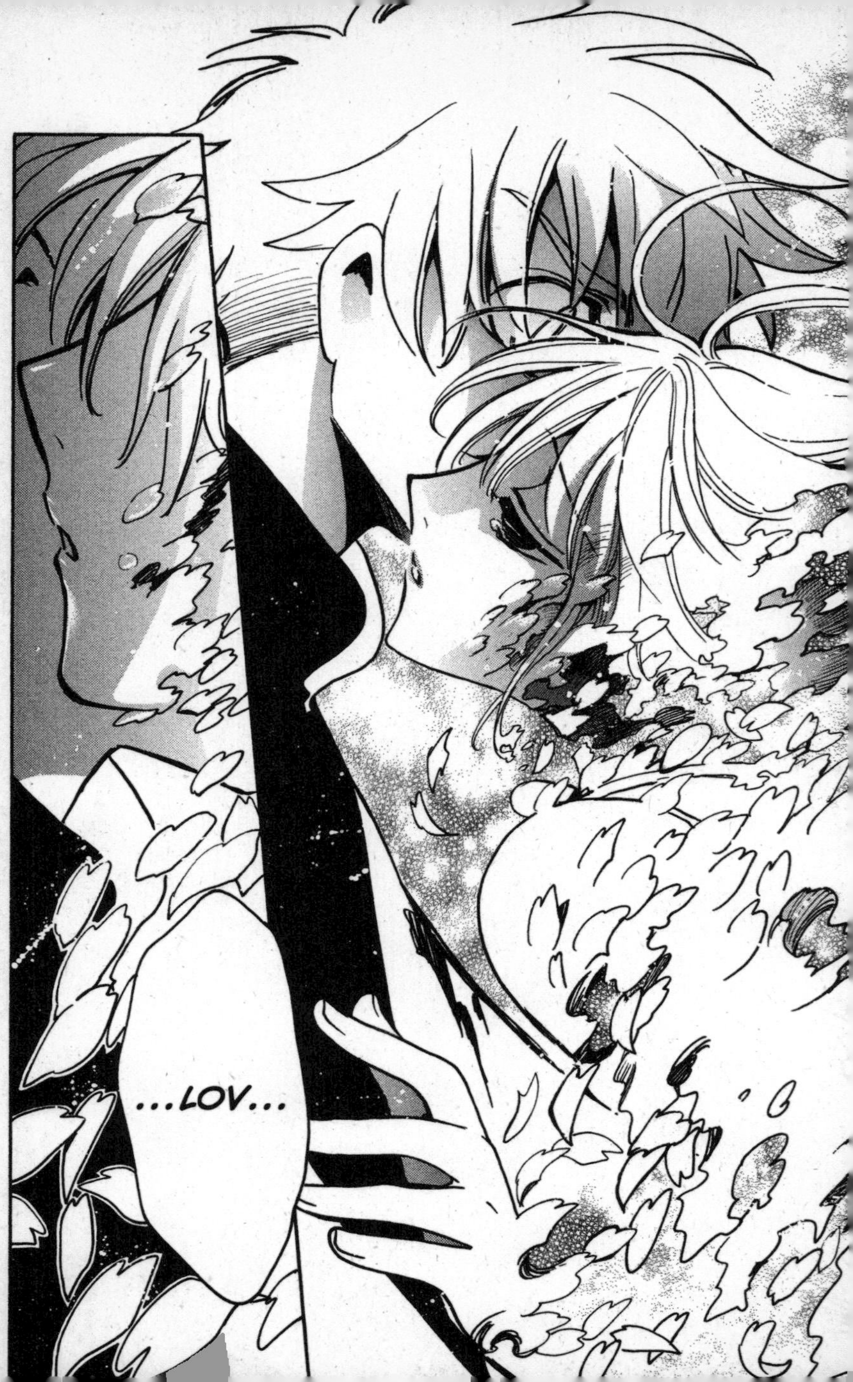
...LOV...

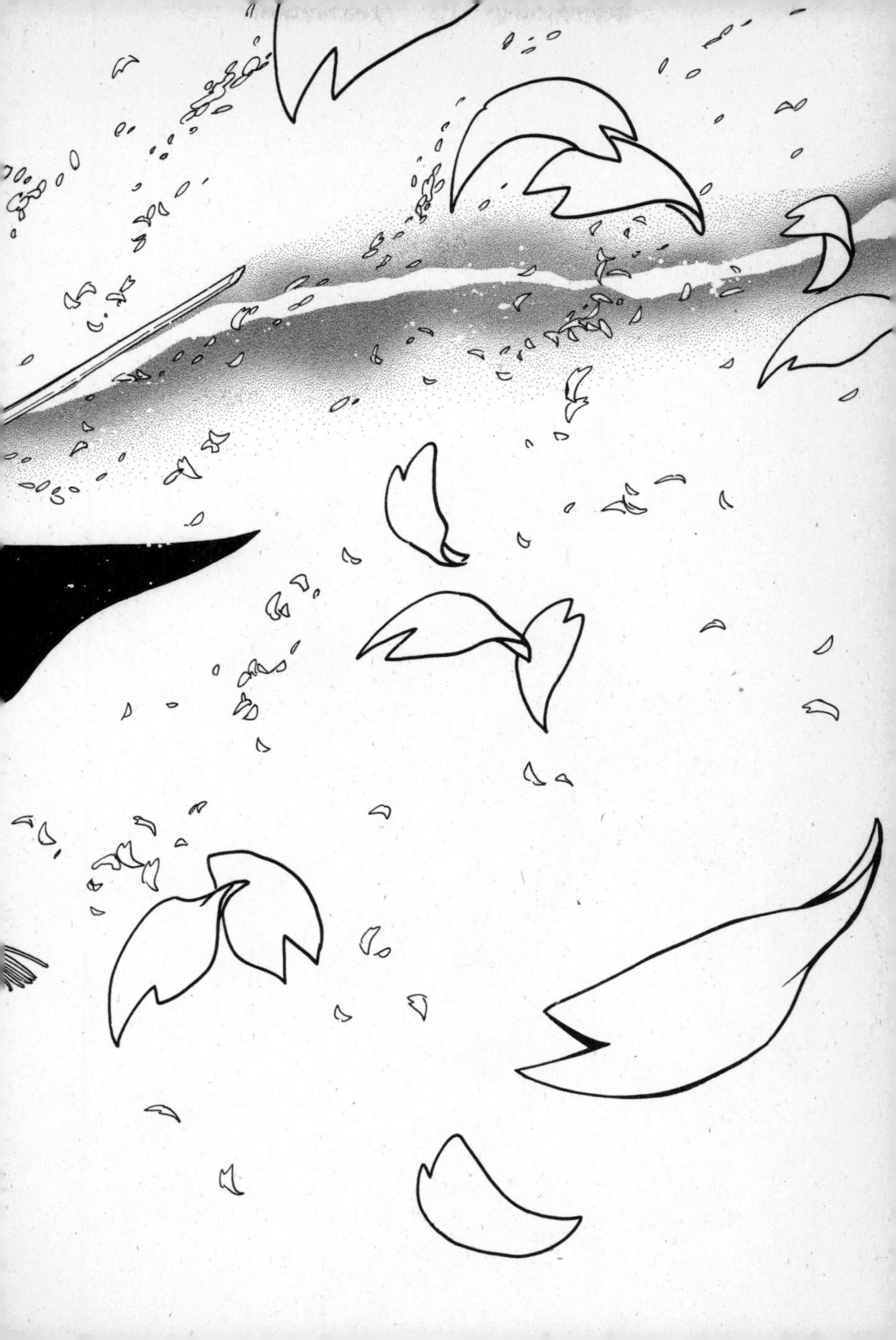

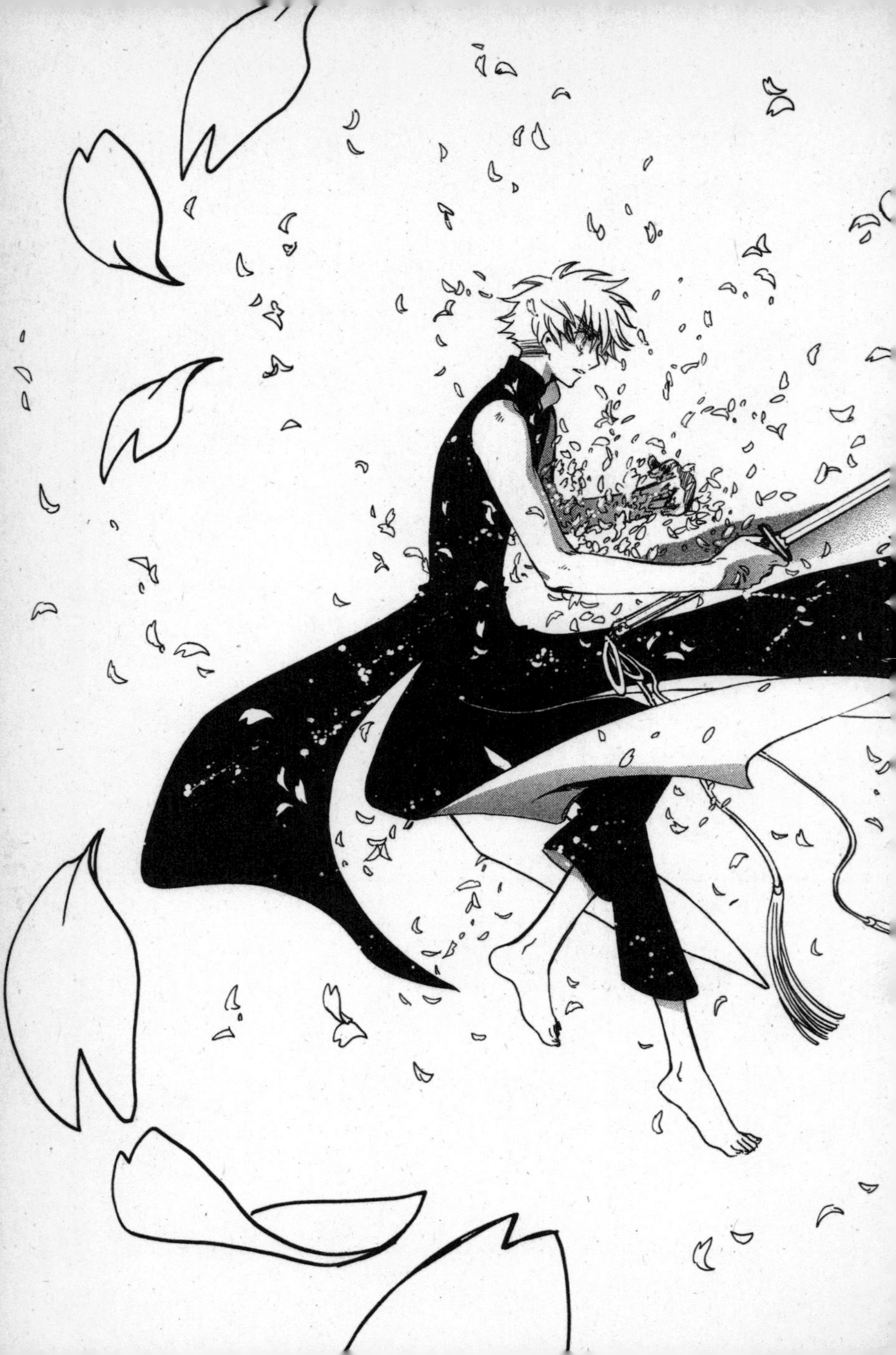

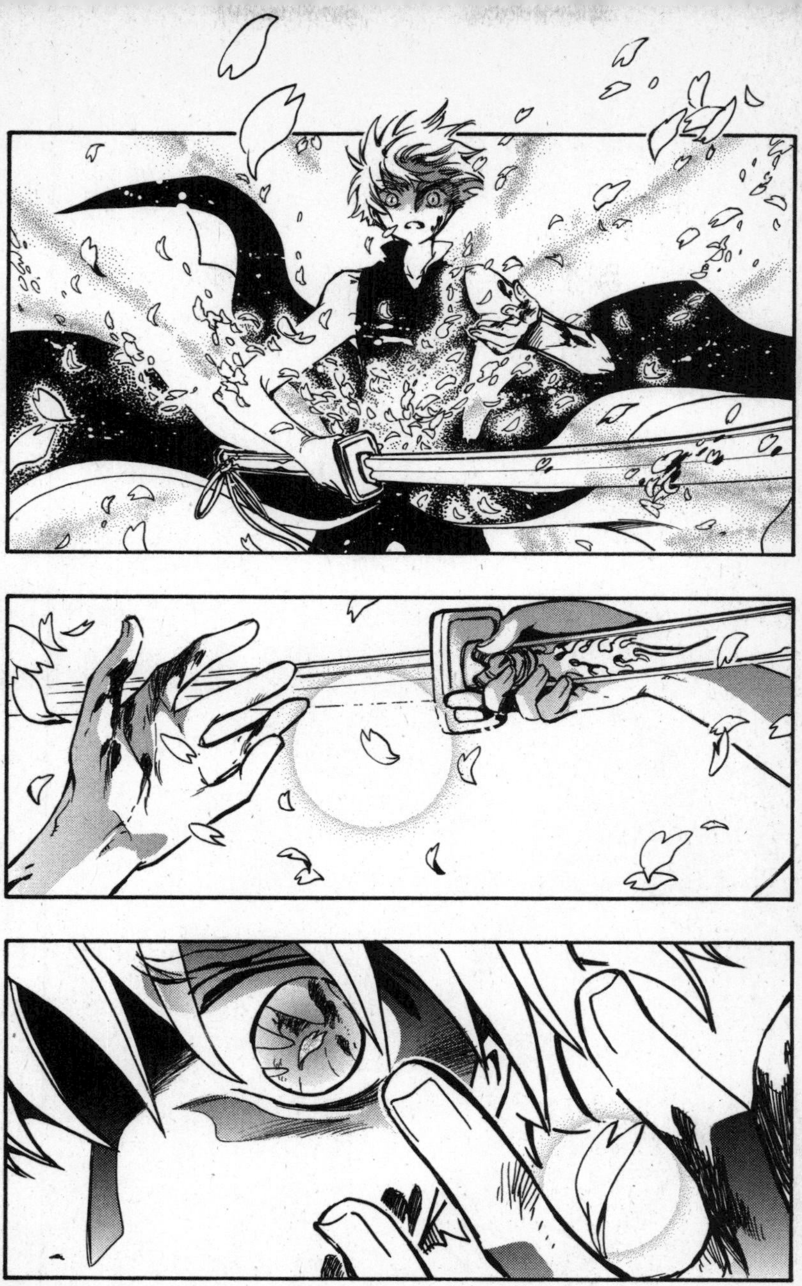

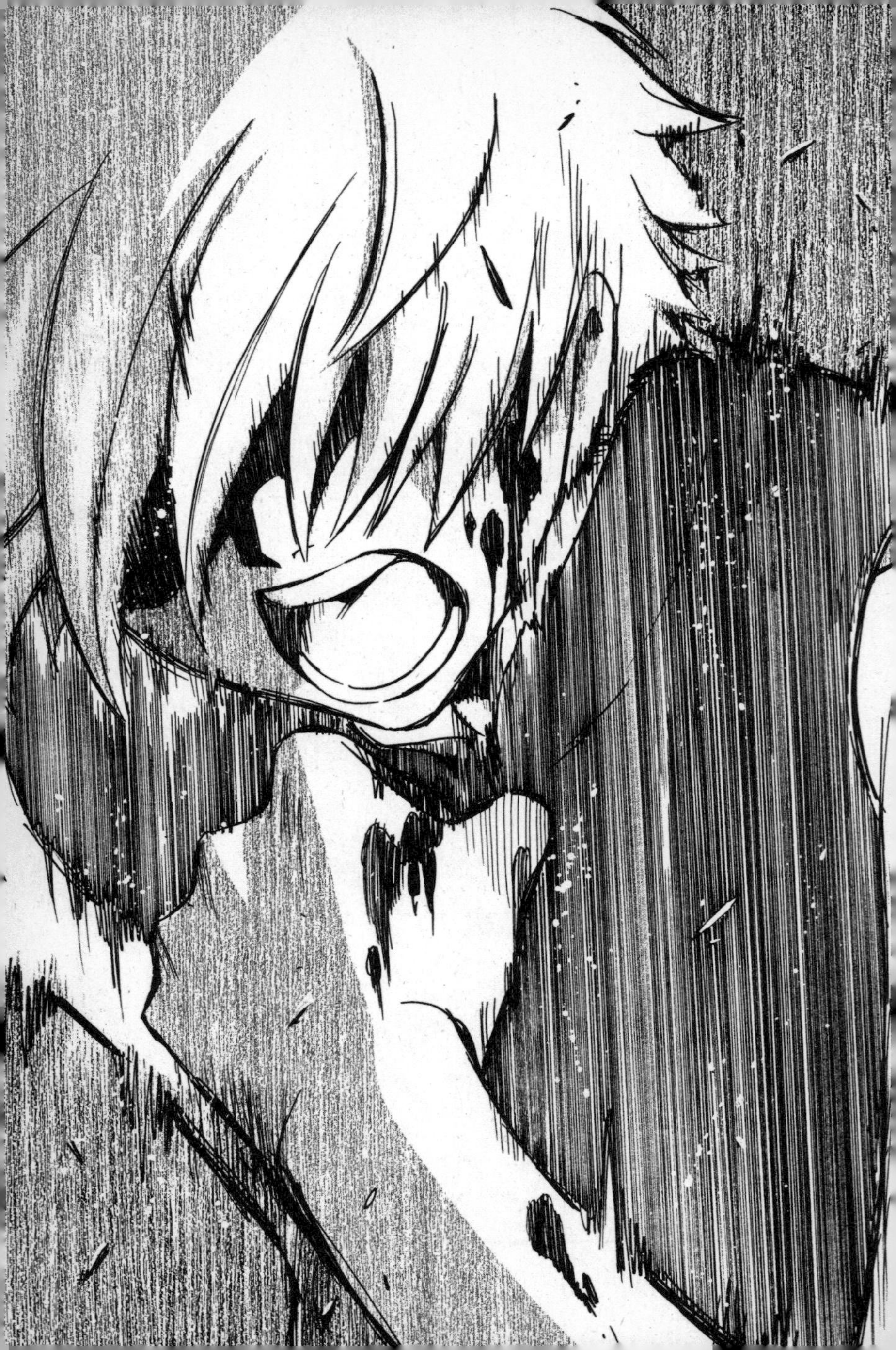

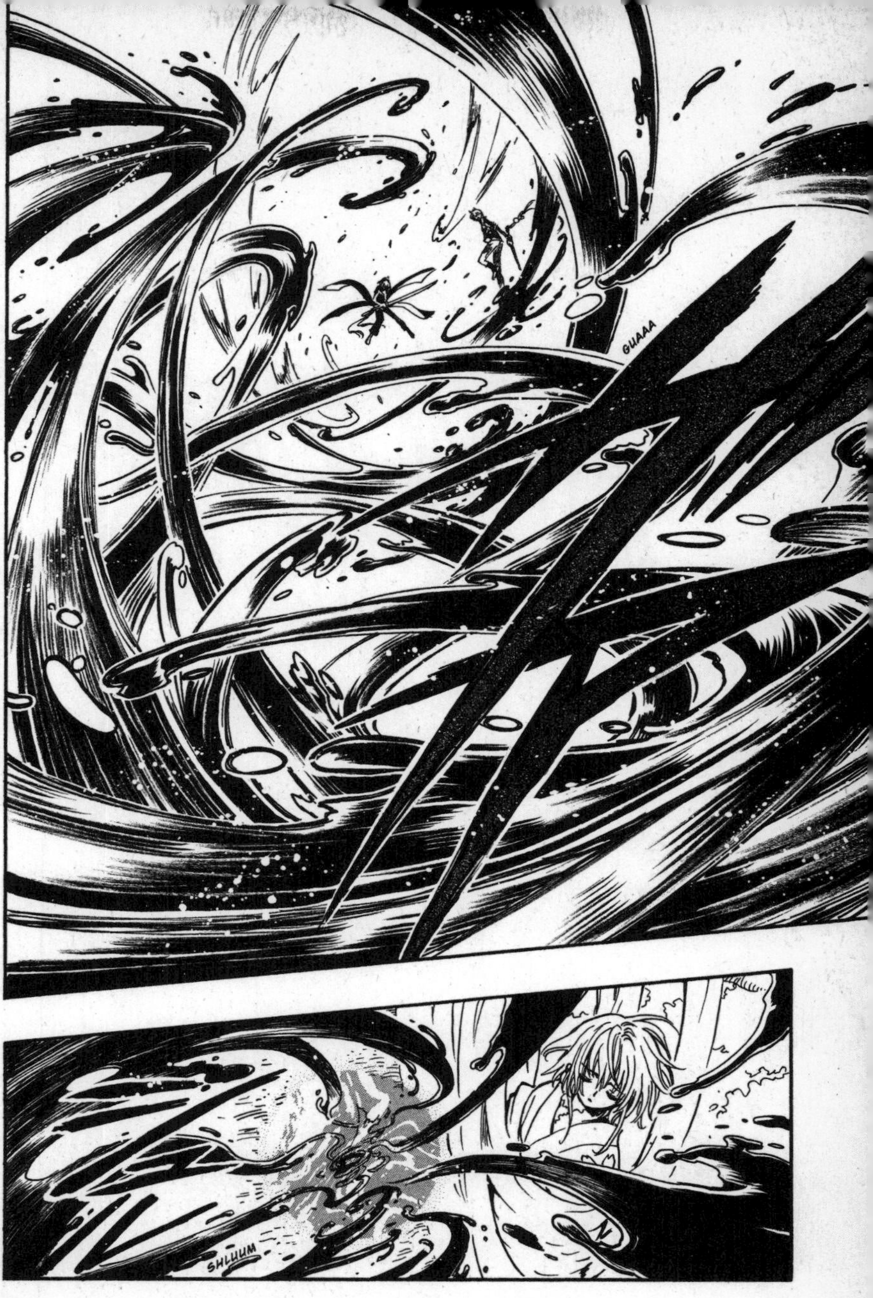
GUAAA
SHLUUM

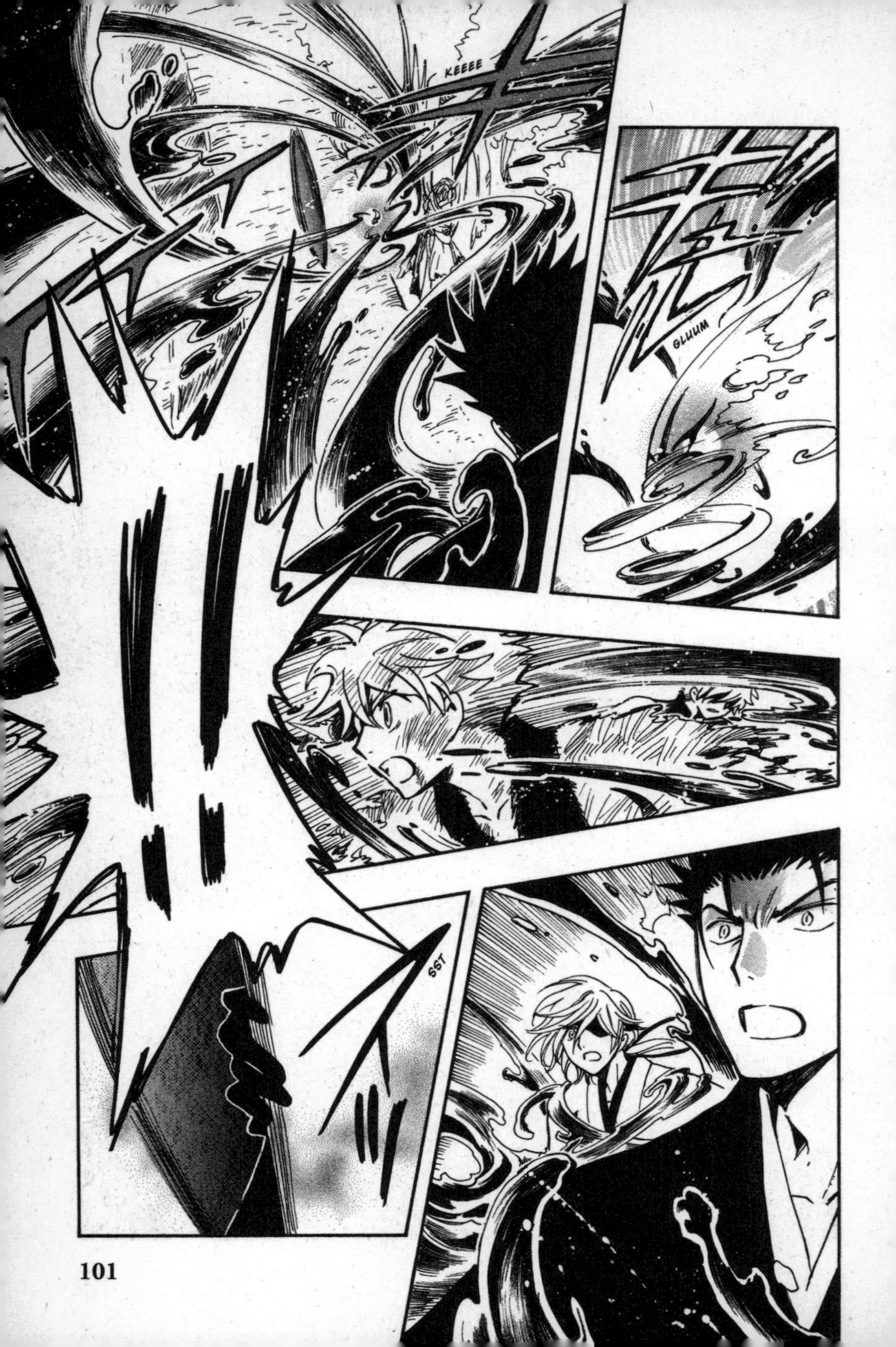
GLLUM
KEEEE
SST

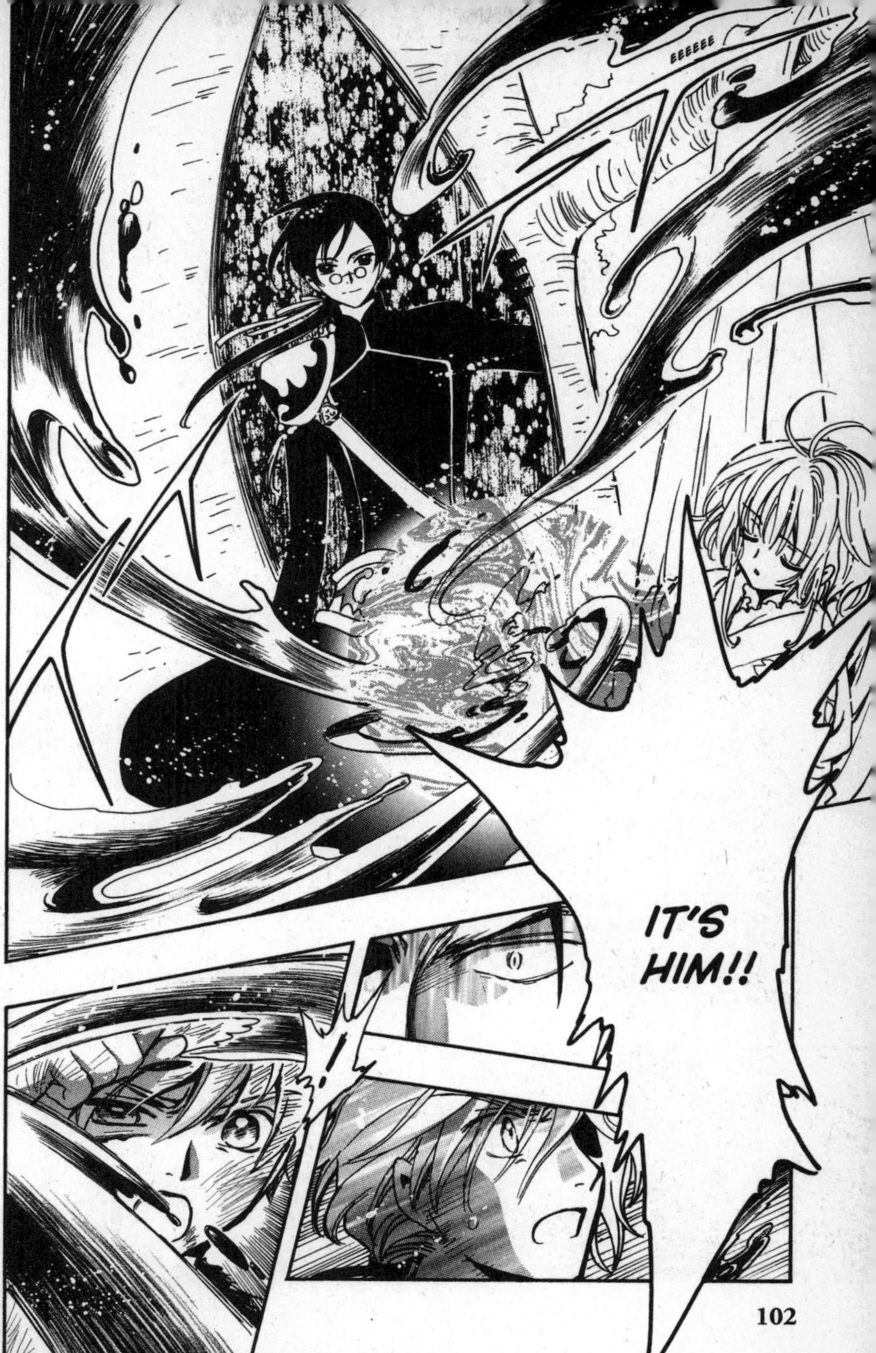
EEEEEE
IT'S HIM!!

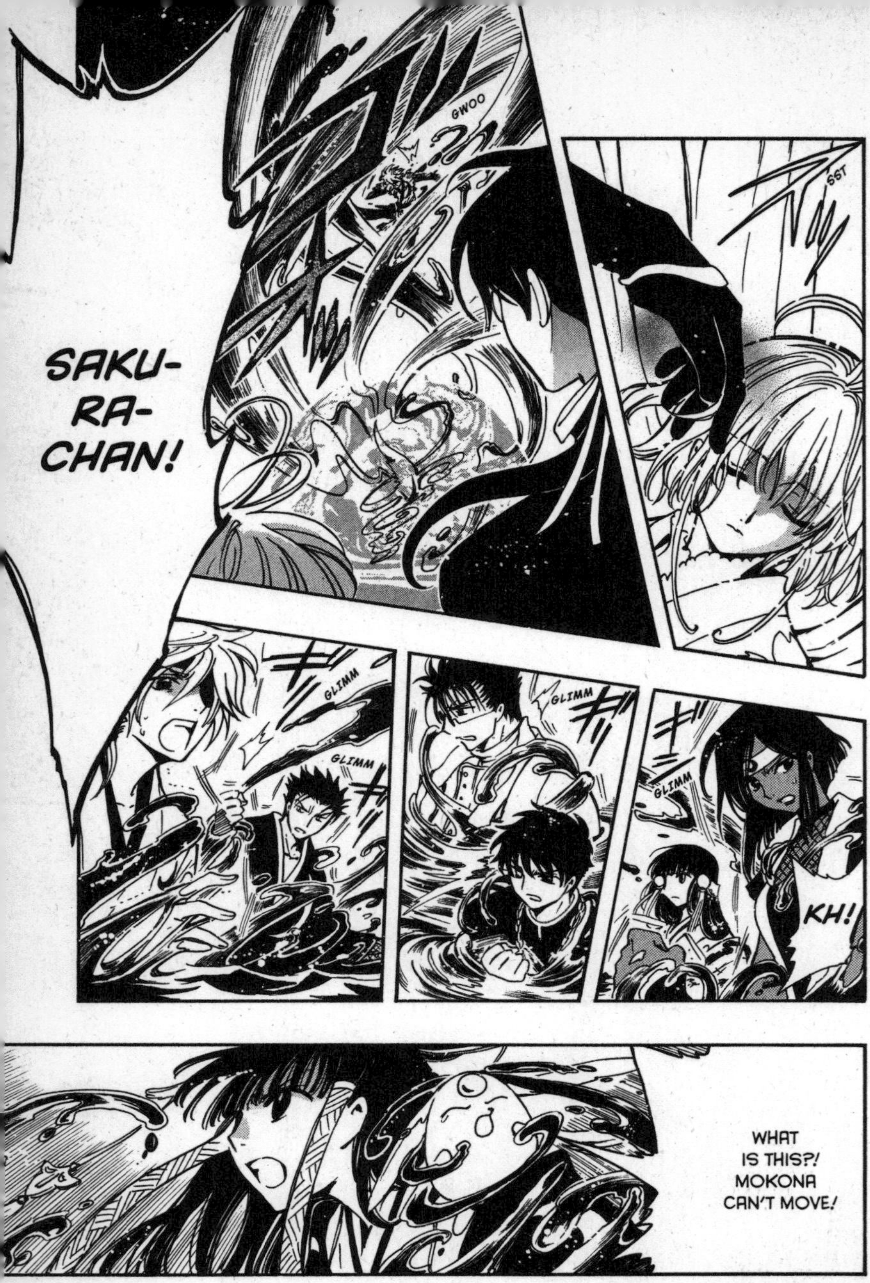
SST
GWOO
SAKU-
RA-
CHAN!
GLIMM
KH!
GLIMM
GLIMM
GLIMM
WHAT
IS THIS?!
MOKONA
CAN'T MOVE!

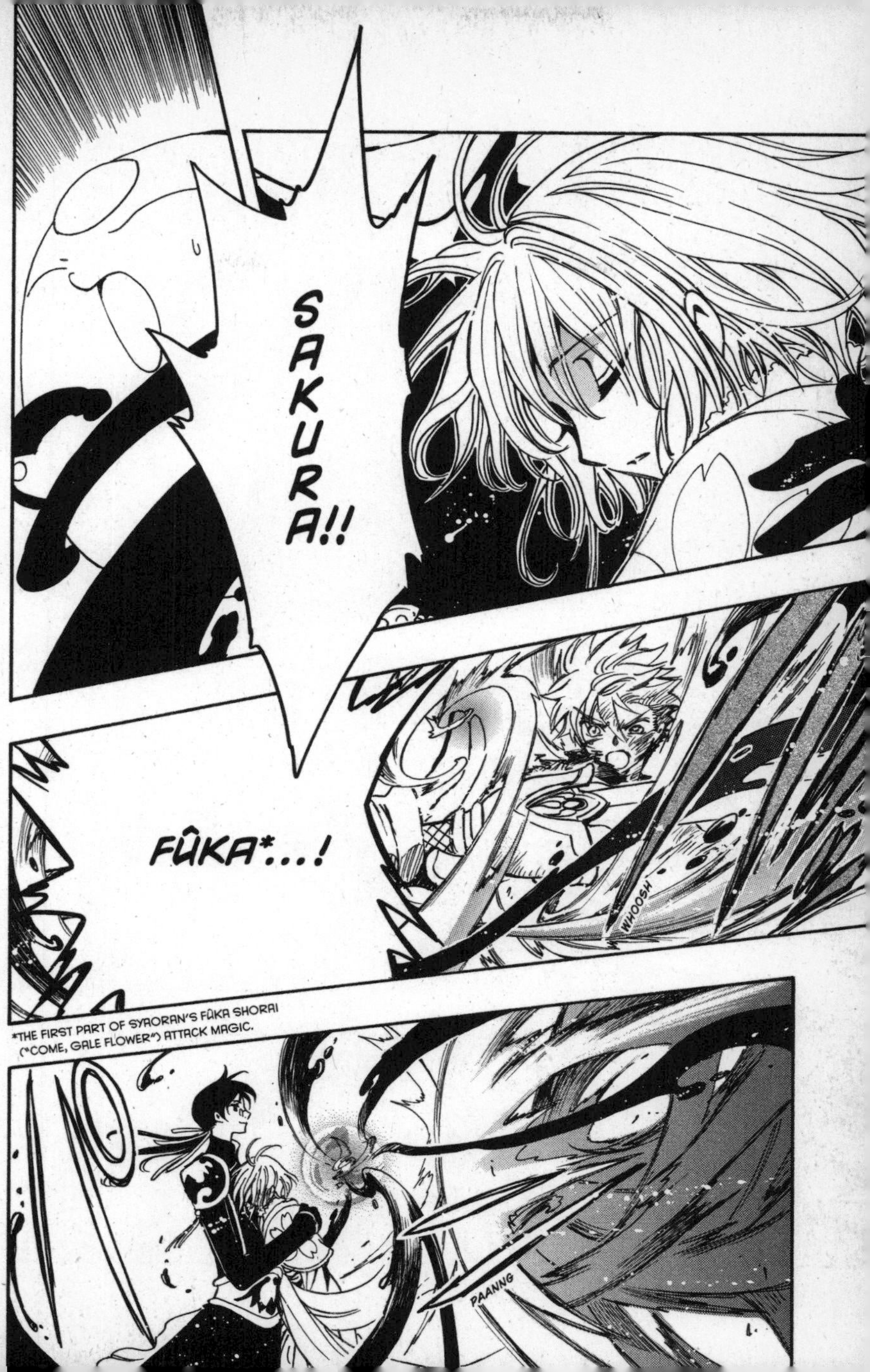
SAKURA!!
FÛKA*...!
WHOOSH
PAANNG

*THE FIRST PART OF SYAORAN'S FÛKA SHORAI ("COME, GALE FLOWER") ATTACK MAGIC.

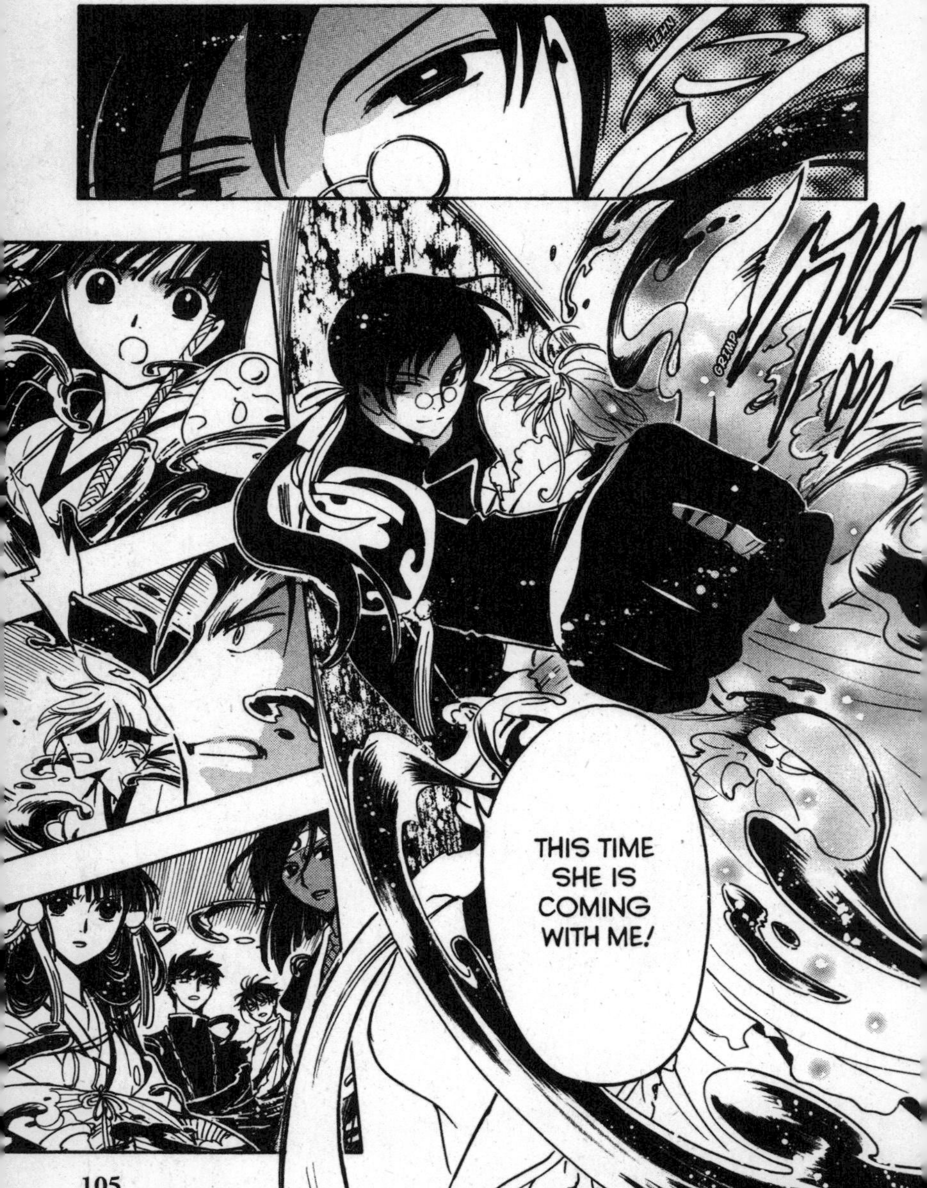
HEHN
GRIMP
THIS TIME SHE IS COMING WITH ME!

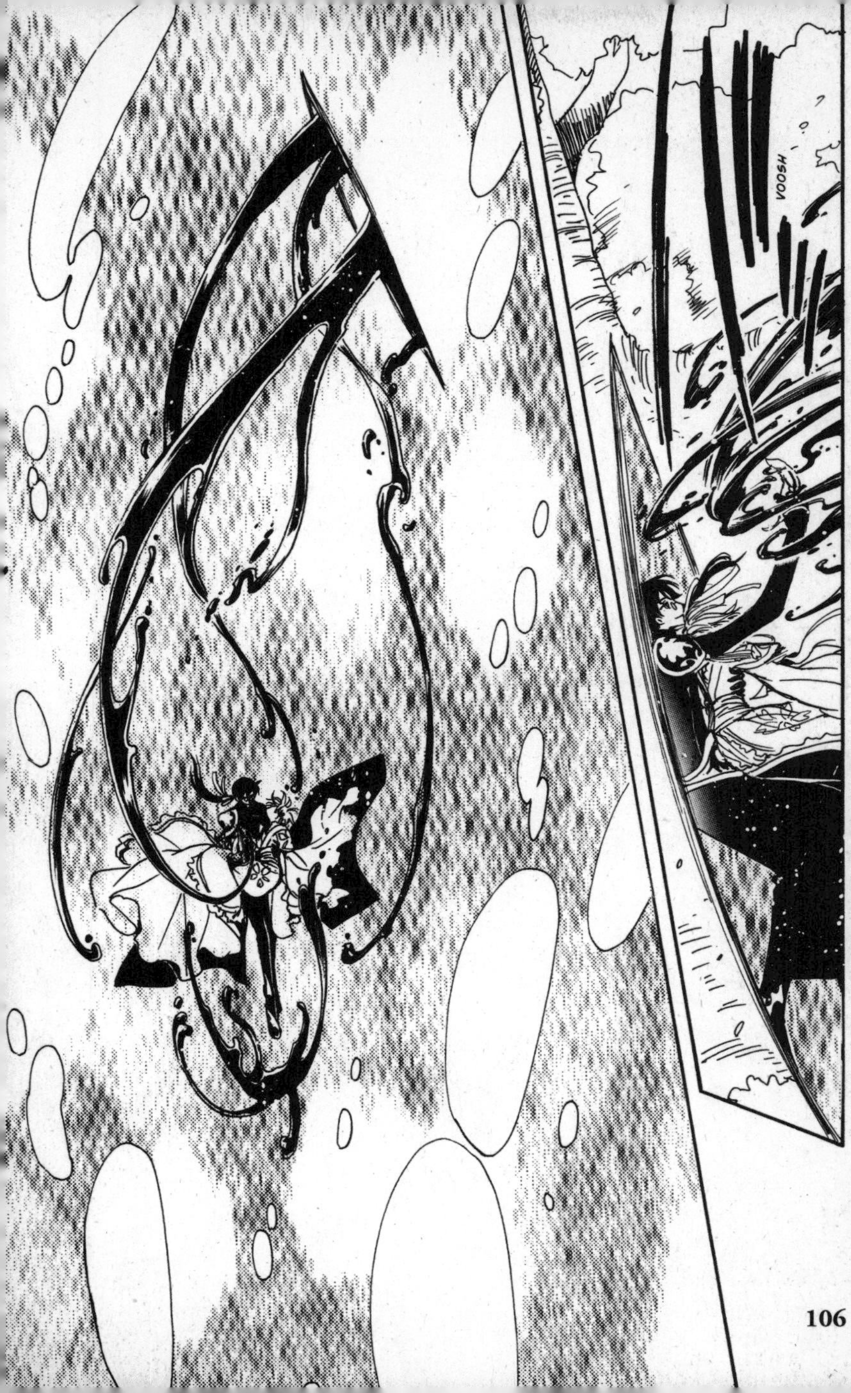
VOOSH

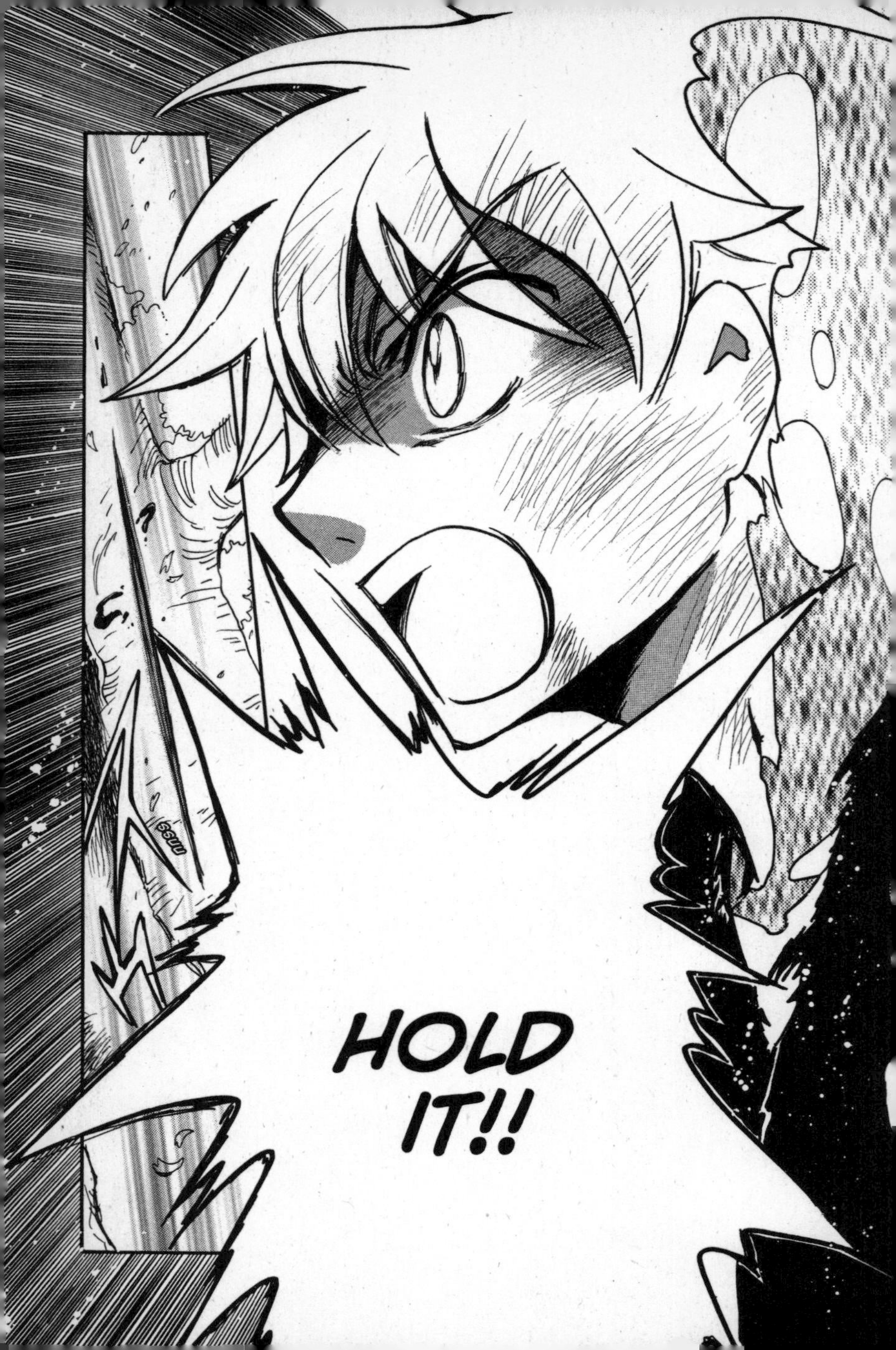
HOLD IT!!

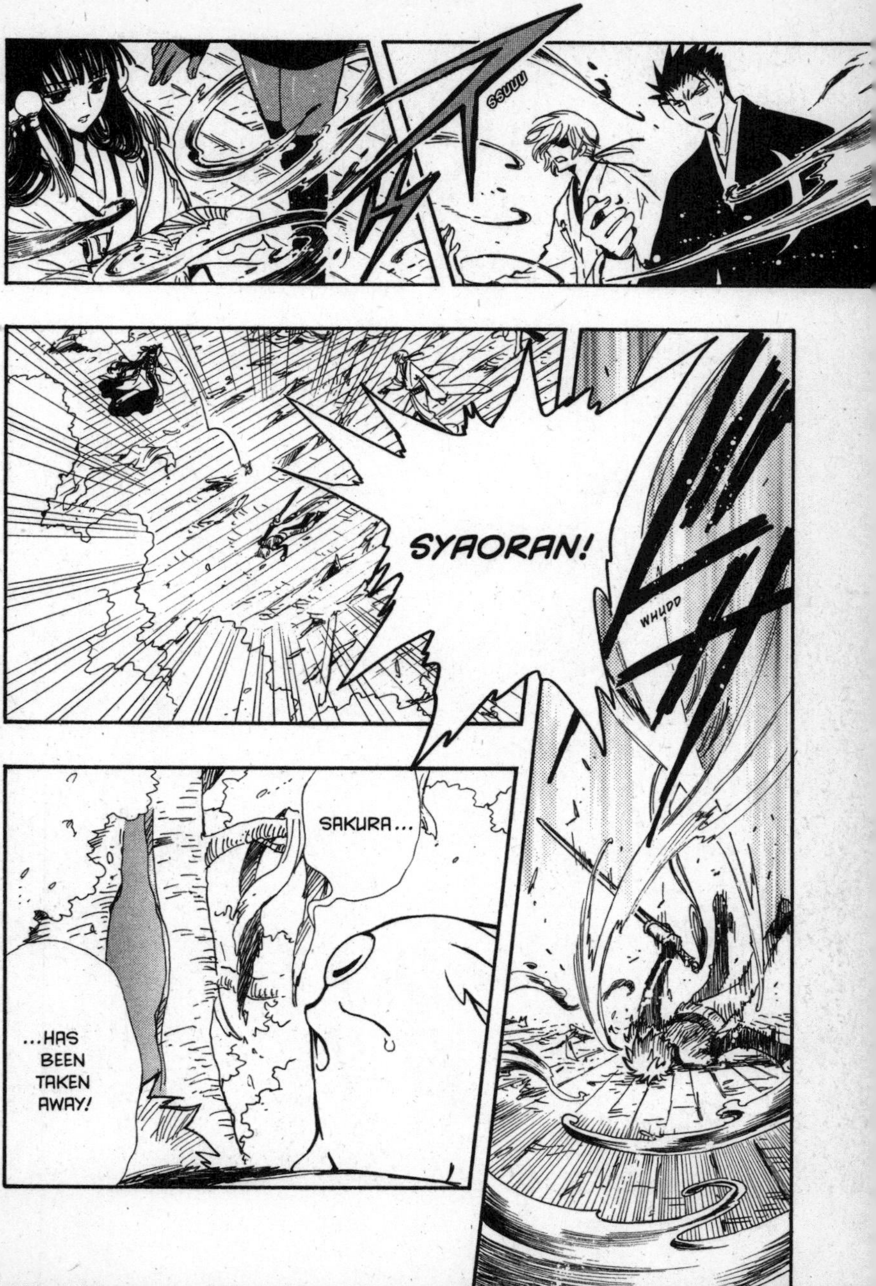
SSUUU
WHUDD
SYAORAN!
SAKURA...
...HAS BEEN TAKEN AWAY!

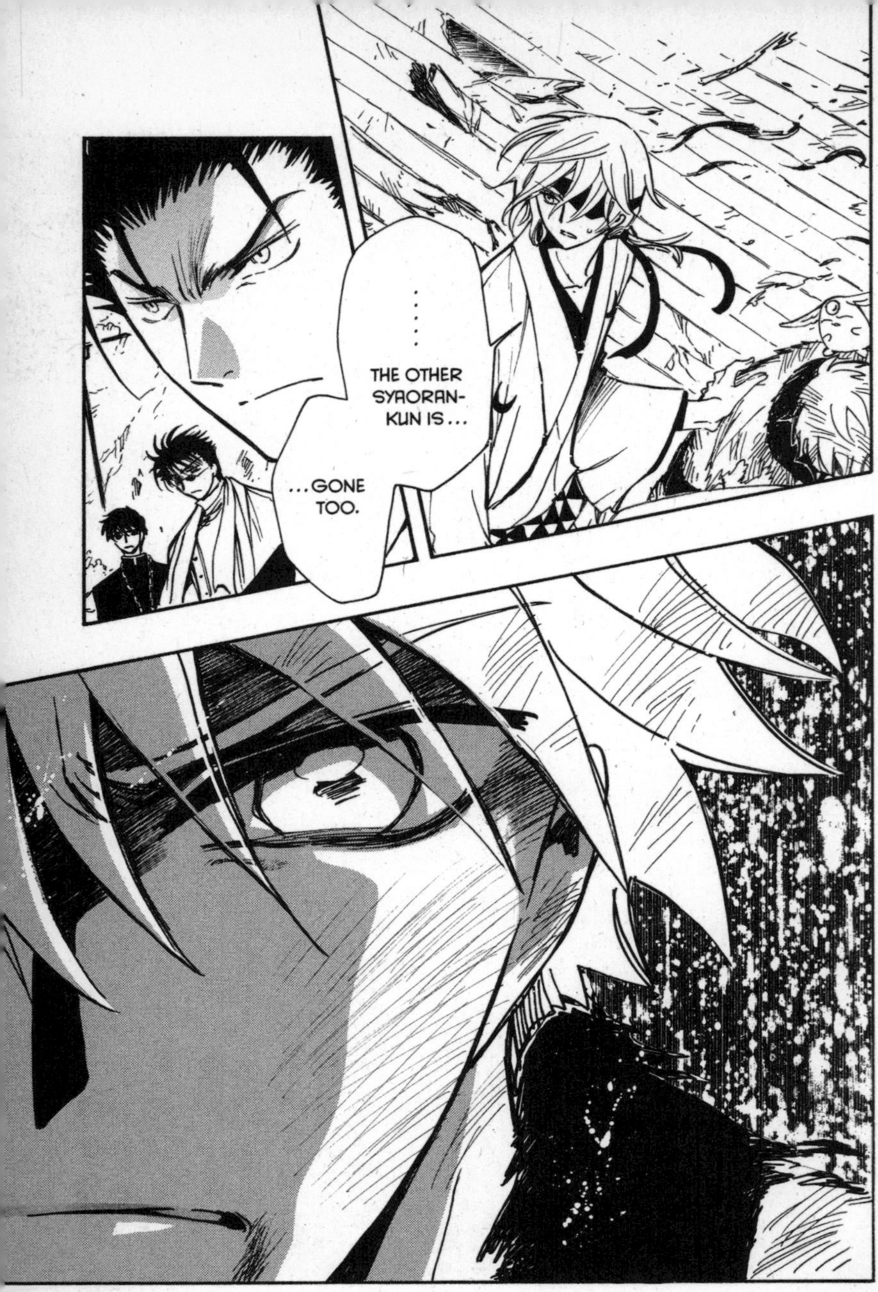
......
THE OTHER SYAORAN-KUN IS...
...GONE TOO.

ツバサ

RESERVoir CHRoNiCLE

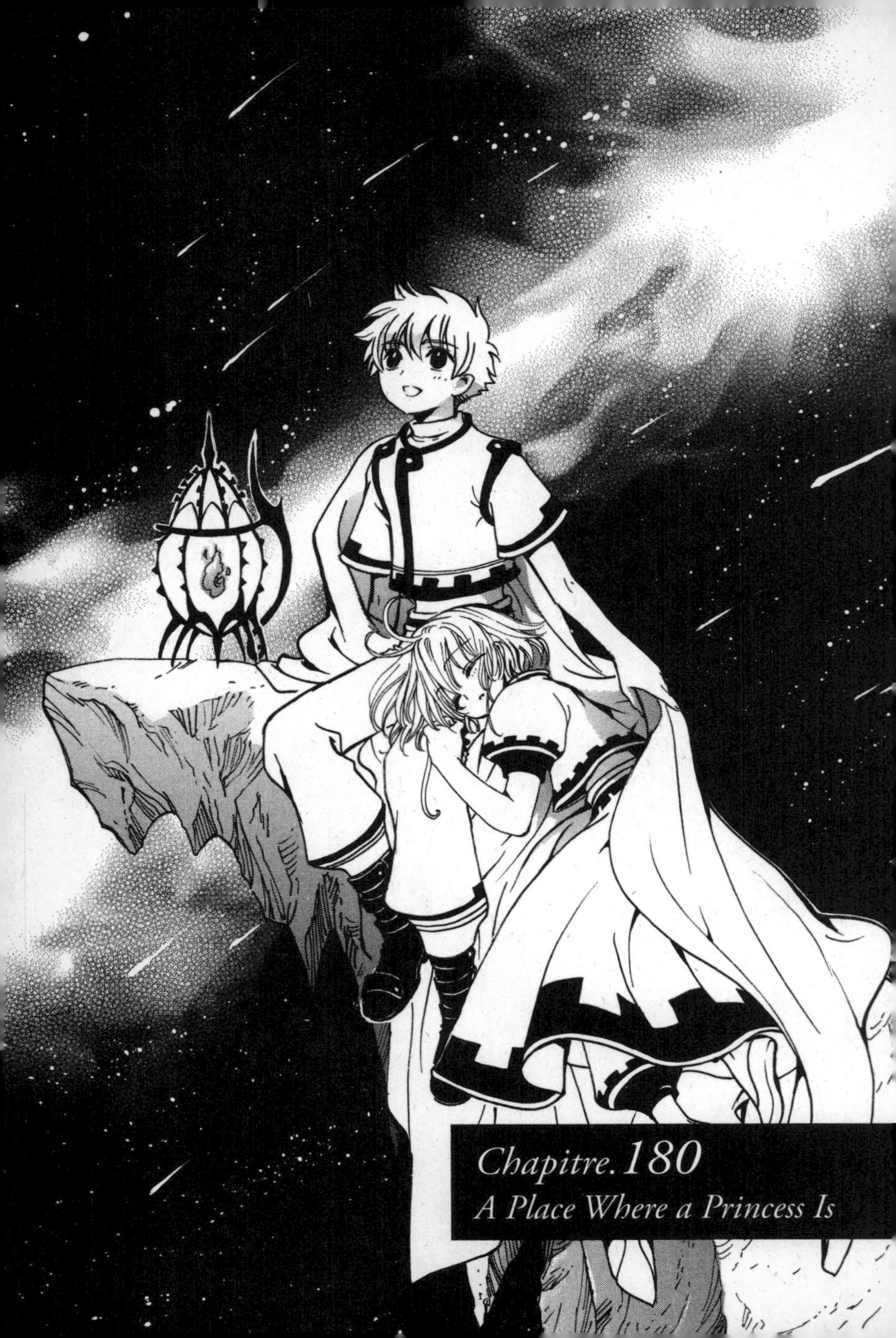
Chapitre. 180
A Place Where a Princess Is

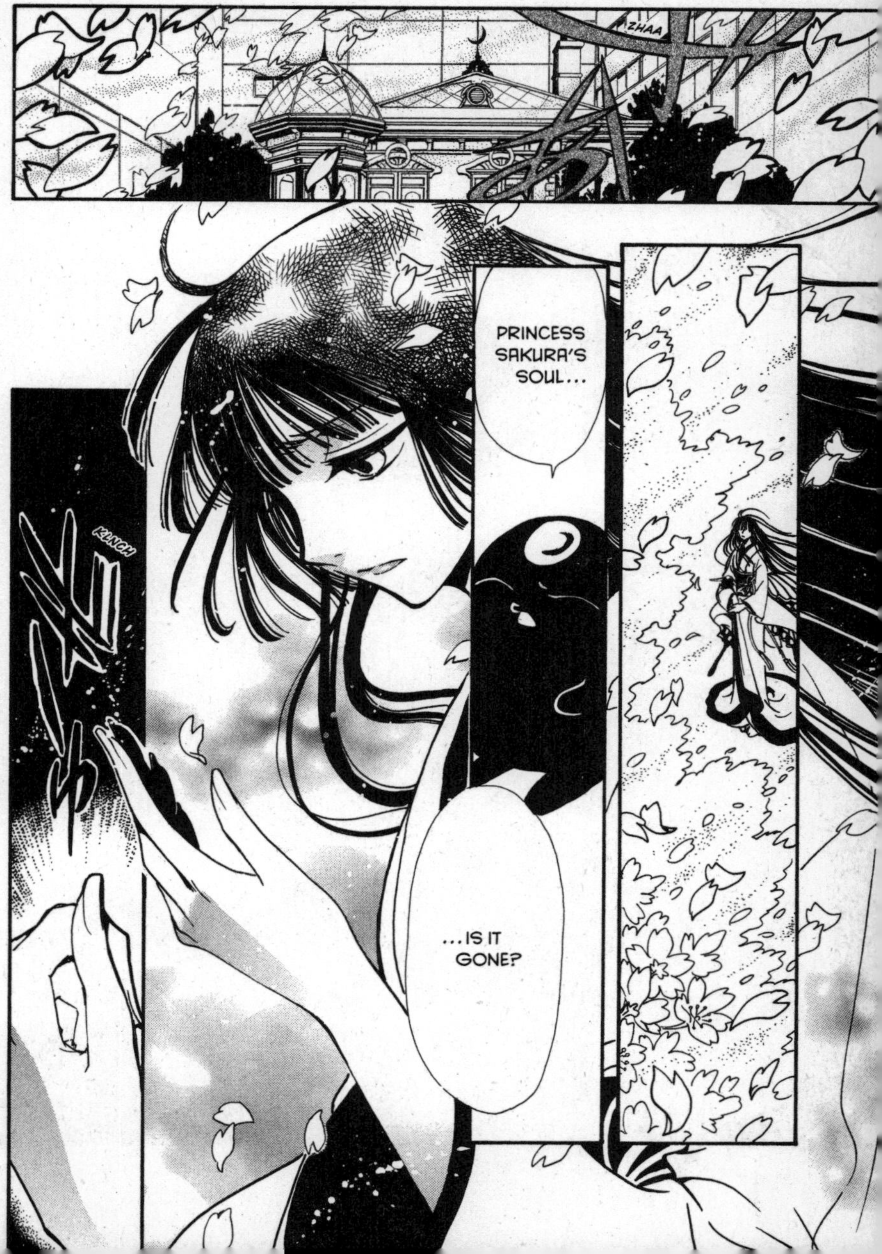
ZHAA
PRINCESS SAKURA'S SOUL...
...IS IT GONE?
KLINCH

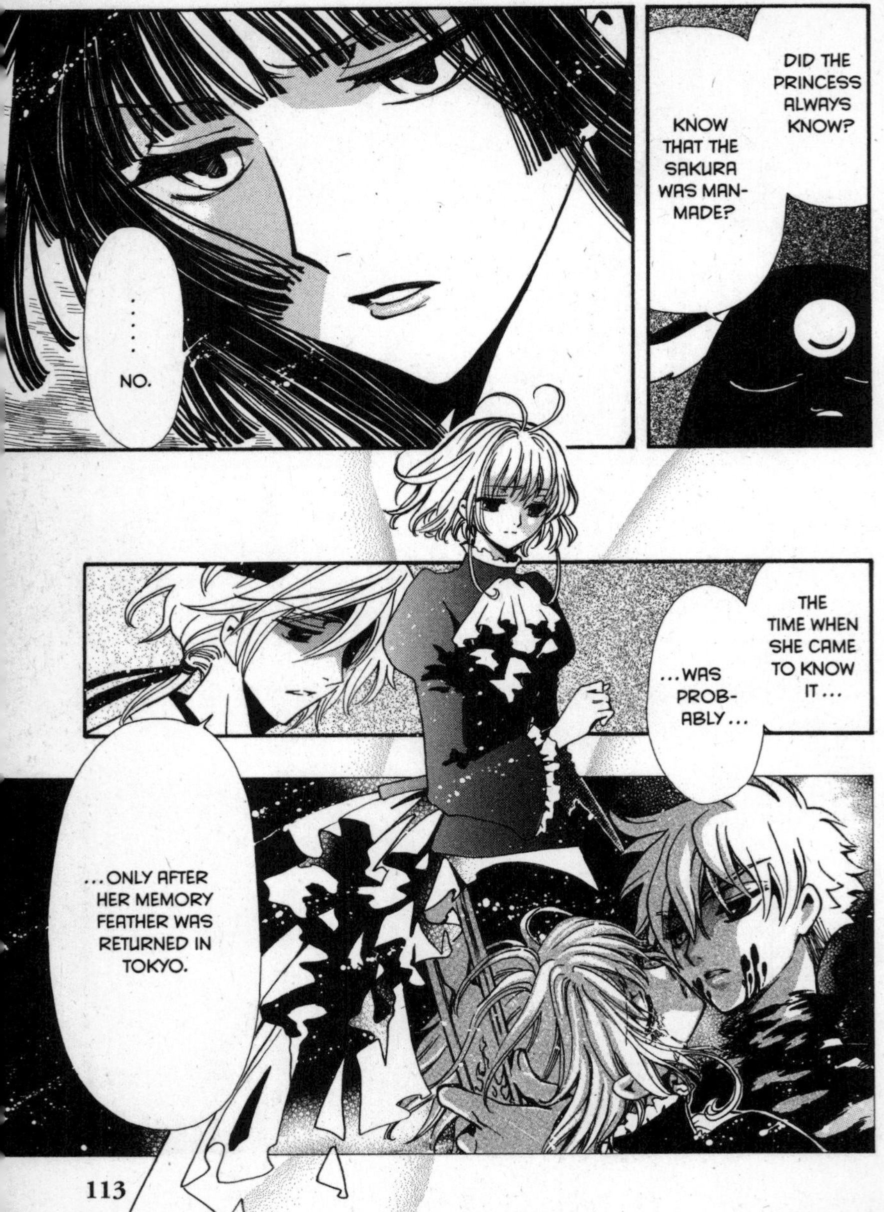
DID THE PRINCESS ALWAYS KNOW?
KNOW THAT THE SAKURA WAS MAN-MADE?
..... NO.
THE TIME WHEN SHE CAME TO KNOW IT...
...WAS PROBABLY...
...ONLY AFTER HER MEMORY FEATHER WAS RETURNED IN TOKYO.

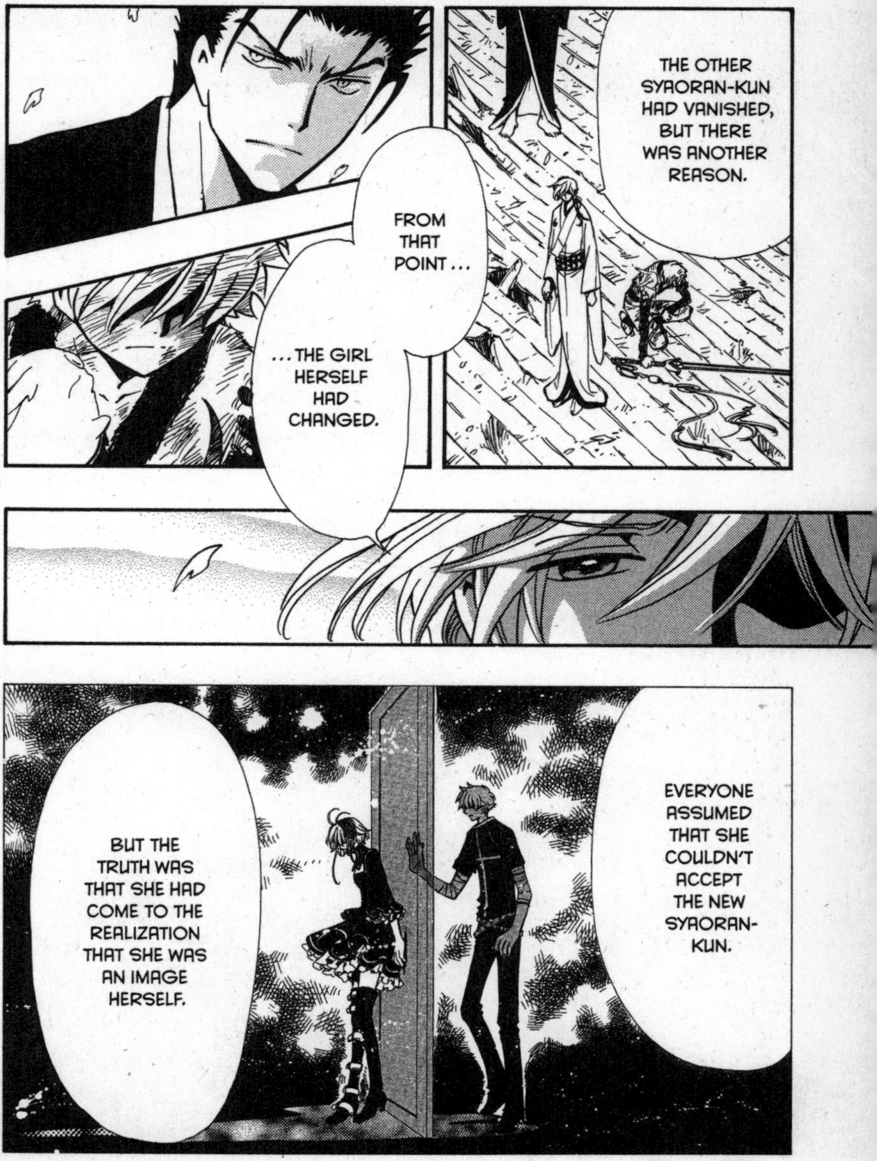
THE OTHER SYAORAN-KUN HAD VANISHED, BUT THERE WAS ANOTHER REASON.
FROM THAT POINT...
...THE GIRL HERSELF HAD CHANGED.
EVERYONE ASSUMED THAT SHE COULDN'T ACCEPT THE NEW SYAORAN-KUN.
BUT THE TRUTH WAS THAT SHE HAD COME TO THE REALIZATION THAT SHE WAS AN IMAGE HERSELF.

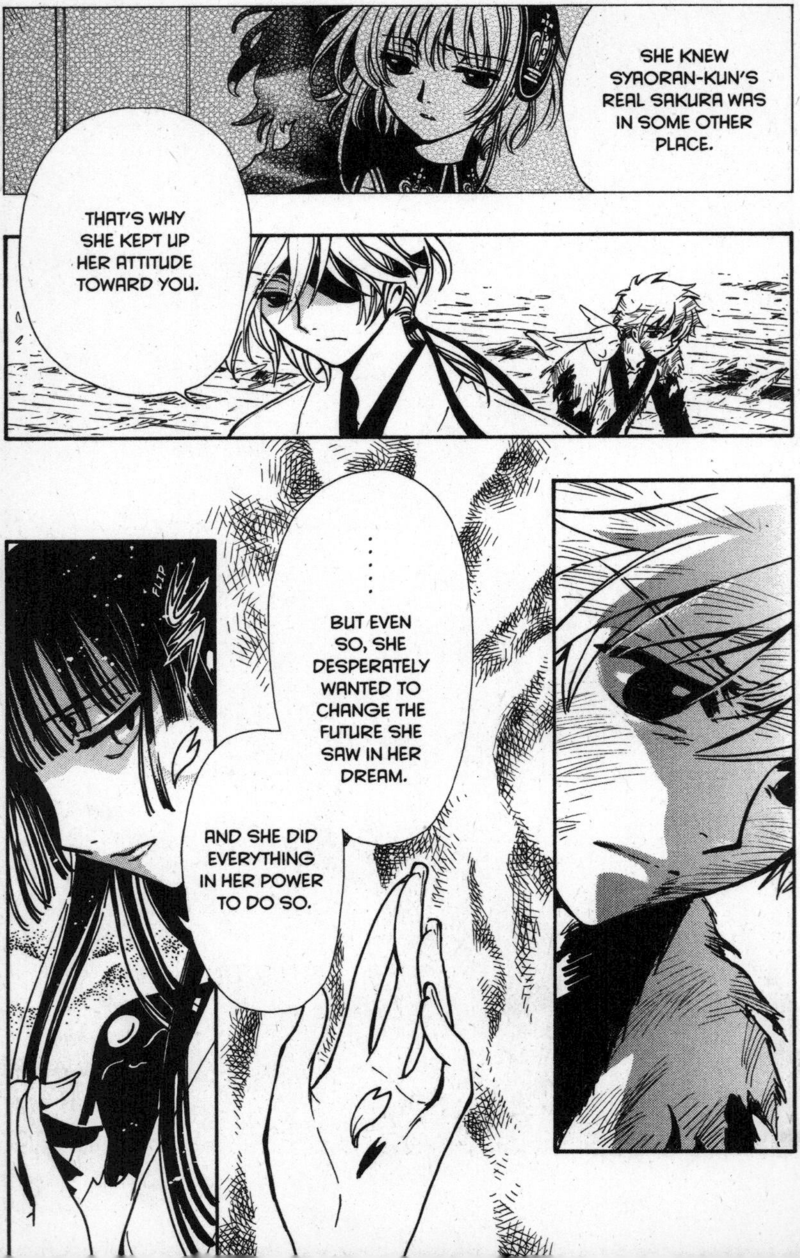
SHE KNEW SYAORAN-KUN'S REAL SAKURA WAS IN SOME OTHER PLACE.
THAT'S WHY SHE KEPT UP HER ATTITUDE TOWARD YOU.
.....
BUT EVEN SO, SHE DESPERATELY WANTED TO CHANGE THE FUTURE SHE SAW IN HER DREAM.
AND SHE DID EVERYTHING IN HER POWER TO DO SO.
FLIP

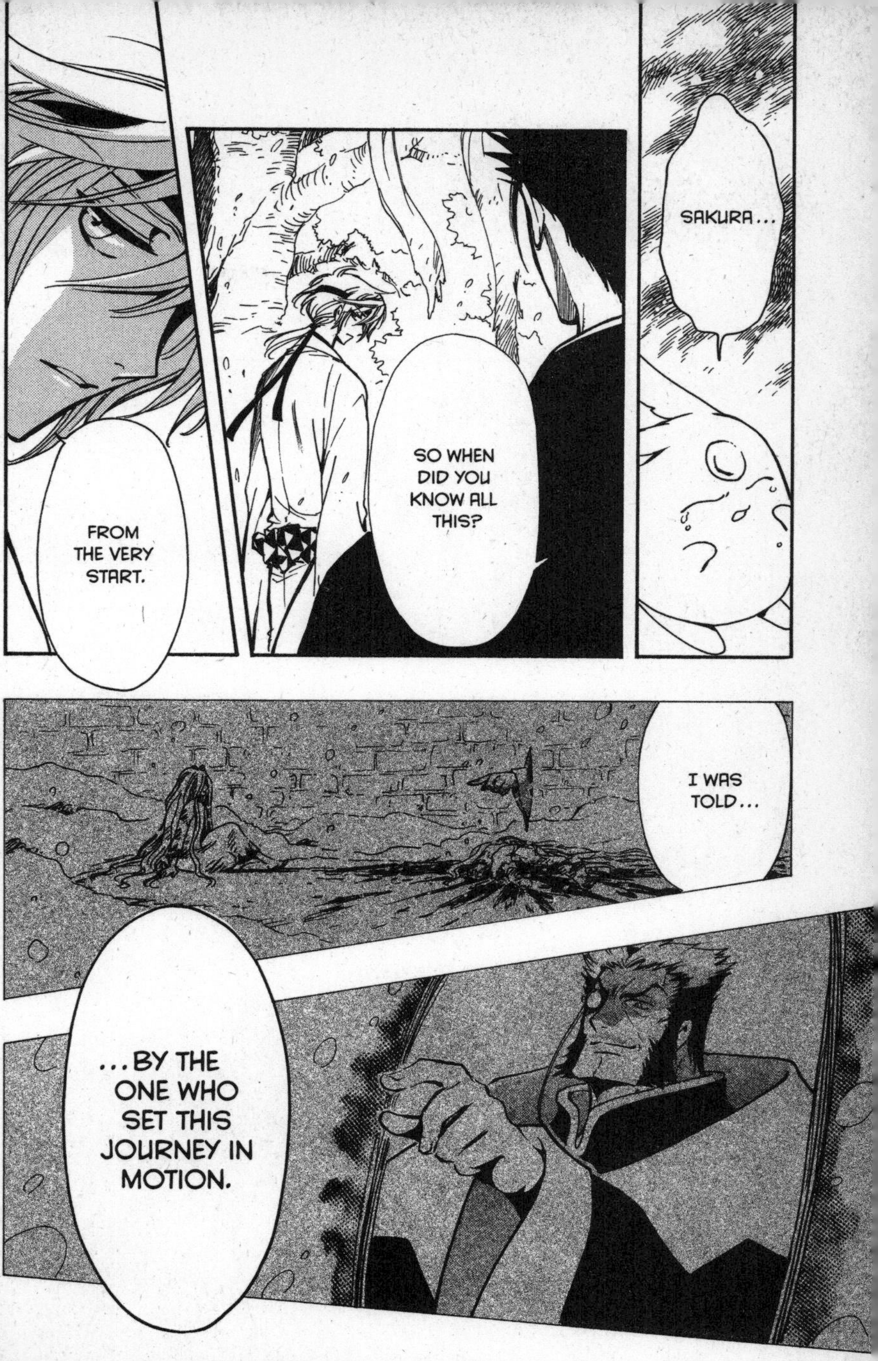
SAKURA...
SO WHEN DID YOU KNOW ALL THIS?
FROM THE VERY START.
I WAS TOLD...
...BY THE ONE WHO SET THIS JOURNEY IN MOTION.

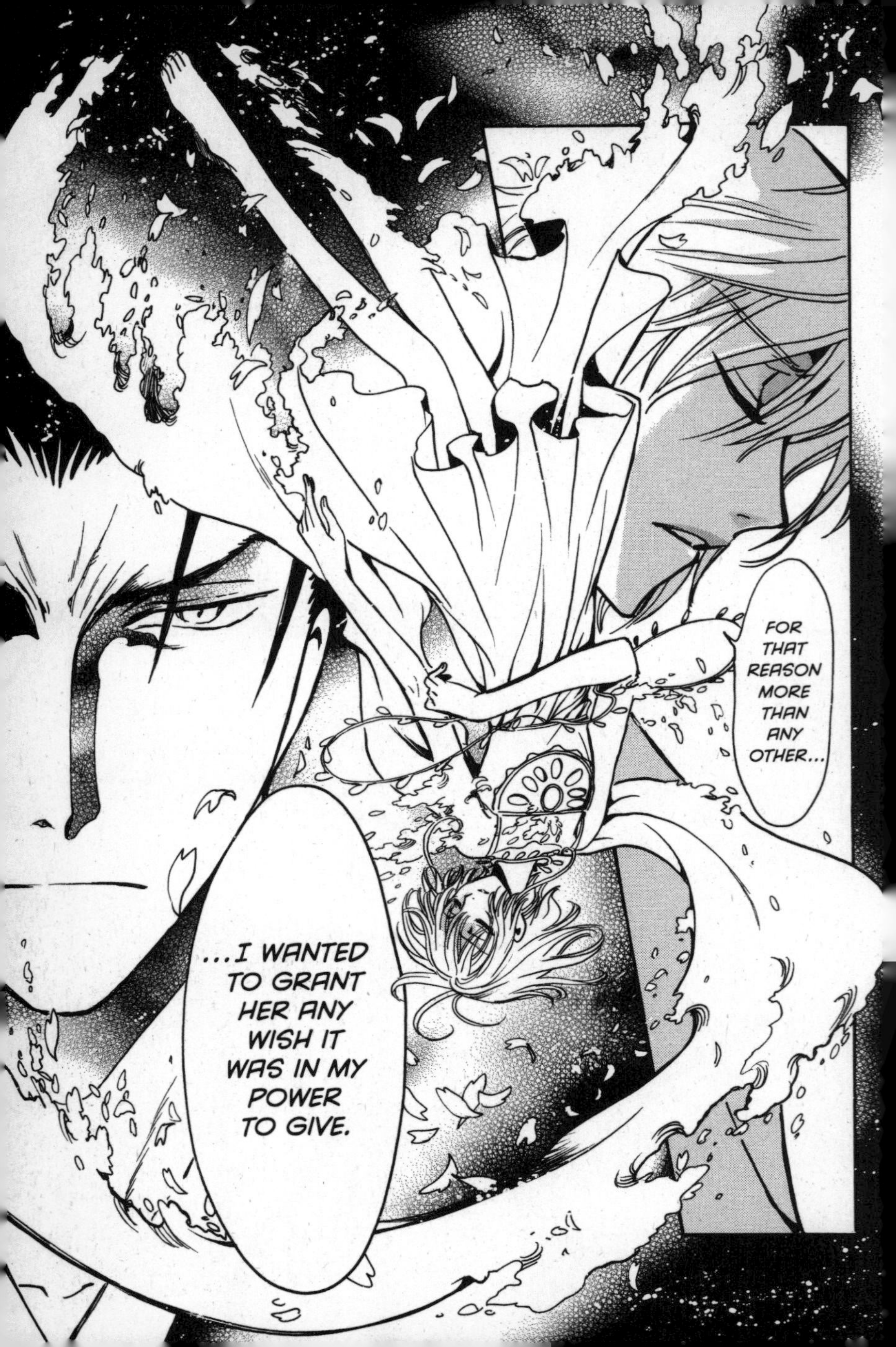
FOR THAT REASON MORE THAN ANY OTHER...
...I WANTED TO GRANT HER ANY WISH IT WAS IN MY POWER TO GIVE.

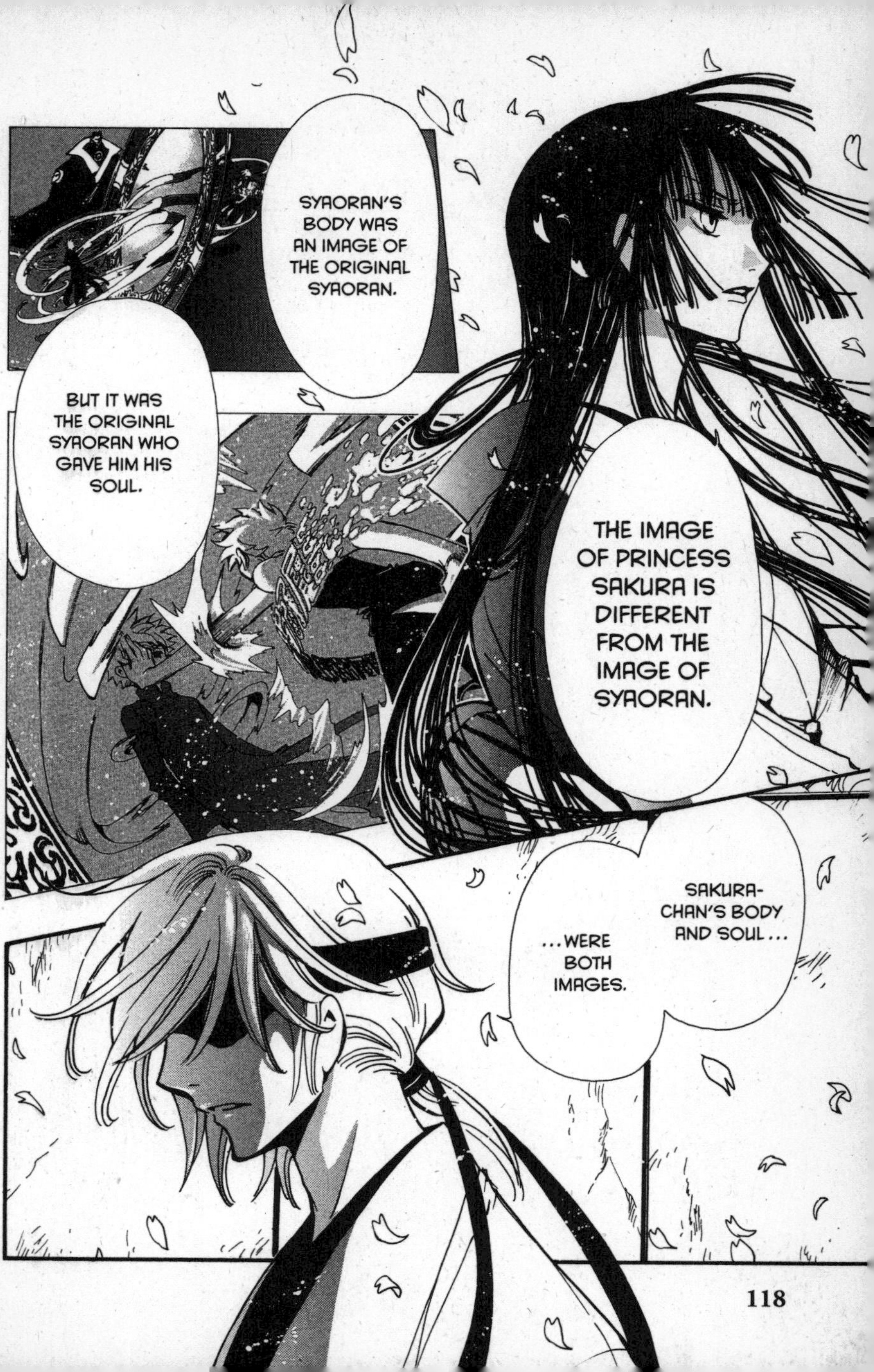
SYAORAN'S BODY WAS AN IMAGE OF THE ORIGINAL SYAORAN.
BUT IT WAS THE ORIGINAL SYAORAN WHO GAVE HIM HIS SOUL.
THE IMAGE OF PRINCESS SAKURA IS DIFFERENT FROM THE IMAGE OF SYAORAN.
SAKURA-CHAN'S BODY AND SOUL...
...WERE BOTH IMAGES.

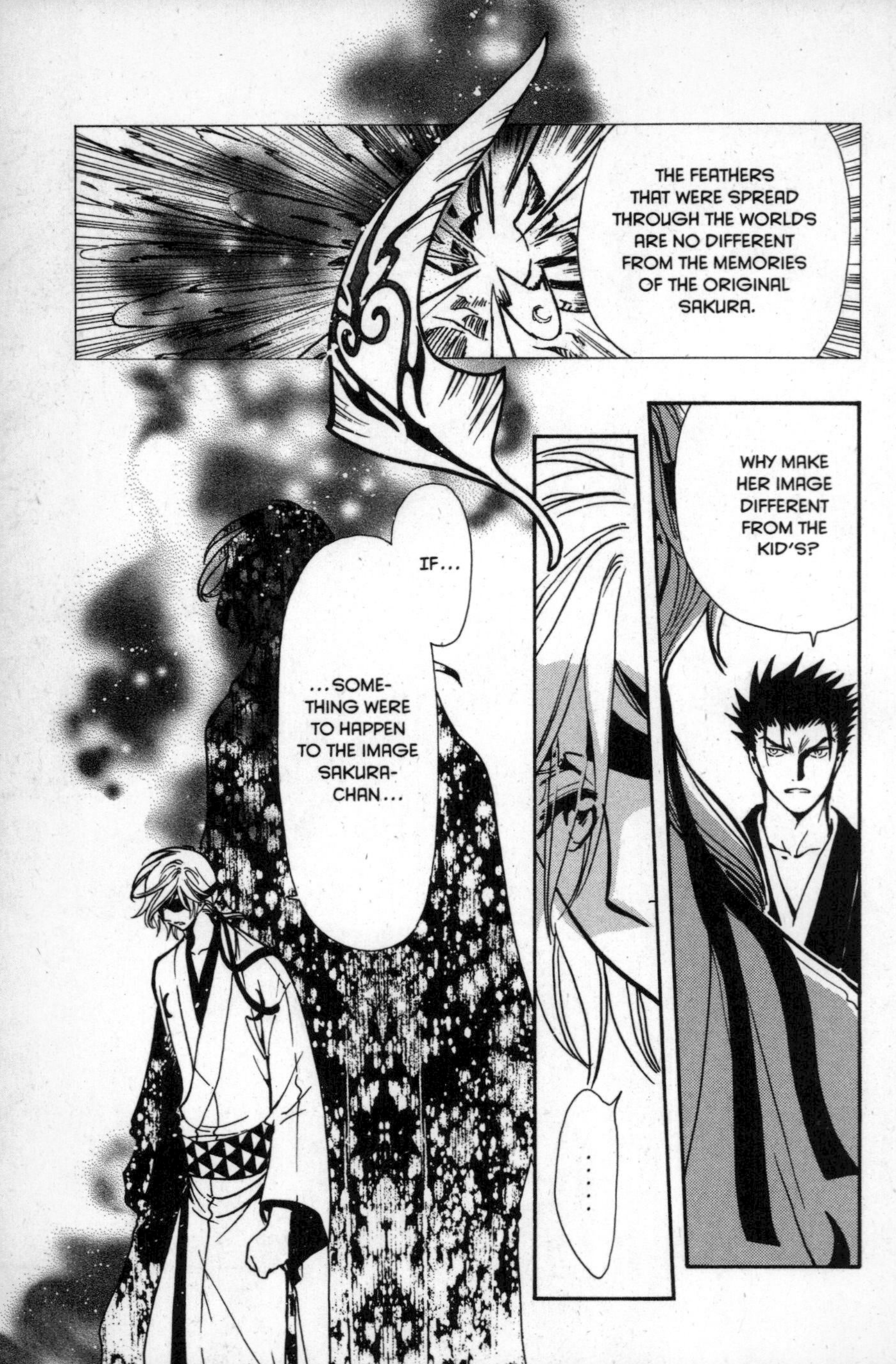
THE FEATHERS THAT WERE SPREAD THROUGH THE WORLDS ARE NO DIFFERENT FROM THE MEMORIES OF THE ORIGINAL SAKURA.
WHY MAKE HER IMAGE DIFFERENT FROM THE KID'S?
.....
IF...
...SOME-THING WERE TO HAPPEN TO THE IMAGE SAKURA-CHAN...

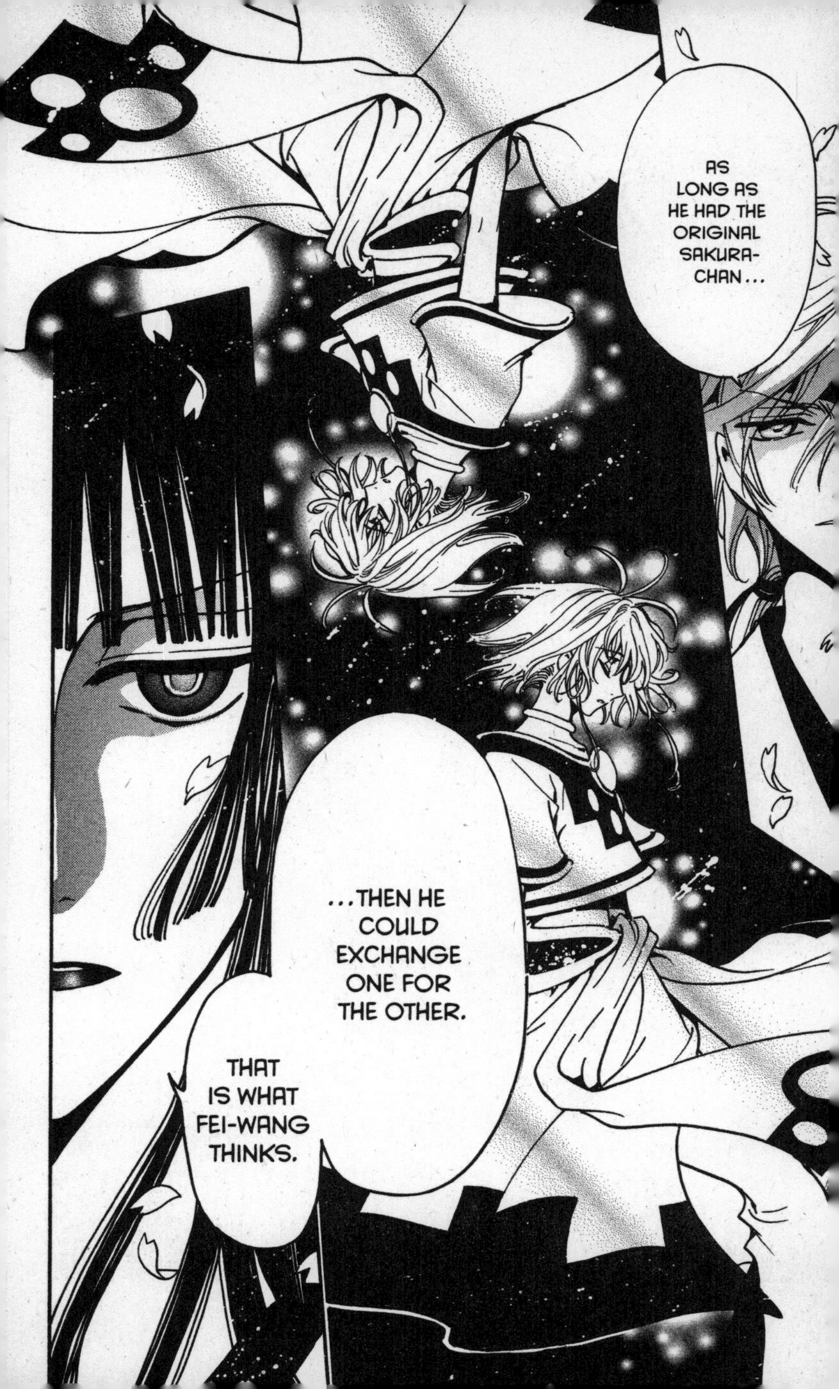
AS LONG AS HE HAD THE ORIGINAL SAKURA-CHAN...
...THEN HE COULD EXCHANGE ONE FOR THE OTHER.
THAT IS WHAT FEI-WANG THINKS.

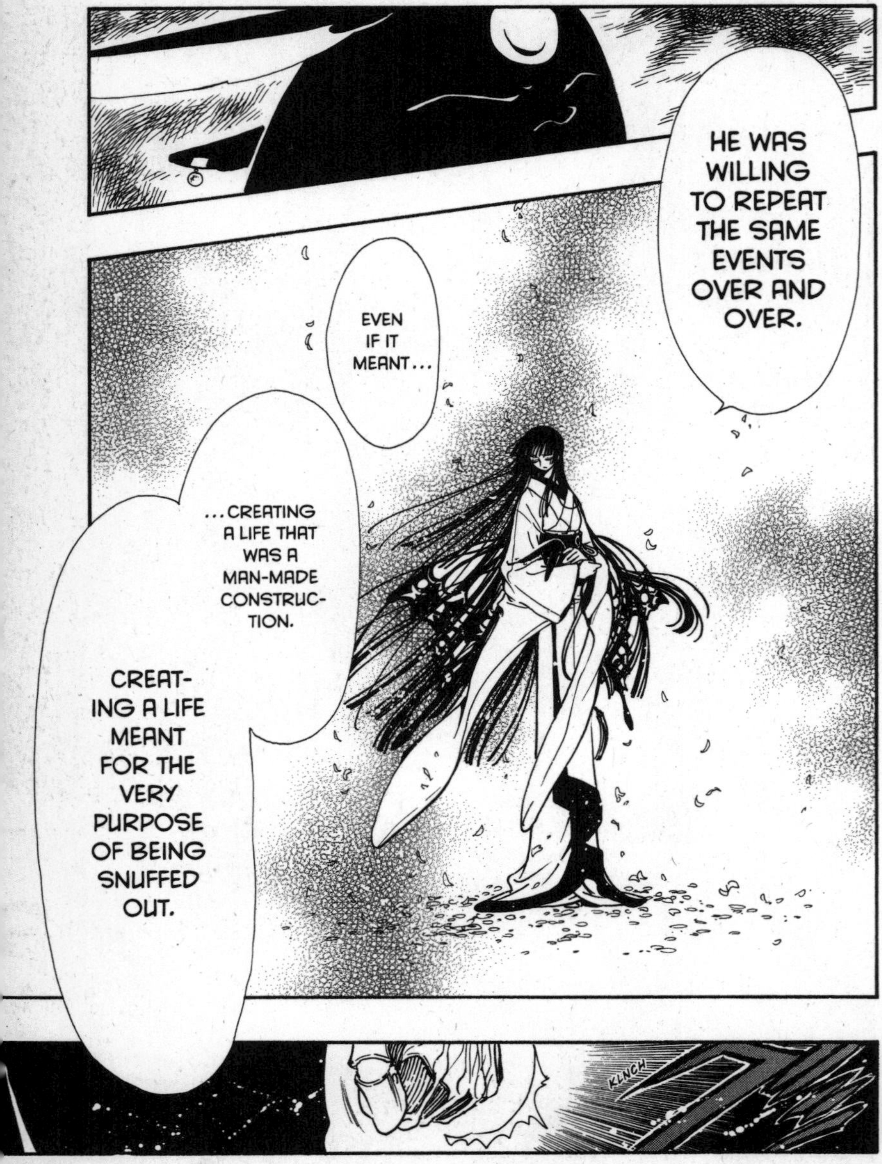
HE WAS WILLING TO REPEAT THE SAME EVENTS OVER AND OVER.
EVEN IF IT MEANT...
...CREATING A LIFE THAT WAS A MAN-MADE CONSTRUCTION.
CREATING A LIFE MEANT FOR THE VERY PURPOSE OF BEING SNUFFED OUT.
KLNCH

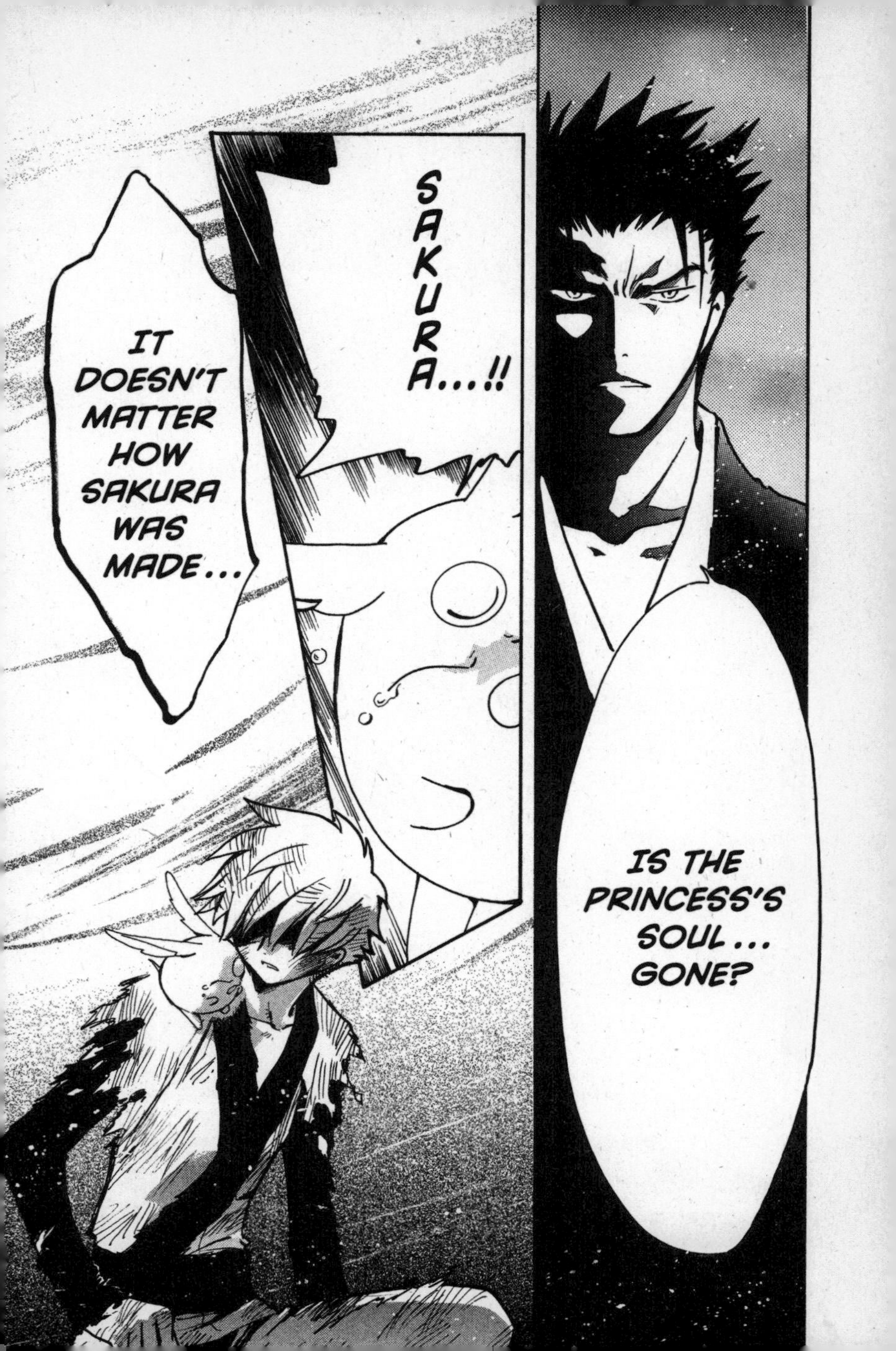
IS THE PRINCESS'S SOUL... GONE?
SAKURA...!!
IT DOESN'T MATTER HOW SAKURA WAS MADE...

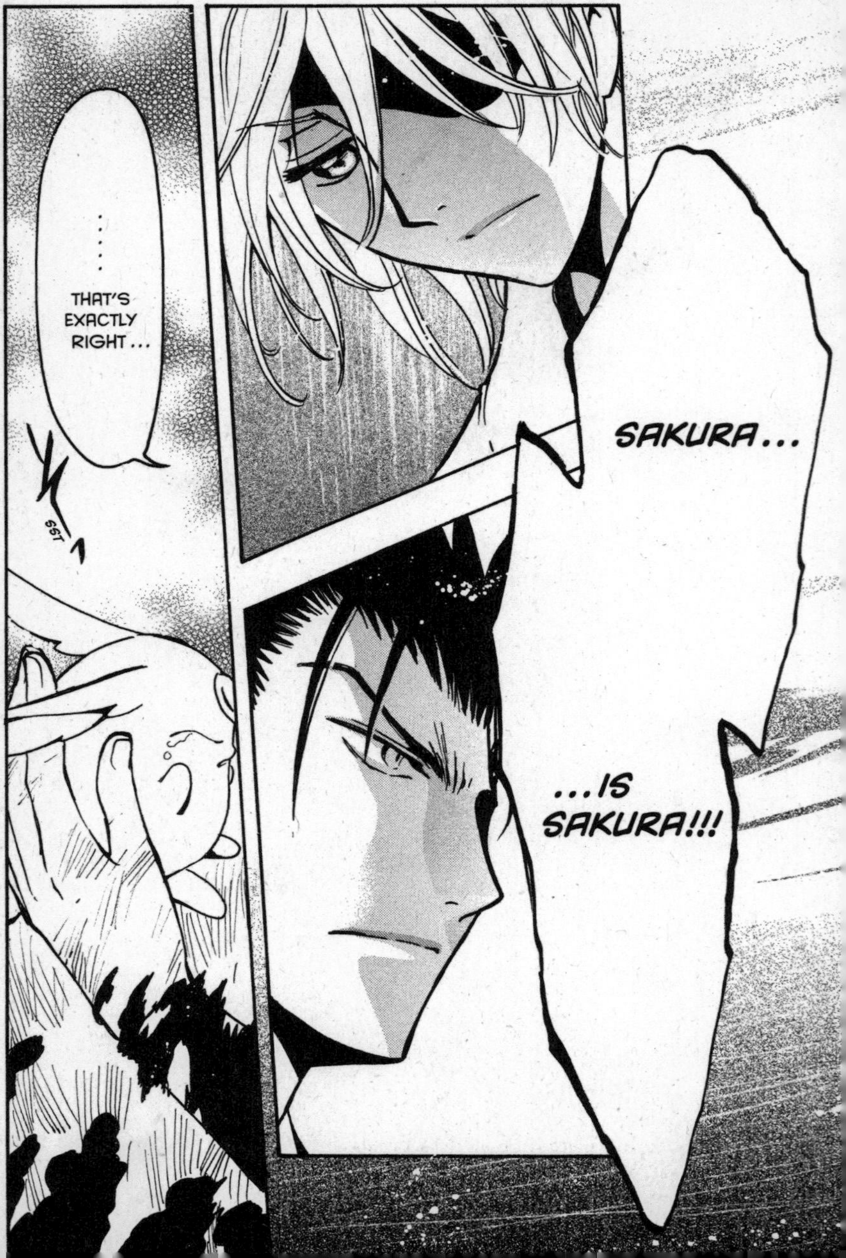
SAKURA...
...IS SAKURA!!!
......
THAT'S EXACTLY RIGHT...
SST

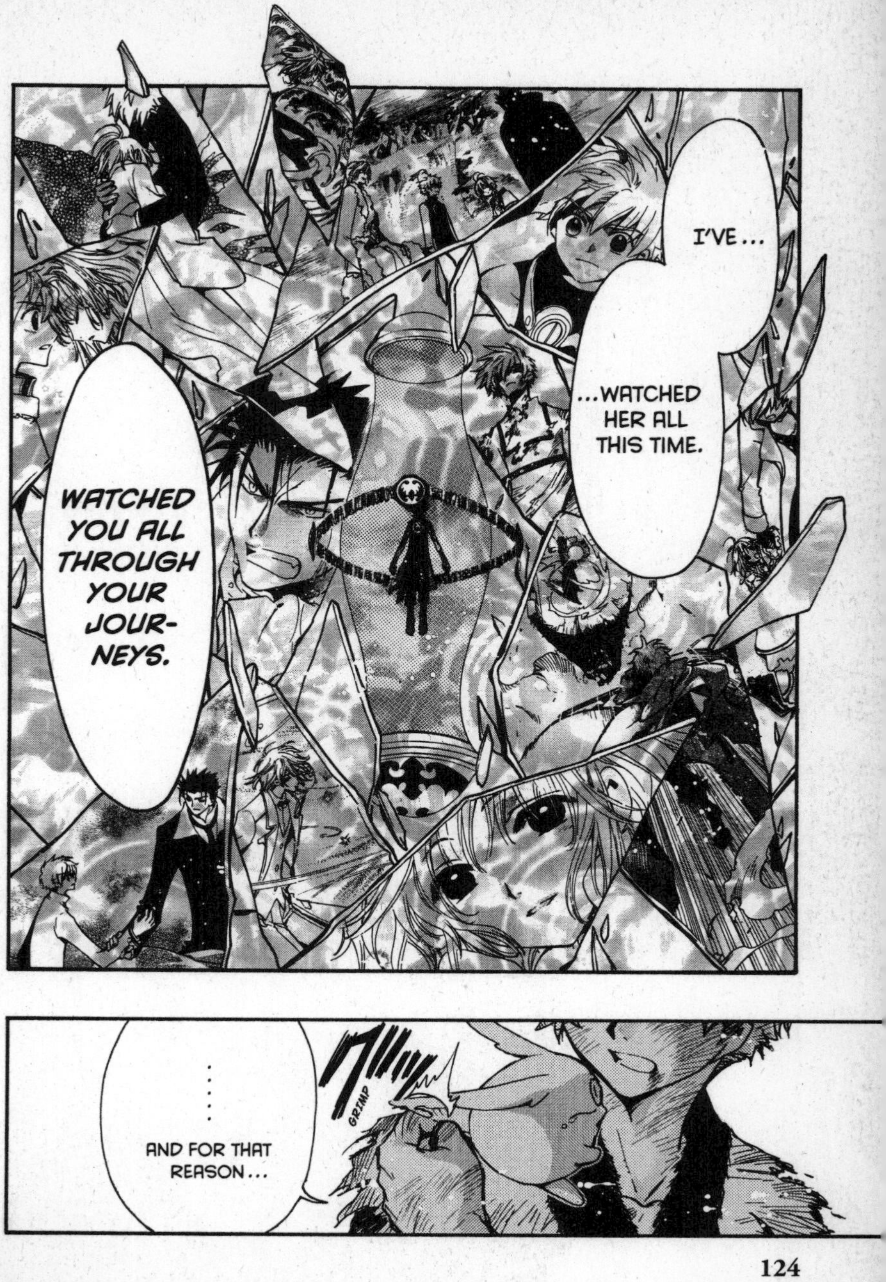
I'VE...
...WATCHED HER ALL THIS TIME.
WATCHED YOU ALL THROUGH YOUR JOUR-NEYS.
GRIMP
.....
AND FOR THAT REASON...

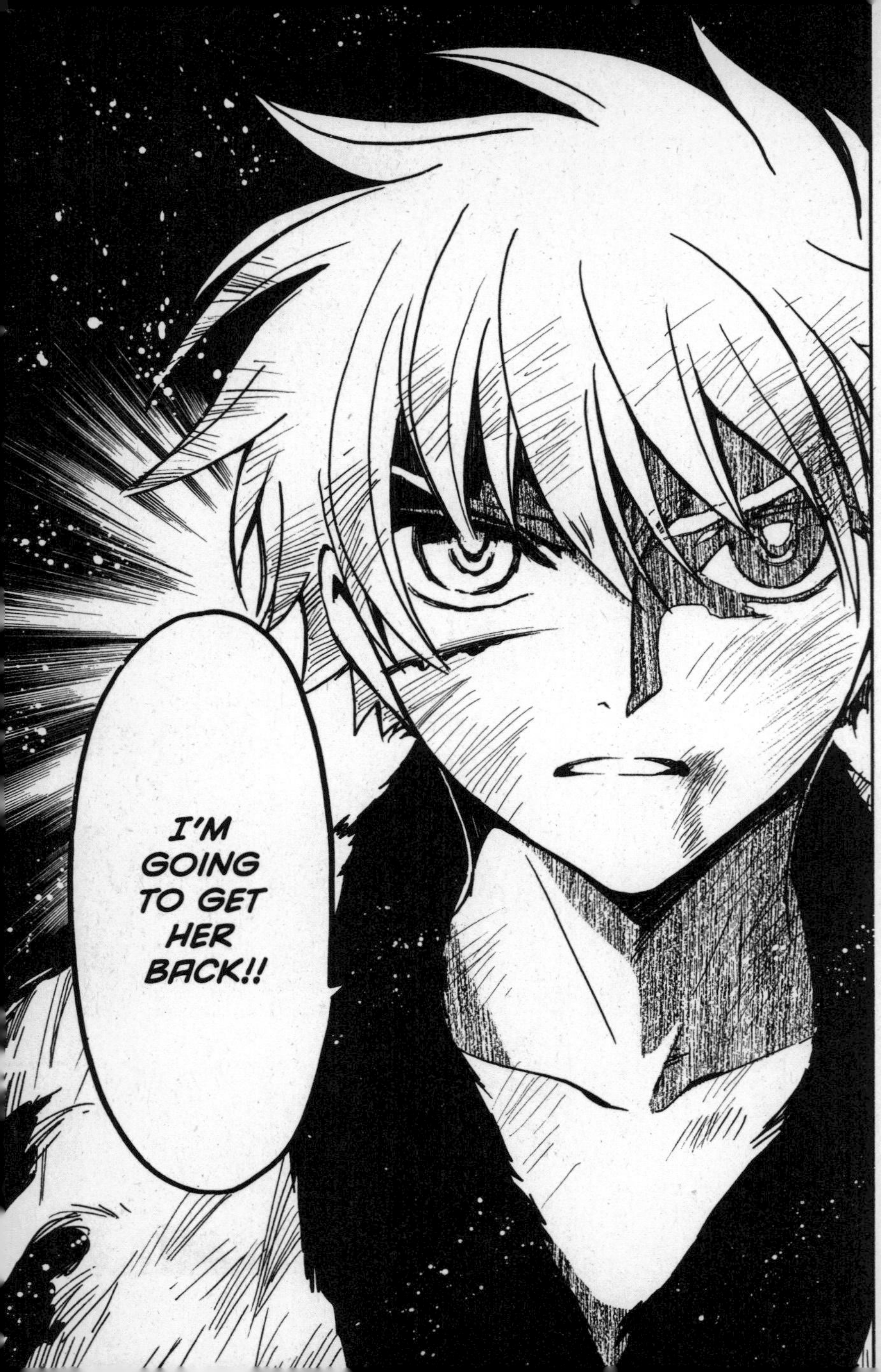
I'M GOING TO GET HER BACK!!

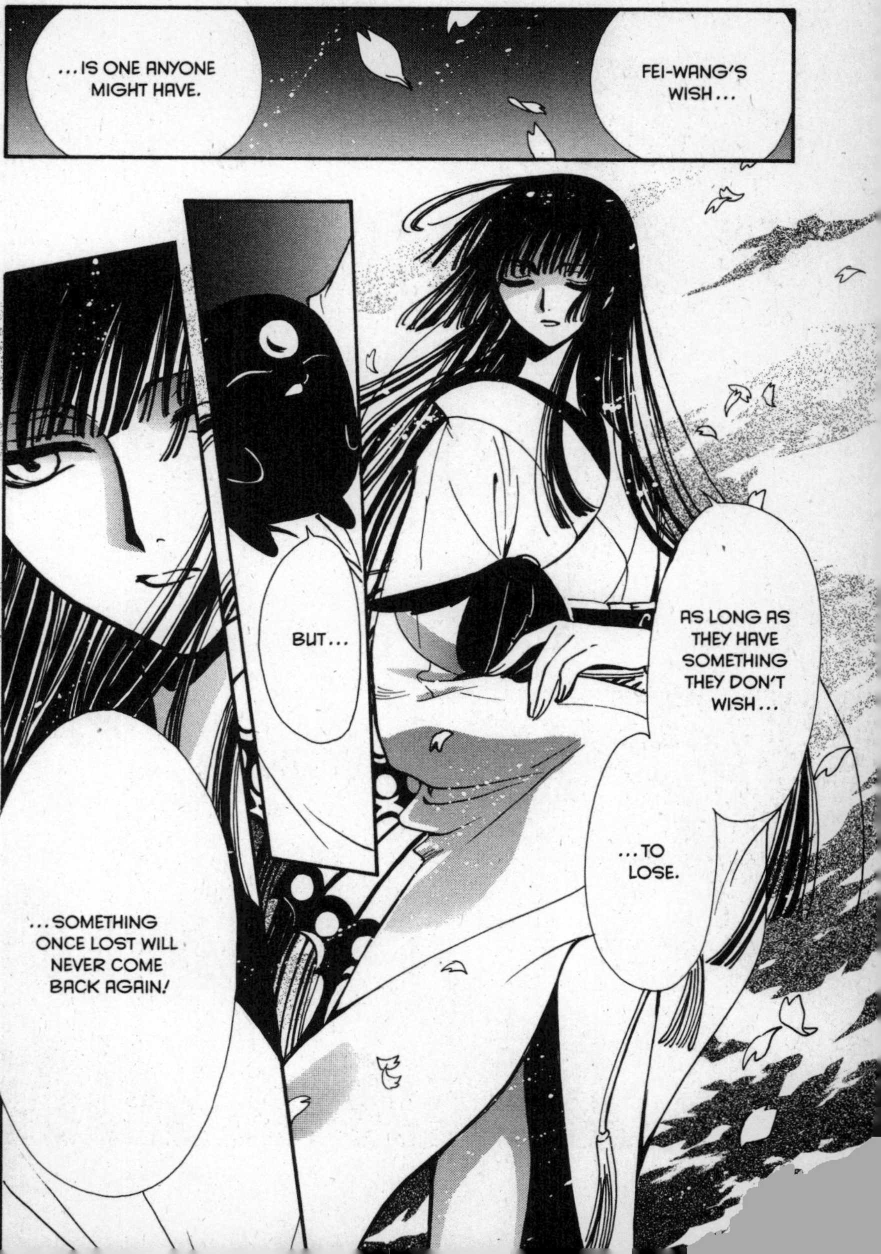
FEI-WANG'S WISH...
...IS ONE ANYONE MIGHT HAVE.
AS LONG AS THEY HAVE SOMETHING THEY DON'T WISH...
...TO LOSE.
BUT...
...SOMETHING ONCE LOST WILL NEVER COME BACK AGAIN!

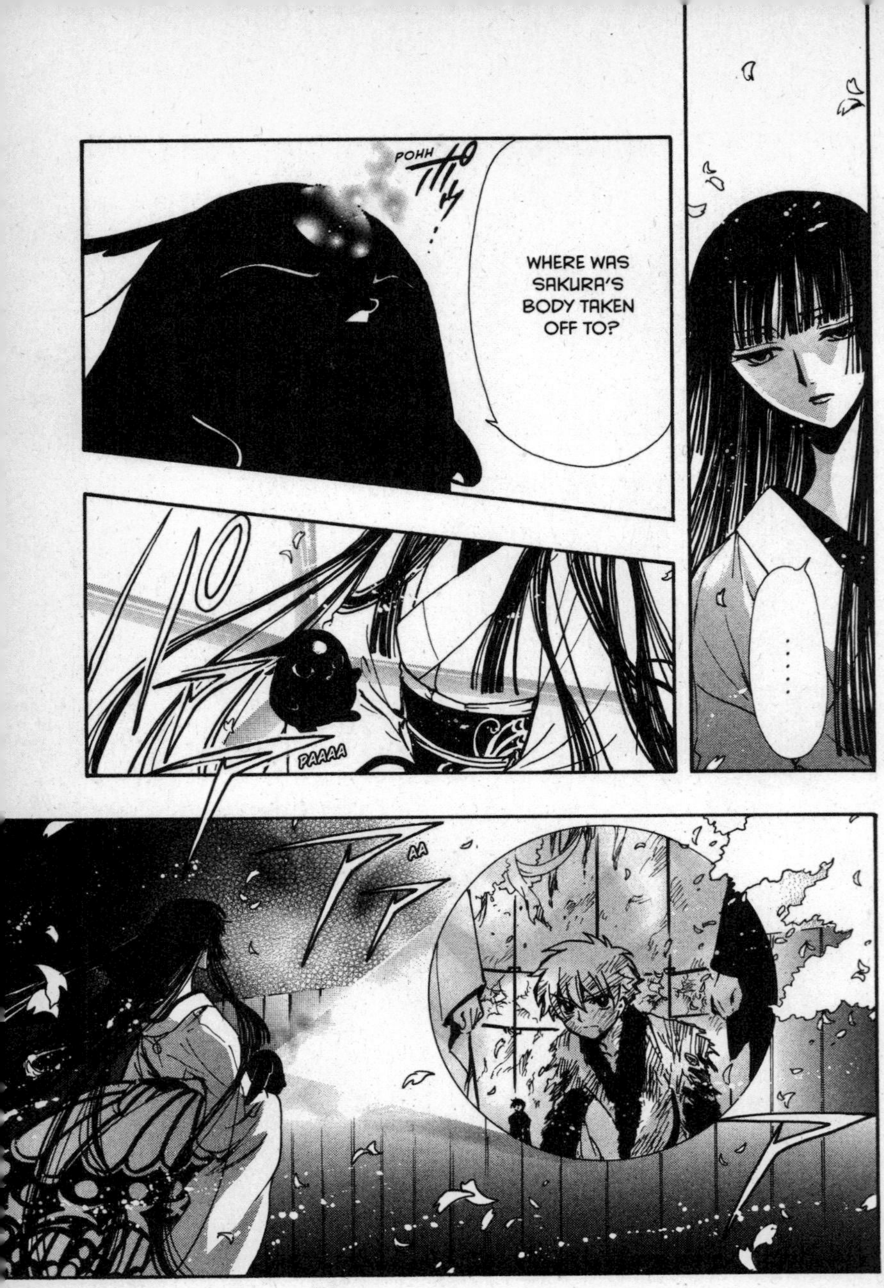
.....
POHH
WHERE WAS SAKURA'S BODY TAKEN OFF TO?
PAAAA
AA

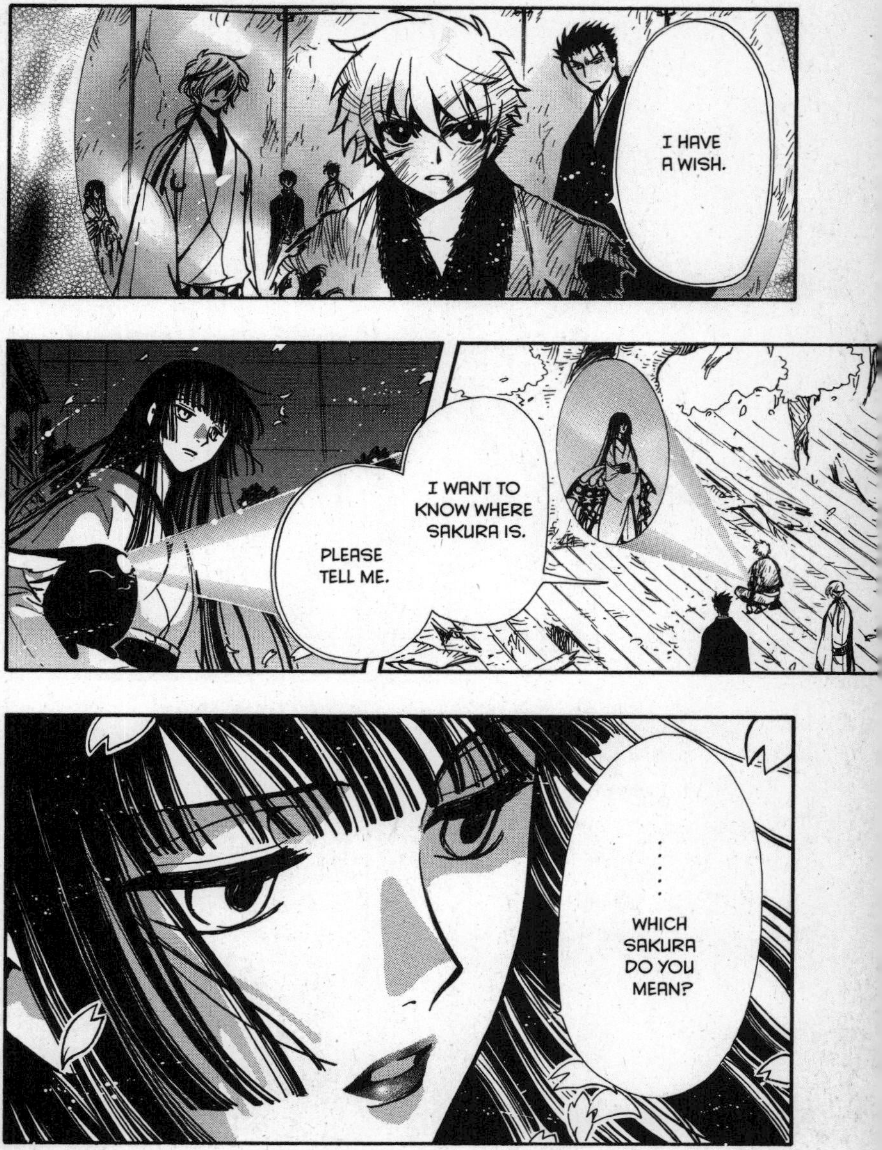
I HAVE A WISH.
I WANT TO KNOW WHERE SAKURA IS.
PLEASE TELL ME.
......
WHICH SAKURA DO YOU MEAN?

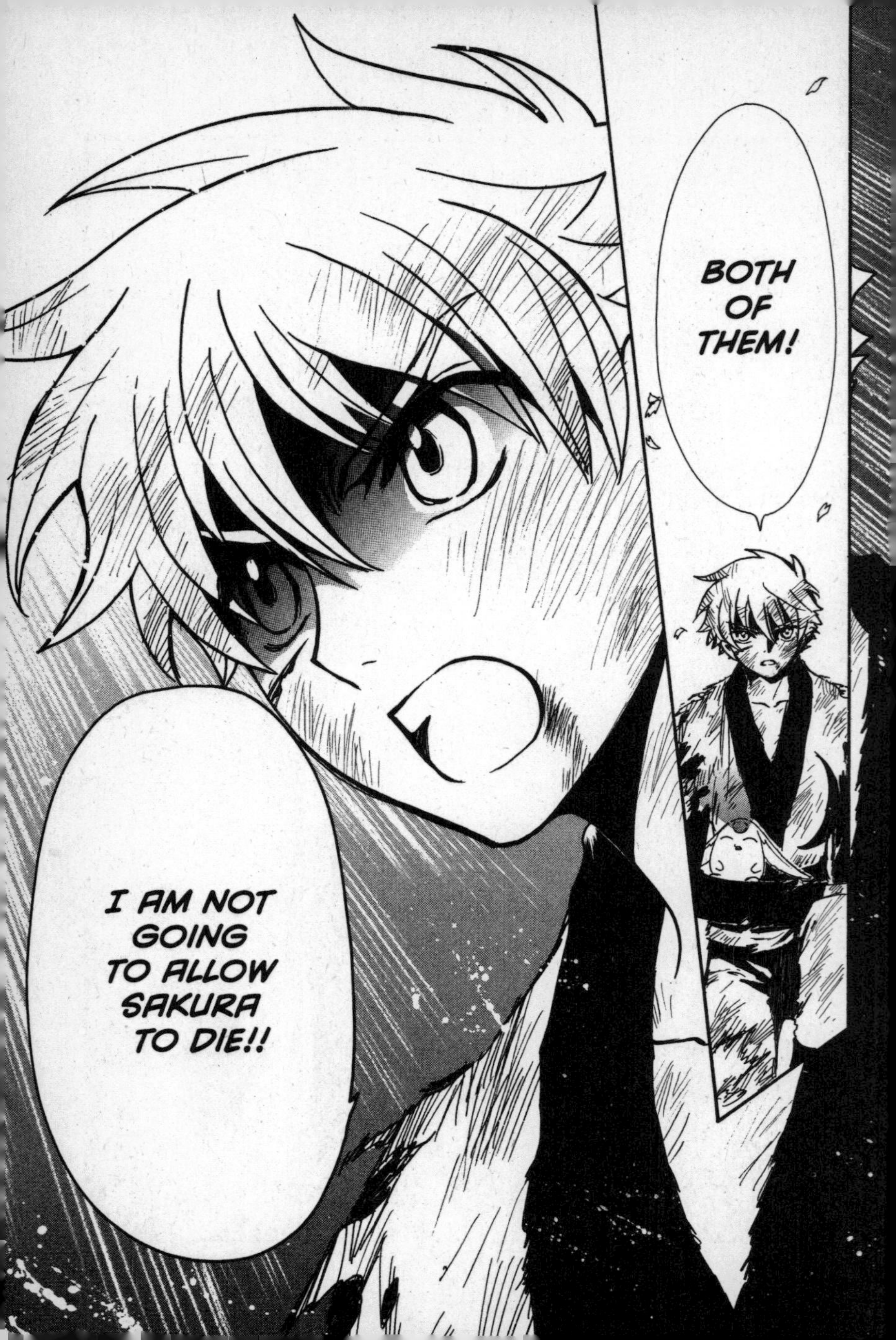
BOTH OF THEM!
I AM NOT GOING TO ALLOW SAKURA TO DIE!!

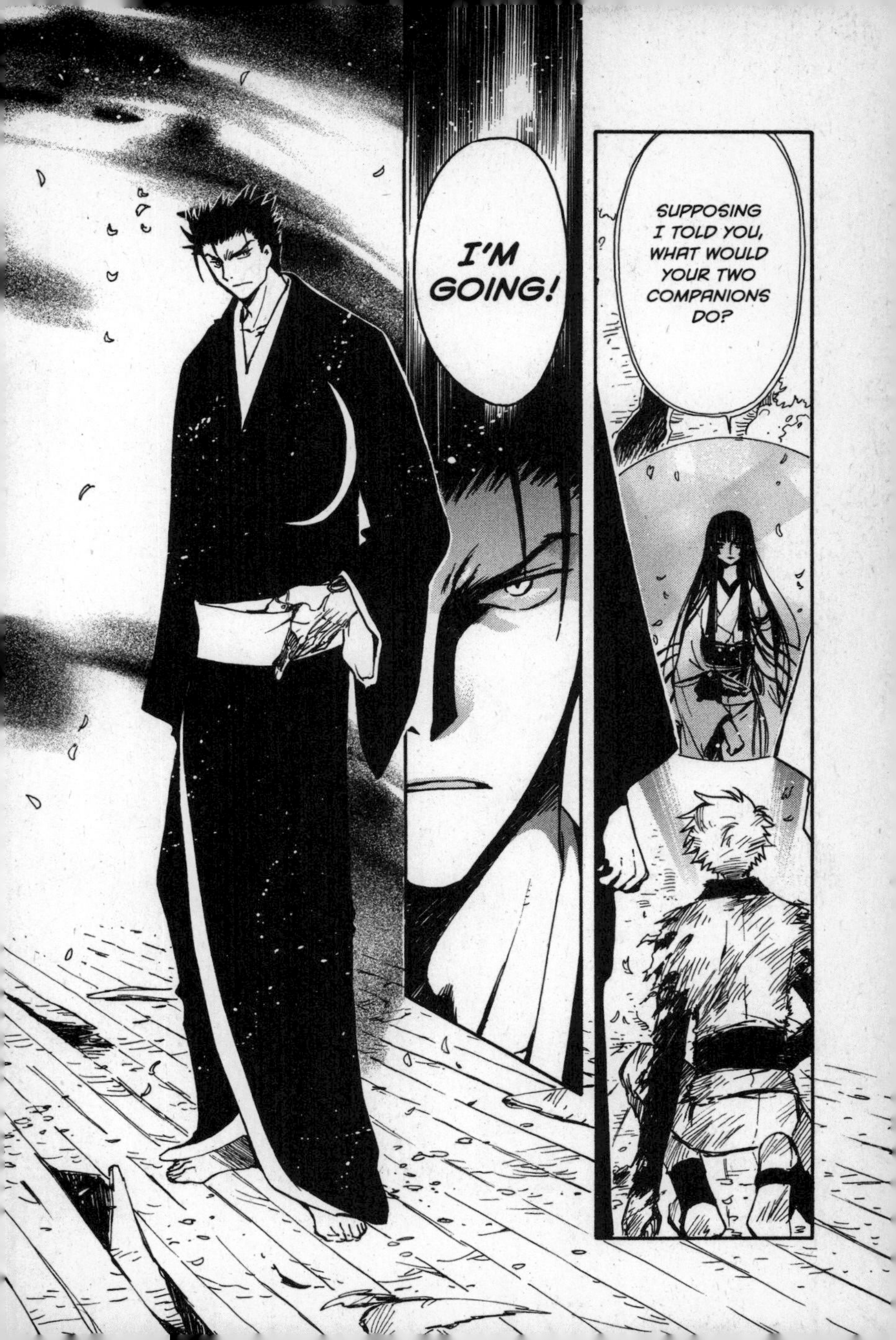
SUPPOSING I TOLD YOU, WHAT WOULD YOUR TWO COMPANIONS DO?
I'M GOING!

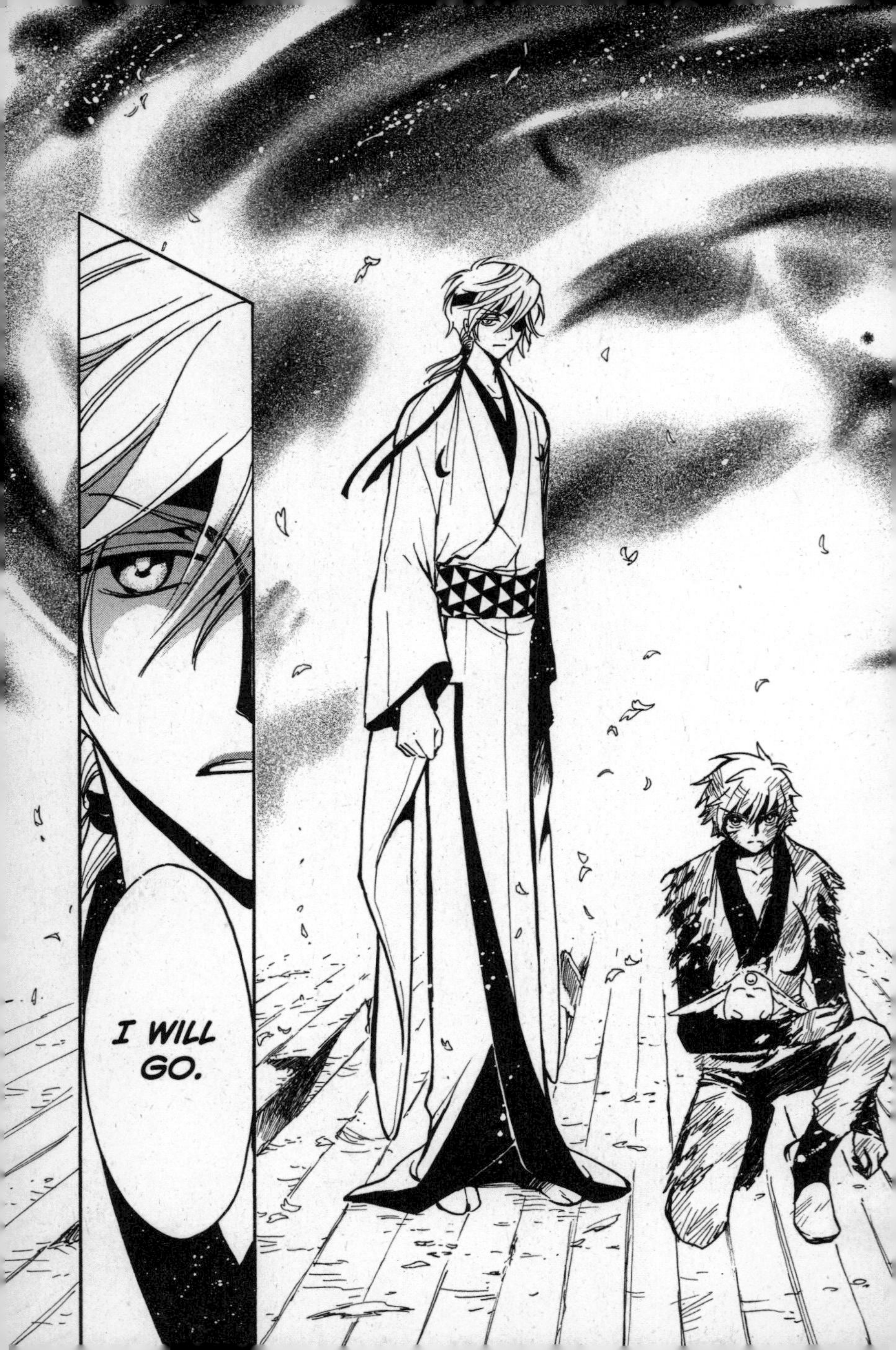
I WILL GO.

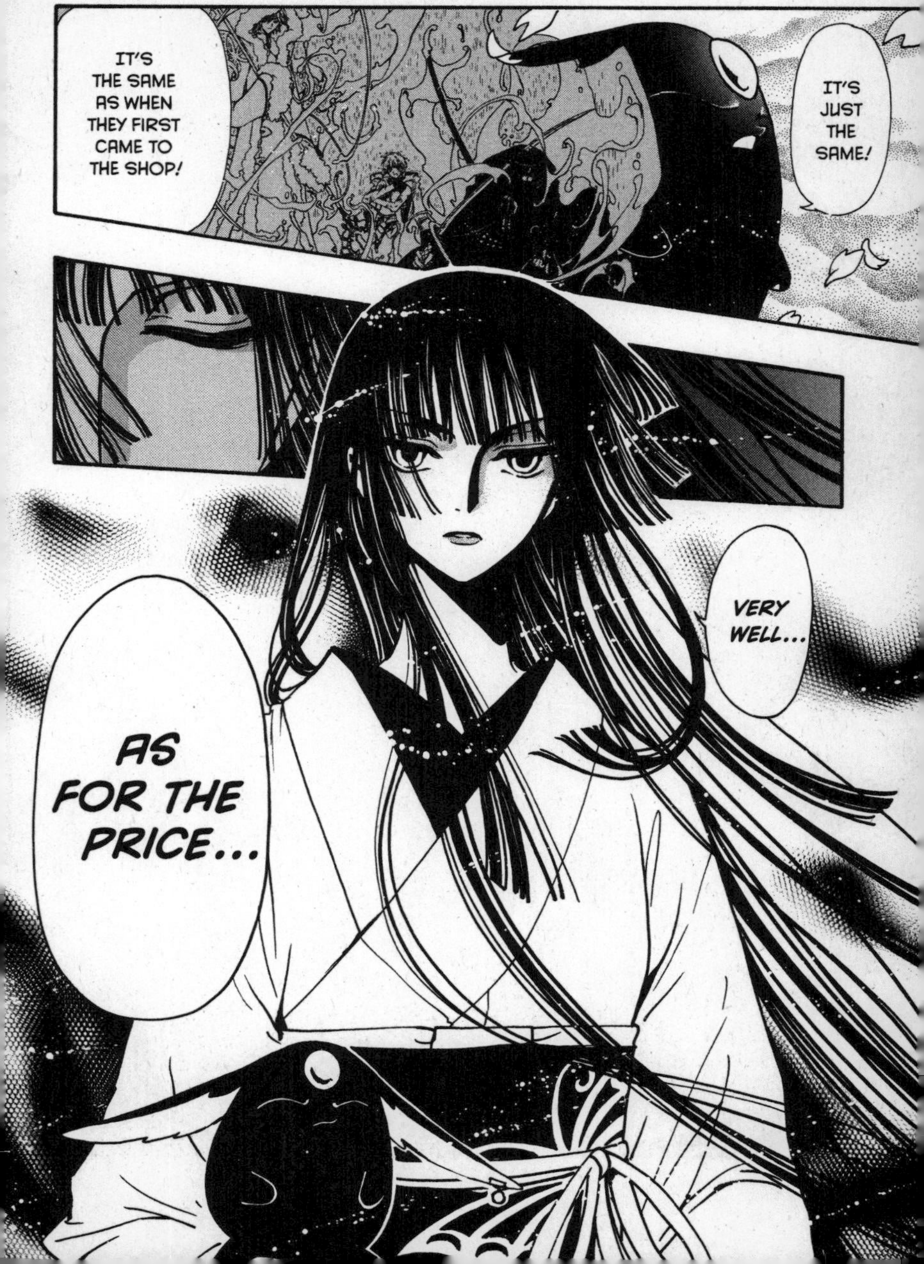
IT'S JUST THE SAME!
IT'S THE SAME AS WHEN THEY FIRST CAME TO THE SHOP!
VERY WELL...
AS FOR THE PRICE...

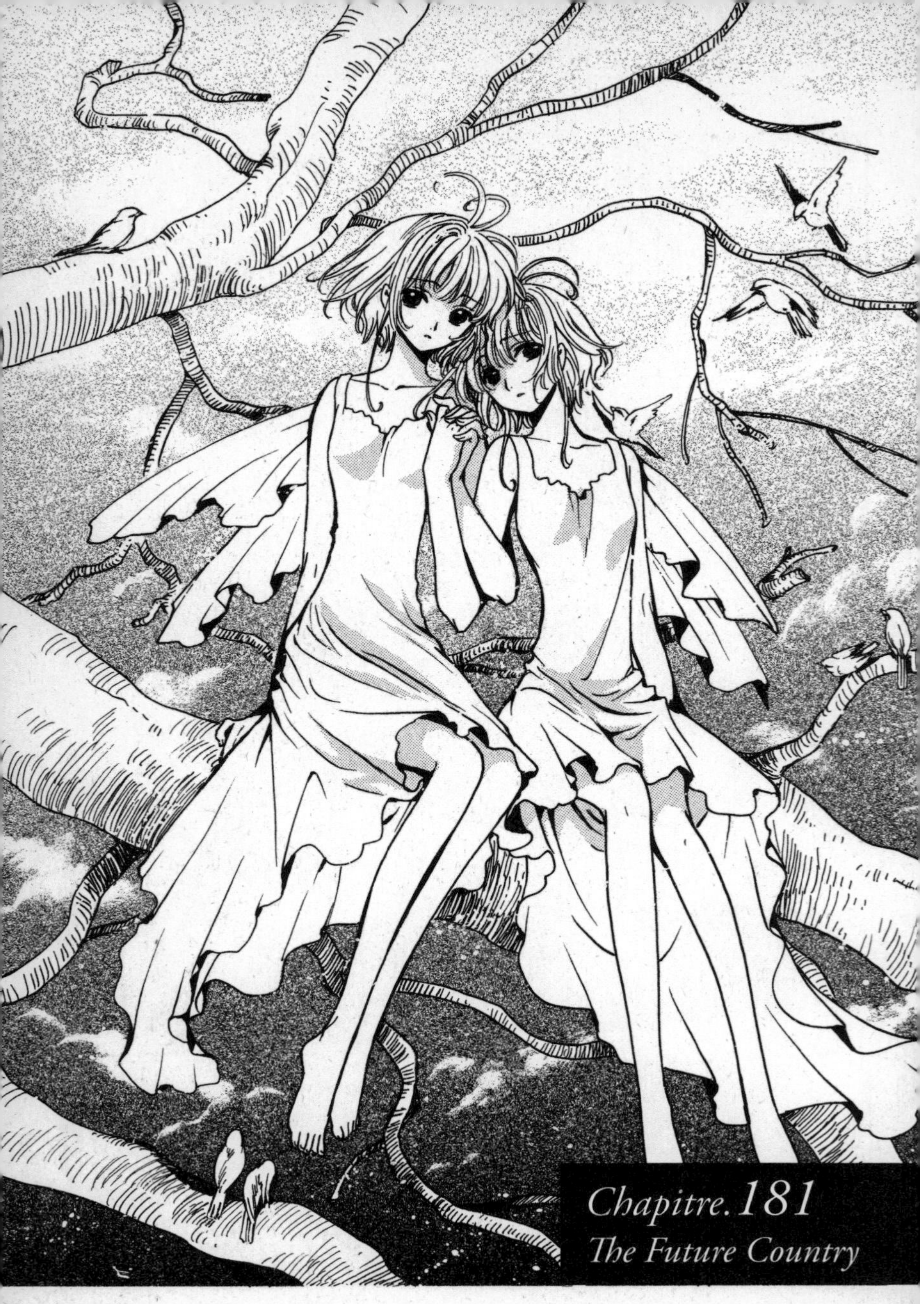
Chapitre.181
The Future Country

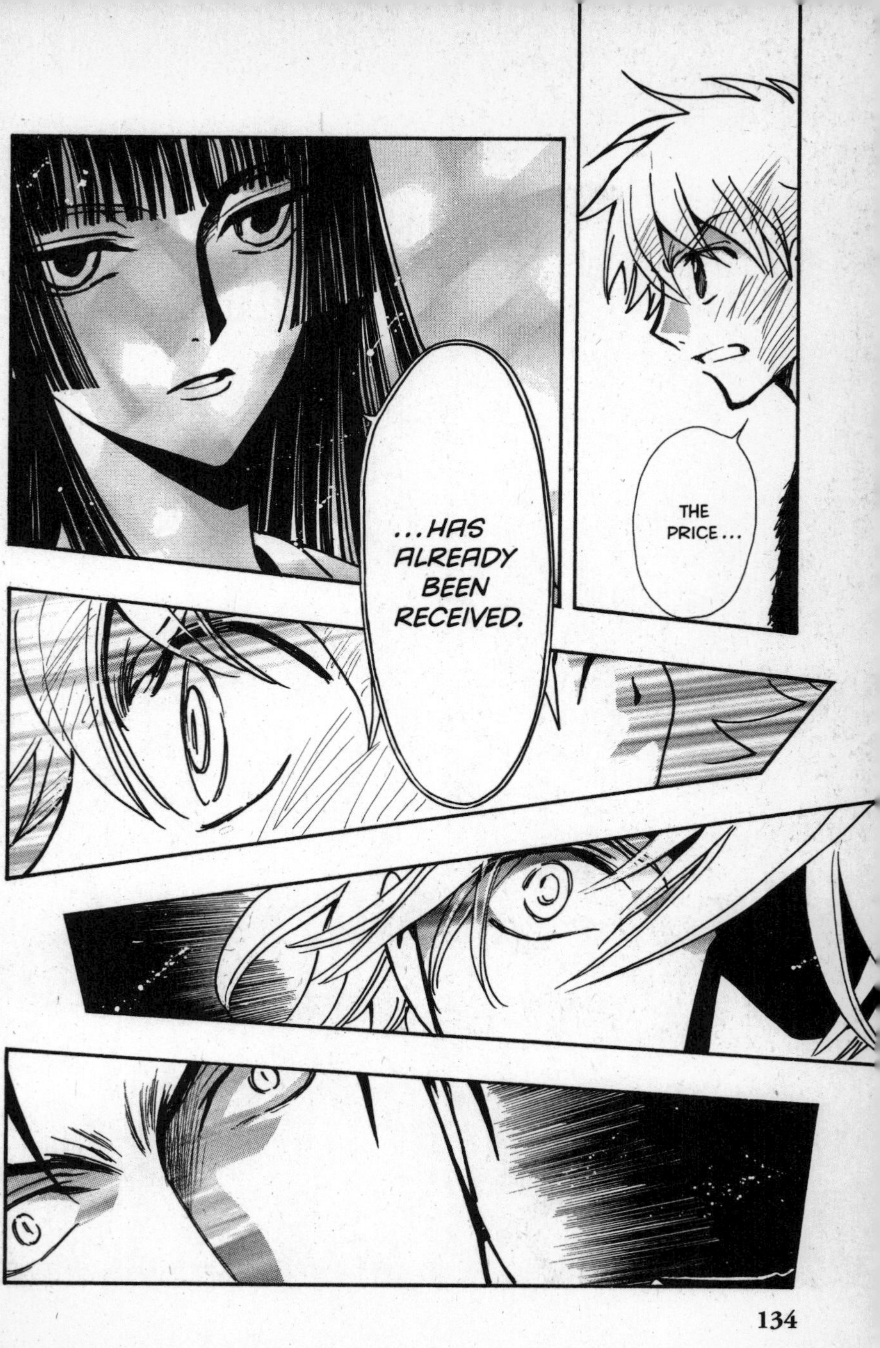
THE PRICE…
…HAS ALREADY BEEN RECEIVED.

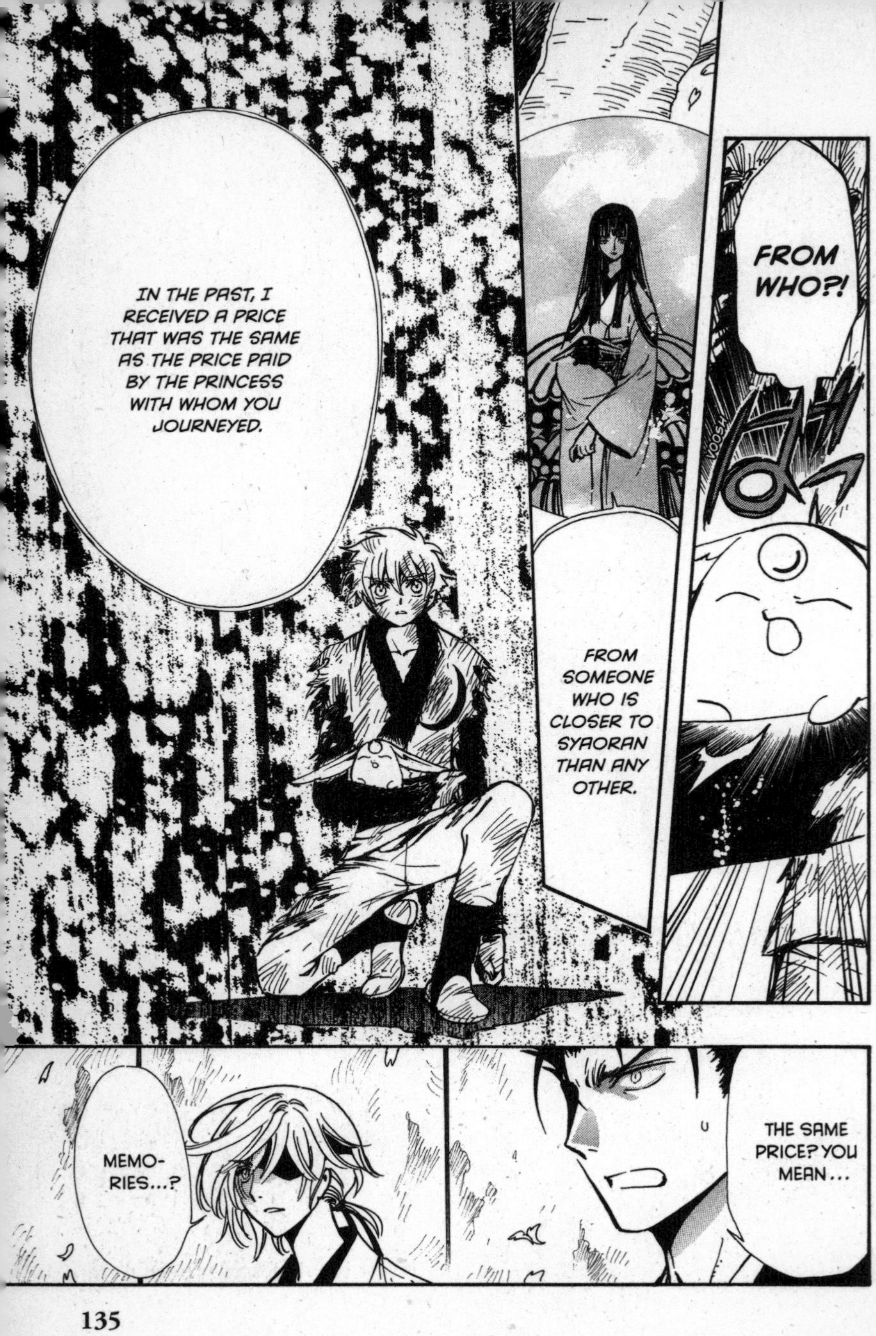
FROM WHO?!
VOOSH
FROM SOMEONE WHO IS CLOSER TO SYAORAN THAN ANY OTHER.
IN THE PAST, I RECEIVED A PRICE THAT WAS THE SAME AS THE PRICE PAID BY THE PRINCESS WITH WHOM YOU JOURNEYED.
THE SAME PRICE? YOU MEAN...
MEMO-RIES...?

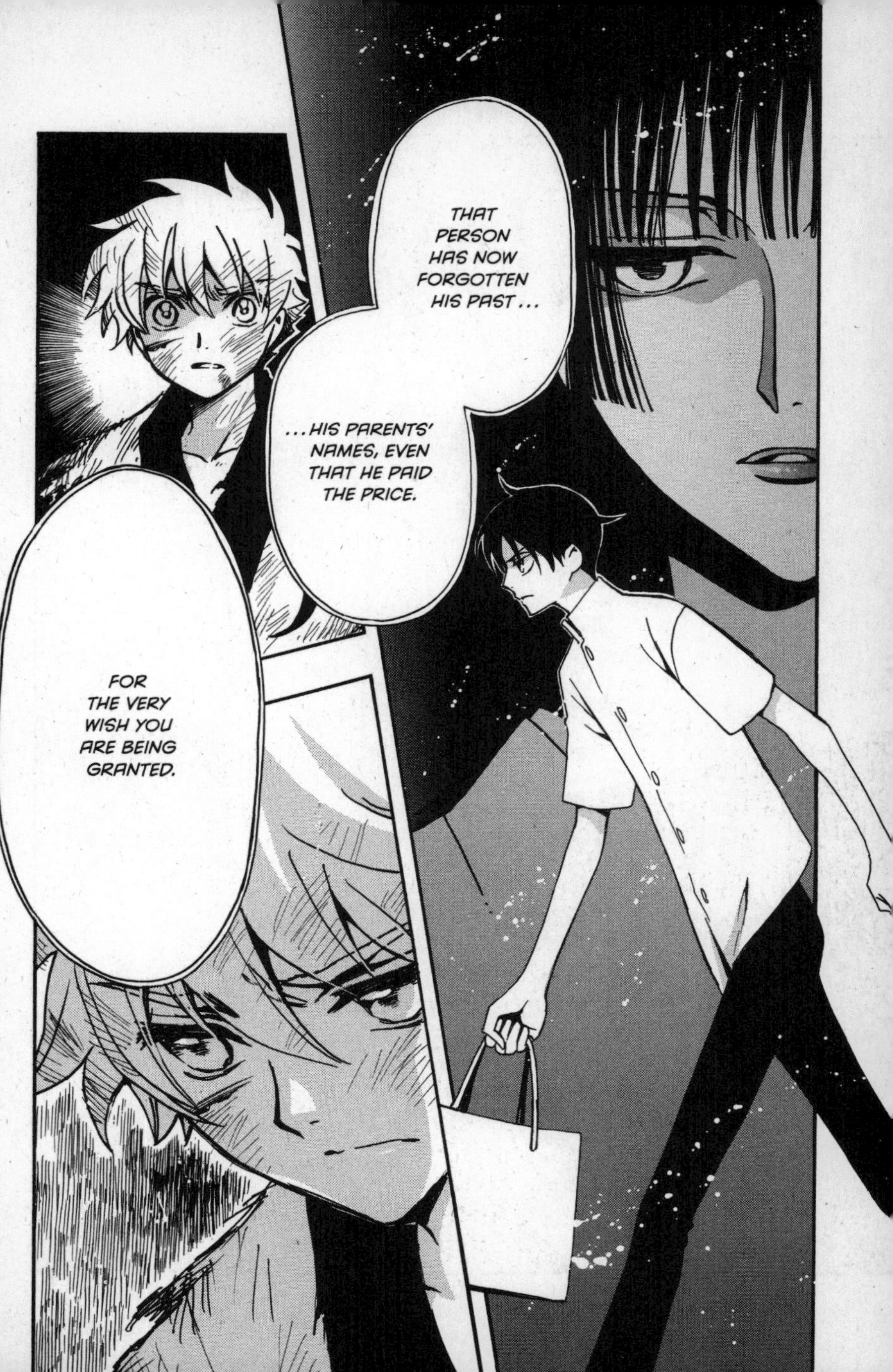
THAT PERSON HAS NOW FORGOTTEN HIS PAST...
...HIS PARENTS' NAMES, EVEN THAT HE PAID THE PRICE.
FOR THE VERY WISH YOU ARE BEING GRANTED.

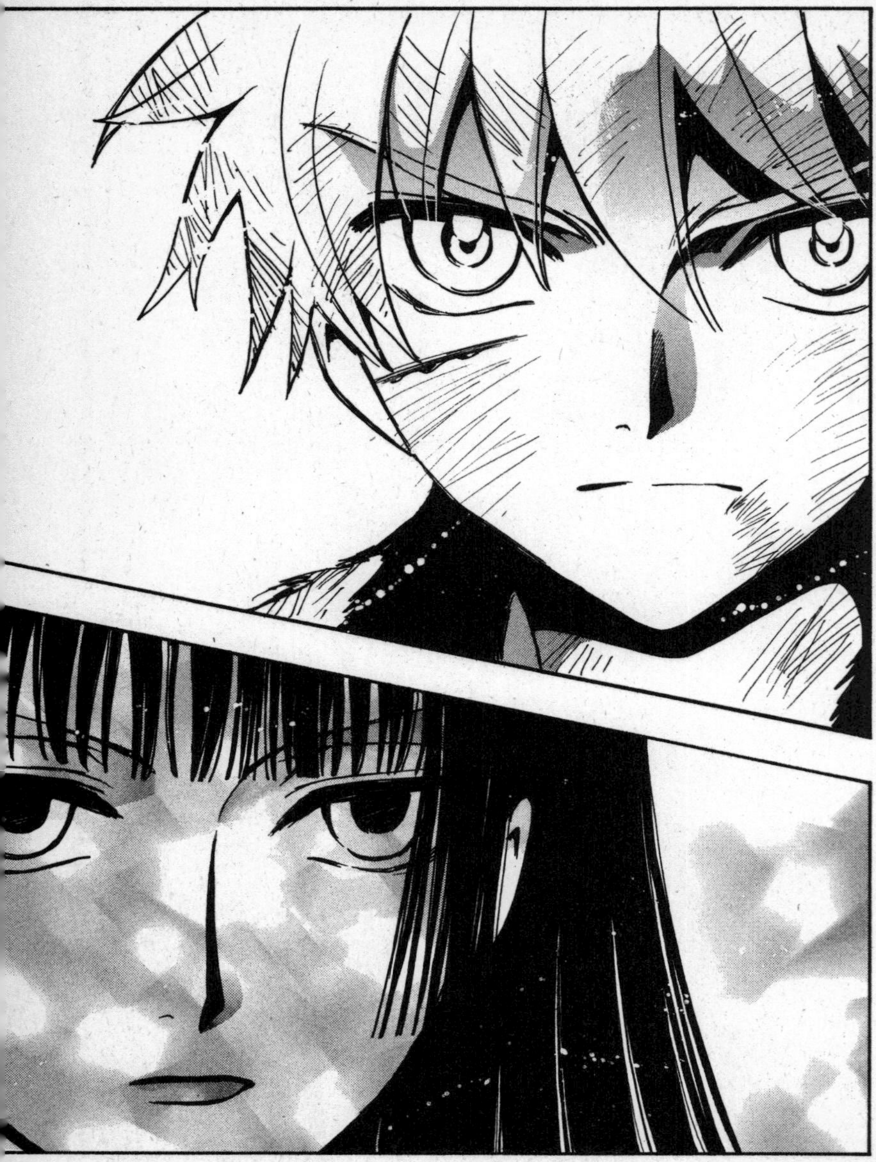

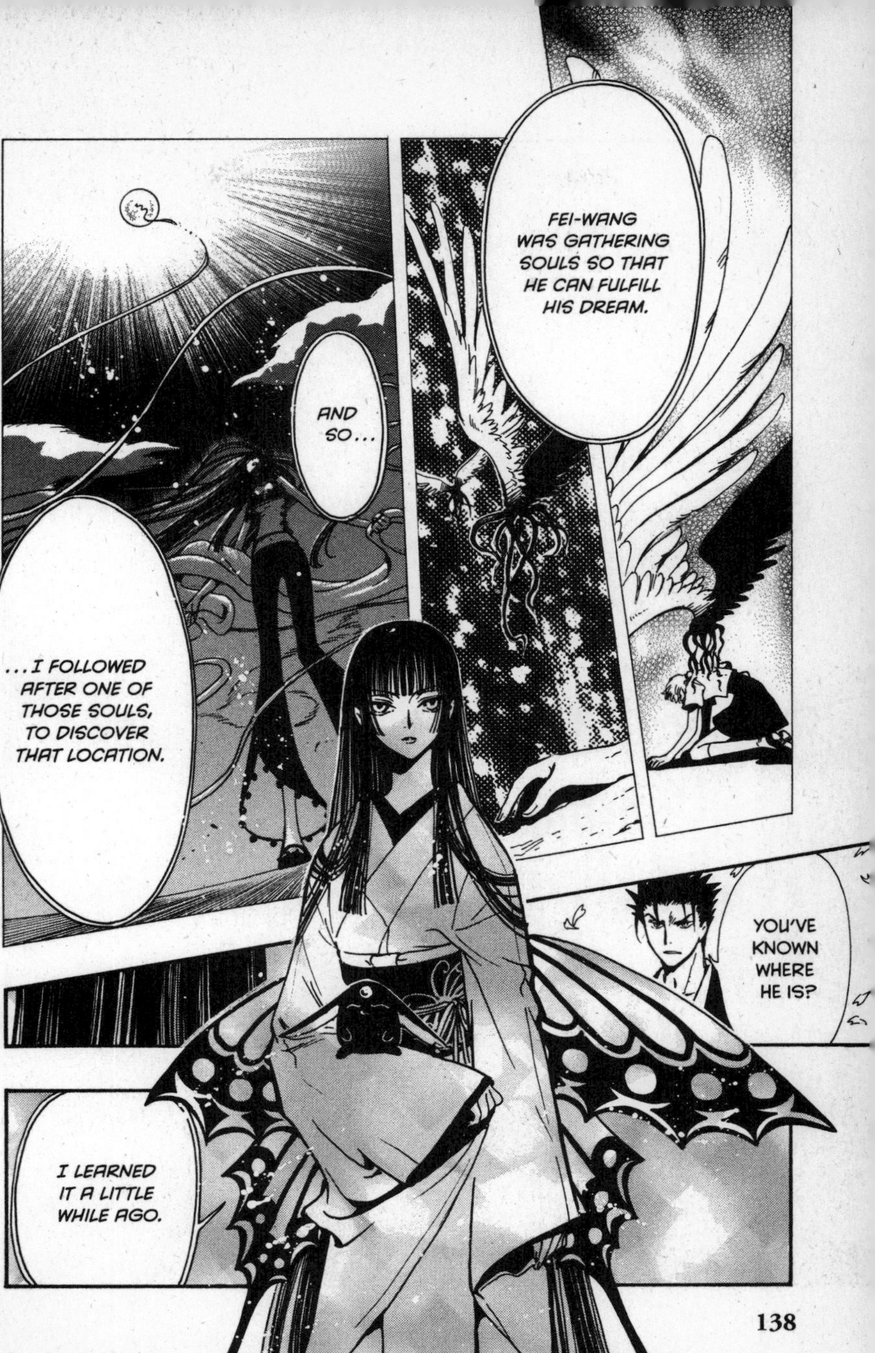
FEI-WANG WAS GATHERING SOULS SO THAT HE CAN FULFILL HIS DREAM.
AND SO...
...I FOLLOWED AFTER ONE OF THOSE SOULS, TO DISCOVER THAT LOCATION.
YOU'VE KNOWN WHERE HE IS?
I LEARNED IT A LITTLE WHILE AGO.

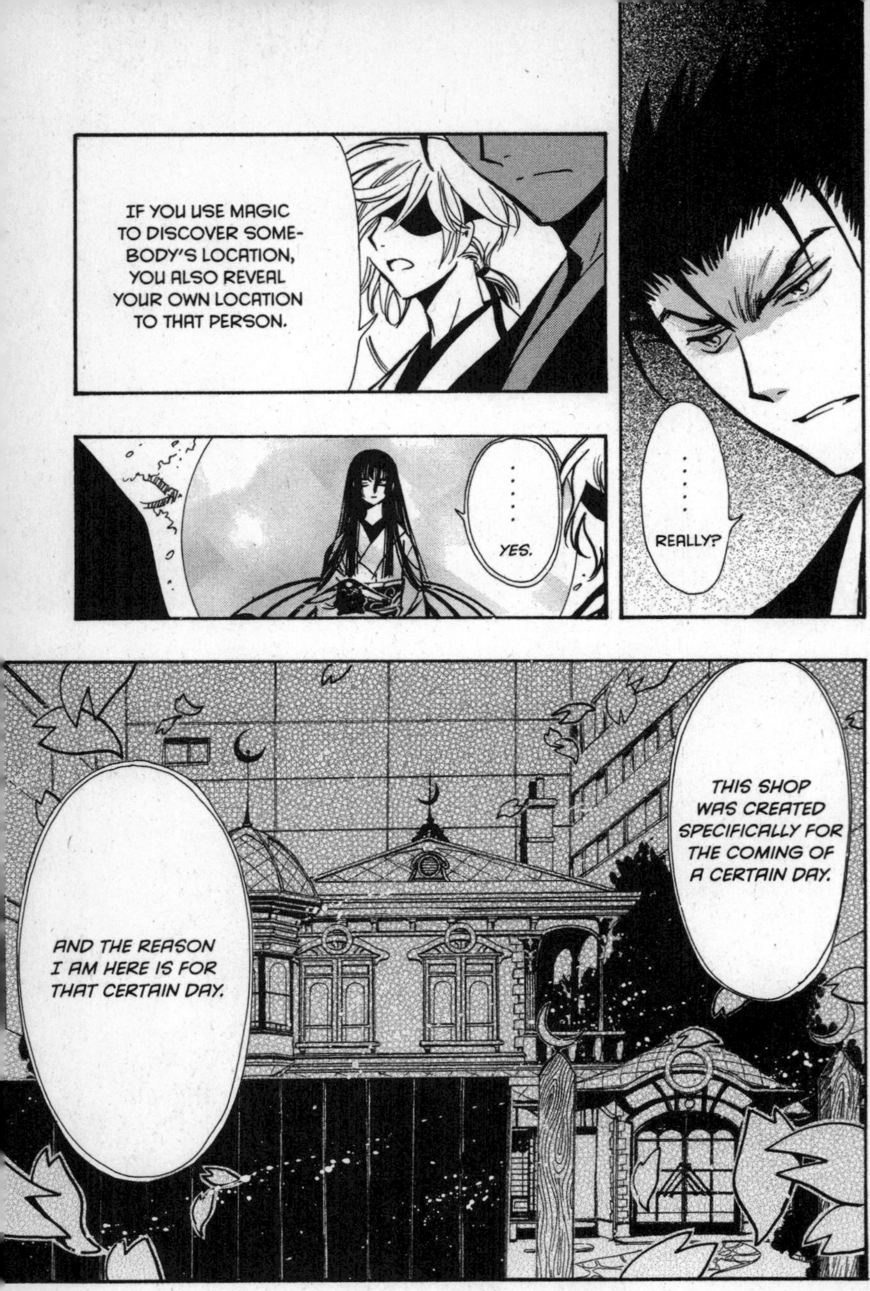
. . . . . REALLY?
IF YOU USE MAGIC TO DISCOVER SOME-BODY'S LOCATION, YOU ALSO REVEAL YOUR OWN LOCATION TO THAT PERSON.
. . . . . YES.
THIS SHOP WAS CREATED SPECIFICALLY FOR THE COMING OF A CERTAIN DAY.
AND THE REASON I AM HERE IS FOR THAT CERTAIN DAY.

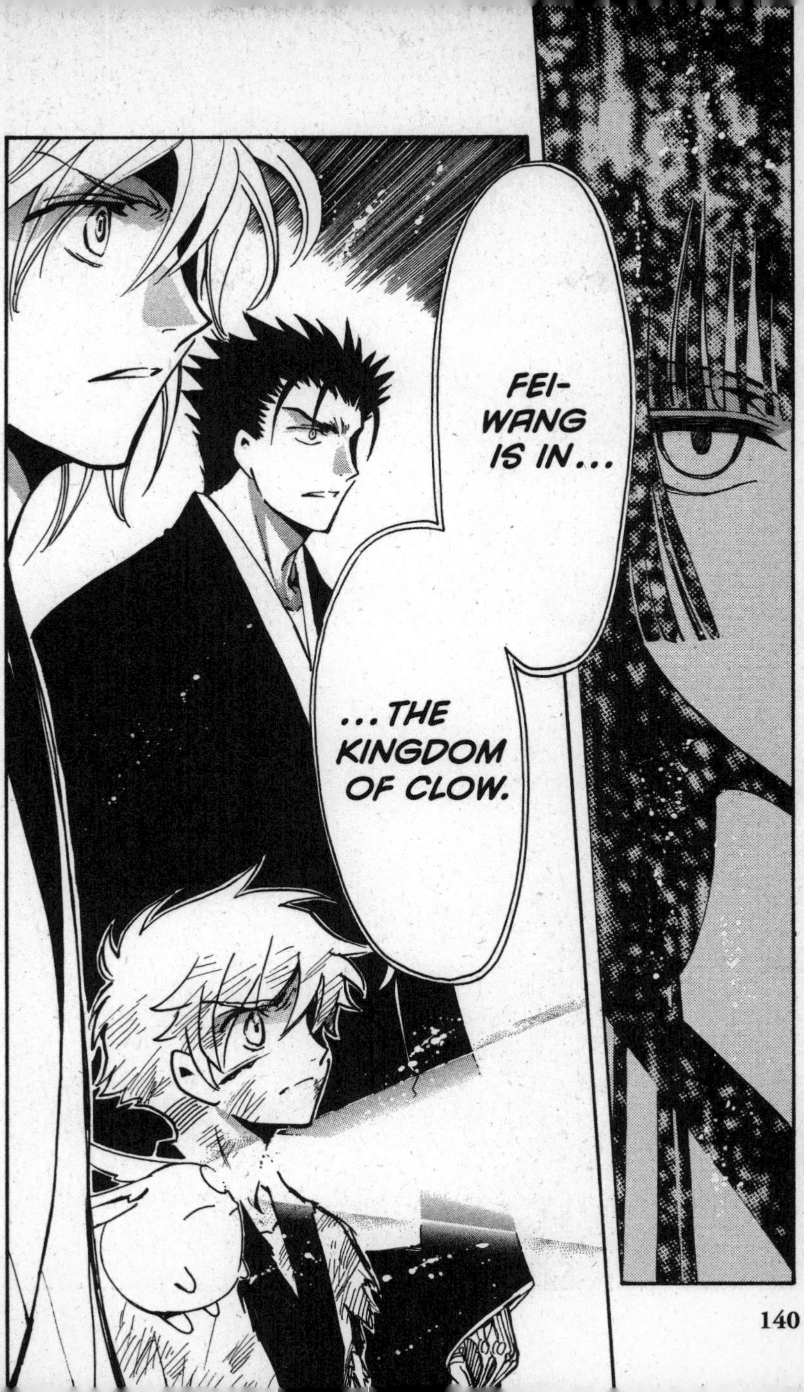
FEI-WANG IS IN...
...THE KINGDOM OF CLOW.

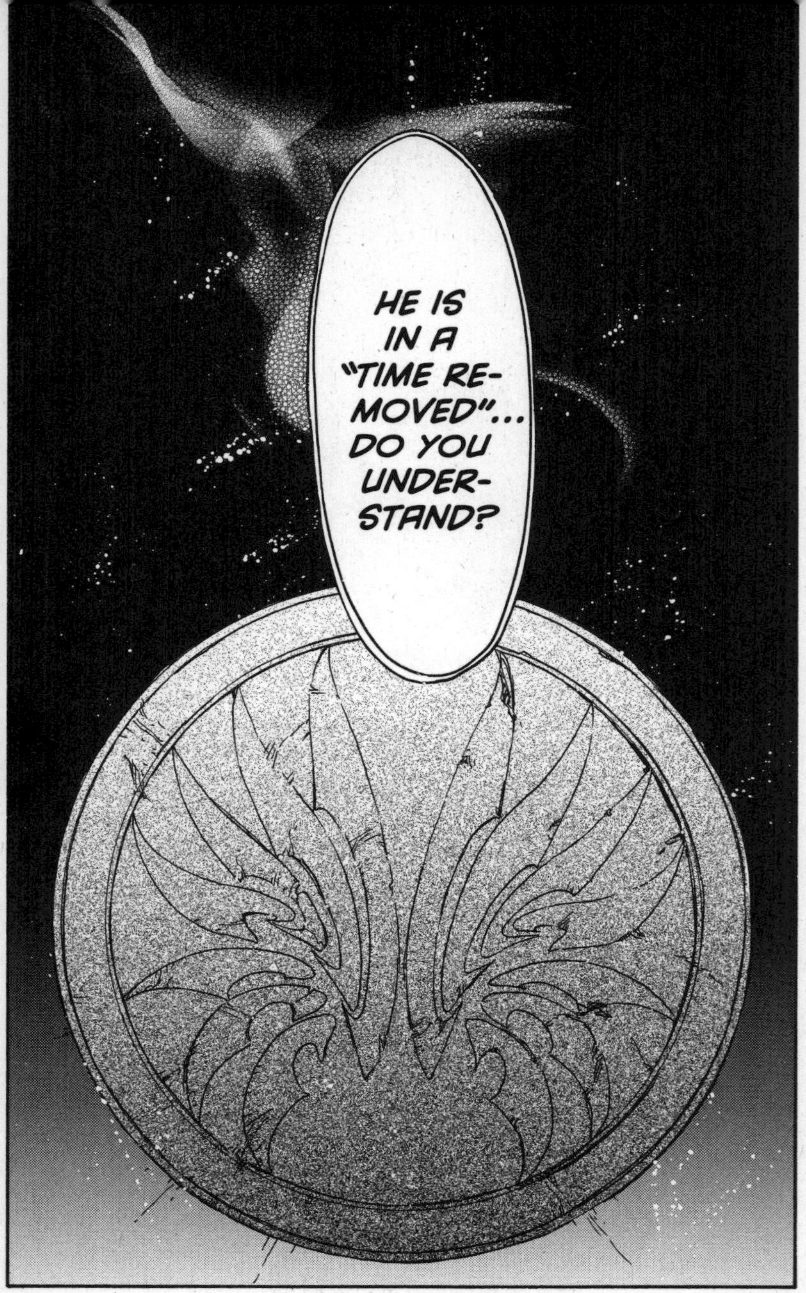
HE IS IN A "TIME RE-MOVED"... DO YOU UNDER-STAND?

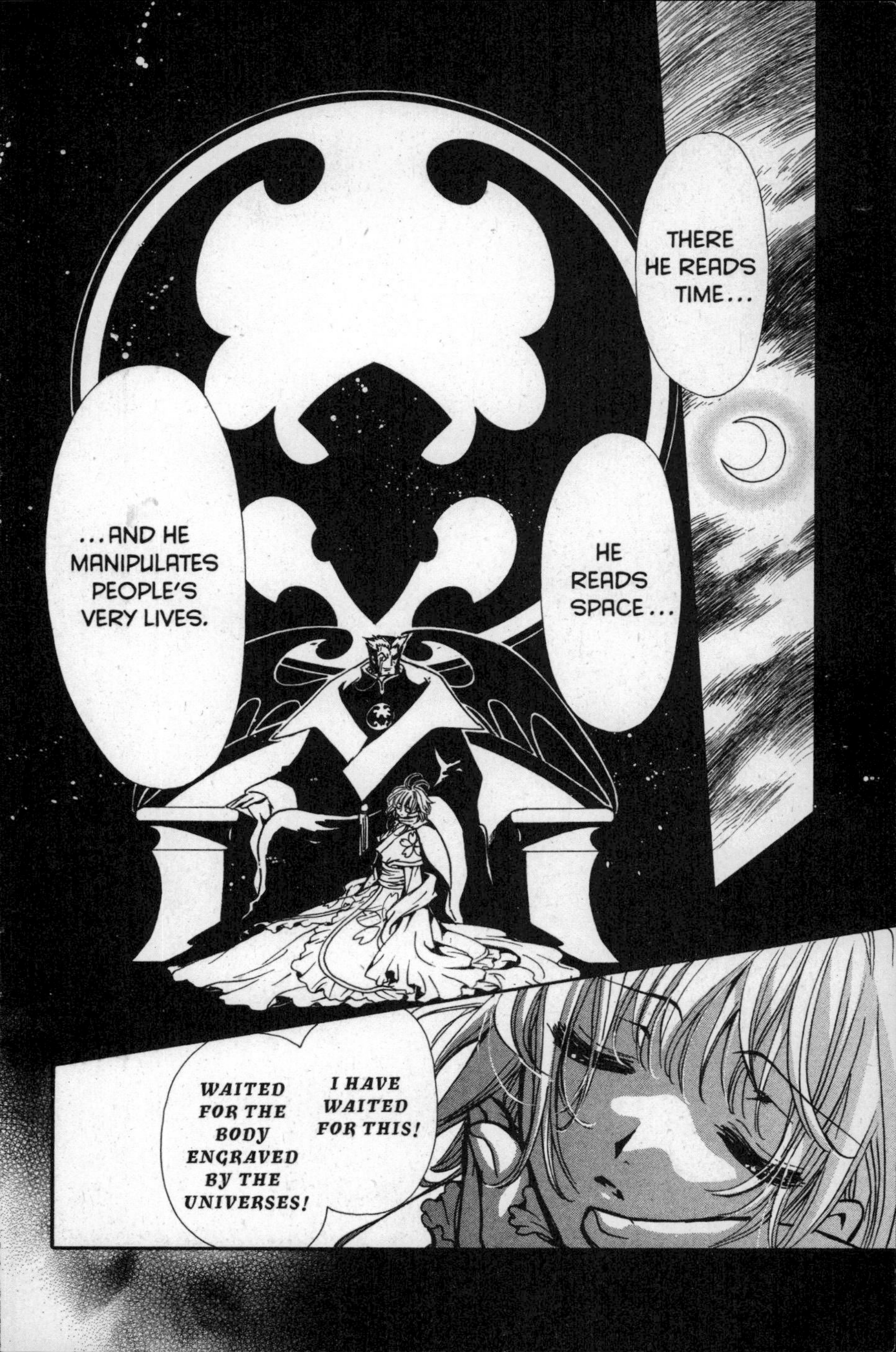
THERE HE READS TIME...
HE READS SPACE...
...AND HE MANIPULATES PEOPLE'S VERY LIVES.
I HAVE WAITED FOR THIS!
WAITED FOR THE BODY ENGRAVED BY THE UNIVERSES!

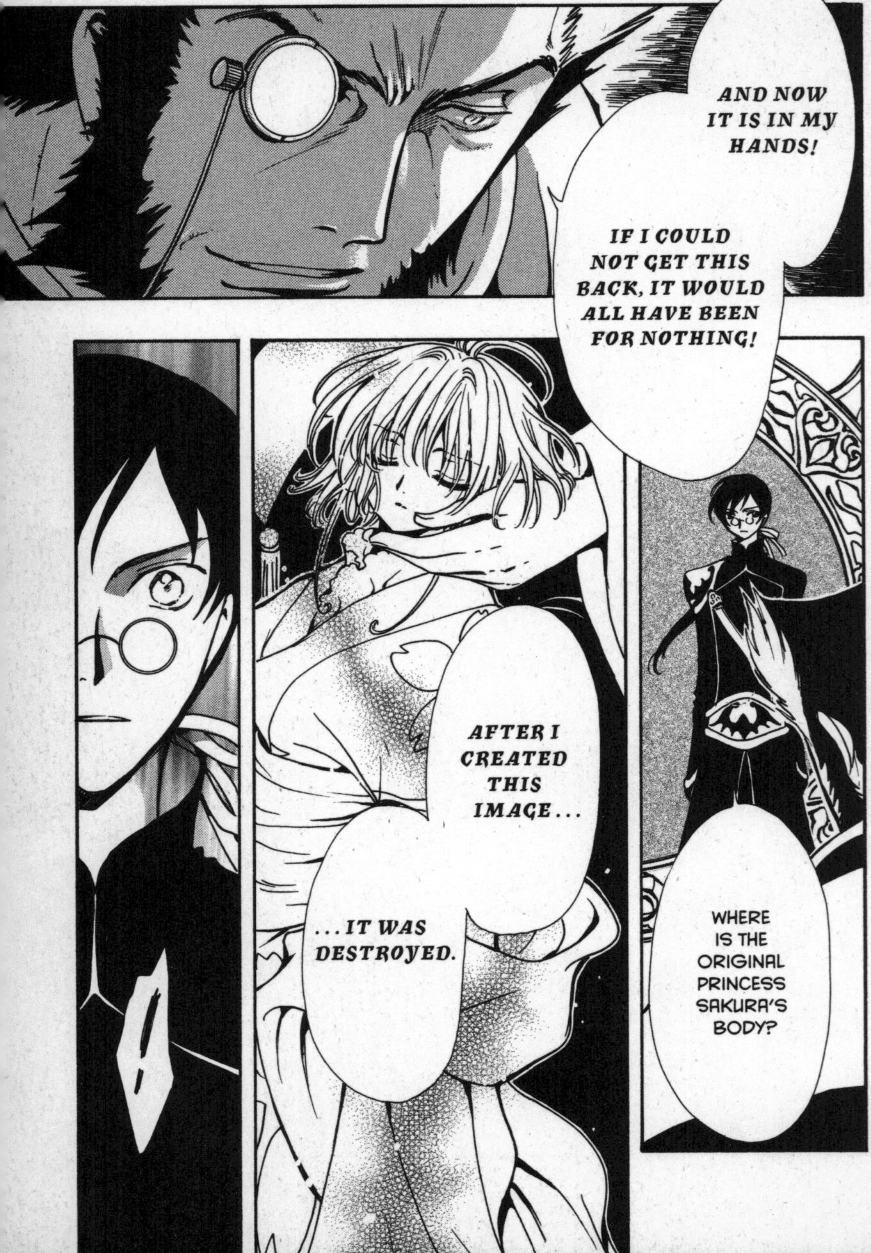
AND NOW IT IS IN MY HANDS!
IF I COULD NOT GET THIS BACK, IT WOULD ALL HAVE BEEN FOR NOTHING!
WHERE IS THE ORIGINAL PRINCESS SAKURA'S BODY?
AFTER I CREATED THIS IMAGE...
...IT WAS DESTROYED.

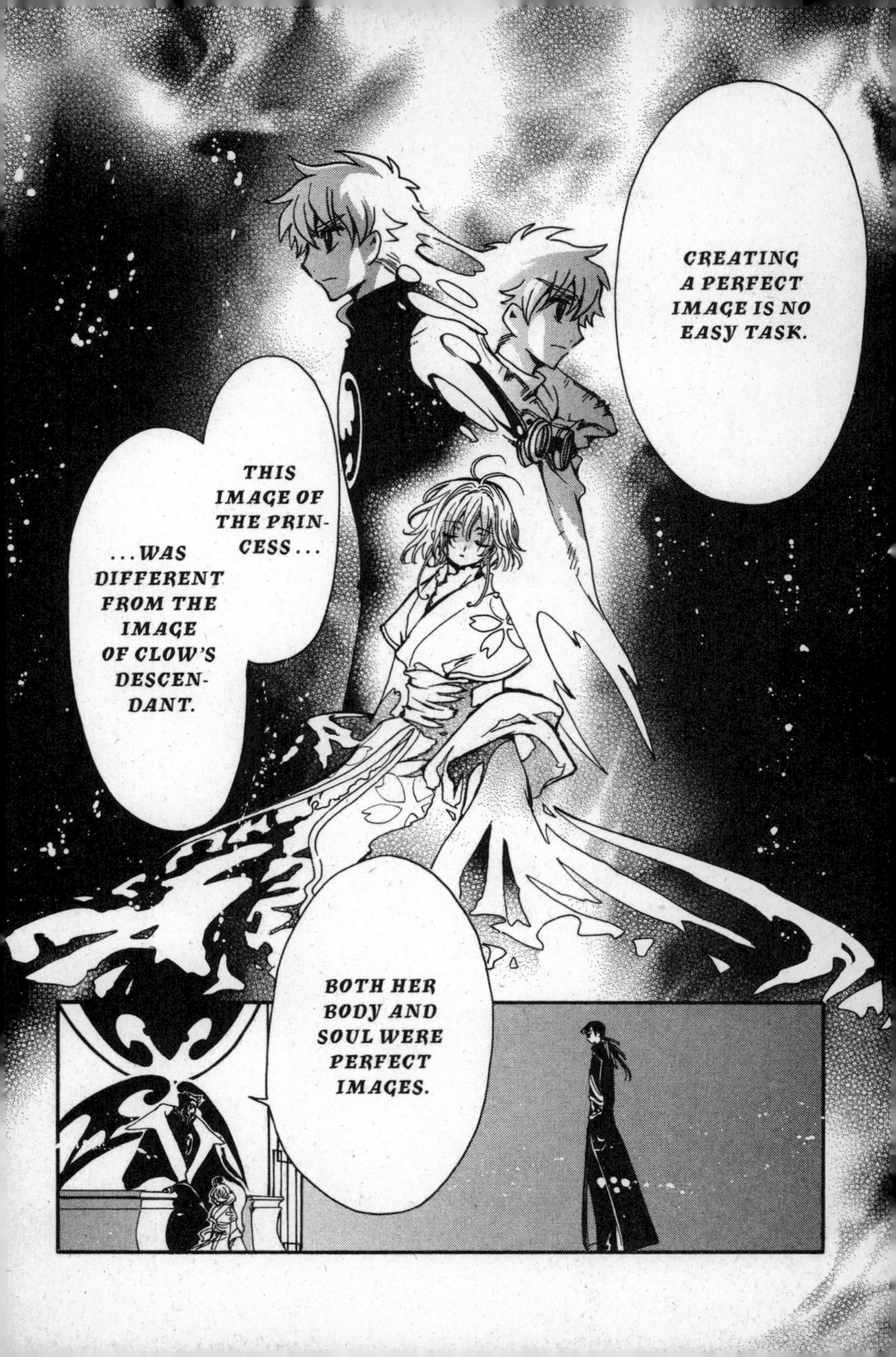
CREATING A PERFECT IMAGE IS NO EASY TASK.
THIS IMAGE OF THE PRIN-CESS...
...WAS DIFFERENT FROM THE IMAGE OF CLOW'S DESCEN-DANT.
BOTH HER BODY AND SOUL WERE PERFECT IMAGES.

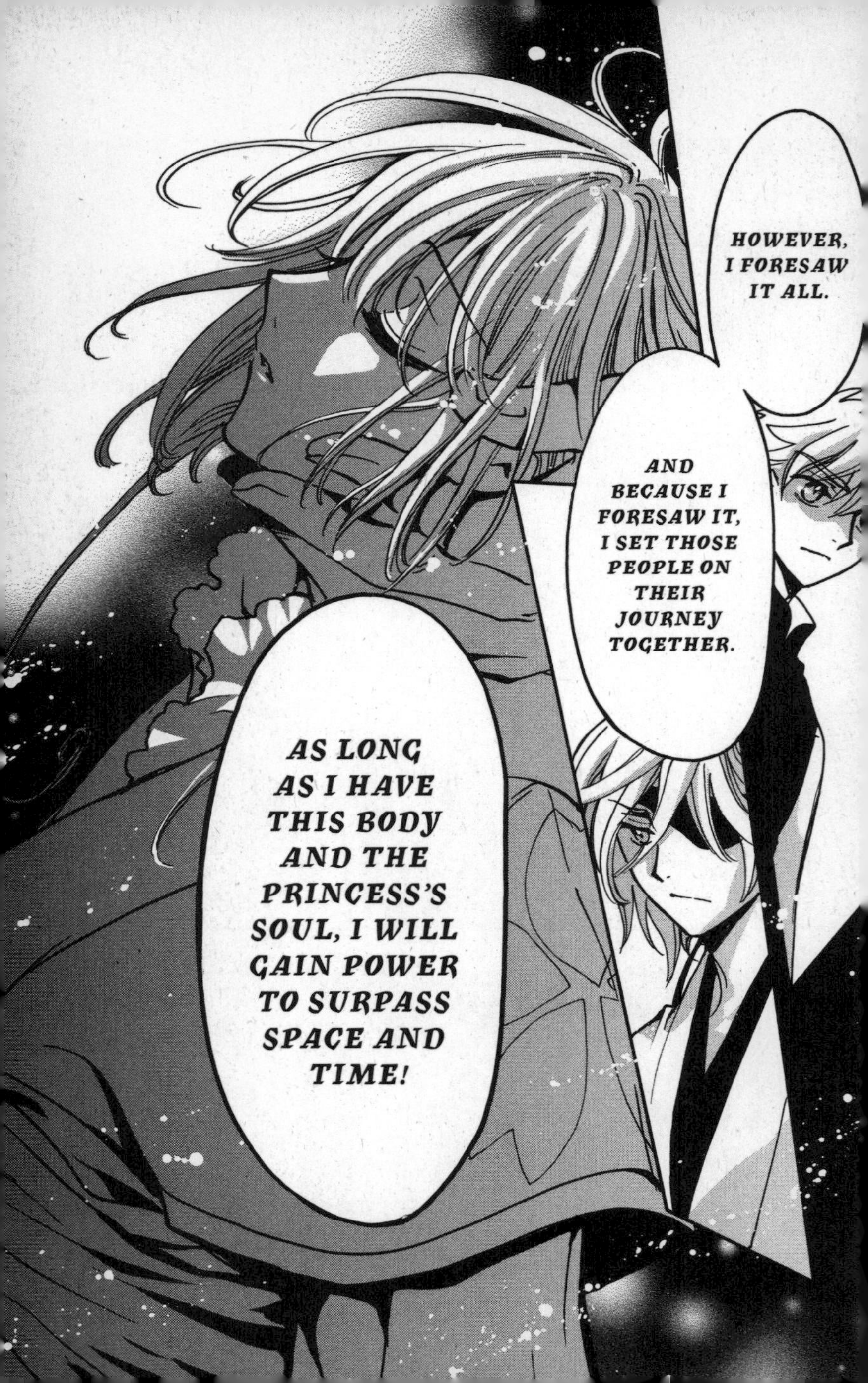
HOWEVER, I FORESAW IT ALL.
AND BECAUSE I FORESAW IT, I SET THOSE PEOPLE ON THEIR JOURNEY TOGETHER.
AS LONG AS I HAVE THIS BODY AND THE PRINCESS'S SOUL, I WILL GAIN POWER TO SURPASS SPACE AND TIME!

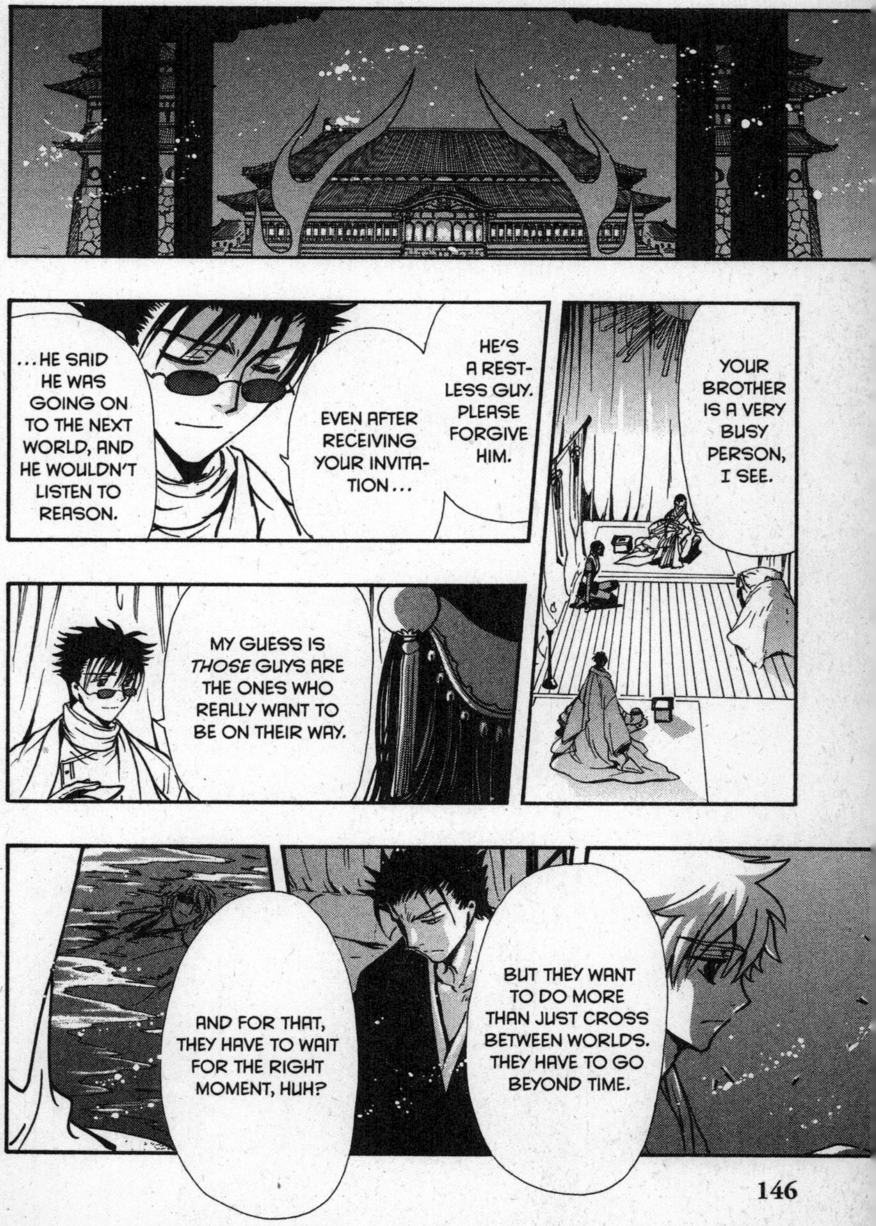
YOUR BROTHER IS A VERY BUSY PERSON, I SEE.
HE'S A REST-LESS GUY. PLEASE FORGIVE HIM.
EVEN AFTER RECEIVING YOUR INVITA-TION...
...HE SAID HE WAS GOING ON TO THE NEXT WORLD, AND HE WOULDN'T LISTEN TO REASON.
MY GUESS IS *THOSE* GUYS ARE THE ONES WHO REALLY WANT TO BE ON THEIR WAY.
BUT THEY WANT TO DO MORE THAN JUST CROSS BETWEEN WORLDS. THEY HAVE TO GO BEYOND TIME.
AND FOR THAT, THEY HAVE TO WAIT FOR THE RIGHT MOMENT, HUH?

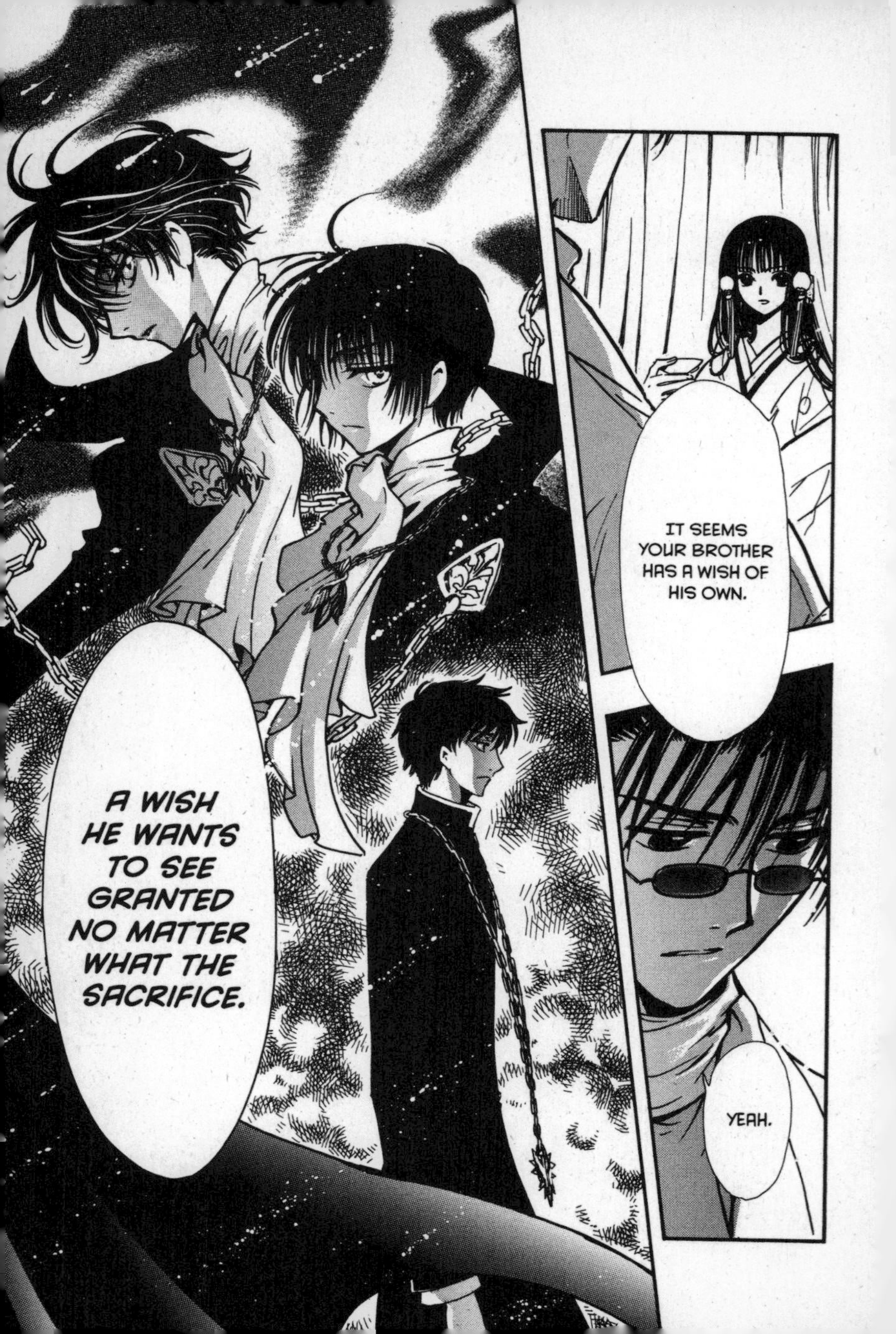
IT SEEMS YOUR BROTHER HAS A WISH OF HIS OWN.
YEAH.
A WISH HE WANTS TO SEE GRANTED NO MATTER WHAT THE SACRIFICE.

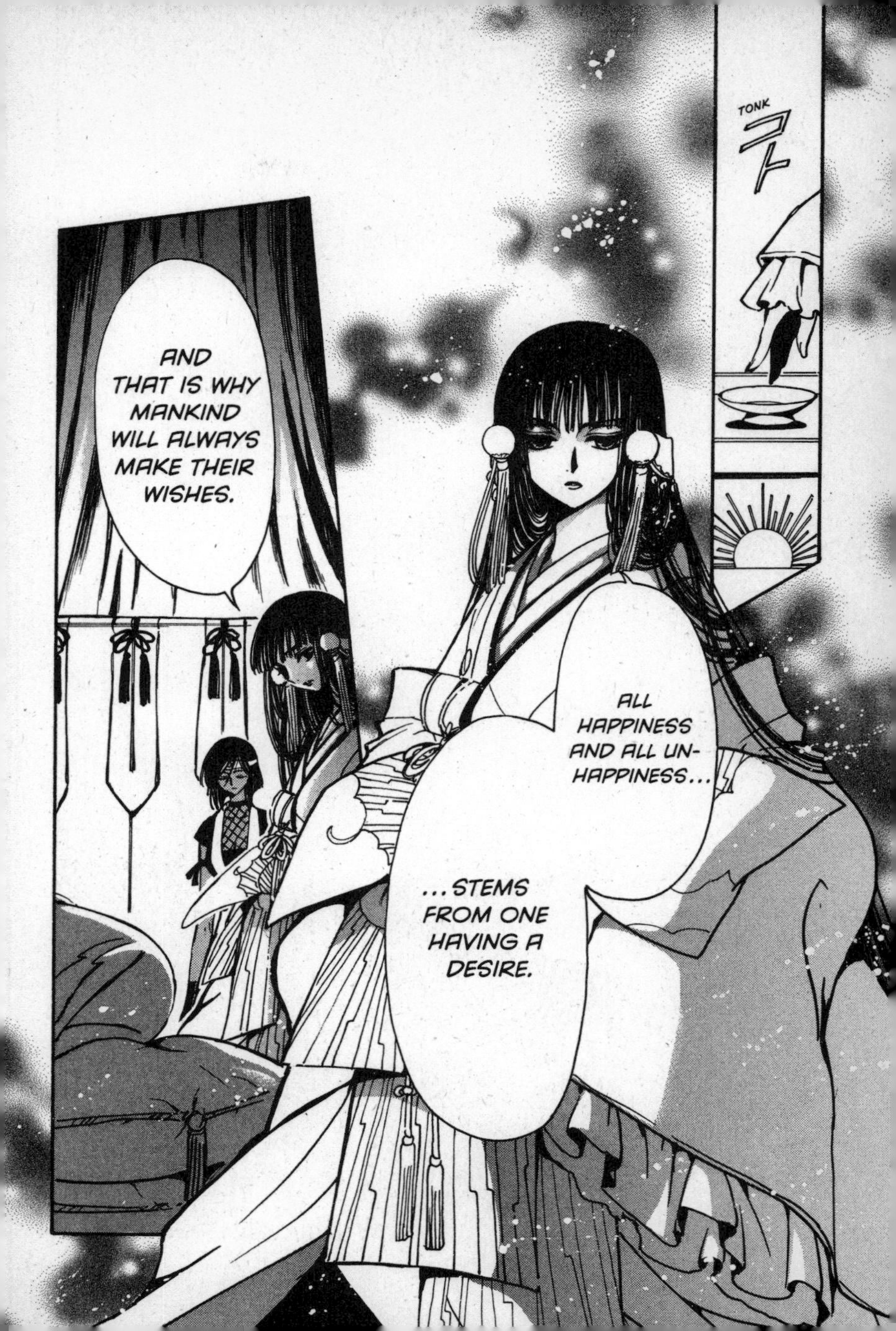
TONK
ALL HAPPINESS AND ALL UN-HAPPINESS...
...STEMS FROM ONE HAVING A DESIRE.
AND THAT IS WHY MANKIND WILL ALWAYS MAKE THEIR WISHES.

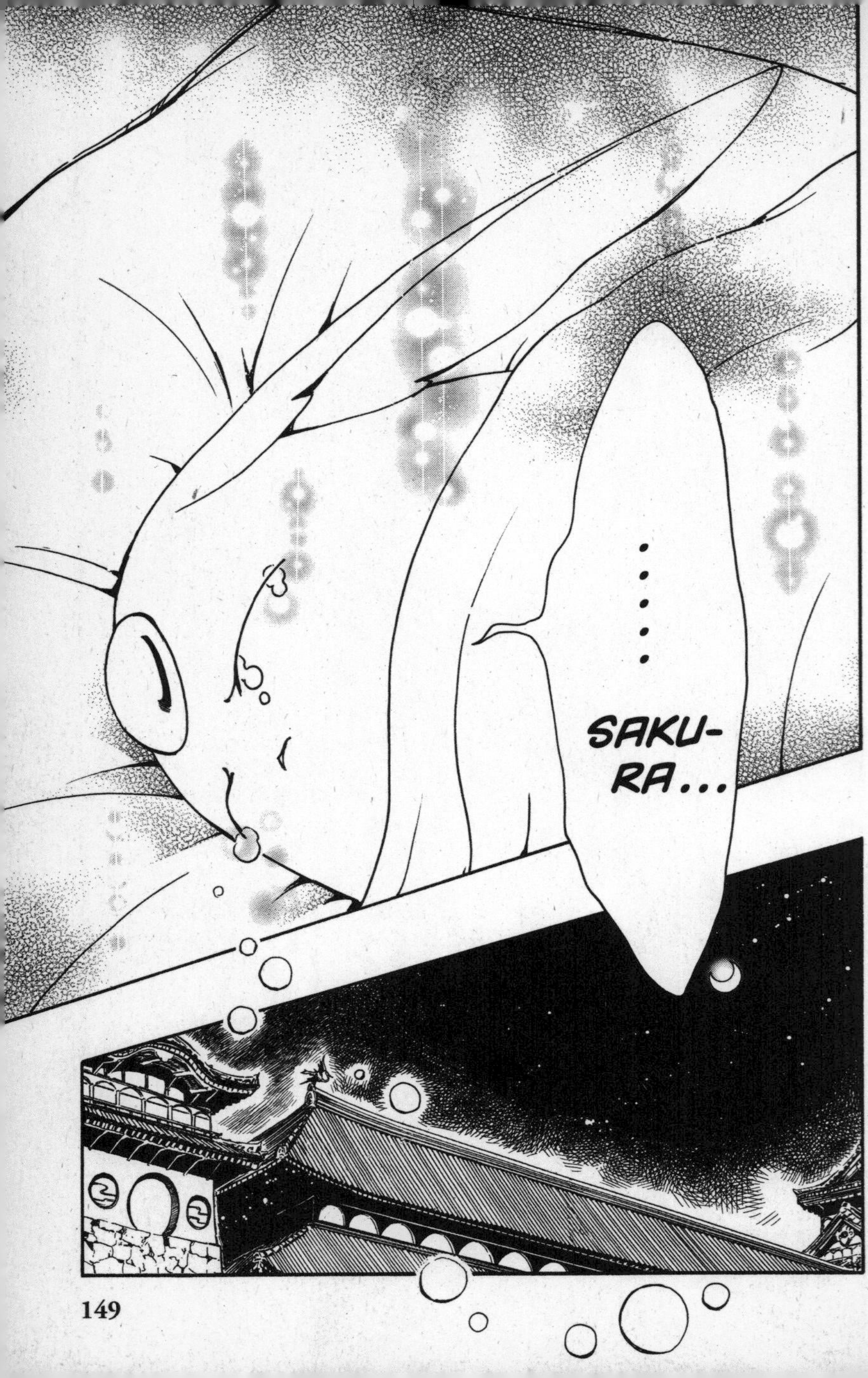
.....
SAKU-
RA...

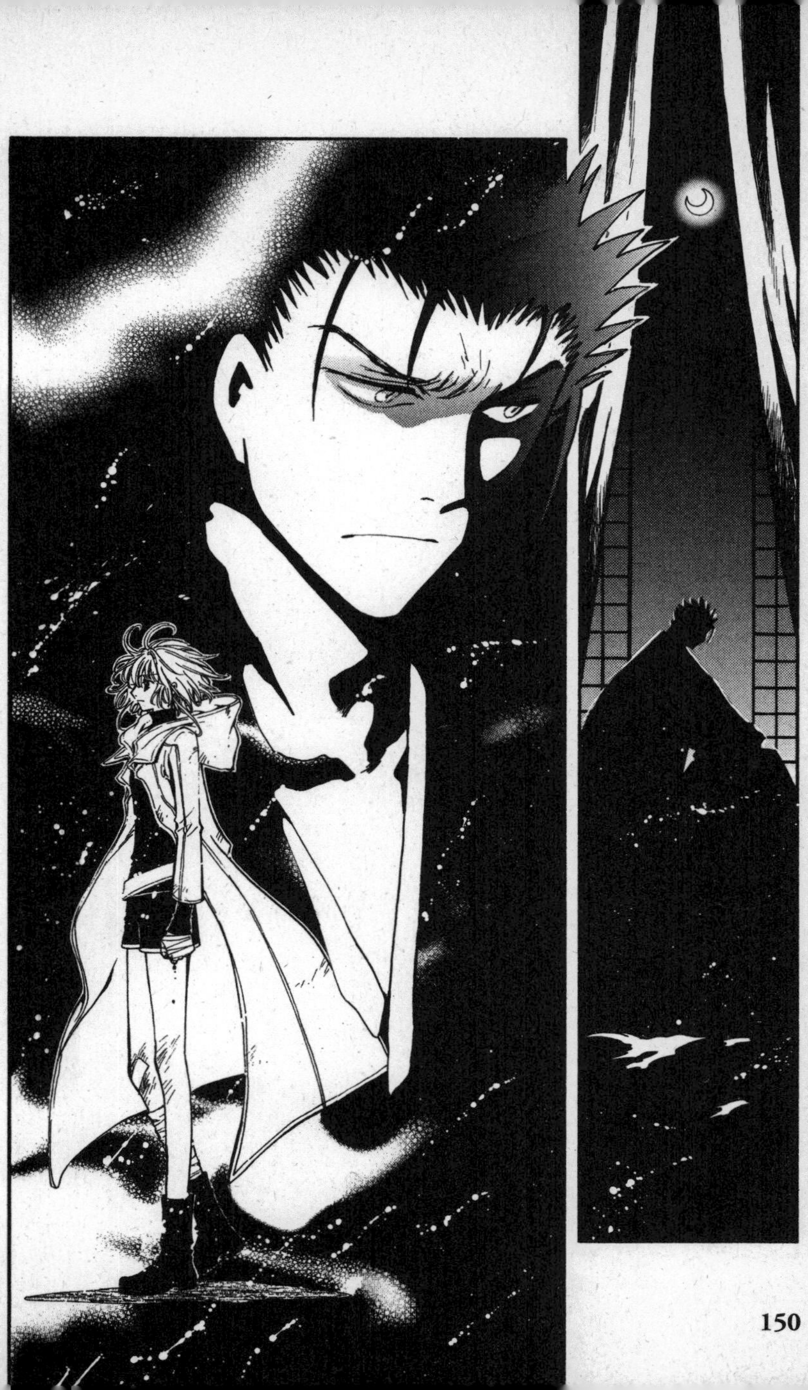

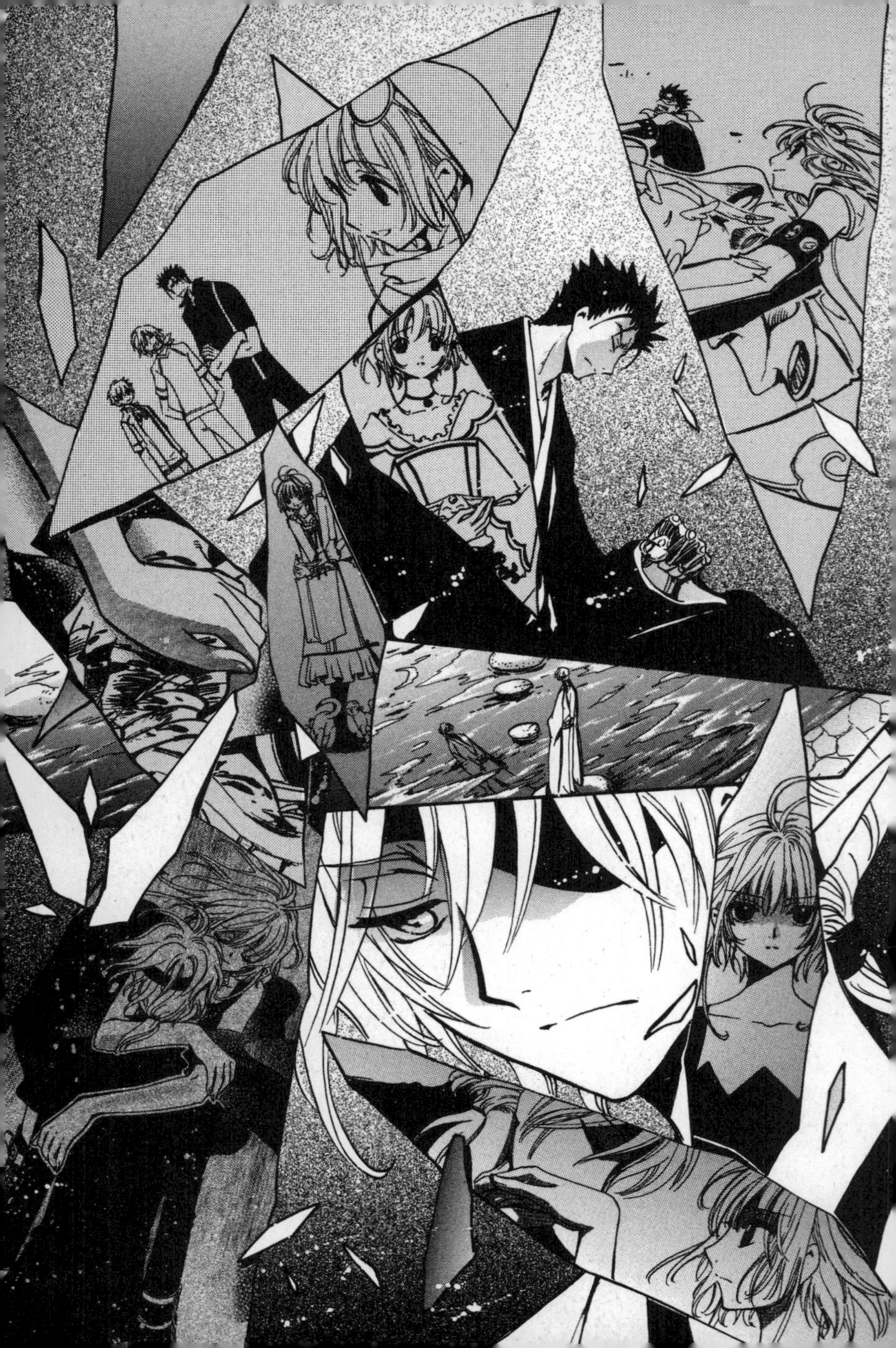

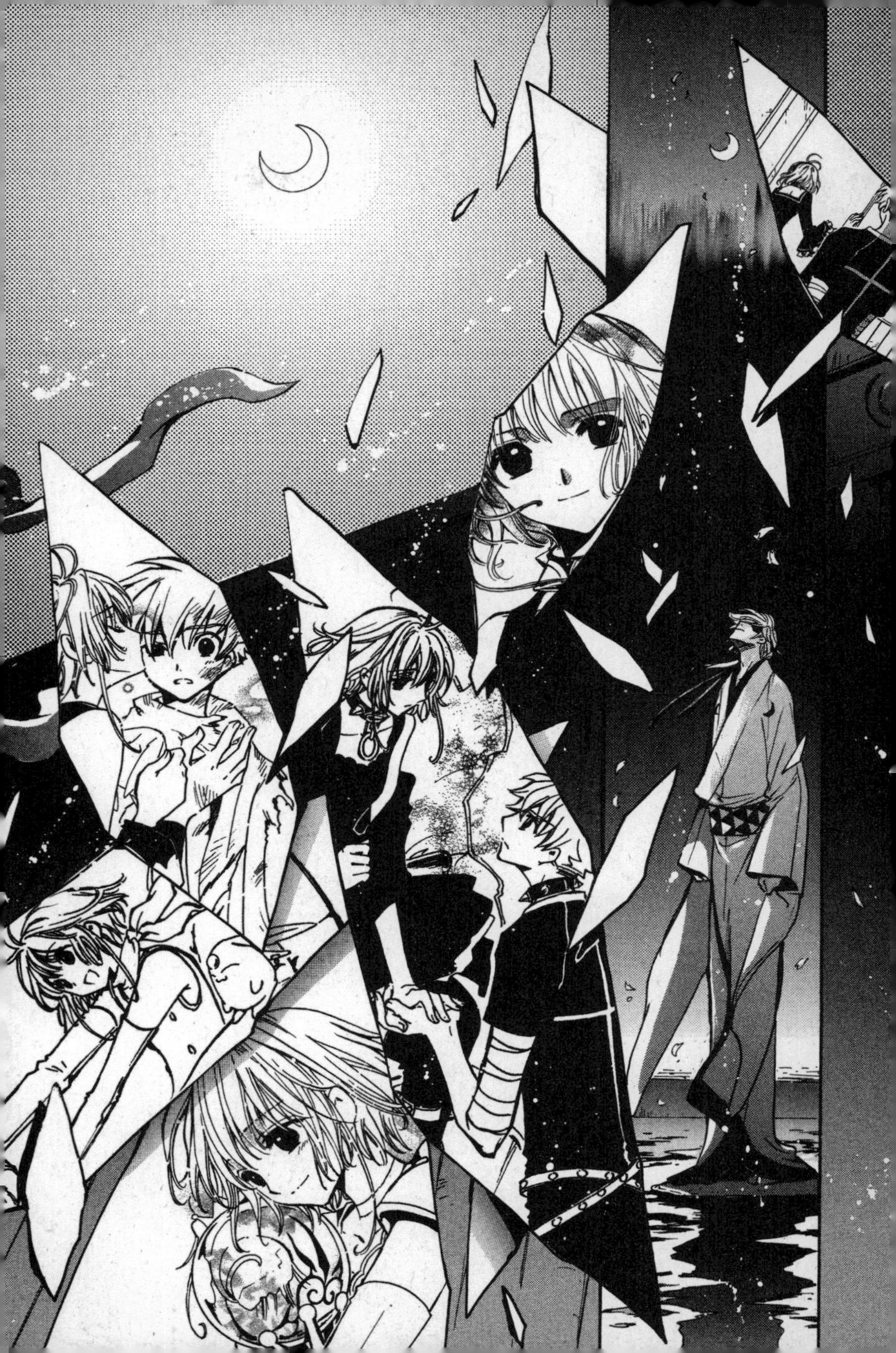

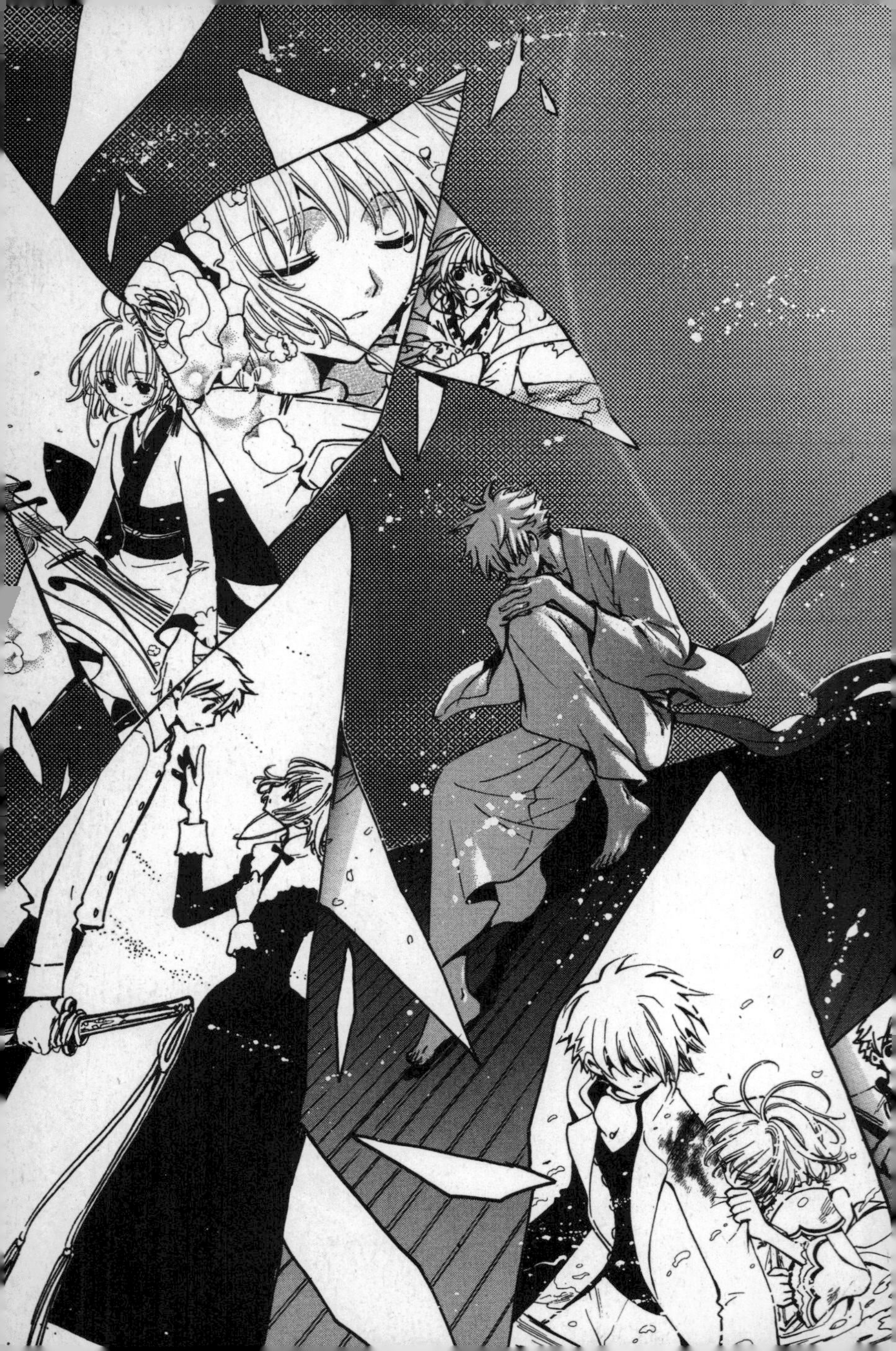

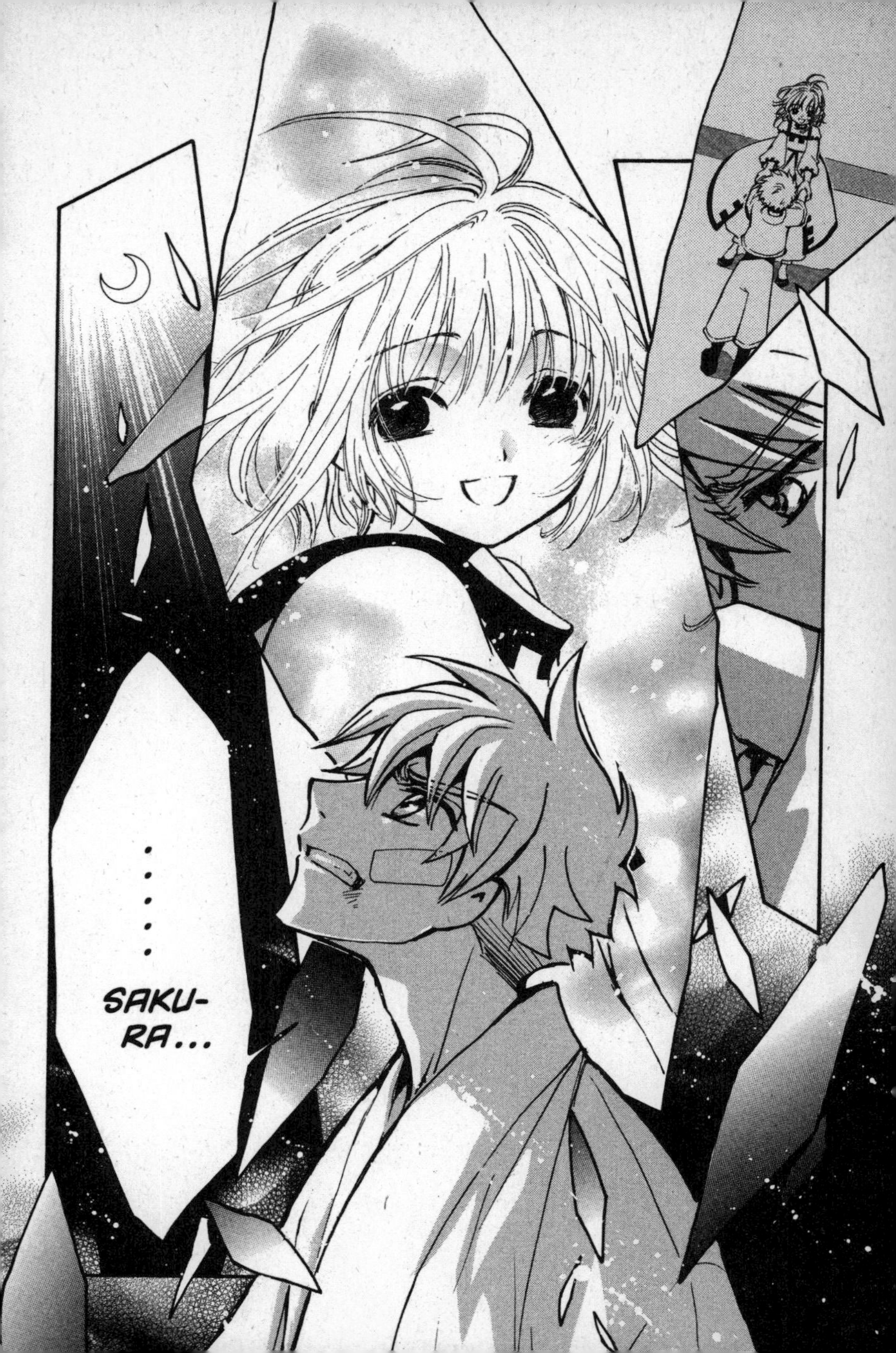

......
SAKU-
RA...

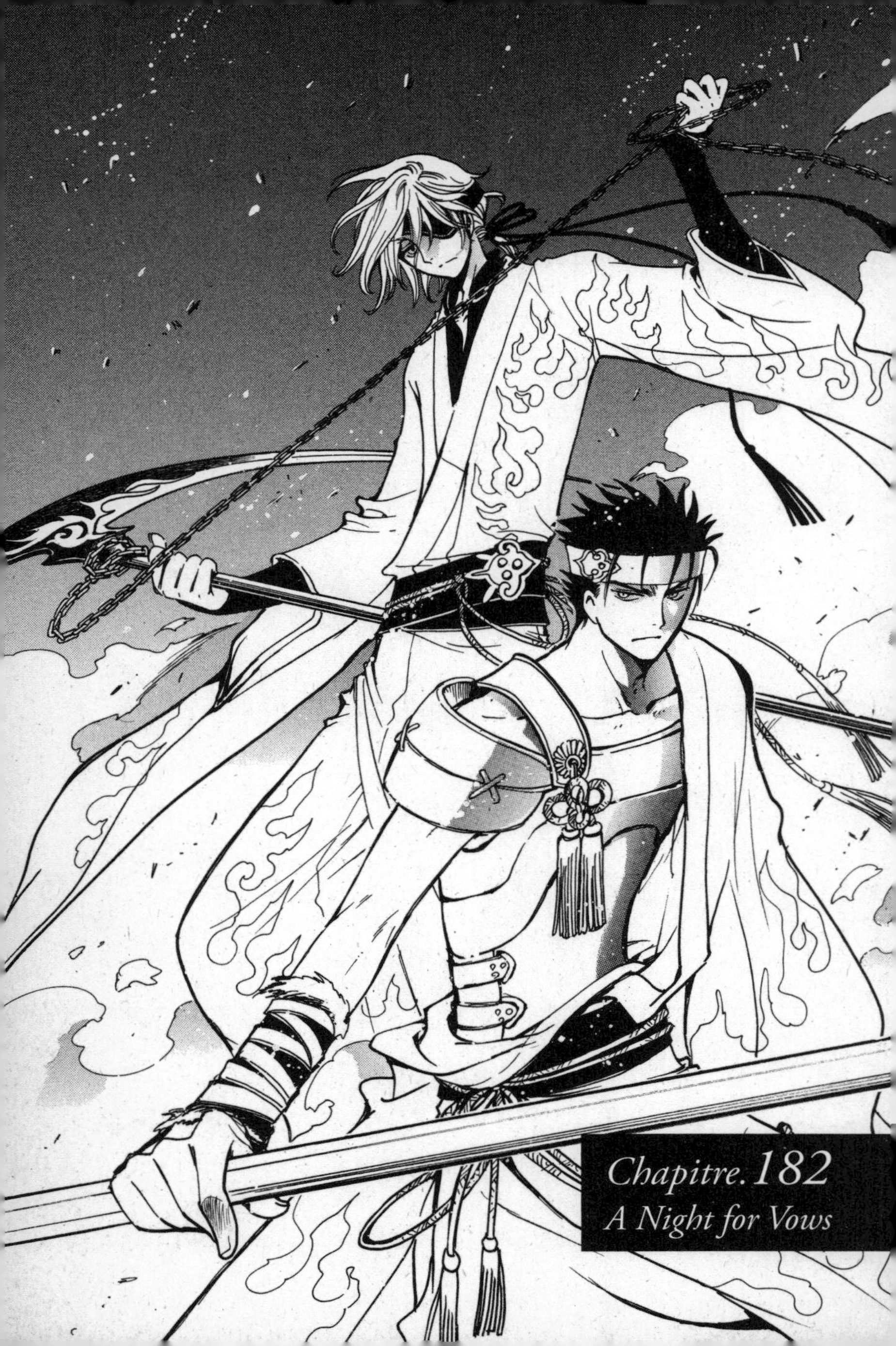
Chapitre. 182
A Night for Vows

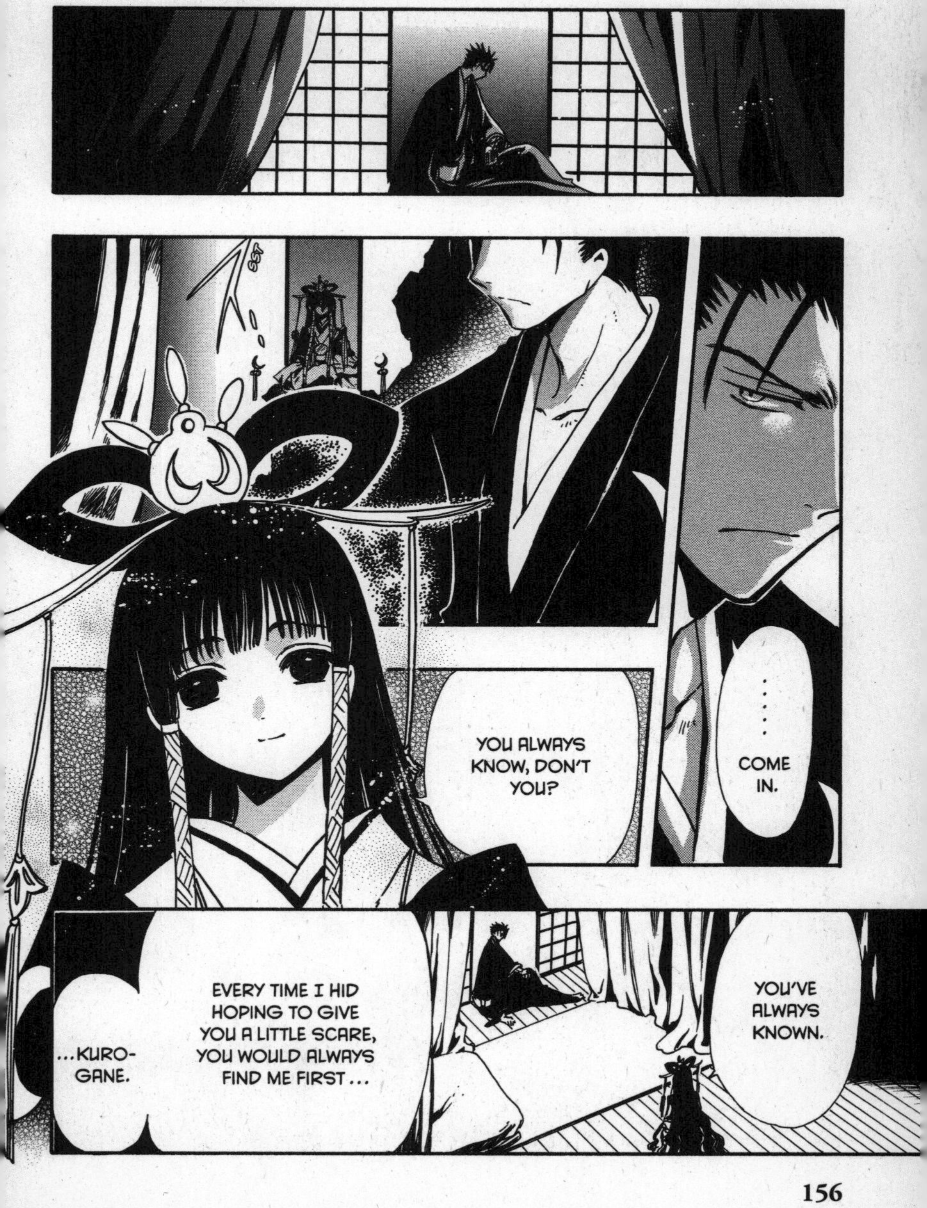

..... COME IN.
YOU ALWAYS KNOW, DON'T YOU?
SST
YOU'VE ALWAYS KNOWN.
EVERY TIME I HID HOPING TO GIVE YOU A LITTLE SCARE, YOU WOULD ALWAYS FIND ME FIRST...
...KURO-GANE.

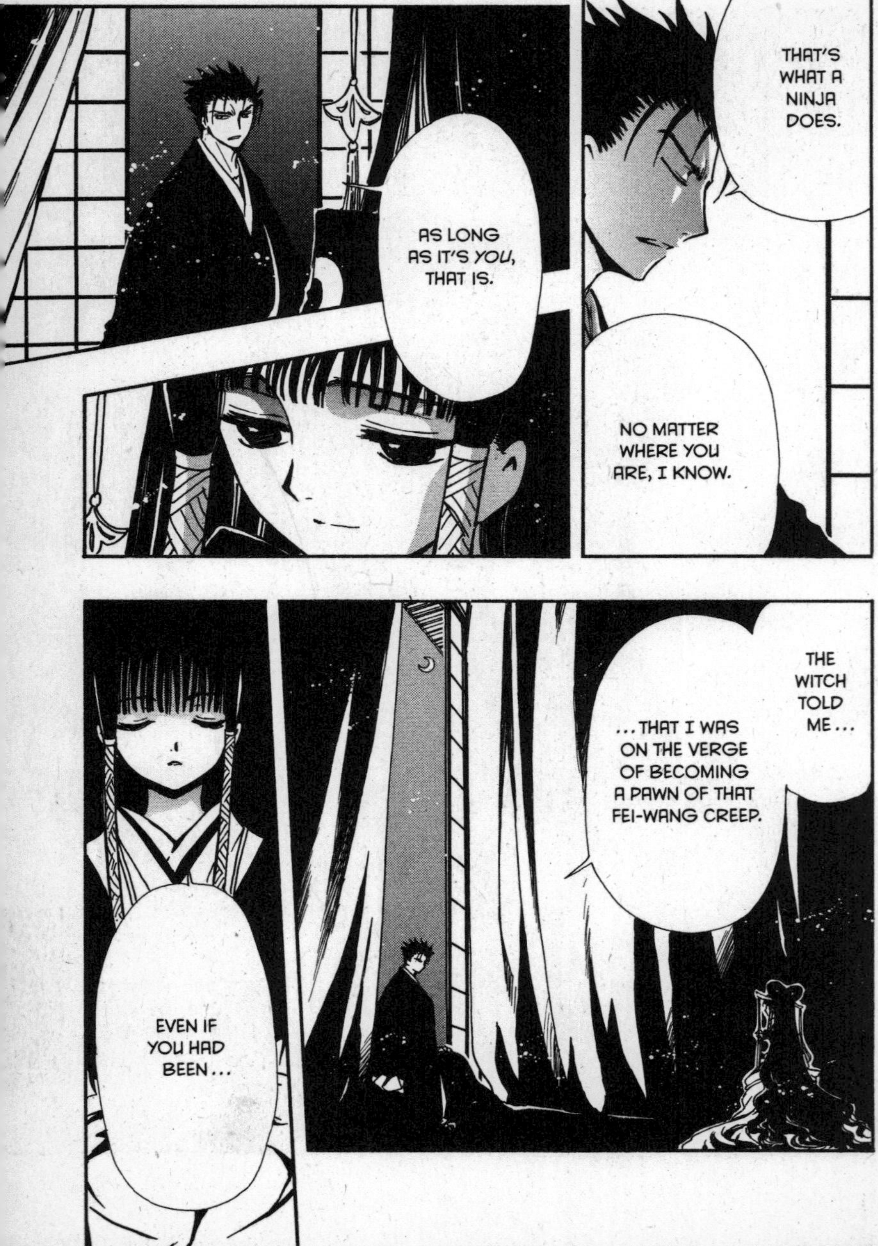
THAT'S WHAT A NINJA DOES.
NO MATTER WHERE YOU ARE, I KNOW.
AS LONG AS IT'S *YOU*, THAT IS.
THE WITCH TOLD ME...
...THAT I WAS ON THE VERGE OF BECOMING A PAWN OF THAT FEI-WANG CREEP.
EVEN IF YOU HAD BEEN...

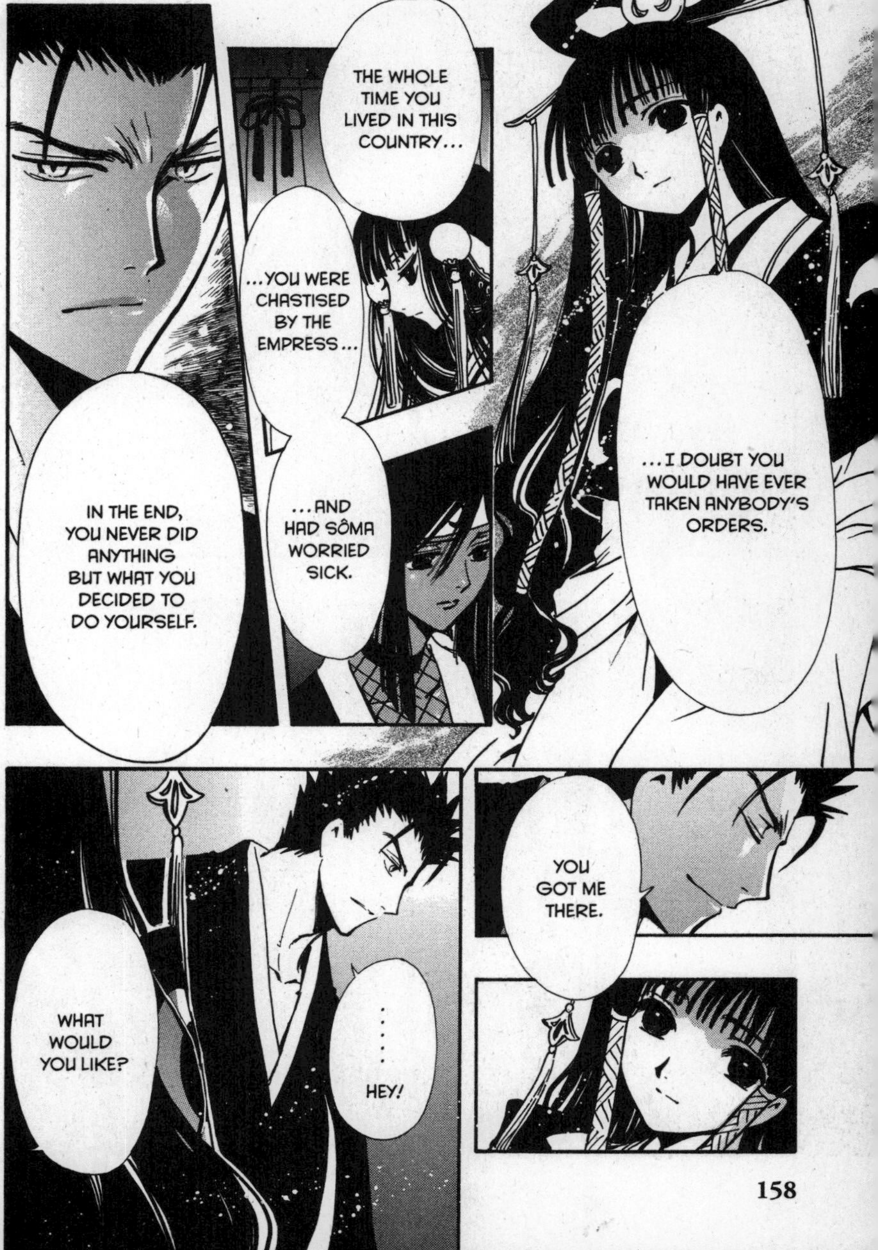
THE WHOLE TIME YOU LIVED IN THIS COUNTRY...
...YOU WERE CHASTISED BY THE EMPRESS...
...AND HAD SÔMA WORRIED SICK.
IN THE END, YOU NEVER DID ANYTHING BUT WHAT YOU DECIDED TO DO YOURSELF.
...I DOUBT YOU WOULD HAVE EVER TAKEN ANYBODY'S ORDERS.
YOU GOT ME THERE.
..... HEY!
WHAT WOULD YOU LIKE?

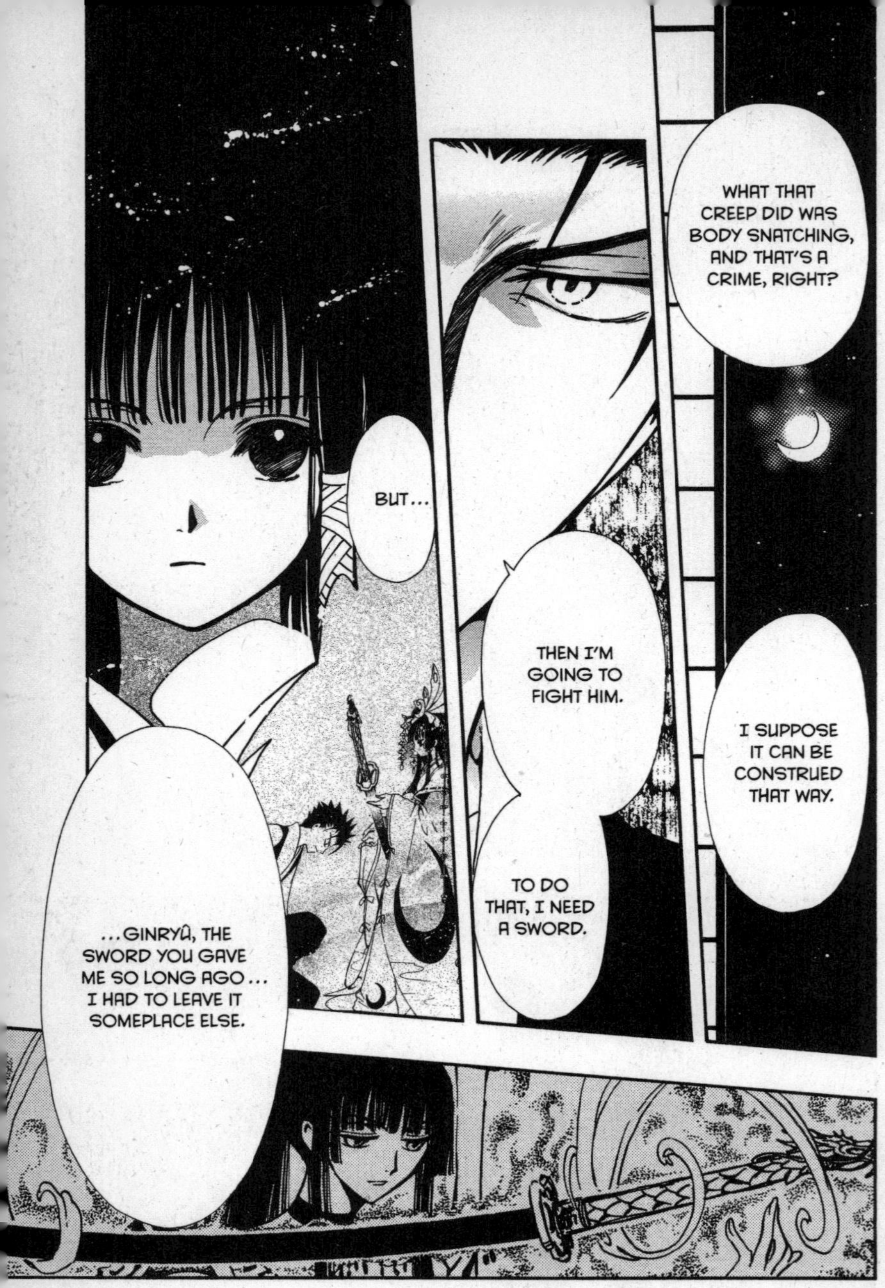
WHAT THAT CREEP DID WAS BODY SNATCHING, AND THAT'S A CRIME, RIGHT?
I SUPPOSE IT CAN BE CONSTRUED THAT WAY.
THEN I'M GOING TO FIGHT HIM.
TO DO THAT, I NEED A SWORD.
BUT...
...GINRYÛ, THE SWORD YOU GAVE ME SO LONG AGO... I HAD TO LEAVE IT SOMEPLACE ELSE.

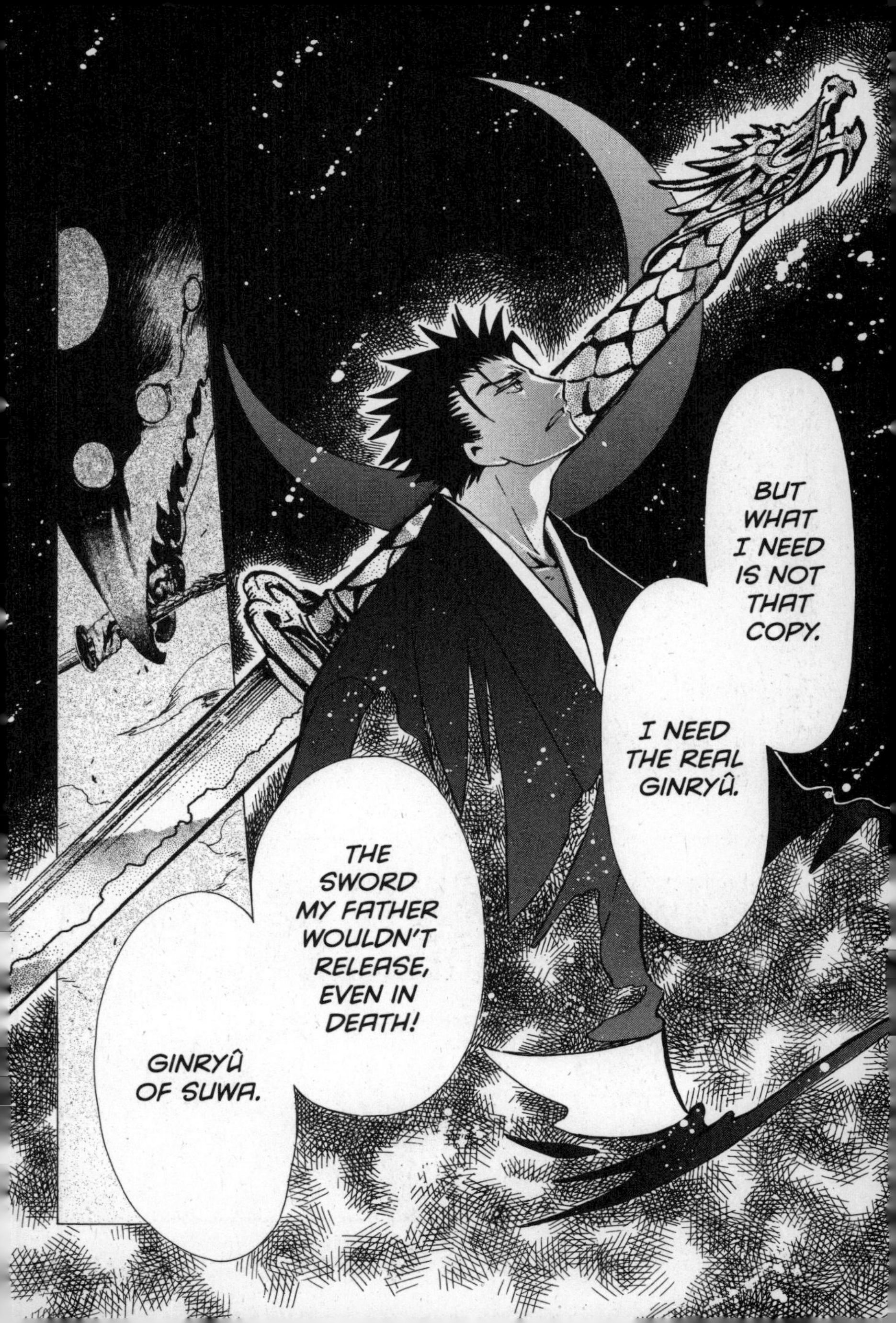
BUT WHAT I NEED IS NOT THAT COPY.
I NEED THE REAL GINRYÛ.
THE SWORD MY FATHER WOULDN'T RELEASE, EVEN IN DEATH!
GINRYÛ OF SUWA.

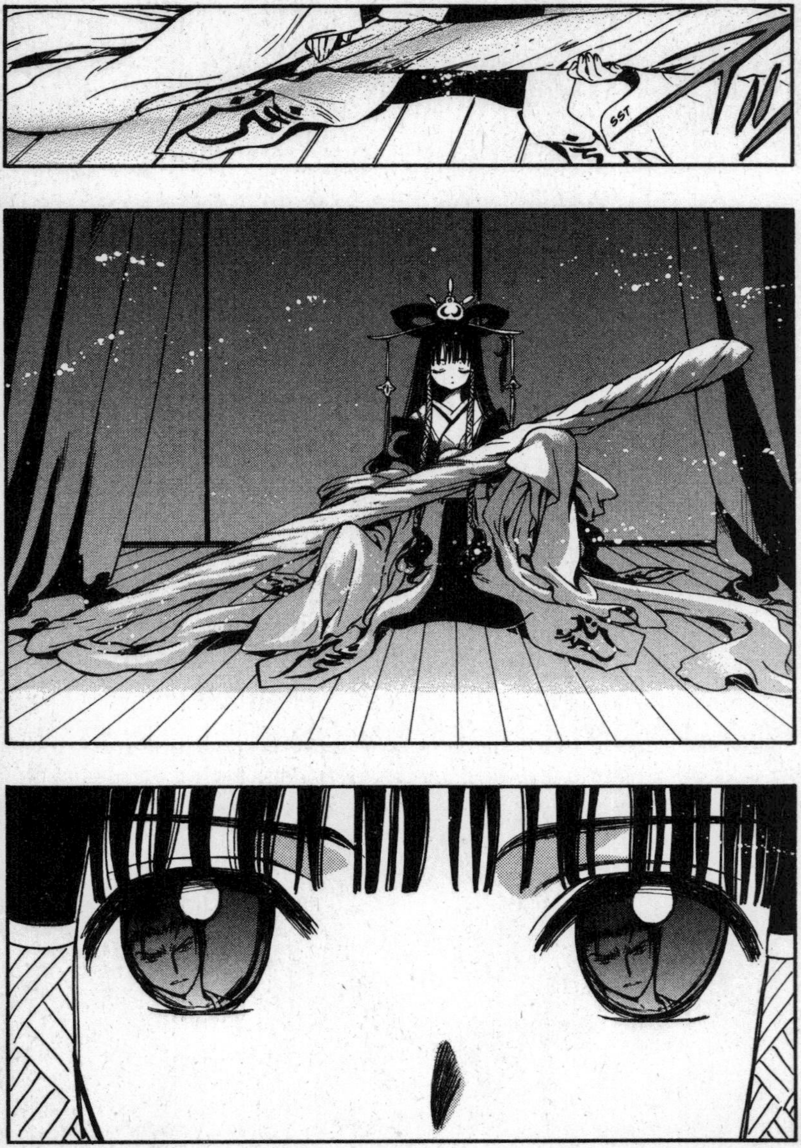
SST

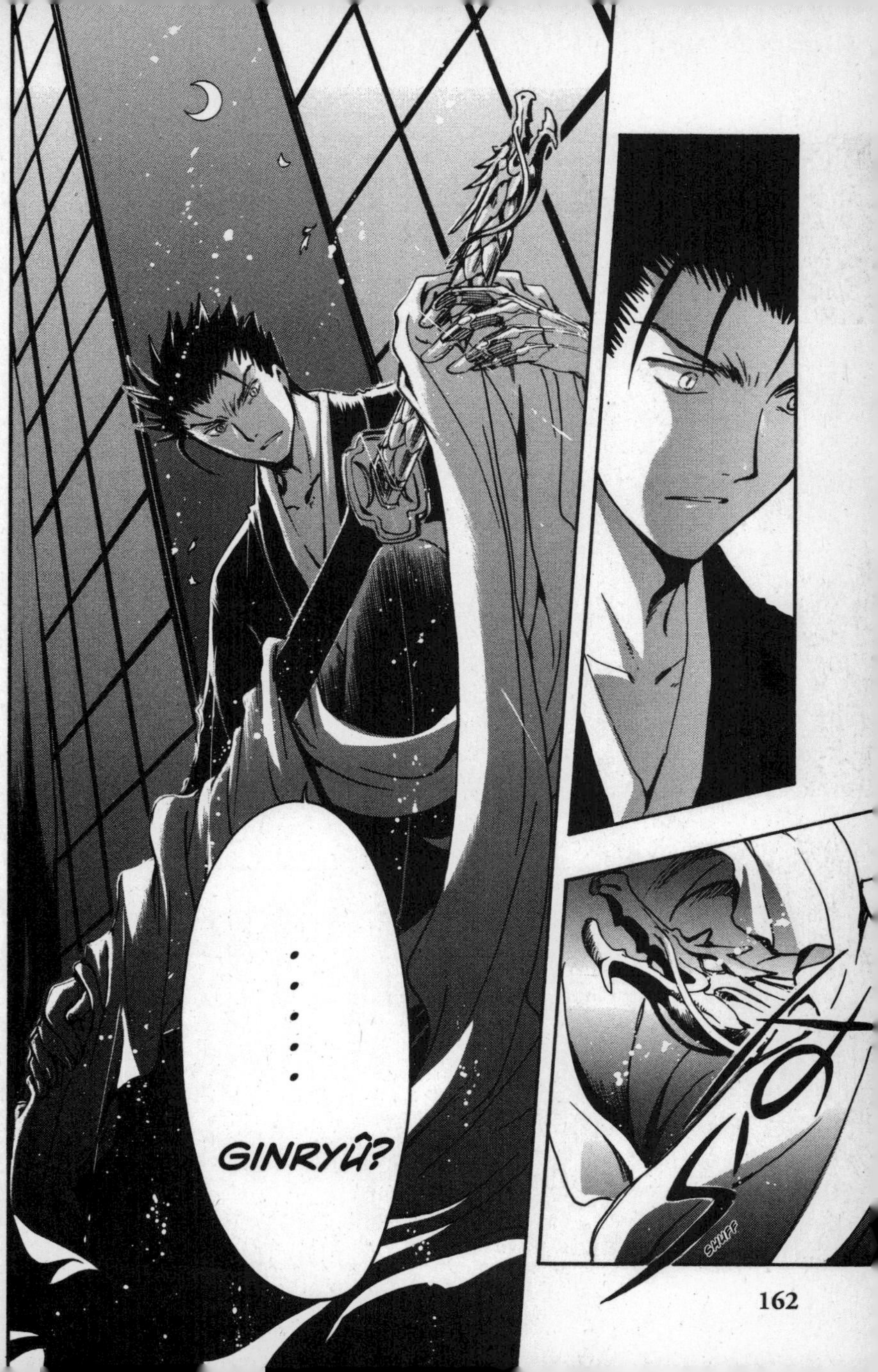
SHUFF
.....
GINRYŪ?

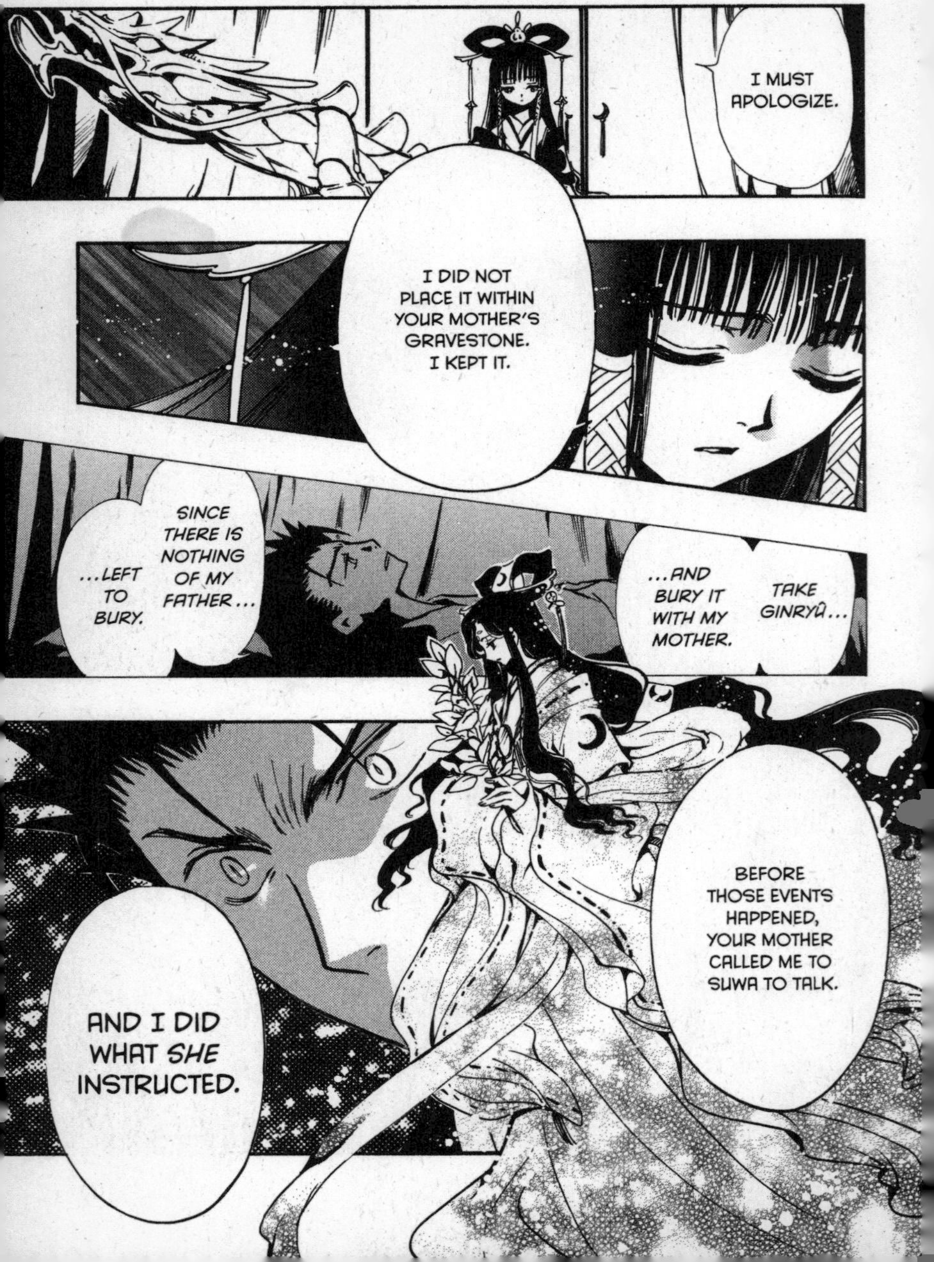
I MUST APOLOGIZE.
I DID NOT PLACE IT WITHIN YOUR MOTHER'S GRAVESTONE. I KEPT IT.
TAKE GINRYÛ...
...AND BURY IT WITH MY MOTHER.
SINCE THERE IS NOTHING OF MY FATHER...
...LEFT TO BURY.
BEFORE THOSE EVENTS HAPPENED, YOUR MOTHER CALLED ME TO SUWA TO TALK.
AND I DID WHAT *SHE* INSTRUCTED.

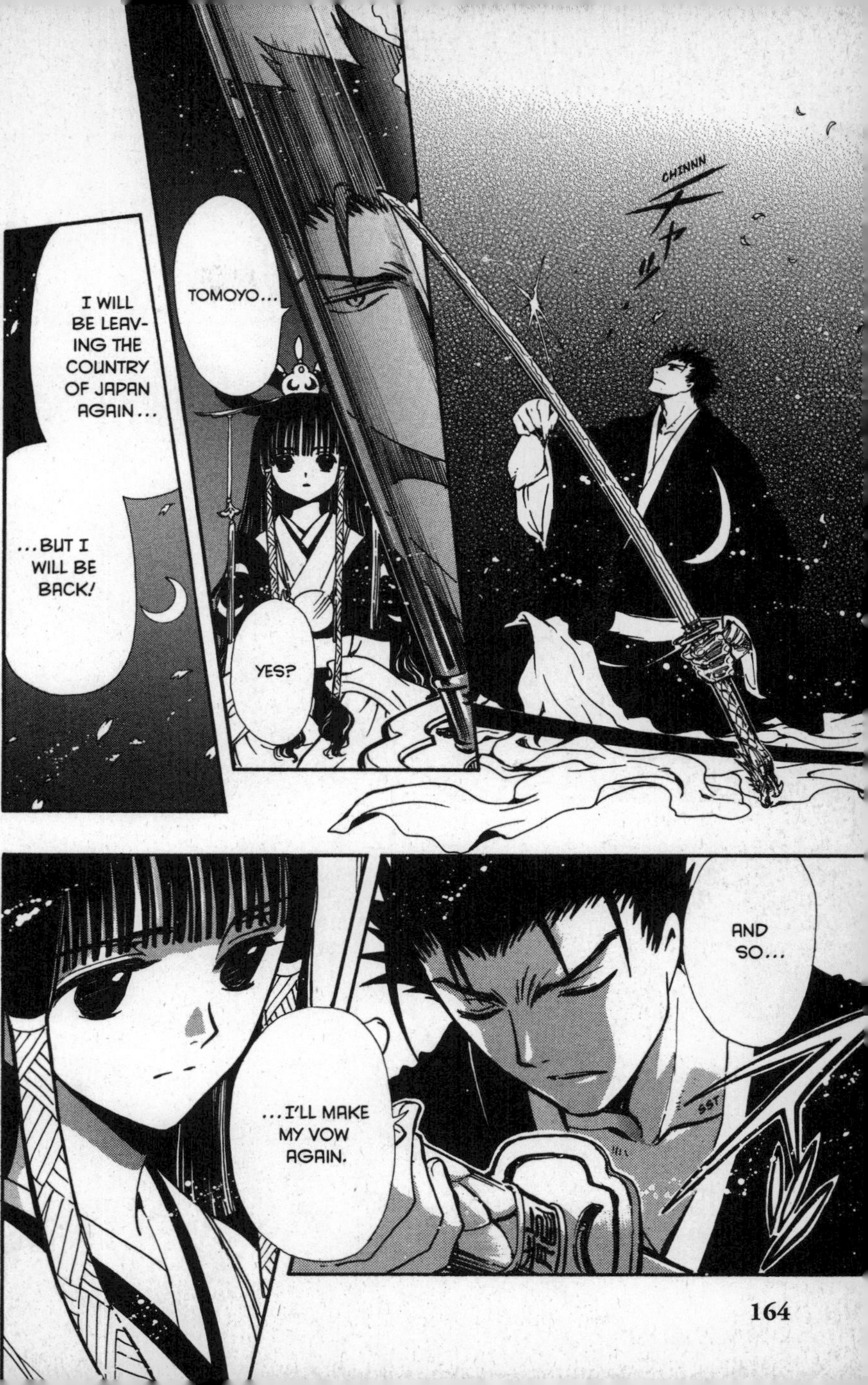
CHINNN
TOMOYO...
YES?
I WILL BE LEAVING THE COUNTRY OF JAPAN AGAIN...
...BUT I WILL BE BACK!
AND SO...
SST
...I'LL MAKE MY VOW AGAIN.

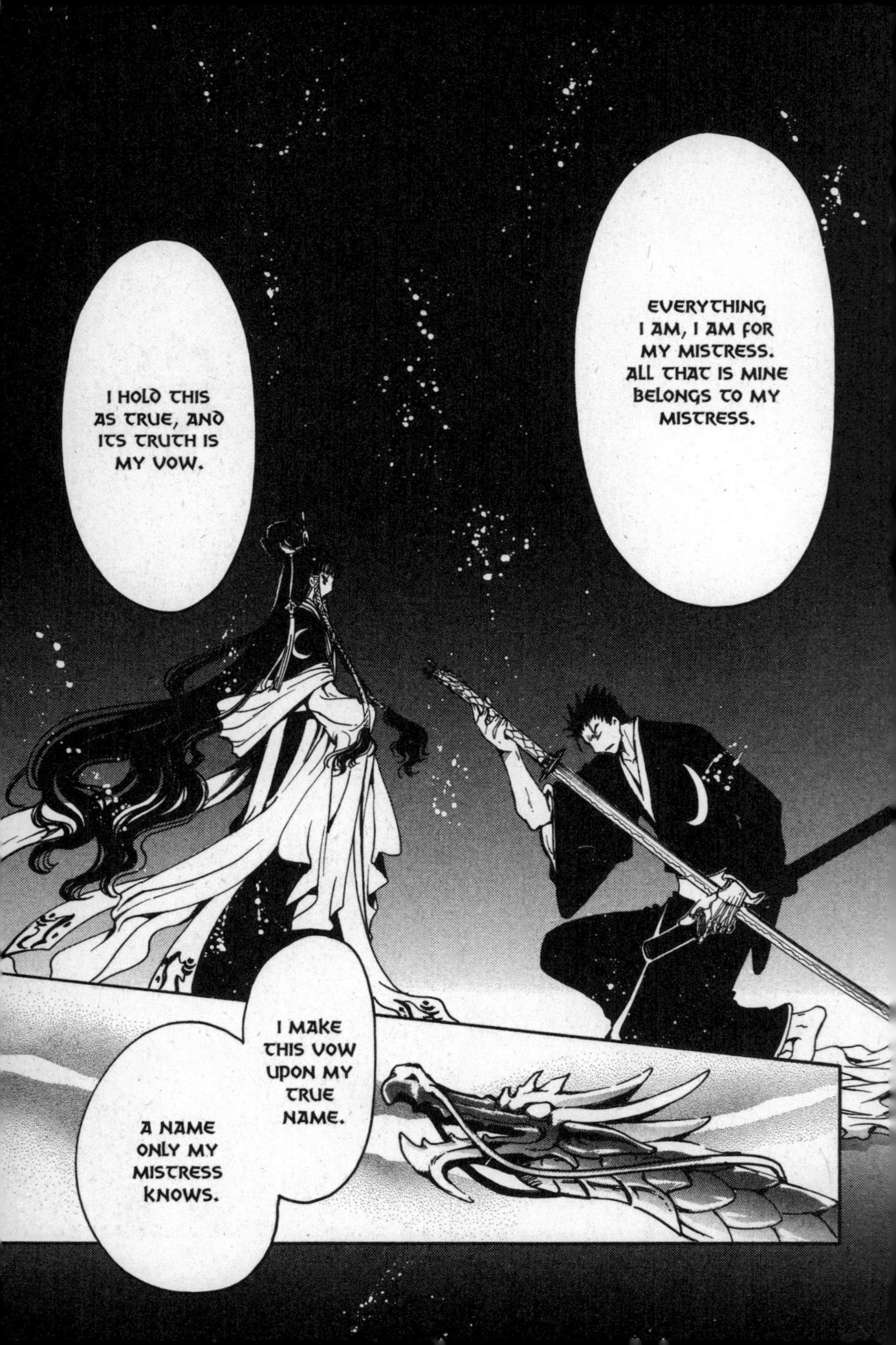
EVERYTHING I AM, I AM FOR MY MISTRESS. ALL THAT IS MINE BELONGS TO MY MISTRESS.
I HOLD THIS AS TRUE, AND ITS TRUTH IS MY VOW.
I MAKE THIS VOW UPON MY TRUE NAME.
A NAME ONLY MY MISTRESS KNOWS.

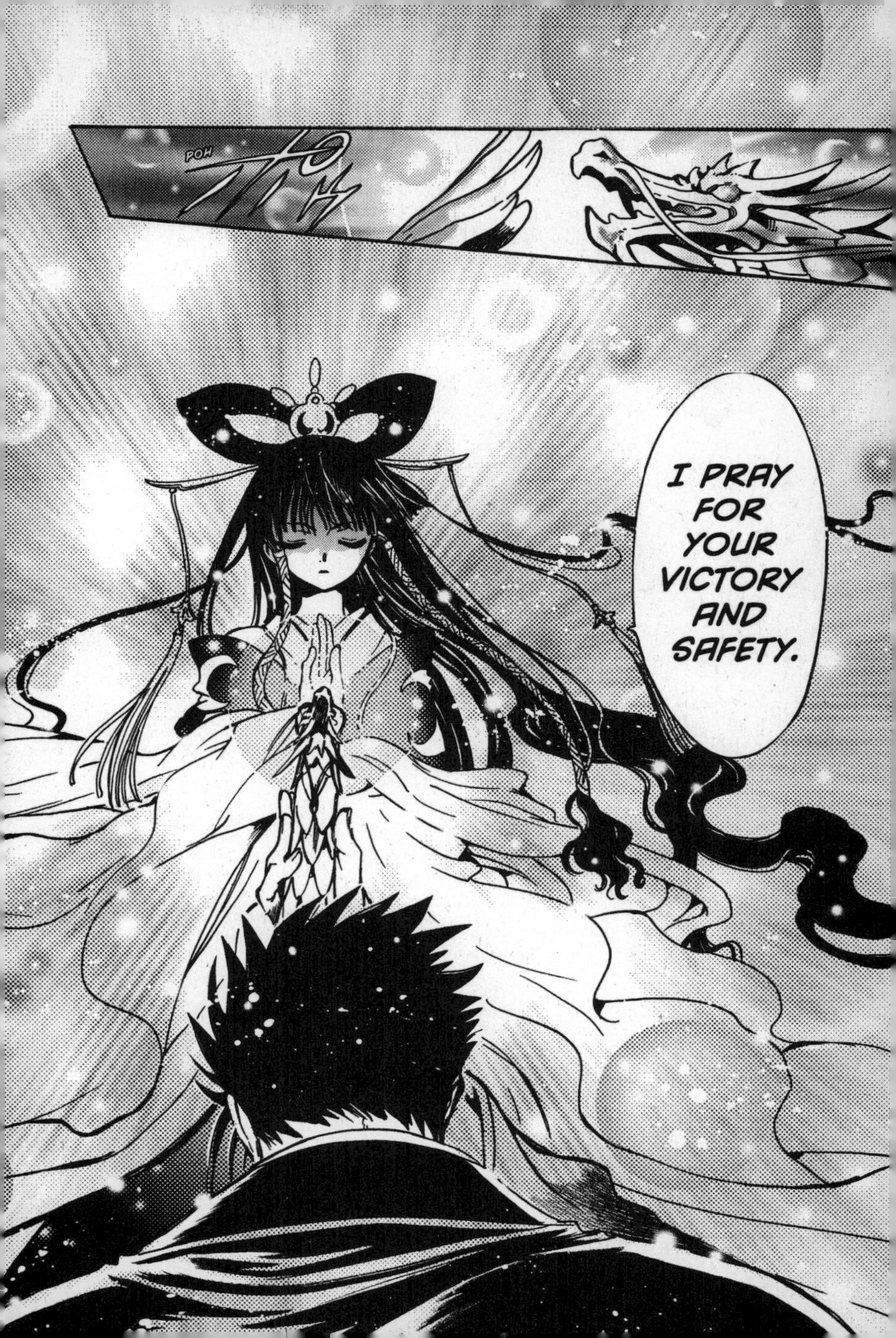
POH
I PRAY FOR YOUR VICTORY AND SAFETY.

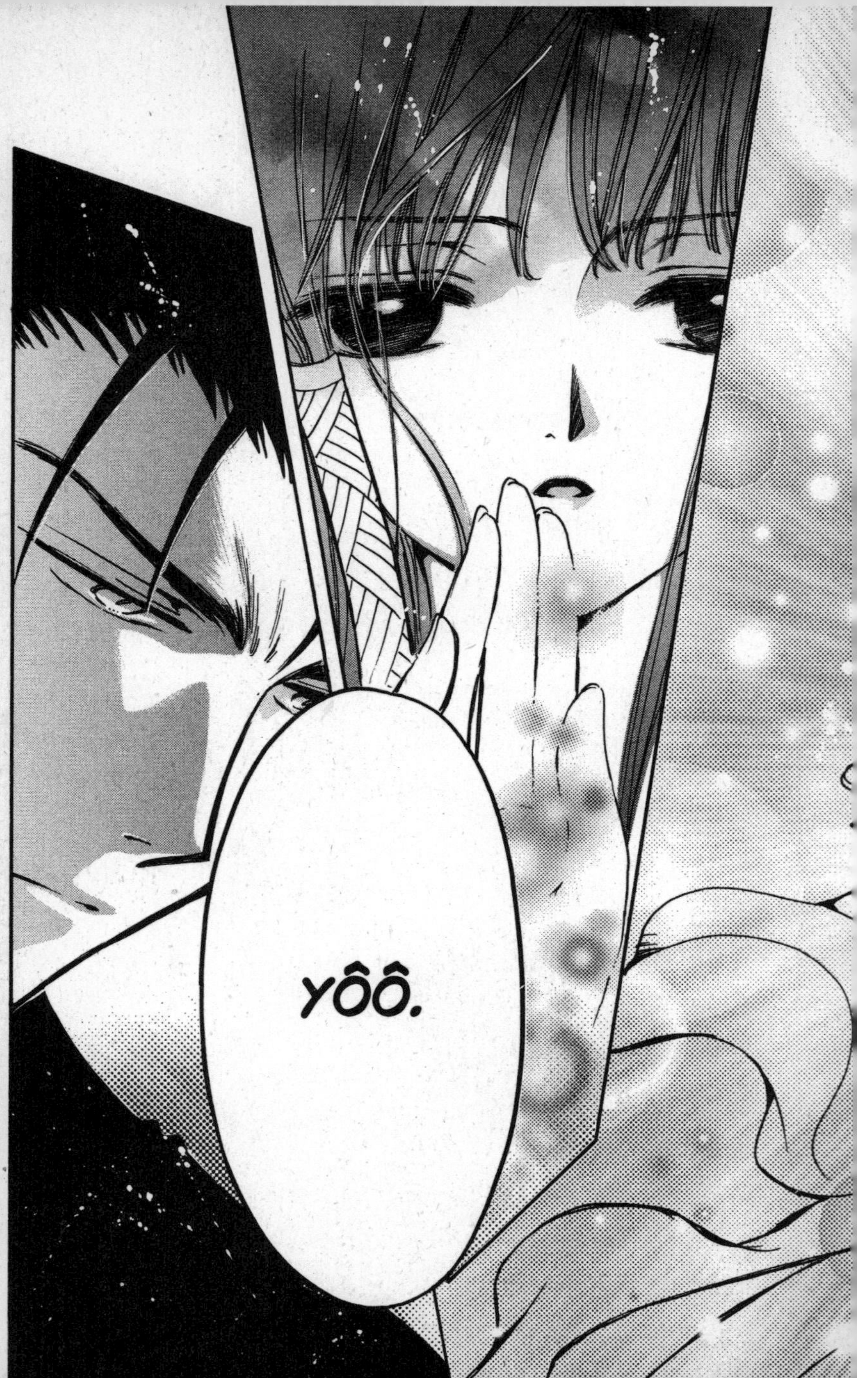
YÔÔ.

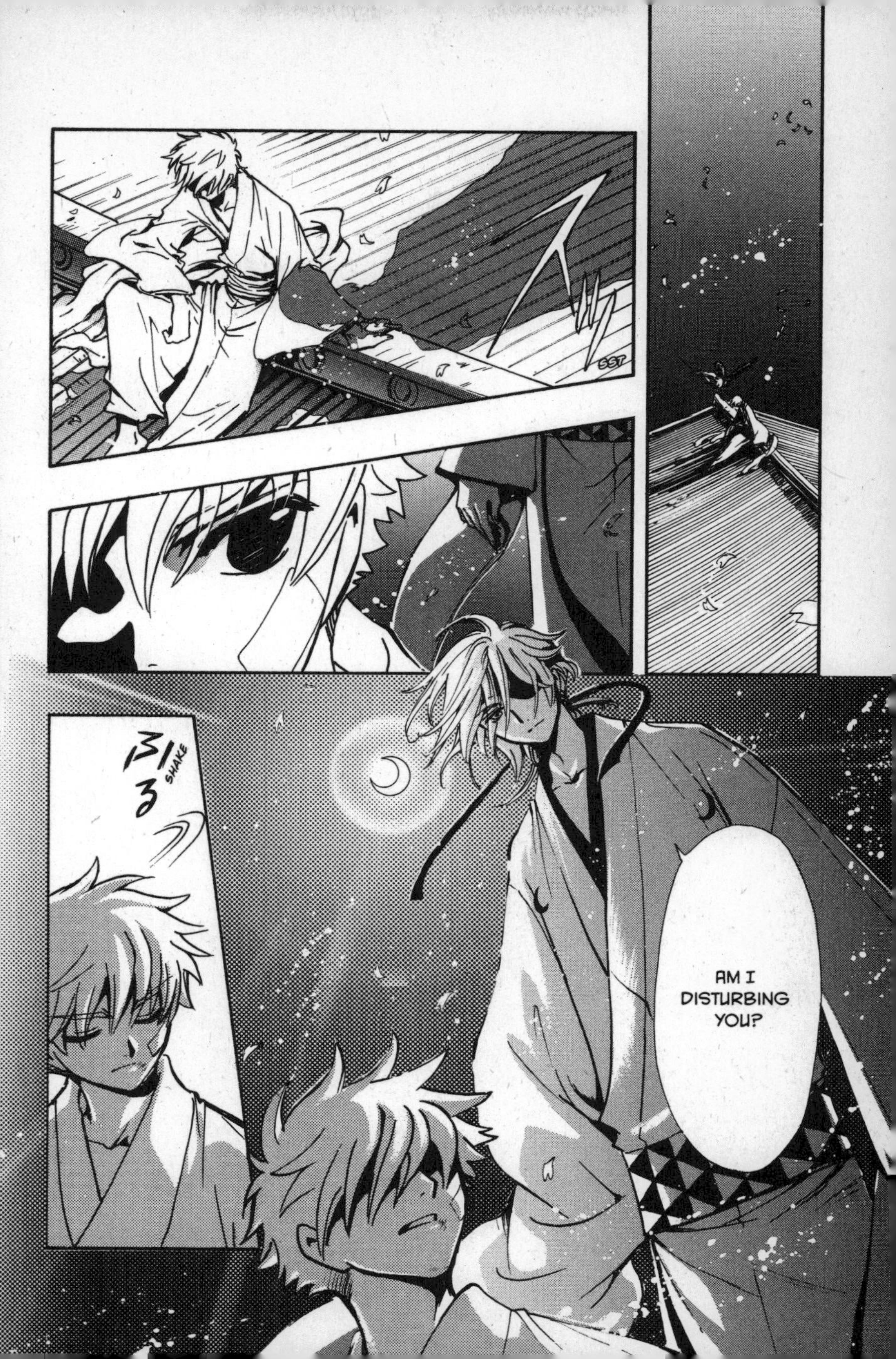
スッ
SST
AM I DISTURBING YOU?
ふる
SHAKE

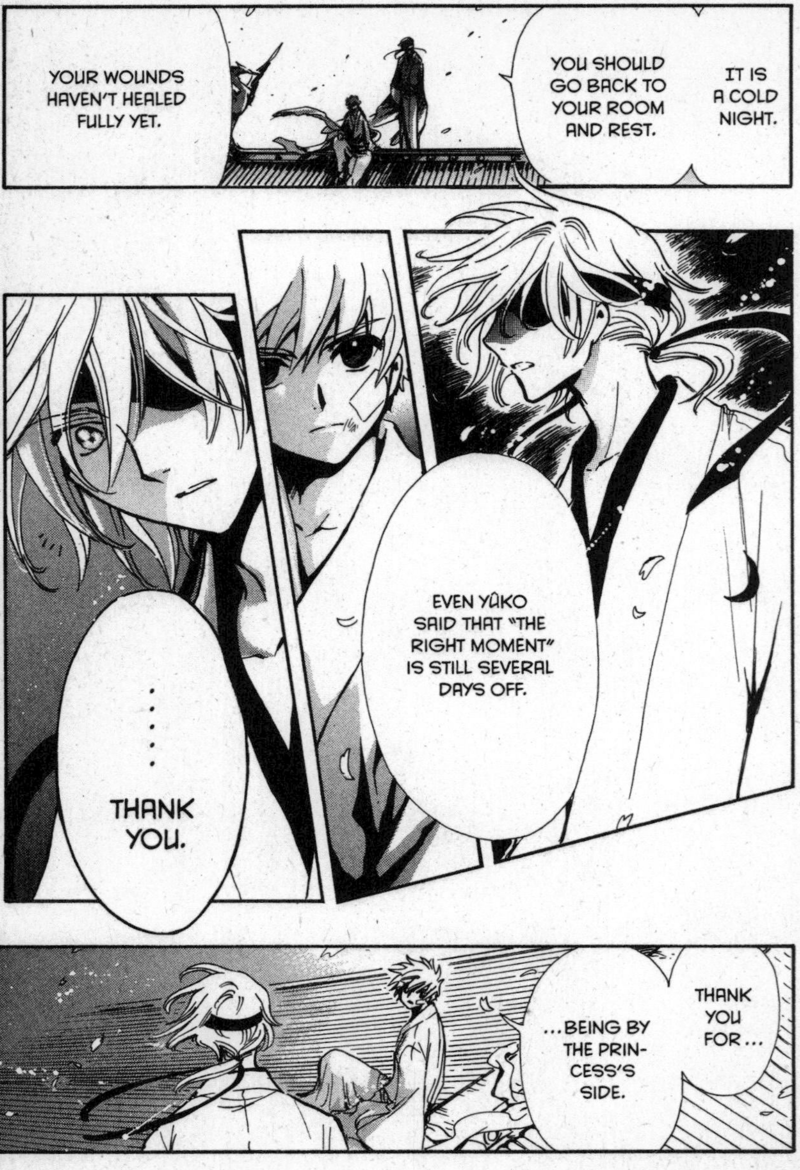
IT IS A COLD NIGHT.
YOU SHOULD GO BACK TO YOUR ROOM AND REST.
YOUR WOUNDS HAVEN'T HEALED FULLY YET.
EVEN YÛKO SAID THAT "THE RIGHT MOMENT" IS STILL SEVERAL DAYS OFF.
...... THANK YOU.
THANK YOU FOR...
...BEING BY THE PRIN-CESS'S SIDE.

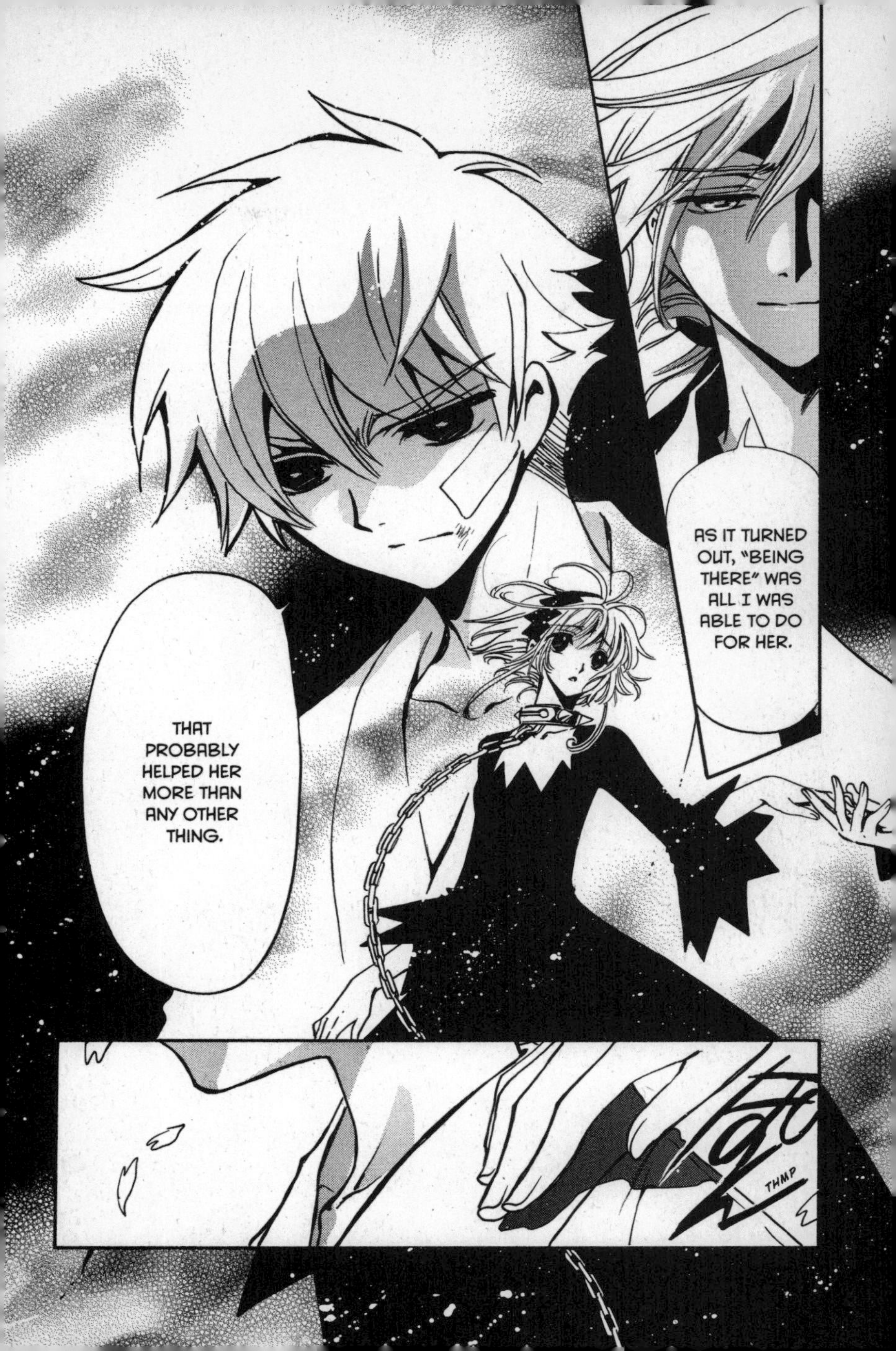
AS IT TURNED OUT, "BEING THERE" WAS ALL I WAS ABLE TO DO FOR HER.
THAT PROBABLY HELPED HER MORE THAN ANY OTHER THING.
THMP

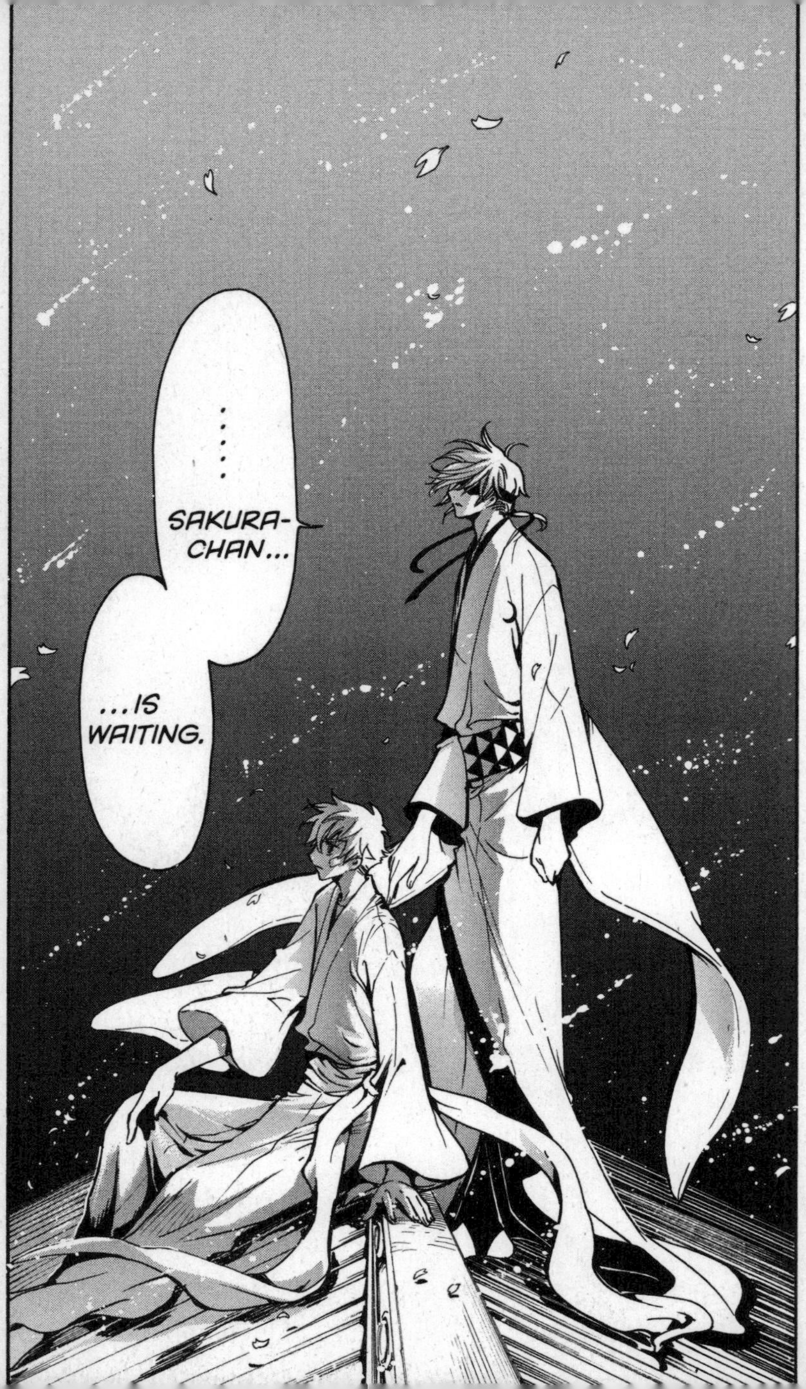
......
SAKURA-CHAN...
...IS WAITING.

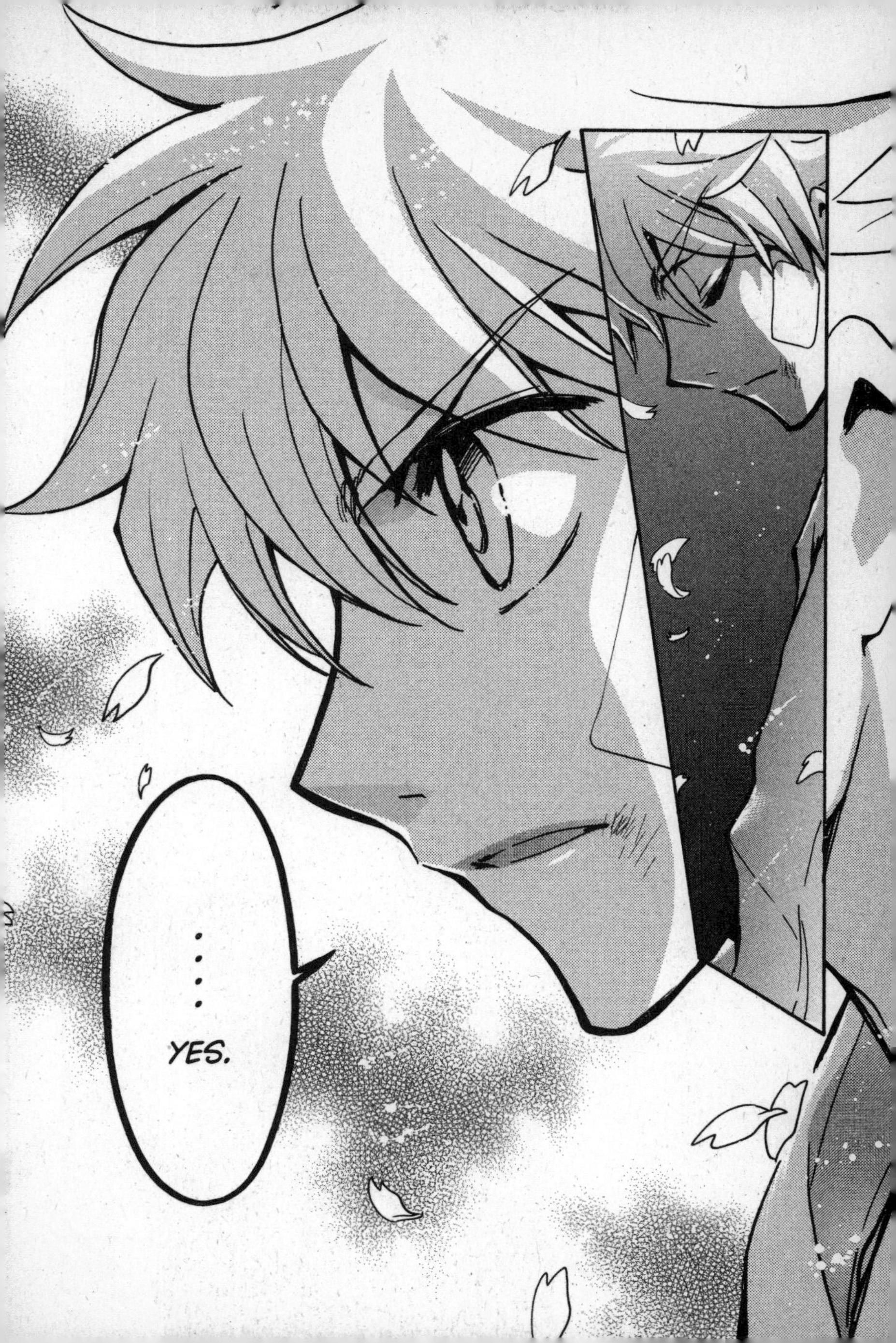
.... YES.

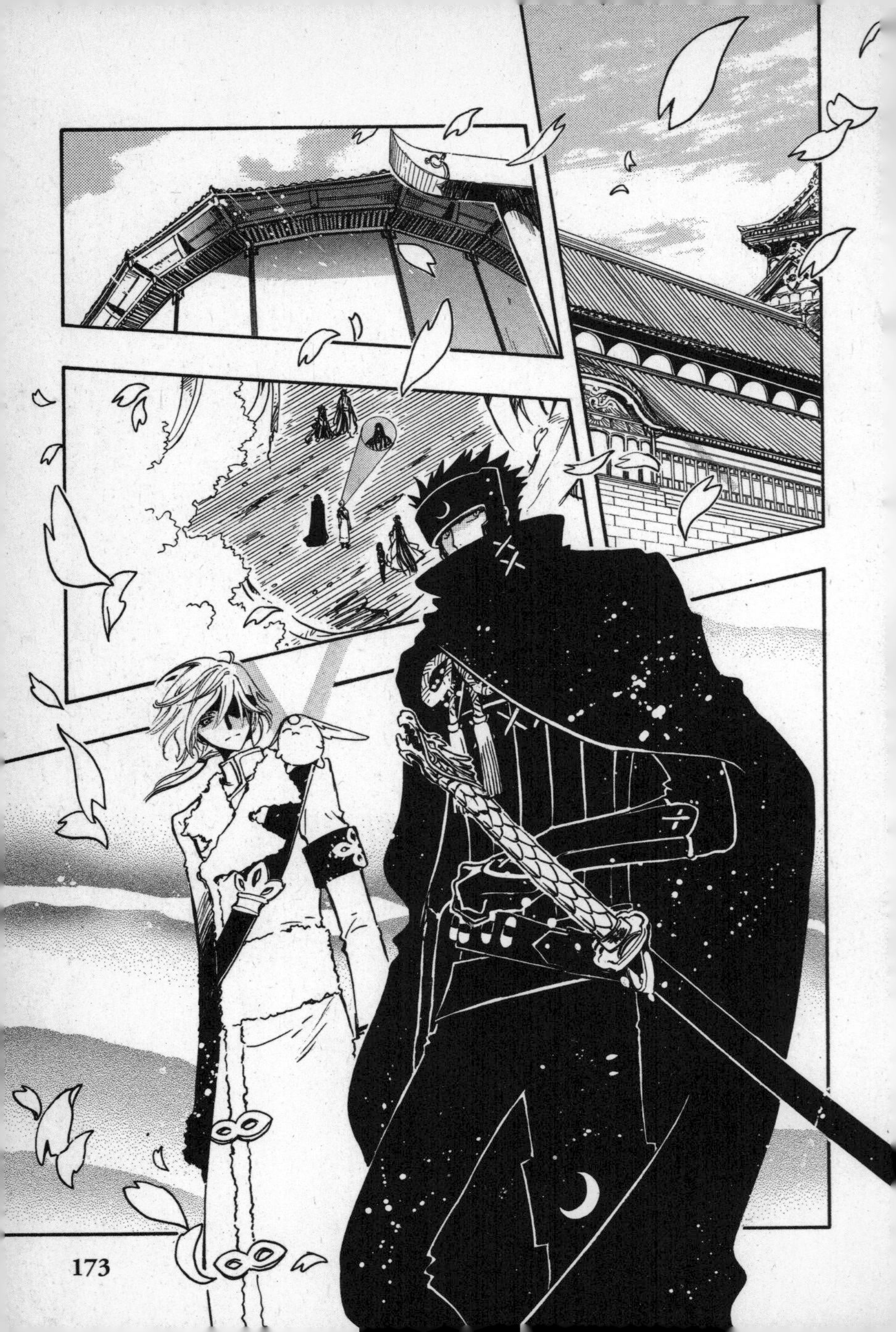

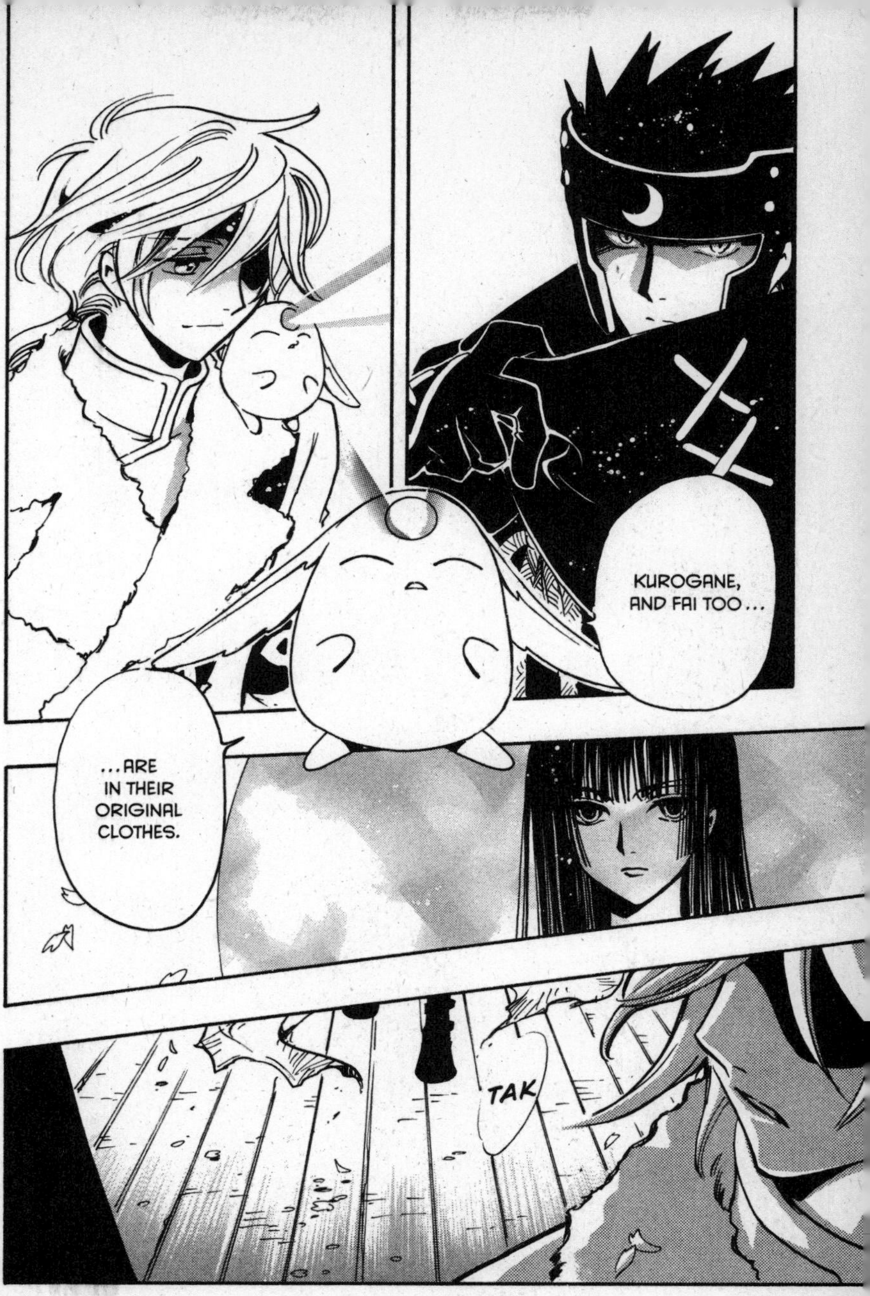
KUROGANE, AND FAI TOO...
...ARE IN THEIR ORIGINAL CLOTHES.
TAK

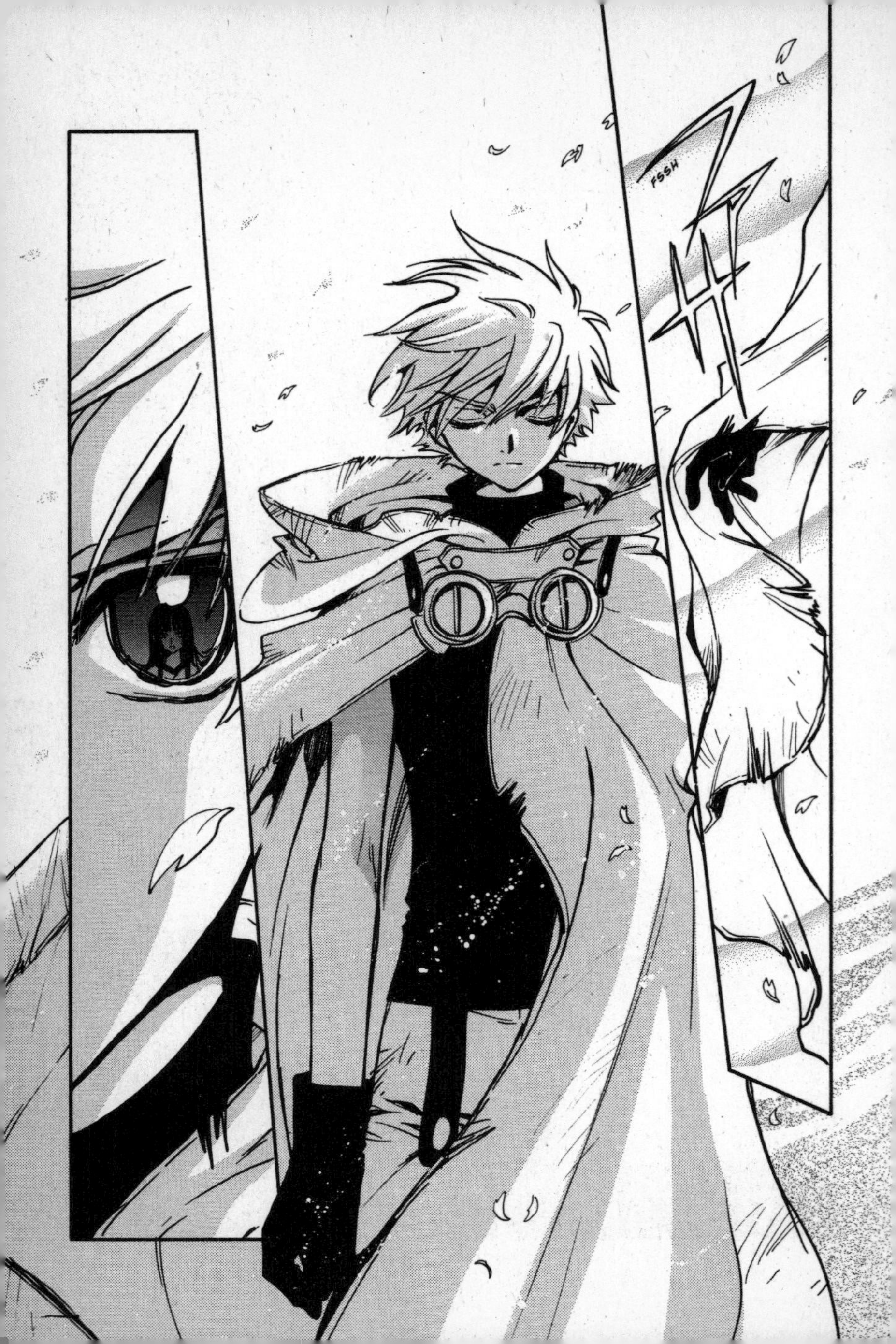
FSSH

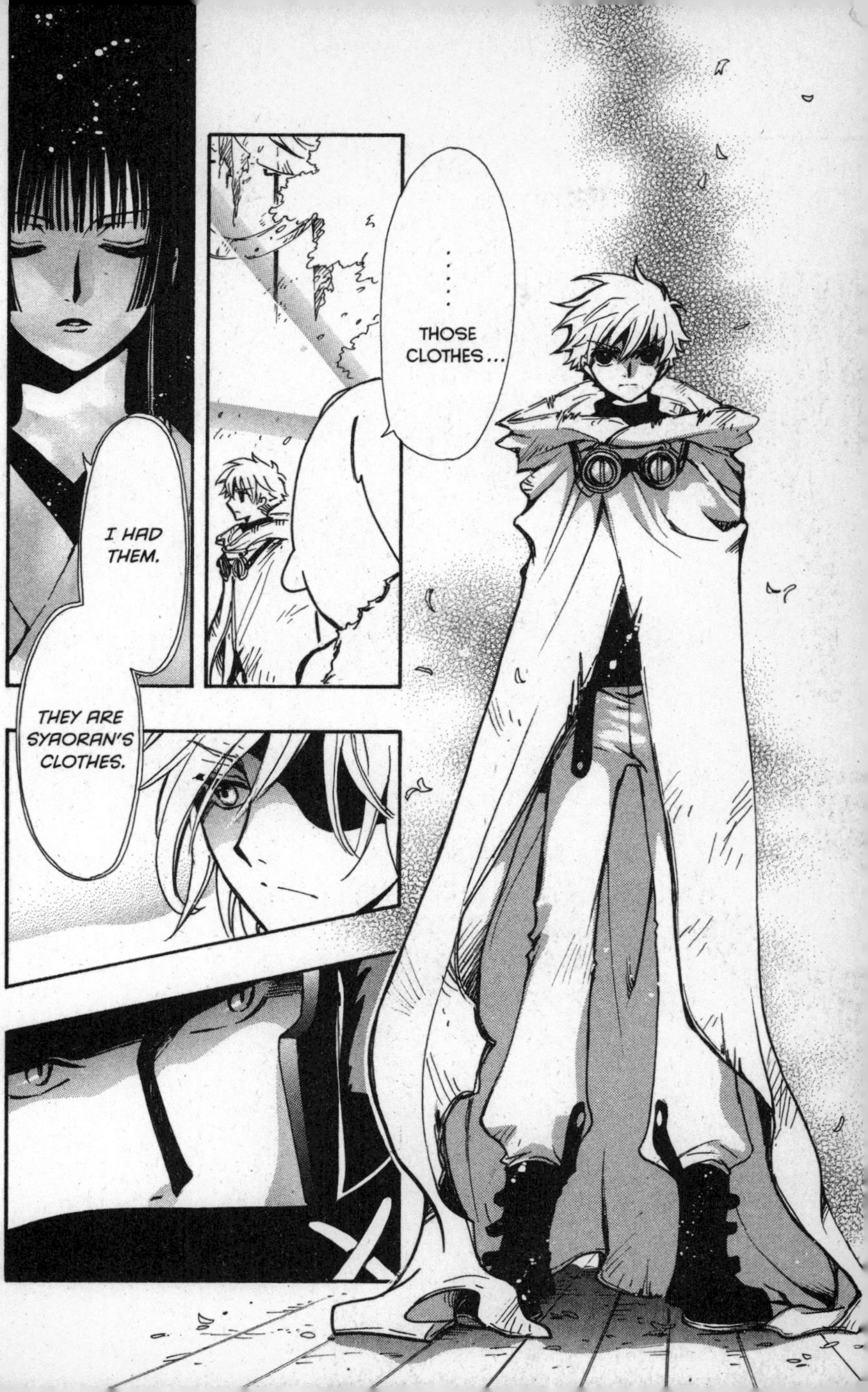
...... THOSE CLOTHES...
I HAD THEM.
THEY ARE SYAORAN'S CLOTHES.

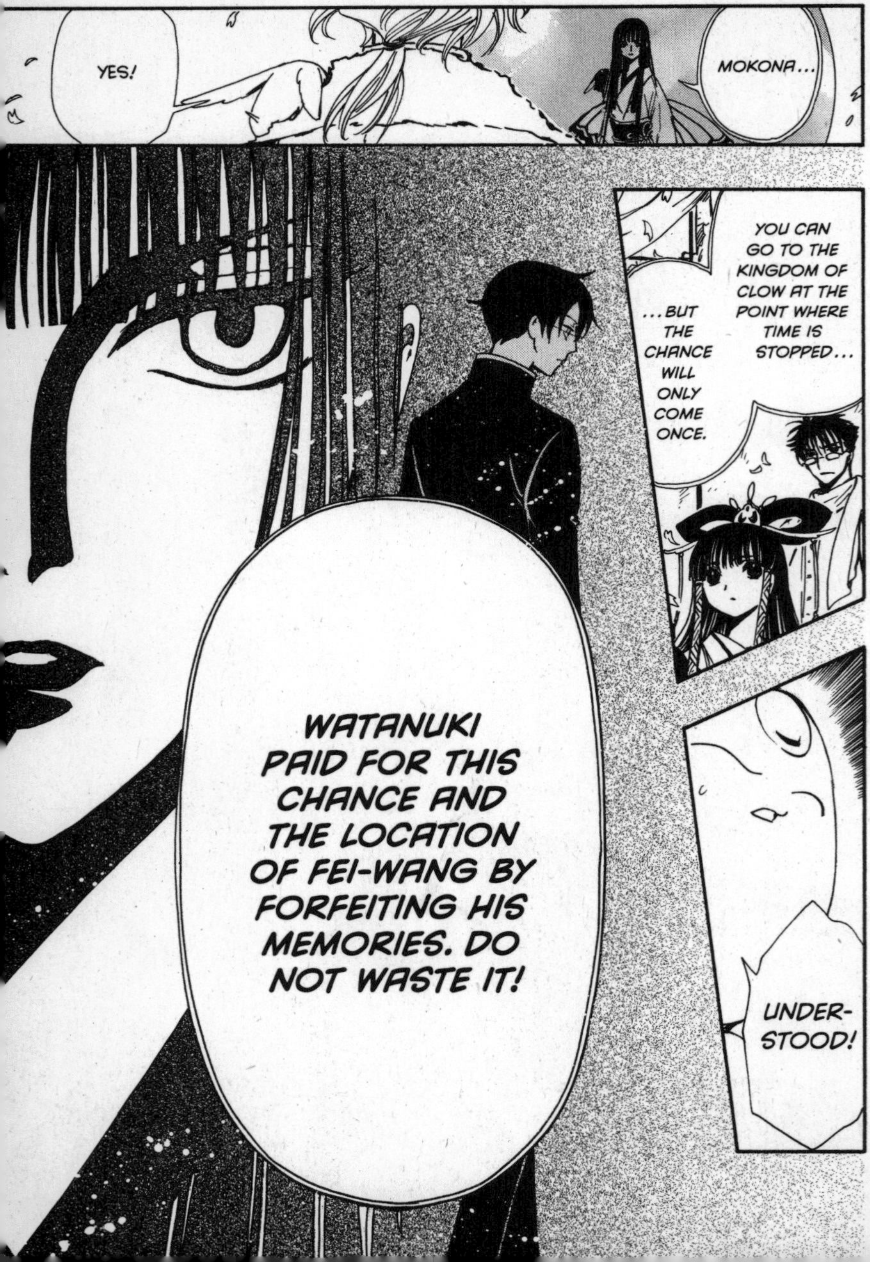
MOKONA...
YES!
YOU CAN GO TO THE KINGDOM OF CLOW AT THE POINT WHERE TIME IS STOPPED...
...BUT THE CHANCE WILL ONLY COME ONCE.
UNDER-STOOD!
WATANUKI PAID FOR THIS CHANCE AND THE LOCATION OF FEI-WANG BY FORFEITING HIS MEMORIES. DO NOT WASTE IT!

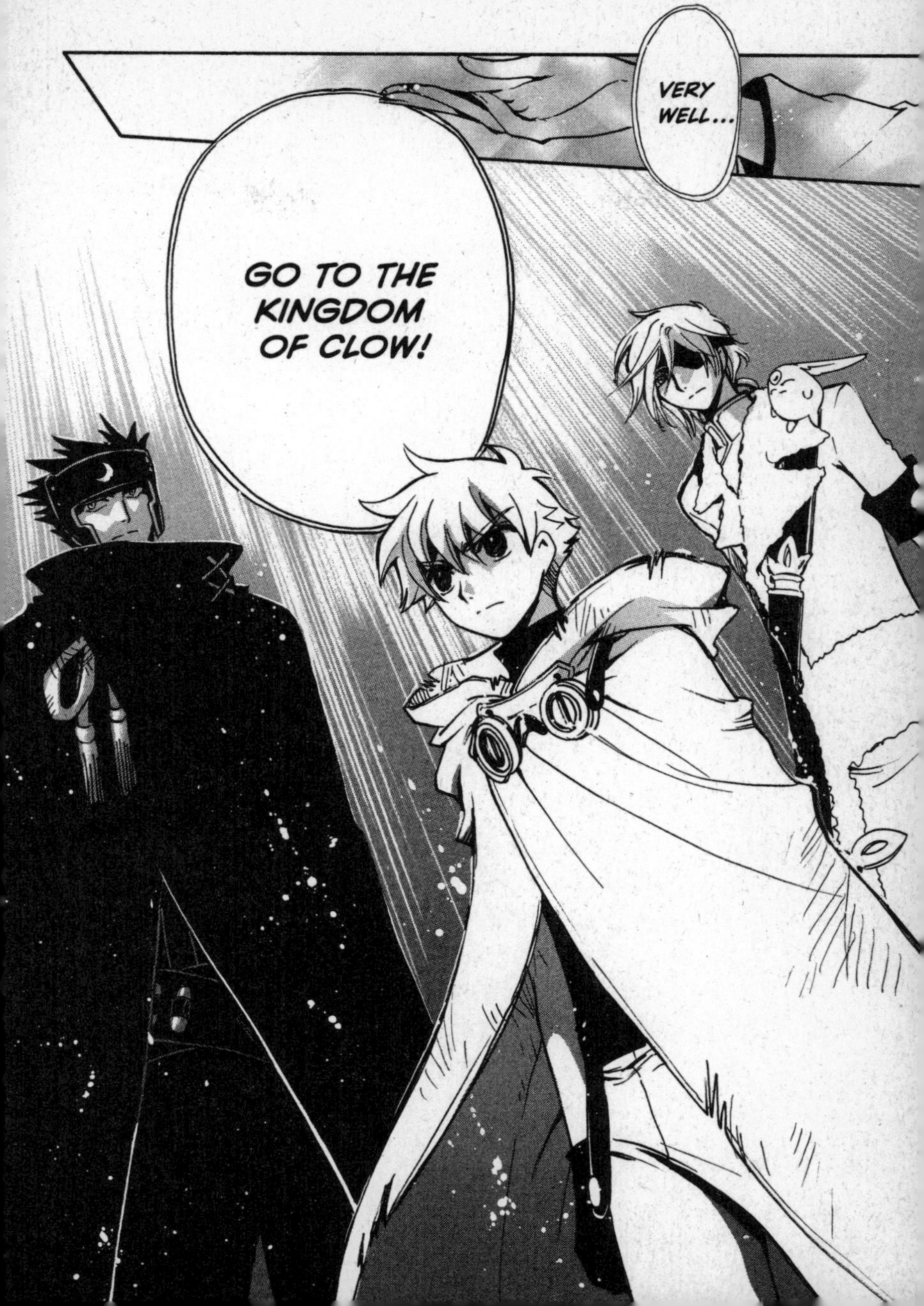
VERY WELL...
GO TO THE KINGDOM OF CLOW!

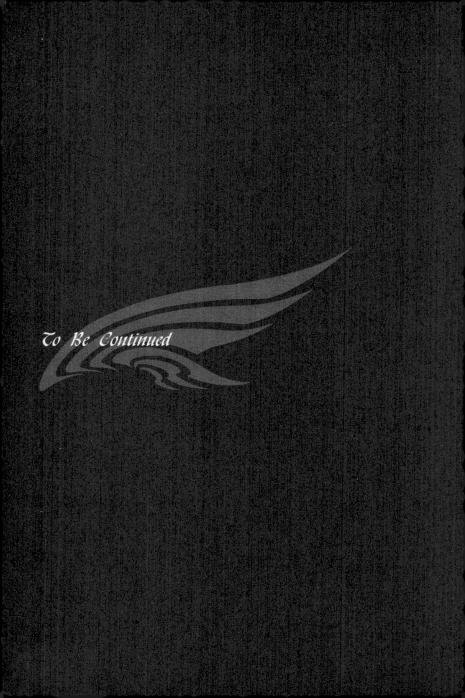

To Be Continued

# About the Creators

CLAMP is a group of four women who have become the most popular manga artists in America—Nanase Ohkawa, Mokona, Satsuki Igarashi, and Tsubaki Nekoi. They started out as *doujinshi* (fan comics) creators, but their skill and craft brought them to the attention of publishers very quickly. Their first work from a major publisher was *RG Veda*, but their first mass success was with *Magic Knight Rayearth*. From there, they went on to write many series, including Cardcaptor Sakura and Chobits, two of the most popular manga in the United States. Like many Japanese manga artists, they prefer to avoid the spotlight, and little is known about them personally.

CLAMP is currently publishing three series in Japan: Tsubasa and xxxHOLiC with Kodansha and Gohou Drug with Kadokawa.

# Translation Notes

Japanese is a tricky language for most Westerners, and translation is often more art than science. For your edification and reading pleasure, here are notes on some of the places where we could have gone in a different direction in our translation of the work, or where a Japanese cultural reference is used.

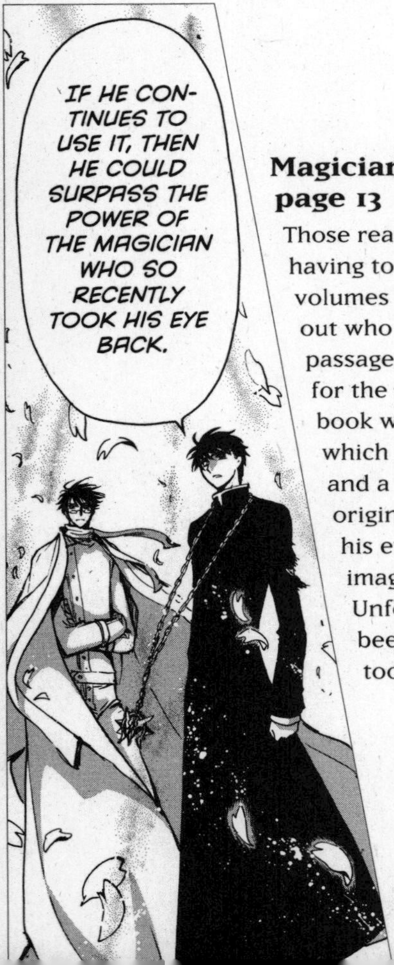
IF HE CONTINUES TO USE IT, THEN HE COULD SURPASS THE POWER OF THE MAGICIAN WHO SO RECENTLY TOOK HIS EYE BACK.

## Magician who took his eye back, page 13

Those readers who are reading this without having to pause three months between volumes will have no trouble figuring out who Seishirô is talking about in this passage. But those of us who have to wait for the quarterly releases of each new book would have to recall volume 16, which was published more than a year and a half ago, to get the reference. The original Syaoran gave the image Syaoran his eye hoping that it would lead the image to develop a soul of his own. Unfortunately that hope seems to have been in vain, and in volume 16, he took his eye back.

## You know what your Sakura feels..., page 89

As sometimes happens in these books, later revelations modify the translations of previous volumes. In this volume, it is finally revealed that Sakura is not the original, but an image of the original, and the original Syaoran knew it. Unfortunately, I, as translator, didn't know it (this volume had yet to be published in Japan at the time that I was translating volume 16). So the line was slightly mistranslated in volume 16. Syaoran's term in the original translation, "my heart," seems to refer to the soul in the form of an eye that the original Syaoran gave to his image. The image of Syaoran assumed that Sakura was the original and that she was only attracted to the piece of the original Syaoran that he possessed. In fact, Sakura was herself an image, and she was honestly attracted to the image Syaoran. I have asked for the line in volume 16 to be modified to reflect the new translation in future printings. If there is no discrepancy between this volume and volume 16, then you have a corrected volume 16.

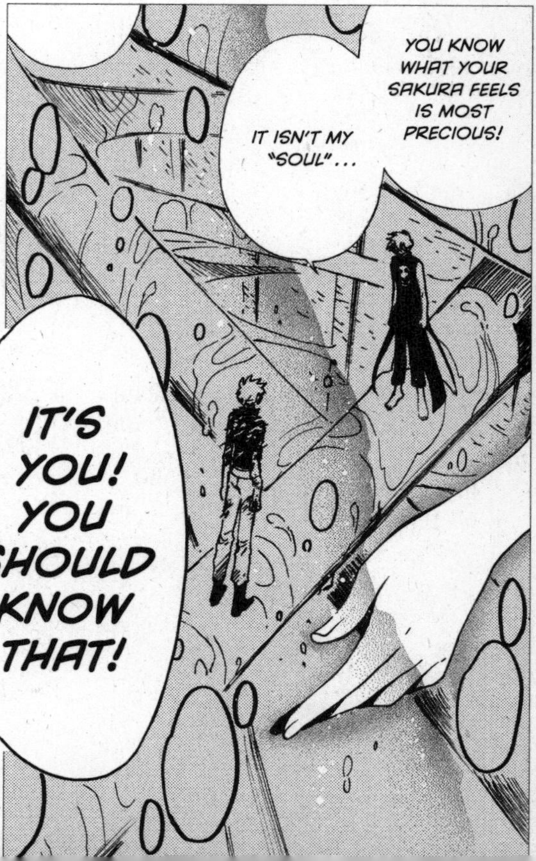
YOU KNOW WHAT YOUR SAKURA FEELS IS MOST PRECIOUS!
IT ISN'T MY "SOUL"...
IT'S YOU! YOU SHOULD KNOW THAT!

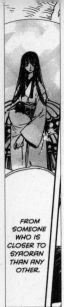

FROM
SOMEONE
WHO IS
CLOSER TO
SYAORAN
THAN ANY
OTHER.

## Closer to Syaoran, page 135

It has been stated in both xxxHOLiC and Tsubasa that
Kimihiro Watanuki's personality is close to Syaoran's.
There seems to be a close connection between them,
and both have paid high prices to the witch Yûko for the
other's sake. As is becoming more obvious in xxxHOLiC,
Watanuki is missing memories. He cannot remember
his parent's names, for example, and he is seriously
beginning to wonder whether his life with Yûko is real or
a part of dreams.

## Yôô, page 167

This is Kurogane's true name, the one
that only he and Princess Tomoyo
know. It is made up of two kanji, one of
which is yô, which means "hawk," and
another kanji to which Tsubasa readers
should be familiar, ô, which means
"king."

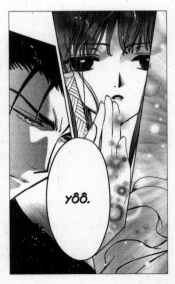

YÔÔ.

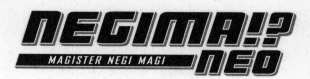
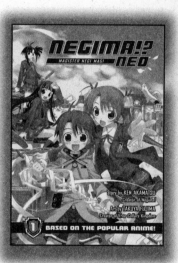
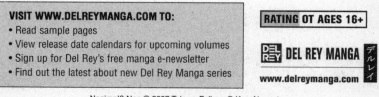

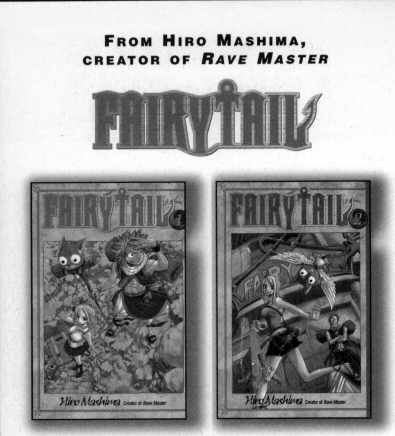
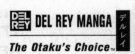

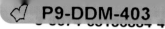
# TOMARE!

## [STOP!]

You're going the wrong way!

Manga is a completely different type of reading experience.

To start at the *beginning*, go to the *end*!

That's right! Authentic manga is read the traditional Japanese way—from right to left. Exactly the *opposite* of how American books are read. It's easy to follow: Just go to the other end of the book, and read each page—and each panel—from right side to left side, starting at the top right. Now you're experiencing manga as it was meant to be!